The Nation and Its "New" Women

The Nation and Its "New" Women

The Palestinian Women's Movement, 1920–1948

ELLEN L. FLEISCHMANN

University of California Press
BERKELEY   LOS ANGELES   LONDON

This book is a print-on-demand volume. It is manufactured using toner in place of ink. Type and images may be less sharp than the same material seen in traditionally printed University of California Press editions.

University of California Press
Berkeley and Los Angeles, California
University of California Press, Ltd.
London, England

© 2003 by the Regents of the University of California

Library of Congress Cataloging-in-Publication Data

Fleischmann, Ellen.
   The nation and its "new" women : the Palestinian women's movement, 1920–1948 / Ellen L. Fleischmann.
      p. cm.
   Includes bibliographical references and index.
   ISBN 0-520-23789-7 — ISBN 0-520-23790-0
   1. Women, Palestinian Arab—Political activity—History—1917–1948. 2. Feminism—Palestine—History—1917–1948. 3. Women in politics—Palestine—History—1917–1948. 4. Panarabism—History. I. Title.

HQ1728.5 .F57   2003
305.48'892'75—dc21   2002009719

Manufactured in the United States of America

The paper used in this publication meets the minimum requirements of ANSI/NISO Z39.48-1992 (R 1997) (Permanence of Paper).

*This book is dedicated to John Benvenuto
with love and gratitude*

Contents

Acknowledgments ix

Note on Transliteration xiii

Abbreviations xv

PART I. CONSTRUCTION OF A "NEW" PALESTINIAN WOMAN

1. Introduction: Inscription into the National Narrative 3
2. Palestinian Women and the Rule of the British Mandate 24
3. The "Woman Question" in Palestine and the Debate in the Arabic Press 63

PART II. THE "NEW" WOMAN IN POLITICS: THE PALESTINIAN WOMEN'S MOVEMENT, 1929–1948

4. The Roots of Movement: Charity and the Nation 95
5. Woman Is All the Nation: The Palestinian Women's Movement, 1929–1939 115
6. The Politics of the Women's Movement: The Question of Feminism, Nationalism, and the "New" Woman 137
7. Pan-Arabism and the 1940s 176

Appendix I: Sources from the Palestinian Press 211

Appendix II: Members of the Arab Women's Executive Committee 213

Notes 219

Bibliography 307

Index 329

Acknowledgments

I feel enormous debt to, and appreciation for, the many people and institutions who helped, encouraged, and supported me during the years of researching and writing this book. The book is the product of a long process that began when I moved to the Israeli-occupied Palestinian town of Ramallah in 1986 and started to teach Middle East studies and history at the Friends Girls School. I was completely inexperienced at teaching secondary school, and had very little formal knowledge of Middle East history. But teaching at a school for Palestinian girls was an exhilarating and inspiring experience. My students were young Palestinian women who had either grown up in the United States or had lived in the Ramallah area for most of their lives. They had an insatiable appetite and enthusiasm for learning that made teaching them a pleasure and a joy. Our experience of the turbulent period leading into and during the intifada contributed to our mutually and simultaneously developing a deep interest in, and appreciation for, their history and politics. I probably learned more from them than they did from me. I thank them all for (albeit unknowingly) sparking my interest in their history, and, again, unknowingly, guiding me to my life's work. They were wonderful students. Although I cannot claim credit for it, some of them are themselves becoming accomplished scholars and researchers. I am very proud of them and honored by our continued association and friendship.

I was also fortunate in my graduate school experience. Georgetown University provided me with an unusually collegial and stimulating intellectual climate in the years during which I engaged in most of the research for this book. Judith Tucker, my advisor, provided crucial support and guidance throughout the long stages of research and writing. She showed particular acumen in suggesting the topic that has engaged my heart and mind for so many years. Many colleagues and friends from Georgetown circles, both then and now, have provided me with valuable advice, comments on my work, sources, contacts, translation help, sustenance, places to stay in the Middle East, and friendship. I thank Ibrahim 'Ali, Bruce Dunne, Mary Ann Fay, Haifaa Khalifallah, Alison McGandy, Garay Menicucci, Sara Scalenghe, Norbert Scholze, Steve Tamari, and Chris Toensing.

Numerous people in Palestine, Jordan, Lebanon, and elsewhere provided me with invaluable support and friendship. They accompanied me on interviews, put me up in their homes, introduced me to contacts and other people who subsequently befriended me, argued with me, fed me, helped translate difficult interviews and handwritten memoirs, and in some cases, put their own work on hold to help me in mine. I thank (the late and missed) Makram Copti, Nada Darwazah, Islah Jad, Farid Kamal, Hilary Rantisi, Zuheira Sabbagh, Rheem Totah, and 'Abd al-Jawad Salih. Farida Salih Mayer graciously provided me with a home away from home in Amman and became an invaluable friend and companion on my rounds of visits to women in Amman. I deeply appreciate Hala and Dumya Sakakini's friendship and patience with my endless questions on my visits to them in Ramallah. My close and dear friend Anna Kennedy is personally responsible for sparking my interest in the Middle East by taking me there for the first time and for sharing our lives in Ramallah and Jerusalem together. I thank her with all my heart. Sharry Lapp has also been a good friend and supporter, sharing those memorably tense and exciting times in Ramallah. The many Palestinian women and men of the mandate generation who graciously gave me their time, recollections and hospitality during interviews receive my deepest appreciation for their contribution to this book.

Numerous colleagues deserve warm thanks for their criticism, sources, conversations, companionship in the archives, reading and encouragement of my work. I thank Joel Beinin, Martin Bunton, Ela Greenberg, Lisa Hajjar, Frances Hasso, Zachary Lockman, Weldon Matthews, Julie Peteet, Ted Swedenburg, and Elizabeth Thompson. Elizabeth Thompson and Julie Peteet's thoughtful comments on the manuscript were invaluable; neither they nor anyone else are responsible for my conclusions, or for my interpretations of their constructive criticism. Special thanks are due to Rosemary Sayigh, who has been extraordinarily generous with her incisive and thoughtful intellectual support, criticism, and friendship, which began in a (pre-email) period during which we had to arduously route our correspondence to and from Beirut and the West Bank via third countries or couriers. Her unmatched interest in, commitment to, and knowledge of the history of Palestinian women continue to be an inspiration.

Thanks are also due to Lynne Withey, director of the University of

California Press, and Kate Warne, the project editor, for their help in all stages of the editing and production process. I would also like to thank Matt Stevens for his careful editing of the manuscript.

I am grateful for the material support I received for research and writing. My research for this book was supported by a Fulbright-Hays Dissertation Abroad Grant, and an NEH post-doctoral grant at the American Center for Oriental Research in Amman; the writing of my dissertation from which this book is derived was supported by a grant from the Mellon Fund and Reverend Royden B. Davis Fellowship from Georgetown University. I thank these granters and institutions for their invaluable support.

I thank my parents, Mary and Jeffrey Fleischmann, for having given me unconditional encouragement for my diverse interests throughout my life. Most importantly, my husband, John Benvenuto, deserves the most thanks of all. He willingly and enthusiastically accompanied me to the Middle East and other parts of the world and has always encouraged and been a major supporter of my work, even when it has interfered with his own work and life. Without his belief in me, I never would have become a scholar. He is that rare thing, a true male feminist. For all of this, I thank him with all my heart.

Note on Transliteration

I have generally followed the system of transliteration used by the *International Journal of Middle East Studies*, with some exceptions: where there are common English spellings of better- known Arabic words (*fellah*, for example) and place names, when citing or quoting from other works that do not use this system, and in some cases, where an individual prefers a certain Latin spelling of their name. I have not transliterated consonants that appear identical in English, and in the case of personal names I have only transliterated the ayn and the hamza, and not the long vowels. I use the prefix "al-" only when I mention a person's full name, dropping it in references to the last name alone. There are some inconsistencies. In the case of Matiel Mogannam, who is cited, quoted from, and discussed in the book, I have kept the English spelling of her first name but used Arabic transliteration of her last name, Mughannam, in order to guide readers who are familiar with Arabic to references that cite her in that language.

Abbreviations

AAC	Anglo-American Commission
AE	Arab Executive Committee
AHC	Arab Higher Committee
AUB	American University of Beirut
AWA	Arab Women's Association
AWE	Arab Women's Executive Committee
AJC	American Junior College
AWU	Arab Women's Union
BCW	Beirut College for Women
CID	Central Intelligence Department
DO	District Officer
HC	High Commissioner
NDP	National Defense Party
PAWS	Palestine Arab Workers Society
PAWU	Palestine Arab Women's Union
PMC	Permanent Mandates Commission
RTC	Rural Training Center for Women
WTC	Women's Training Center

PART I

Construction of a "New" Palestinian Woman

1. Introduction

Inscription into the National Narrative

But it's not here. And this is history.[1]

From 1929 until 1947, headlines such as the following blazoned across the pages of the Arabic press in British Mandate Palestine: "We Women are Not Less Nationalistic than Men," "Protest of the Ladies Over the Oppression of the Government," "The Arab Woman—Always in the Vanguard and the Forefront of the Ranks," "Our Women and the Homeland," and "Demonstration of the Ladies of Jaffa Yesterday—Magnificence, Organization, and the Recitation of Nationalist, Fervent Speeches."[2] The press amply documented the extensive involvement of the Palestinian women's movement in the unfolding national struggle during the mandate period, reporting on women's demonstrations, congresses, memoranda to the government, arms smuggling, meetings with government officials, fundraisers, aid and visits to prisoners, and participation in regional and international women's conferences. Clearly, during this crucial period of history Palestinian women were doing something.[3] Yet, notwithstanding the profusion of contemporary press coverage, Palestinian women are almost completely absent from the writing on this crucial period of Palestinian history.

In her article, "Palestinian Women: A History in Search of Historians," Rosemary Sayigh issues a challenge to historians to remedy this lacuna, and puzzles over the "vast disparity between the long, rich history of Palestinian women's involvement in the national struggle of their people and the writing of this history."[4] This book is a response to her call, and I hope the first among others to follow. My intent is to inscribe Palestinian women into their national narrative through exploring not only what they did within the nationalist/political arena, but also the social, cultural, and economic context within which they operated in this particular period of history.

Palestinian Arab women in the British Mandate period (1920–48)[5] found themselves in the midst of a maelstrom that comprised not only the famously intractable "conflict" (the Arab-Israeli conflict), but also a myriad of social, cultural, and economic transformations that caused as much rupture and disjuncture in Palestinians' lives as the political struggle that continues to dominate their existence as a people. In this book, I argue that gender constituted an integral part of the disrupted process of nation-building, which not only became synonymous and simultaneous with anticolonial resistance but—uniquely in the Palestinian case when compared to the rest of the Arab East during this period—endures, seemingly indefinitely. Put simply, Palestinian nation-building not only became indistinguishable from the national liberation struggle but also became confused with it.[6] Women played an important role in this process, which began during the mandate period. They launched a dynamic and active women's movement that participated in all of the major events and reacted to the crises that occurred in this era. The lengthy, ongoing nature of the nation-building project had implications for the women's movement and Palestinian society overall. For one thing, it played a major role in engendering extensive transformations, debate, and contestation about the place of women and gender—the so-called woman question—in all aspects of Palestinian society. The "woman question," however, was really an internal argument about the nation's history and identity, as these came into question and under threat in this period. These issues were further complicated by the part played by the presence of the British Mandate government, which curiously assumed its ability to maintain the "social" status quo and not "interfere" with the natives, while imposing a colonial system of rule that promised support to another national movement whose stated goal was complete transformation of the land, politics, and society of Palestine. As a result, the women's movement necessarily internalized and reflected the ambivalences and conflicts inherent in both confused and confusing British policies, and in the reactions of Palestinian society overall (and of the male-led national movement in particular) to these processes. Despite these ambivalences and influences, however, women were able to assert a feminist agency and autonomy from the male nationalist project and colonizers' imposition of neotraditional custom.

This book consists of two parts. In the first, I examine the background out of which the Palestinian women's movement arose, paying particular attention to social, cultural, and economic factors that influenced and affected the primarily middle- and upper-class women who constituted the core of the movement. Embedded in the narrative, which takes into account British government policies, the changing economy, women's education and welfare (the subjects of Chapter 2), and discourse on gender in the press (covered in Chapter 3), are the sometimes unconscious and subtle processes that went into constructing women's multiply inflected sense of identity. All of these factors contributed to women's motives and ability to become actively engaged in founding and running an autonomous women's movement in a period during which women lived under restrictions—albeit under challenge and transformation—of their mobility, role in society, and public visibility.

The second part of the book then chronicles and analyzes the actual development of the women's movement, from its earliest organizational roots to the end of the mandate. The overlap and continuity in women's organizing defy simple linear chronology. Although the British Mandate obviously strongly shaped women's outlooks and opportunities, a simple periodization of premandate and mandate activities is not altogether meaningful, nor are other externally imposed chronological categories. Chapter 4 delineates the formation of women's charitable associations beginning in the Ottoman period; the relationship between notions of gender and charity; the earlier women's organizations in Palestine, the impetuses behind their establishment, and the political and social implications of Palestinian women organizing. Chapter 5 charts the movement's major activities and key events during the seminal first decade of its existence, from its establishment during the 1929 Palestinian Women's Congress to its participation in the 1936–39 strike and revolt. Chapter 6 provides a detailed narrative and analysis of the movement's leadership and political strategies, as embodied in the Arab Women's Association (AWA)[7] and, later, the Arab Women's Union (AWU). These groups led and dominated the women's movement during most of the period studied. I examine the movement's leadership, internal organization, public tactics, strategies, discourse, and its complicated relationships to the male-led national movement and British Mandate government. Chapter 7 analyzes the pan-Arab elements of the women's movement, and chronicles its trajectory, and other, new forms of organizations prevalent in the last decade of the mandate, up until the dispersal and destruction of Palestinian Arab society in 1948.

But in order to make sense of the narrative, it is necessary to also investigate and negotiate the larger, multiple, complex, and shifting terrain of which it is a part: nationalism, feminism, and colonialism.

NATIONALISM, FEMINISM, AND COLONIALISM

The emergence of the Palestinian women's movement must be situated within the complex intersection of feminism, nationalism, and colonialism. Recently this nexus of "isms" has begun to develop into a veritable genre of its own, drawing the attention of scholars of Third World women's studies and colonialism. The trend is in part a result of our entry into a so-called postcolonial[8] period that has stimulated analysis of the mixed legacy of former nationalist movements in their new incarnations as nation-states in granting women equal status to men. Such studies involve investigating the gendered nature of nationalism; it has become almost axiomatic that "national liberation now" does not necessarily lead to "women's liberation later," since "women who are not empowered to organize during the struggle will not be empowered to organize after the struggle."[9] Historically, during often-protracted nationalist conflicts, nationalism has almost always taken primacy over struggles for gender equality, which was deferred until independence. A complex, ambiguous, and tense relationship between feminism and nationalism has been the result. This dynamic has been further complicated by the configurations of various colonial structures that interfered with indigenous social practices. Nationalists were able to successfully ascribe injustices and social inequalities to the distortions (political, economic, social, cultural) brought about by colonial rule. Colonial governments, for their part, manipulated gender systems through selectively upholding and disrupting local norms and practices.

Unlike other Third World countries—such as South Africa and India, to give two examples—Palestine has yet to enter the state of "postcolonialism." Indeed, one could argue that Palestinians are more firmly entrenched in a protracted colonial situation, considering the rate at which Arab-owned land continues to be confiscated and settled by Jewish Israeli colonists, and controlled by Israel—a situation that, at the time of this writing, does not seem likely to change any time soon. Yet the questions raised in postcolonial studies—analysis of the intertwined strands of nationalism, feminism, and colonialism—provide a relevant framework for studying the history of Palestinian women. One reason is the durability and continued importance of Palestinian nationalism. These fly in the face of contemporary attitudes about nationalism and national liberation, which are cast as irrelevant and atavistic, having fallen out of political favor along with other ideological remnants from the recent past.[10] The "exceptionally harsh, intractable" nature of the struggle, and the continued deferral of Palestinian nationhood have contributed to this durability.[11] Another reason is Palestinian society's long encounter with diverse forms of colonialism, the effects of which it is still experiencing.

Until relatively recently, Palestinian women's participation in the nationalist struggle had been perceived as a "necessary [albeit] not sufficient condition" for their emancipation as women.[12] Palestinian women frequently expressed their belief that "the struggle for women's liberation is not distinct from the rest" and does not contain "any contradiction either between the assertion of . . . national identity—Palestinian and Arab—and women's liberation."[13] Starting with Palestinian women's involvement in the nationalist movement in the 1920s, and up through the intifada of the late 1980s–early 1990s, nationalism was seen as having a "releasing effect" on women, providing them with a public role and outlet for political expression.[14] It was widely considered the only appropriate oppositional response for women living under colonial (British and later Israeli) hegemony. For some time, Palestinian women did not question or problematize the tensions between their nationalist participation and the gender inequalities in their society. They frequently expressed the difficulty inherent in promoting what they perceived of as narrow, feminist issues when their whole nation was under attack: no Palestinian—male or female—had political rights, and men in particular were singled out for violent treatment.[15] Demands for gender equality were (and still are) perceived as divisive. Yet in the 1980s a critique of the tensions began to emerge and has since begun to intensify and evolve, despite continued, tenacious adherence to the primacy of the national issue over feminist ones in many circles.[16]

Part of what has created the tensions between feminism and nationalism in the Palestinian and other Third World contexts are limited, Western-oriented definitions of feminism that ignore the realities of imperialism and colonialism and universalize Western women's experiences as representative of "women." Western women are not innocent in their role in upholding or representing those political systems against which Third World women and men have been struggling. Third World women's experiences with colonial hegemonies have made them deeply suspicious of Western feminists, since "northern culture (of which feminism is a part) is not neutral in relation to other cultures but is integral to Western political and economic domination."[17] Third World feminist scholars have interrogated Western feminists' sole focus on gender asymmetry in determining power differentials, articulating instead a feminism that takes into account the "intersections of the various systemic networks of class, race, (hetero)sexuality, and nation."[18] Women living under colonial hegemonies could not—still cannot—ignore the fact that social and political inequalities of men and women alike were consolidated, controlled, and maintained by colonial state structures. They do not define themselves solely by gender. Crucial to understanding Third World feminisms is a "notion of agency which works not through the logic of [gender] identification but through the logic of opposition" to colonial structures of domination.[19]

The problem cannot necessarily be articulated as a conflict between

"Western" or "Third World" feminisms. The recent epistemological trend towards multiculturalism and the "politics of difference," which has resulted from Western self-criticism on the issue of representing the "Other," threatens to reproduce the very binary categorizations it eschews, this time unproblematically privileging the "indigenous."[20] Marnia Lazreg calls for "some awareness of a common denominator between people of different cultures, a *human* bond. The notion of 'cultural universals' or that of the 'human mind,' however problematic, are expressions of such a common link between various peoples."[21] Feminism can share some universal "sets of organizing principles" that ought to highlight common ties between women, despite its different incarnations within specific cultures and historical periods.[22] One problem, as Lazreg points out, is that "to think of feminism in the singular is sociologically inappropriate."[23] Another problem is that Western historians of feminism have been too mired within their regional specialties to discern the common patterns and links between the diverse ideological strands of feminisms in different parts of the world.[24]

The question of feminism in Third World women's movements, which may not have explicitly defined themselves as "feminist," needs to be historicized in a way that challenges not only overly Westernized definitions of feminism, but also internal, indigenous feminist critics who reject their own historical antecedents, the early "bourgeois" women activists who were involved in charitable, religious, or social organizations. We need to recognize that "feminism, perhaps outside the terms and definitions as we know it today, has existed in a variety of forms" within Third World societies throughout history.[25] The problem lies in a tendency by feminists of all ilks (and their critics, one should note) to "judge historical feminism and its advocates by contemporary expressions of both feminism and feminist theory."[26] Karen Offen cautions historians of the dangers of using the words "feminism" and "feminist" "anachronistically and with great abandon" without defining or scrutinizing "the full content of the ideas" so labeled. She calls for a "historically sound . . . more dynamic, more supple and more comprehensive" definition of feminism that "can bear the weight of the historical evidence and make sense of it."[27] In tackling the task herself, she identifies two modes of (Western) feminism that evolved historically: "relational" and "individualist." Relational feminism is "a gender-based but egalitarian vision of social organization" that "featured the primacy of a companionate, non-hierarchical, male-female couple as the basic unit of society." It "emphasized women's rights *as women* . . . in relation to men," whereas individualist feminism featured "the individual, irrespective of sex or gender, as the basic unit" of society, emphasizing "more abstract concepts of individual human rights and . . . the quest for personal independence."[28]

Offen, it should be noted, was discussing the history of Western feminism. But here one can make a case for finding commonalities between Western and Third World feminisms—specifically Palestinian feminism—without necessarily attributing ideological or practical origins to one or the other. Third World feminisms have evolved and practiced similar forms of feminism without naming or categorizing them as such. As Sharon Sievers notes, "Feminism may be the name that has been given to a particular set of organizing principles and ideas about women, but universally such sentiments—the moral passion that precedes organizing principles—are present long before we have names for them."[29] The concepts behind relational feminism are useful for societies such as Palestinian society, which has tended to stress communal or collective well-being rather than that of the individual. Relational feminism worked toward greater appreciation for "women's work" and their role in society, reinforcing the family unit and existing domestic arrangements. It "combined a case for moral equality of women and men with an explicit acknowledgment of differences in women and men's sexual functions in society."[30] Temma Kaplan, writing about early twentieth-century Spanish women activists, articulates a concept of "female consciousness," which, combined with relational feminism, is also particularly appropriate to Palestinian women's activism: "Female consciousness centers upon the rights of gender, on social concerns, on survival. Those with female consciousness accept the gender system of their society . . . women with female consciousness demand the rights that their obligations entail."[31] Neither female consciousness nor relational feminism challenged either patriarchal practices[32] or group solidarity, both of which are embedded in Palestinian nationalism, which has proven adroit at rephrasing traditions or customs in official discourse in order to heighten and maintain national unity.[33] Palestinian nationalism has converted Palestinian society's emphasis on communal values into "a culture of [nationalist] resistance" built upon "expressions of ethnic identity and group solidarity." Often it is women who transmit and embody this culture.[34]

One can see elements of female consciousness and relational feminism in the construction of a particular hybrid that some have called "nationalist" or "national" feminism.[35] What distinguishes national/ist feminism from other feminisms is the valorization of an idealized "nationalist woman," a figure that is a syncretic hybrid of conflicting features: both "traditional"[36] and "new woman," mother and fighter, for example.[37] This figure is appropriated by both patriarchal nationalists and female national feminists alike. She embodies both preservation of a culture and nation under attack by colonialist hegemonies and deconstruction of the indigenous patriarchal institutions that formed the very pillars of that culture and nation.

Nationalists (particularly the male leadership) have dealt with the inherent contradictions in the figure of the nationalist woman in various ways. "Tradition" was perceived as a major impediment in the struggle to achieve national independence. Yet male (and many female) nationalists were unwilling to interrogate and upset their societies' gender systems and domestic divisions of labor. Women became the site of contestation, since they were "represented as the atavistic and authentic body of national tradition (inert, backward-looking, and natural) embodying nationalism's conservative principles of continuity."[38] Patriarchal nationalism thus transformed and reinscribed new meaning to women's domesticity, politicizing it, elevating it to new heights, and imbuing it with nationalist significance. According to Partha Chatterjee, Indian nationalists situated women as protectors of the national culture and its "spiritual" realm, as embodied by the home (versus the "world"). In the process, a "new patriarchy" evolved out of nationalist and reformist currents. This new patriarchy "conferred upon women the honor of a new social responsibility, and by associating the task of 'female emancipation' with the historical goal of sovereign nationhood, bound them to a new, and yet entirely legitimate, subordination."[39] Thus the potent combination of nationalism and "new womanhood" effectively reinforced patriarchal structures and helped blunt the sharp edges of disquieting social change.

The politicization of domesticity is epitomized by the appropriation of the institution of motherhood in nationalist discourse. In Palestine, the "mother of the martyr" is revered and assigned special status.[40] In South Africa, women such as Winnie Mandela were celebrated as "mothers of the nation" after independence was achieved. In India and Bengal, "the good woman, the chaste married wife/mother . . . became the iconic representation of the nation."[41]

Yet despite nationalism's ostensibly conservative and negative effect on and/or legacy to women, it cannot be denied that, historically, it has provided an impetus for women to defy social and cultural norms and become involved in realms of activity from which they had previously been excluded. It has offered an opening, a foot in the door, so to speak. Frances Hasso cautions feminists to assess women's involvement in a more nuanced way by situating them "simultaneously as actors, symbols, and authors—using, being used by, and constructing nationalism on their own terms."[42]

Third World women have not necessarily responded docilely to the iconography, symbolism, and roles imposed on them by patriarchal nationalism. African women, for example, while accepting the maternal valorization in nationalist discourse, "transformed and infused the ideology of motherhood with an increasingly insurrectionary cast" as "mothers of the revolution."[43] Women have created their own indigenous feminisms, which often have involved subverting and reworking "tradition," redefining "feminism" and political activism in their own terms and historical contexts. "When men revolt, their behavior still falls within, rather than violates, masculine cultural norms."[44] For women to revolt, they must find ways to express dissidence, militancy, and resistance that defy the usual, gendered modes of discourse and redefine women's acts to be as "political" as men's.

Palestinian women marked out their own spheres of activity and developed their own "language of refusal and militancy" within the women's movement, creating their own forms of indigenous, nationalist feminisms.[45] These were profoundly affected by their class, their strongly felt nationalist feelings, and their perceptions of the articulations of power among themselves, Palestinian men, and the British colonial authority.

A HISTORY IN SEARCH OF HISTORIANS

In attempting to write a history of the Palestinian women's movement, I was interested in interrogating the triadic relationship between nationalism, feminism, and colonialism. But I confronted an unusual situation: there is a surprising silence that shrouds the subject of Palestinian women in almost all historical writings on Palestine. There is a small but growing body of material in autobiographies, personal memoirs, and oral histories that either address women's experiences or contain accounts of women, but for all intents and purposes, there is almost no written history that focuses on the experience of Palestinian women.[46] To be sure, this has begun to change since the research for this book was completed; yet research is still limited primarily to a handful of articles in books and journals.[47]

It is perplexing that Palestinian and Middle East historians have exhibited little interest in such a seminal part of Palestinian history as the women's movement. This is all the more surprising considering that writers on Palestine continually invoke the history of Palestinian women's role in the national struggle without undertaking the research and writing of this history. Furthermore, contemporary Palestinian women activists derive lessons from, and draw parallels between, their current situation and this history without seriously examining it. Nahla Abdo, for example, says:

'No going back' is a statement quite often reiterated by women activists in the ongoing Palestinian *Intifada*. With an indirect reference to the Algerian experience and a direct one to their own history of subjugation, Palestinian women appear to be making a historical breakthrough.[48]

Yet this "history of subjugation," so easily assumed and referred to, has yet to be fully researched and written. The lack of information on the history of Palestinian women has important implications. There is little data on women's function in or relationship to economic structures, education, culture, law, the family, political institutions, or agriculture, for example—all areas of study that could inform the context of women's "history of subjugation." The researcher has few experts and only a very small body of knowledge to consult other than raw, uninterrogated primary sources.

Why then has the history of Palestinian women's involvement been relegated to such obscurity? There are several factors that provide partial explanations. The global dispersal of the Palestinian people—first in 1948 and subsequently in 1967—and their existence in widespread, multiple diasporas have resulted in the commensurate scattering of the sources for their history. It is impossible to overestimate the effect of 1948 on Palestinian society and its national political and cultural institutions, which have either disappeared completely or had to rebuild themselves, often in insecure, conflict-ridden regions of the world.[49] Some scholars cite the dispersal as the "major reason for the paucity of studies on Palestinian women."[50] Another effect of the dispersal of the Palestinian population has been the confiscation, control, and restriction of access by the Israelis to the archival materials, personal papers, and the like that remain in geographic Palestine.[51] This scattering of, and lack of access to, potential sources constitutes a very real problem for scholars of Palestinian history. It has not, however, prevented them from studying in depth the (male-led) Palestinian national movement, nor other topics in Palestinian history. The problem of studying Palestinian women extends beyond the difficulty of locating sources.

A second limitation has been the epistemological primacy of the national struggle as the key determinant in analyses of Palestinian politics and society. There has been a tendency to situate women entirely within its context without examining the full range of their historical conditions and experiences anterior to the conflict. Thus, the history of Palestinian women is assumed to be simplistically "understood through an examination of the history of her struggle alongside that of her people."[52] The understandable preoccupation with the current and future political situation among those writing about Palestinian women has resulted in the evolution of two major genres of literature, both focused on contemporary developments: Palestinian women's role in the "revolution" (national liberation movement of the 1960s–1970s led by the Palestinian Liberation Organization, or PLO); and their participation in the intifada and contemporary Palestinian politics since the 1980s.[53]

From surveying the literature on Palestinian women, one gains the impression that "prior to nationalism, women have no history, no resistance, no independent agency."[54] The national struggle, for the most part, is defined as occurring in the post-1948 era. Most of the (usually brief) references to women during the mandate period or earlier in these two genres tend to reiterate two conflicting themes: women played a heroic, revolutionary role and "participated in every matter of the struggle or revolutionary work in every part of Palestine"; or women's role was restricted due to "social traditions" and the "backwardness" of Palestinian society.[55] The corollary to the latter is the simplistic adage that pre-1948 women's leaders were "bourgeois" and ineffective because they were elitist, not politically "aware," and did not "suffer what the ordinary women suffered in the way of repression, ignorance, and backwardness."[56] There is little use of primary sources, nor are the constantly reiterated nationalist themes in this literature critically examined. The discursive style of the writings wavers contradictorily between celebratory and almost hagiographic to critical and dismissive, reflecting more the particular writer's contemporary political agenda and attendant revisionist historical view rather than presenting nuanced, researched analysis.[57] Writers often combine elements of both styles. Characterizations of women's role as "revolutionary" derives from a tendency in 1970s–1980s literature on Palestine to reinscribe such events as the 1929 Wailing Wall incident as nationalist "revolutions," when other accounts indicate they were, rather, inchoate popular expressions of anger, fear, and protest.

Other, scant historical references to Palestinian women are located within the historiography of the mandate period, where women are mentioned (if at all) in passing or in footnotes; or ghettoized and isolated in a special section in which they suddenly and briefly appear, only to be completely disregarded in the rest of the national narrative.[58] For the most part, the dynamic, involved women's movement that endured throughout the mandate period is relegated to a few paragraphs in both bodies of work.[59] The lack of interest in pre-1948 history among those who write about Palestinian women is particularly baffling in light of the thriving interest in, and growing corpus on, the history of women's participation in oppositional politics and nationalist movements in other parts of the world.[60]

Yet another explanation as to why the pre-1948 period in particular is neglected can be attributed to the disjuncture between the experiences of younger and older generations of Palestinian women. "Past factors tend to influence, or distort, our experiences of the present." This is particularly resonant to Palestinians, whose past has a "living active existence in the present," and whose future is continually and seemingly endlessly, predicated on contested versions of history.[61] These contestations involve not only divergent historical narratives between Palestinians and Israelis, but also among Palestinians.[62] The generations who did not experience the *nakba* ("disaster," the common Arabic term for the events of 1948) pass judgment on their elders' historical experiences. Criticisms for the mistakes, factionalism, class divisions, and reactionary nature of the "generation of the disaster" inform most histories of this era.[63] The Palestinian women's movement is guilty by association with a period in history that is renowned—perhaps infamous—for the colossal failure of Palestine's leadership and the loss of the country. Yet failure alone does not account for lack of a written history, despite the maxim that history belongs to the victors; histories of that (male) leadership abound.[64]

INTERSECTIONS OF HISTORIES: WOMEN'S, THIRD WORLD, AND MIDDLE EAST HISTORY

The absence of Palestinian women in historical writing also derives from the status of Middle Eastern women within the genre of women's history, and women's history within the field of Middle East history. In her seminal work, *Gender and the Politics of History*, Joan Wallach Scott announces that "Virginia Woolf's call for a history of women . . . [in *A Room of One's Own*] has been answered." She depicts women's history as "marked by a remarkable diversity in topic, method, and interpretation," which includes "a vast array of topics studied" and "a vast accumulation of writings." Indeed, women's history has spawned growing, sophisticated, rich corpora in specializations such as work, reproduction and sexuality, and politics, to name a few.[65] Yet her celebratory account of the status of "women's history" is implicitly exclusive; missing in both text and notes documenting the "vast array" of historical studies are references to works on Arab, Middle Eastern, or Third World women—categories in which Palestinian women are situated. Despite recent proliferation, expansion, and change in the extent, substance, and subjects of women's studies, "Third World women" still remain marginalized to a great extent within Eurocentric Western historical scholarship, both as subjects of study and as scholars.[66] The need for solid, empirically based research grounded in the historical experiences of Third World women is compelling; such studies remain scarce.[67]

Despite marginalization of Third World women's history within the field of women's history, the literature is theoretically rich and helps contribute to understanding the Palestinian situation. The dearth of appropriate paradigms or literature in Middle East history led me to draw substantially upon Third World women's history and subaltern studies. Indian women's experiences with British colonialism and their involvement in the Indian nationalist struggle, for example, made their history especially relevant to the Palestinian context.[68]

A few words about terms seem called for here. There is growing criticism of the assumptions underlying use of the term "Third World women" that deconstructs its multiple meanings, both in its entirety (as "Third World women") and singly ("women," or woman, and "Third World"). Rajeswari Mohan flatly asserts, "There is no collective will, visibly marked body of people, or community based on shared experience that inherently corresponds or exists anterior to the discursive configuration of the third world woman."[69] Mohan and other critics are reacting against a tendency to essentialize, universalize, and categorize the experiences of "Third World women," which undermines the complexities, differences, diversities, and divisions inherent in "Third World" as in other histories. (It must be added that the same objections can be raised against use of the term "Western women.") Chandra Talpade Mohanty dissects the problem of "woman" in "Third World woman":

> The assumption of woman as an already constituted, coherent group with identical interests and desires, regardless of class, ethnic or racial location or contradictions, implies a notion of gender or sexual difference or even patriarchy (as male dominance—men as a correspondingly coherent group) which was applied universally and cross-culturally.... What is problematical, then, about this kind of use of 'women' as a group, as a stable category of analysis is that it assumes an ahistorical, universal unity between women based on a generalized notion of their subordination.[70]

She offers a definition of "Third World woman" that highlights "the common context of political struggle against class, race, gender and imperialist hierarchies that may constitute third world women as a strategic group."[71] Yet this definition assumes another kind of unity, one based on struggle, that does not take into account women who may not necessarily be engaged in the types of struggles identified by Mohanty. Despite the debate over terminology and definitions, scholars treading warily in the contentious, identity-conscious, intellectual atmosphere prevalent today require the use of meaningful categories of analysis without having to resort to constant footnoting and explanations of their multiple and even potential meanings. For this and other reasons, I do not jettison the use of "Third World women," but rather reject any definition that posits a "singular, monolithic and paradigmatically victimized subject."[72] Instead, recognizing Third World women's diverse, multiple identities and historical experiences requires using the term "judiciously in appropriate circumstances."[73]

I use this term despite the fact that it does not reflect the consciousness of the subject under study, the Palestinian women's movement of the 1930s and 1940s. Of course, women living in Palestine before 1948 did not perceive themselves to be living in the Third World, a term that did not even exist in this period. Yet, as I argue throughout the book, the women involved in the movement did articulate a conscious sense of collective identity and political strategizing with other women who lived under colonial regimes—to the extent of corresponding with them, appealing to them for support and offering it in turn, and inviting them to and participating in conferences together. Thus, the term has some meaning in this respect; it accurately depicts the sense of common identity expressed consciously and acted upon by Palestinian women involved in the movement. As a historian, I am taking the prerogative of imposing this category of analysis in order to help readers see the universal aspects as well as the broader political context of the Palestinian women's movement.

This leads us back to another term: "Palestinian women" as enfolded within the understanding of "Third World women." Feminist theorists have deconstructed meanings of "woman" which posit a "universal, self-producing binary opposition" between "man" and "woman," and instead have proposed using "gender," a more "useful category of analysis." Scott defines gender as "a constitutive element of social relationships based on perceived differences between the sexes, and . . . a primary way of signifying relationships of power."[74]

Yet, as we have seen above, Third World feminists warn against all-inclusive categorizations that do not take into account sources of power differentials *among* women. One must thus beware of referring to a homogeneous, undifferentiated collectivity, "Palestinian women," since the heterogeneity of Palestinian society, with its urban-rural, class, and religious differences, has resulted in distinctions and social inequalities among Palestinian women.[75] When I speak of Palestinian women, the particular context is crucial. This work deals primarily with a relatively privileged, elite segment of Palestinian women. I include Palestinian women from other social classes (the majority of "Palestinian women") where possible and appropriate. But this study, due to the character of the movement itself, focuses on a particular class of women.

The field of Middle East history has also been implicated in the dearth of studies on Palestinian women's history. Scholarship on women and gender, while proliferating and constituting some of the most exciting work in the field of Middle East history, nonetheless remains marginalized within it, although this may change in the coming years.[76] Yet it comes nowhere near the extent and scope of women's history in other (Western) fields. As is the case with Third World women's history, the need for solid, empirically grounded history is still urgent.

Margaret Meriwether and Judith Tucker note another aspect in the field of Middle East women's history, which is "the apparently small concern to most women researchers and activists" from the region about the lack of serious historical study. They attribute this to a number of factors, including the feeling among women that they wish to make a "clean break" with a history of oppression and instead look to a better future; the "history they know and can know" is one of elite women, whose past they do not wish to "enshrine"; and, on a very practical level, the field has trouble attracting women scholars due to poor research facilities, among other reasons.[77]

The relative poverty of women's history within the field of Middle East history is also related to the fact that, despite some progress, the discipline overall tends to highlight the political and diplomatic at the expense of social, economic, and cultural history, which affects the study of women and gender.[78] In the mandate literature referred to above, for example, most monographs focus primarily on political factors without taking into account social, economic, or cultural structures. "Politics . . . has been socially constructed, or, more accurately, male-constructed."[79] "Politics" in the Palestinian case, tends to connote the nationalist struggle, seemingly divorced from its economic and social content.[80] In this context, "women's issues" (and by extension, their activities) are perceived of as "social" and not "political."[81] Because women, by and large, participated informally in "politics," the economy, and culture, they were not granted historical or political agency. Furthermore, men "have had the power to define what knowledge is," and what constitutes "political"; "by making political women 'invisible', men reinforce the dualistic world view of themselves as political and women as apolitical."[82] Women often were involved in spontaneous, unorganized activity that was unrecorded, or not designated as "political" or "historical."

SOURCES

Because of the silence concerning Palestinian women's history in written works, the trajectory of this study has been dictated more than is usual in such research by its primary sources, which comprise for the most part oral history interviews, the Arabic press, and British government documents. I also utilized autobiographies, memoirs, and publications of the women's organizations, such that existed. The archives of the women's organizations were either lost like many other Palestinian historical records, or, if they exist (I never located any), are unavailable. What emerged was the articulation of three distinct voices: Palestinian women's memories—largely about their personal lives, involvements, and daily life during the period—in the interviews; Palestinian male points of view from the press; and British (mostly male) colonialist voices.[83] Missing are Jewish voices.[84]

Oral History and Private Memory

In the course of the research, I interviewed approximately seventy Palestinians, most of them women. By a cruel twist of fate, all of the major leaders of the women's movement (as represented in the written records) were already deceased by the time I began this research. The long-term president of the AWU, Zlikha al-Shihabi, died several days before I arrived in Jerusalem to begin the research. Indeed, a number of women I interviewed passed away not long afterward. Because of this, I have had to extrapolate and infer—perhaps more than is usual—from the evidence that was available the attitudes and objectives of the leadership of the women's movement. I did, however, interview women who had participated in the movement's activities, some relatives of the leadership, and some men who had known certain leaders. Although I initially tried to locate "politically active women," ultimately my choice for interviews was unsystematic and entirely dependent upon contacts and the good will and assistance of the friends and colleagues who provided me with names, introductions, and, in some cases, accompanied me and helped translate. People had diverse ideas about who was "suitable" to be interviewed. I ended up interviewing older women who were usually distinguished for their active role in women's organizations (in the present as well as past) or their education and stature in society. But I also interviewed a smaller number of village women who usually requested anonymity. Both the village and educated women were "ordinary" in the sense that they were not national figures (with one exception), nor were they major leaders in the past or present. The older educated women were not necessarily "ordinary" for their time, but neither were they some of the more famous *shakhsiyyāt* (well-known, notable women).[85]

My use of oral history originated out of a need to fill in the gaps and silences in the written records. Many of the interviews were informal conversations that were studded with stories, opinions, and historical information casually imparted by the "history-givers" but carefully noted by me.[86] Oral history has been little used in the traditional field of Middle East history. For this and other reasons, I had little experience with the complex methodological processes and problems involved in conducting interviews.[87] Over time, I found myself increasingly drawn to the "call" of women's stories, and aware of the personal nature of doing oral history. The wise words of a psychiatrist to his young resident-in-training (Robert Coles) seem particularly relevant for historians:

> The people who come to see us bring their stories. They hope they tell them well enough so that we understand the truth of their lives. They hope we know how to interpret their stories correctly. We have to remember that what we hear is *their story*. . . . [Later the older doctor cautions: "Remember, what you are hearing is to some extent a function of *you*, hearing."][88]

These words strike at the heart of the oral history project. When I began rather self-consciously to "interview," I narrowly focused my questions on the formalities and details of the women's movement without realizing the importance of trying to weave together the texture of women's everyday, personal, individual lives. I did not *hear* the stories at first because my own research agenda and expectations obstructed the hearing process; the stories women told me seemed to have little to do with my "topic." I unconsciously attempted to impose on the history-givers "a type of narrative shape . . . and a pattern of remembering" that were alien to them.[89] Women offered me their own narrative, their own story, in essence telling me a story within a story: their emphases ultimately steered me toward subjects I had not imagined writing about. Women provided me with their own "evaluations, explanations and theories, which often constitute[d] a principal value of the account and [were] intrinsic to its representations of reality."[90]

Although "'narrative' has become one of the charged code words in the current struggles over history," I believe that we historians should not abandon our story-telling function.[91] The attack on narrative is part of the "postmodern claim that verbal constructs do not correspond in a direct way to reality, [a claim that has] arisen precisely when women and non-Western peoples have begun to speak for themselves."[92] Hearing and then trying honestly to tell women's stories—especially in their own words—gives them agency and a voice in their own history that has been woefully absent.[93] Few Palestinians of this generation were not directly and personally affected by history with a capital H, and thus had much to offer. As Luisa Passerini observes, "It is an irony of history . . . that what is written about it so largely ignores the personal lives of individuals in the very period (the past hundred years) when individual subjectivity has been transformed, becoming an important area of scientific study and political interest."[94] Using oral history was thus a conscious decision to deepen the overall context, add women's voices, and clothe the "political" narrative with its personal context.

Oral history is not unproblematic. The relationship between "truth" and "facts," and "interpretation" and "representation" always quivers with tension. The oral historian must ultimately listen to the way memory is reconstituted, which reveals as much as the objective information contained in the account itself. This kind of listening involves surrendering a certain amount of authorial control, since the history-givers dictate the narrative through their choices of what to suppress or emphasize, highlighting themes, myths, or popular stereotypes important to them and their agenda. These reveal much about individuals' concepts of relations of power, self, and identity. They also highlight history-givers' notions of history itself.

What people chose to forget was telling; the late Hind al-Husayni, renowned for founding an orphanage for the surviving children of the Dayr Yassin massacre in 1948, informed me that she did not participate in demonstrations or join "anything" (such as a women's group) until she founded the orphanage, Dār al-Tifl al-'Arabi.[95] Yet other women mentioned her, and I found repeated press articles detailing her prominence in student protest activity during the 1936 revolt.

Hind al-Husayni's "forgetting" was part of a complex process Ted Swedenburg calls historical "salvage work," as well as the product of the workings of private memories that "cannot . . . be readily unscrambled from the effects of dominant historical discourses."[96] Palestinian interlocutors understand that "private memory must be transformed into public history" as part of the Palestinian nationalist project to keep memories alive in order to contest the pro-Zionist historical narrative dominant in the West.[97] "Palestinian attempts at historical self-representation must be understood, therefore, in relation to their narrative absence in the West."[98] By talking to a foreign researcher, Sitt Hind wished to stress her current, ongoing nationalist work, capitalizing on the institution's and her own renown in order to highlight the misfortune of the Palestinian people as exemplified by the tragedy of Dayr Yassin. Her previous involvement in the 1930s, in her own, perhaps subconscious, memory was relegated to irrelevancy. After all, the revolt failed, and furthermore was barely known in Western historiography and political discourse. She chose to demote it in a hierarchy of personal memory in which a more useful segment of her personal history was presented to an outsider who might convey the plight of her people to the West.[99] This common tendency on the part of history-givers forced me to reexamine my own research priorities and pay attention to Palestinian notions of what is important historically. I also learned to dig further and not to accept information—from whatever source—at face value. One must weave together the strands of oral memory with documentary evidence and not rely on one to the exclusion of the other.

The Press

A major surprise in my research was discovering the abundance of press coverage of Palestinian women in the Arabic newspapers. Women were not mentioned in secondary sources on the press, which had led me to believe that I would not find much information about them in newspapers.[100] I have included a chapter devoted entirely to this topic for a number of reasons. The extensive and wide-ranging press coverage of women spoke volumes about the discursive ferment on gender issues in Palestinian society. Men and women alike read and wrote in the press about the "woman question," which is the focus of Chapter 3. The central issue in these contestations extended beyond the ostensibly limited topic of "women" to constitute virtually the future of the nation and Palestinian society's sense of its historical identity. Second, the women's movement and the press developed an unusually symbiotic relationship, to the extent that one suspects the press played the role of promoter and mouthpiece at certain crucial moments. I explore these issues in Chapter 6.

British Documents

The British documentary sources used in this study consist of Colonial and Foreign Office records and personal papers or memoirs of British officials or individuals who worked and/or lived in Palestine during the mandate period. The government documents articulate a distinctive discourse of their own, revealing by their very configuration government attitudes about gender: women are present primarily in files that deal with education, social welfare, health, and "Moslem affairs."[101] The one notable exception is police files that were kept on the activities of the women's movement, particularly during the 1930s.

There is a onesidedness and lack of symmetry in the information imparted in the British government archives, attributable in part to the lack of an official Palestinian national archive. British officials have different emphases than would Palestinian officials, if their own voices in the records had been preserved. (A few have.) On certain subjects we simply do not have a Palestinian interlocutor.

Shards of History

> When all's said and done, carved stones, pages on which the author or the copyist labored, mosaics, all those are just fragments of humanity as well, in fact those parts of ourselves which we hope to be immortal.[102]

All of the major primary sources in this study are characterized by both partialness and partiality. The fragmentation of the data was frustrating; I felt "teased" by fascinating events and topics that appeared in the sources, usually reported cursorily or vaguely, only to vanish without further trace.[103] Because of this fragmentation, the data itself played a strong role in shaping my investigation of certain topics, groups, and themes—often unanticipated—that were more richly documented than others. This is the reason I have focused for the most part on the role of the elite women who were active in the women's movement. Sources on peasant women, who constituted the majority of Palestinian women during the period studied, were elusive. Doubly marginalized by social class and gender, peasant and poorer urban women as well have traditionally not been deemed worthy historical subjects—not even in their own view sometimes. I hope that further research will rectify their absence in history writing, including my own.[104]

The second issue of subjectivity and point of view of sources is not, of course, unique to the history of Palestinian women. It, also, is related to the problem of fragmentation. Because I was the first to locate Palestinian women in many of these sources, I felt both an obligation and freedom to utilize the data multivocally, changing voices between and even among the different sources in an attempt to foreground each source's subjectivity rather than lay claim to some Rankeian ideal of historical objectivity. The oral history interviews, for example, provide a female, Palestinian counterpoint to the largely male, British point of view expressed in the Colonial and Foreign Office documents. I found myself constantly aware of issues of voice and representation in the sources. Part of my project, then, involves not only construction of a history but also a self-consciousness about how I do it.

Researching Palestinian women's history requires that the scholar become detective, explorer, and archeologist. The mentality and tenacity of a detective is helpful in pursuing clues in attempts to close the gaps in knowledge. In order to find women in historical sources, one must seek them in the first place. I explored uncharted waters without a map or guarantee that the data I inferred and hoped was "out there" even existed. And, indeed, as often as not, I did not find what I was looking for but something totally different. The rewards were great. Oral history, in particular, provided me with a vivid evocation of the mandate period; I was able to invoke a distinct feeling for many aspects of the lives of Palestinian women from diverse backgrounds through hearing endless stories and engaging in discussions with them about their lives. I felt like I knew certain personalities, could visualize neighborhoods and villages, and even mentally recreated a certain texture of the time from the images and descriptions that recurred and resonated from women's stores of memory. Without the existence of Palestinian national archives, the tasks of imaginatively speculating where information might be found, and searching for it, took on major importance. I have had to write archaeologically, piecing together multiple shards of oral and written memories and documents. The ultimate product is a history that resembles reconstructed pottery assembled of small holes contiguous with richly painted shards.

2. Palestinian Women and the Rule of the British Mandate

The entry of the British into Jerusalem to take control of Palestine on December 11, 1917, signaled the beginning of profound transformations in the lives of Palestinian Arabs. Within the span of three decades, the country experienced not only waves of successive crises and turmoil such as the Wailing Wall incident of 1929, the violent upheavals of 1933, the general strike and great revolt of 1936–39 (*al-thawra al-kubra*), and of course, the ultimate disaster (*al-nakba*), the war of 1948, but also tremendous socioeconomic and cultural change as well. Great Britain's explicit obligation to Jewish colonization under the terms of the Balfour Declaration distinguished Palestine from other British colonial undertakings such as those in India and Egypt. Analogous to other British colonies, Palestine ultimately bore the cultural, political, social, and economic imprint of British imperial hegemony. This was particularly the case with those Palestinians, primarily of the upper and middle classes, who came into direct contact with British officials and the government institutions that carried out mandate policies. Concepts such as "British justice" entered the Palestinian discourse on notions of fairness, legality, and rights. British ideas on education, "character" development, hygiene, and universal (middle-class) womanhood—to name but a few—were reflected in the workings of governmental institutions, which in turn influenced Palestinian cultural and social practices.

Paradoxically, however, many who lived through it recall much of the mandate period as one of relative—albeit precarious, uneven, and temporary—stability.[1] This may be a function of historical retrospective on the part of Palestinians. The mandate period was the most recent and possibly last time in their history when they lived as a national entity in the entirety of their land.[2] In comparison to the massive dispersal and shattering events that came in the wake of 1948—the 1967 war; Black September (1970); the

24

Lebanese civil war; the invasion of Lebanon and Sabra and Shatila massacres; the intifada; the Gulf War; and the complete breakdown of stability and order which, as of this writing, has been the outcome of the failure of the dysfunctional, flawed Oslo Accords—the mandate period may indeed be perceived as one of stability. After it ended, exile, diaspora, and national disintegration became a way of life affecting all Palestinians. Furthermore, many of the social, economic, and cultural changes witnessed during this era were part of a period of transformation that had already begun during the last half-century of Ottoman rule. In some ways, the British Mandate government continued a process of change, both gradual and uneven, which had already become familiar to Palestinians.

One aspect of this period that has not received much scholarly attention is social change and Palestinian interpretations of it. Studies of the status of women and changing perceptions of gender help construct a more comprehensive historical vision than studies that focus exclusively on national and international politics, diplomacy, or economics. The Palestinian women's movement can only be understood within the context of the forces of change and continuity that shaped women's individual and collective experiences. One important aspect affected those experiences: the policies and practices of the British Mandate government. The argument here is that, although the government, in fact, had no explicit, articulated policy regarding women, ultimately its institutions, practices, and overall governmental policies worked to construct a kind of de facto policy that simultaneously neglected, disciplined, and repressed women. (To be fair, its predecessor, the Ottoman government, was as feeble in dealing with the needs of half its population.) Yet despite this sometimes almost passive policy of neglect, a small core of educated, "modern," "new women" emerged, having benefited from social change that both preceded and continued throughout the mandate period. These women would found and run the Palestinian women's movement.

WOMEN AND GENDER IN LATE-OTTOMAN PALESTINE

The area known as Palestine was conquered by and incorporated into the Turkish Ottoman Empire in the sixteenth century, under whose rule it remained until it came under the League of Nations Mandate granted to Great Britain in the post–World War I settlements. In the late-Ottoman period, Palestine was divided into various administrative units of the provinces of Beirut and Syria. Beginning as far back as the eighteenth century, it had begun to experience a series of economic, political, social, and cultural transformations brought about by the integration of the region into the world economy and increased commercialization of agriculture; the Tanzimat (reforms) enacted by the Ottoman government in the mid-nineteenth century; and the encroachment of European political, cultural, and economic interests in the region. These resulted in the growth of regional and international trade; modest but growing urbanization, particularly in Jerusalem and the coastal cities of Jaffa and Haifa; and a slow but steady shift in political influence from rural to urban elites.[3]

The Tanzimat was explicitly oriented toward strengthening and centralizing the political power of the Ottoman government through modernization. Reforms included the foundation of a secular educational system, "streamlining land-tenure relations" in order to increase taxation, liberalization of the status of religious minorities, and the establishment of a constitution (which was quickly abrogated, however).[4] Accompanying this process was the development of urban government in the mid-nineteenth century, marked by the establishment of municipal and district councils, and new court and land registration systems, all of which "engendered considerable bureaucratic activity" in the cities.[5] The growth and prosperity experienced by the larger towns of Palestine were also stimulated by increased European religious and cultural penetration, which had an impact on the expansion of trade.[6] The city of Jaffa became the major port of arrival and embarkation for an increasing number of Christian pilgrims and visitors, while Jerusalem was transformed from a "relatively minor provincial town" into the "biggest city of Palestine and the political and cultural center of the country."[7] Improvements in communications and infrastructures such as the building of roads, railway, telegraph lines, and the development of a postal service closely linked urban and rural areas, making the boundaries between their worlds more permeable. Civic and political life evolved with the founding of social, literary, charitable, and political associations. European (and to a lesser extent, American) Christian missionaries played a major part in founding some of these institutions—schools in particular.

The people of Palestine, however, experienced these modernizing processes "in uneven, contradictory, and internally differentiated ways," depending upon their various overlapping class, gender, religious, and regional identities.[8] Continuity coexisted, often uneasily, with change. Throughout the period studied, Palestine remained an agrarian society, although it is important to note the diversity within this characterization. The rain-fed, fertile coastal plains differed from the dry-farmed hilly regions and the southern desert, for example, making it difficult to generalize about the economic conditions and social formation of the Muslim Arab peasantry who constituted the majority living in Palestine's more than 850 villages. Although peasant landowning patterns in the late-Ottoman period varied from region to region and according to topography, agricultural use, and local custom, most peasants were small family farmers without substantial landholdings.[9] The specter of debt and the "rapacious" demands of tax collectors increasingly haunted them, and many lost their land as repayment for loans to debtors, moneylenders, or bigger landowners. As a result these people became either tenant farmers or agricultural wage laborers.[10] The Ottoman land reforms, by and large, tended to benefit larger landowners.[11]

Rural society was characterized by informal systems of mutual support and governance based on kin networks, local village government, and customary law. Villages were "knit together in a variety of economic, political, social, and cultural networks" with larger villages and towns constituting "social hubs" and commercial centers for smaller ones.[12]

Work on the family farm and kin relationships constituted the center of peasant life. Family members worked the land, performing most of the seasonal labor required. Although the division of labor was gendered, with men doing the plowing, threshing, and winnowing, and women performing the domestic work, food processing, field work, and animal husbandry, the latter's contribution was "much valued" and crucial to the success and survival of the family farm.[13]

Marriage was "central to social relations" in Palestinian society, "reinforc[ing] social ties within the community."[14] Marriages tended to be arranged by male relatives of the bride and groom, and generally took place when both were young, although frequently the choice of bride or groom was made by mothers, while the conclusion of formalities and contractual aspects were dealt with by the senior male relatives.[15] Under Islamic law, marriage is a contract by the two parties involved. The husband pays the wife a dower, the *mahr*, which constitutes her personal, not conjugal, property. He is responsible for his wife's maintenance and has some control over her personal mobility, while she owes him obedience. A woman's status and security depended on her family situation and material prospects. "Patrilocal marriage and the ease of divorce made women transient members" of their husband's family, resulting in greater dependence, reliance upon, and closer bonds to their natal families than their conjugal ties.[16] In the case of divorce or widowhood, a woman lived with her closest male relative (usually her father or a brother), who was responsible for her maintenance.

Under Islamic law, women's property is their own absolutely. During this time period, it was usually acquired through the *mahr* or inheritance. Although the *mahr* often comprised gold or money, women sometimes received land or movable property such as farm or herd animals instead. Women's inheritance might also consist of such property, especially land or orchards.[17]

Peasant women experienced greater personal mobility than urban, middle-, and upper-class women, and generally did not veil or practice seclusion. There was a common perception that they were "much more the equals of their husbands" than were town women.[18] Their productivity was valued, and they often exerted great influence within the extended peasant household, particularly the older women who ran the household. Their experience of the social changes that accompanied the political and economic changes in this period were noticeably different from those of women from the middle and upper classes. Although there was a kind of stability and continuity in the type of labor they performed and in their role within the family, this changed somewhat during the mandate period, when male agricultural workers migrated to city and town employment.

Palestine's small middle class during the late nineteenth and early twentieth centuries—merchants, small manufacturers, teachers or professionals, and members of the Islamic religious bureaucracy (*'ulamā'*)—tended to reside in the towns or cities. Larger percentages of Christians were concentrated in the cities and towns, in many of which the influence of Christian missionary institutions was more pronounced. The towns and cities contained, as well, "artisans, petty traders, service and day workers" who constituted a poorer working population.[19]

The women of upper- and middle-class urban families were more restricted and secluded than rural and poorer urban women, whose outdoor work responsibilities required greater personal mobility. Urban elite women rarely left their homes unattended by male relatives, and, up through the first decades of the twentieth century, Christian women as well as Muslim women often veiled and dressed modestly.[20] Social mixing of men and women rarely occurred outside of the family. Although few middle- or upper-class women worked outside of the home, domestic labor within the home was considerable, due to the high standards and importance of Arab hospitality and cooking, not to mention the lack of modern amenities such as running water in the house. The Arab middle- or upper-class housewife tended to perform as well as supervise the household labor. Musa al-'Alami, from a prominent Jerusalem family, recalls that the work his mother performed was "killing." Sometimes food preparation for a large group of guests could take as long as fifteen hours.[21] We have little data on the labor of poorer urban women. Clearly they were involved in informal economic sectors such as domestic service, midwifery, petty street vending, peddling, and even, in some cases, prostitution.[22]

Like their rural sisters, urban women's primary "institution of belonging" was the family unit, and marriage played a key role in their lives.[23] As an institution, marriage was important in creating and maintaining social and business alliances between families or different kin groups. Wealthier urban women, in addition to acquiring property through marriage and inheritance, sometimes invested in and managed their own property, usually real estate. Wajiha al-Husayni, born in 1908 into the notable Jerusalem Husayni clan, inherited a great deal of property, mostly land, from her father when she was young, and supervised the management of her own estates, for example.[24] Women might also contribute some of their own capital to their husband's business or to major family expenses, such as building a house.

Starting in the mid-nineteenth century, upper- and middle-class families gradually began sending their daughters to schools—primarily schools founded by foreign Christian missionaries. The Ottoman government in Palestine, unlike that of Muhammad 'Ali and his successors in Egypt, did not aggressively pursue the kinds of "educational modernization and technological and social reform" that led to governmental educational establishments for women.[25] The missionary schools played a larger role in Palestine and Greater Syria in the dissemination of education for girls. The first, St. Joseph's, was established in Jerusalem in 1848 by the French Catholics. By the late nineteenth–early twentieth century, there were over 1,300 foreign missionary schools in Palestine and Syria.[26] Most of these early private schools were founded in the towns and cities, such as Acre, Haifa, Jaffa, Jerusalem, Nazareth, and Nablus. Although the numbers of students at first were small and overwhelmingly Christian, increasingly, Muslim families of the upper and middle classes sent their daughters to these private schools, since the Ottoman government did not establish many government schools for girls.[27]

Women also began to work outside the home in Palestinian urban society in the late nineteenth–early twentieth century. They were few in number, primarily middle class and Christian or members of other minorities, and tended to be teachers in missionary or foreign-run schools. Melia Sakakini (born in 1890), sister of the noted educator and nationalist Khalil Sakakini, exemplifies this type of "pioneer."[28] Educated at the Arab Orthodox School in the Old City of Jerusalem, she later attended the Russian-run Teachers Training College in Bayt Jala and became a teacher and headmistress in

Jaffa.[29] Slowly, more upper- and middle-class women began to become visible as teachers, students, members of, and workers in, benevolent institutions and even, in rare cases, in occupations such as nursing.[30] Unveiling came slowly as well. By most accounts, some Palestinian middle-class women began to discard the veil in the 1920s, but the practice of veiling varied considerably from region to region, and, although gradually diminishing by the 1930s, was "still widely in vogue" according to some accounts.[31]

There is a general perception that during the late nineteenth and early twentieth centuries Palestinian society witnessed a gradual liberalizing tendency. A major factor that played a role in the social changes that led to this trend was the enormous intellectual influence of the writings and ideas of Islamist reformers such as Muhammad 'Abduh, Rifa'ah Rafi'al-Tahtawi, and the controversial Qasim Amin. Their impact, along with that of state-sponsored modernizing initiatives, played a major role in the development of new discourses that led to a "questioning and rethinking of the role of women." Women as well as men began to write about gender roles, women's education, marriage, and legal rights under Islam (among other matters) in the women's press that began to evolve in the late nineteenth century, as well as the mainstream press.[32] Although the press in Palestine developed much more slowly, and a women's press never materialized, the new ideas and debates influenced the literate Palestinian classes, albeit, perhaps, at a slower pace than in Egypt (see Chapter 3). These developments—the slow but steadily increasing dissemination of education, women's beginning to work outside the home, new discourses on women, and modernizing reforms of the Ottoman state—all played a role in the overall but uneven liberalizing trend in the region.

A final factor that also contributed to this trend was European influence. The complex and ambivalent legacy of European colonialism in Middle Eastern societies has become the subject of much interest, criticism, and debate, but cannot be discounted. What is important to note is that European influence and European colonialism were not necessarily monolithic. Many European missionaries, for example, while interested in proselytization and often socially conservative, were also genuinely concerned with providing education to girls, whereas the record of the British colonial government in expanding educational opportunities to girls—in both Egypt and Palestine—was undeniably dismal. Exposure to European culture and social mores, which accompanied the presence of missionaries, merchants, and diplomats, was disturbing, stimulating, and sometimes alienating, but it is also crucial to remember that these reactions went both ways. European economic, political, and cultural encroachment was one factor among many.

Furthermore, the European presence—and particularly its economic and cultural impacts—affected Palestinians differently according to their social and economic class and whether or not they lived in rural or urban society. New ideas about women were less likely to reach and affect overworked Palestinian peasant women than they would newly educated middle class urban women, for example. Nonetheless, among Palestinians who remembered late-Ottoman rule and the onset of the mandate there is the perception that the British initiated a life that was "more free and liberal" for women.[33]

BRITISH GOVERNMENT POLICIES AND GENDER

After the British took control of Palestine in 1917, they ruled under a military administration until 1920, when the government was converted into a formal mandate under the League of Nations as negotiated in the San Remo Conference following the armistice.[34] The purposes of the mandate from the beginning were contradictory: to facilitate the establishment of the "Jewish National Home," as declared in the Balfour Declaration, while simultaneously safeguarding the civil and religious rights of the "non-Jewish communities" and encouraging self-governing institutions.[35] Unlike Iraq and Syria, whose mandates provided for eventual independence, Palestine was ruled under a more ambiguous mandate, dealt with by the British "as just another colonial possession."[36] The text of the mandate does not mention the future political status of the country at all, although there are frequent references to the development of the "Jewish National Home," the precise meanings of which were nebulous and ill defined, making these concepts susceptible to variable and changing political interpretations. (In fact, the Jews and their rights are explicitly mentioned in six articles, whereas the word "Arab" does not appear anywhere in the document.) In reality, though, the Palestine government acted as "an extension of the British state."[37] The British directly controlled legislative, judicial, military, and foreign affairs and supervised religious ones.

The guiding principle of the British administration in Palestine toward the Arab population was protection of the status quo and resistance to innovation.[38] This was part of a "conscious colonial policy" that ensured that "the daily life of the people, hallowed as it was by both religion and custom, was as far as possible not interfered with in any obtrusive way."[39] Translated into practice, the policy was not necessarily benign or passive. The British maintained certain religious or tribal structures in order to facilitate administration, mediate conflict, and impose control, retaining those "customs" or practices that benefited their objectives in certain ways while creating or developing others that suited their purposes. In their concern with upholding "tradition," they reinforced social fragmentation and stratification, as well as created racialized religious categories for each individual, as Jew, Muslim, or Christian. The irony of this concern—which at times seemed almost obsessive—for not changing the social status quo was that their very presence in and of itself was, in fact, profoundly intrusive, provoking significant transformations in Palestinian politics, culture, economy, and society. Furthermore, this policy was unevenly pursued by individual government officials who did or did not necessarily agree with, or interpret it, in the same way.

Gender and the Mandate Government

Nowhere did the British government articulate an explicit policy on women. There were no commissions on women or departments of women's affairs. The issue of gender, while not entirely ignored, was embedded within other concerns. Over the twenty-eight-year course of the mandate, the British government's work with women focused on social conditions, which were dealt with as though divorced from political and economic factors.

Where they did pay attention to the problems or special conditions of Arab women, British officials conflated them with those of children, squarely situating motherhood as the central element in the government's definition of woman's function. Most government programs were geared toward supporting and buttressing women's role as mothers, training young women in "mothercraft" through the school system, for example, or targeting mothers in infant welfare programs under the auspices of the Department of Health. Even programs that did not directly engage mothers, such as midwife training and licensing, were geared toward supporting the institution of motherhood. These programs were consistent with British domestic welfare policies that linked child and maternal welfare with national development.[40]

Another area in which the British demonstrated interest in women was the regulation of lower-class women, such as prisoners, domestic servants, midwives (who were often poorer villagers), and prostitutes. This was part of the ostensible British mission of carrying out social reforms in order to bring the country "into line with the enlightened principles regarding the treatment of women and children which would be expected of an English Administration."[41] The government's policies were directed towards promoting better "hygiene," controlling venereal disease, and "reforming" conditions for women prisoners—most of whom (under the "enlightened"

British justice system) were incarcerated for petty crimes such as watering buffalo milk, running away from home, or stealing chickens.[42] Some of the earliest pieces of legislation passed by the government included the registration of midwives, and the Young Offenders Ordinance, which allowed the courts to commit female offenders up to the age of eighteen to a reformatory or industrial home.[43]

The British government was notoriously conservative and parsimonious in its budgetary policies and development plans for Palestine.[44] Palestine, a poor country with few natural resources and a largely undeveloped, agricultural economy, was to pay for itself, reinforcing colonial policies that a "self-supporting colony" not be financially dependent upon the home economy.[45] In an economic survey of sixteen colonies in the British colonial empire in 1937, the government of Palestine spent the least percentage of its budget (7.2 percent) on social services.[46] Despite a regressive tax burden on a poor population, and the British home government's resistance to furnishing loans for development, the Palestine government consistently ran in the black. Over the years, the percentage of its expenditures allocated to social services and public works decreased while those for security rose significantly.[47]

The government relied as much as possible on charitable organizations and religious groups to fill the gaps in social services. These groups had no official status or representation in the government, however. The Palestine Women's Council, for example, founded in 1921 and headed by Lady Samuel, the wife of the first high commissioner, was merely a "consultative body," which received the "warm support" of the administration, but no financing or official recognition. The government expressed itself "willing to refer to the Council questions affecting women and children in Palestine," but could not "bind itself to give effect to any resolutions" that the council passed.[48] Most of its members were European. Thirteen out of thirty-six of its affiliated organizations were Jewish, whereas only one was Arab. In its 1923–24 report, it lists only one Arab woman on its roster. One of its first acts was to obtain the appointment of a woman, Miss Margaret Nixon, as government welfare inspector in charge of the concerns of women and children. The struggle to get her appointed illustrates the council's ineffectual role and the government's laissez-faire attitude about women's welfare. Nixon was privately funded through leftover funds from the Syria and Palestine Relief Fund in the first year of her work, but the government had to be persuaded to accept the funding and make the appointment. The words of the chief secretary, attempting to refuse the funding when it was offered by Frances Newton, a member of the council, sum up rather neatly the government's attitude about women's welfare: "It cannot be said, can it, that the appointment of a woman welfare inspector is indispensable to the carrying on of the Government's administration?"[49] Other than its initial work focused primarily on prison reform, the Palestine Women's Council did not last long, nor was it very active much beyond its founding years in the early 1920s.[50]

Attitudes Toward Women and Gender in British Colonial Society

The British officials entrusted with carrying out government policies and working in departments that dealt with Arab women were influenced by contemporary orientalist notions of Middle Eastern women which were based upon very limited direct experience.[51] Their attitudes played a major part in their formulation of policy and execution of (limited) programs of development that affected women. Most Westerners' images of and ideas about Arab women had come from travelers' accounts, which tended to focus on upper-class women's life in the harem, and were characterized by voyeurism, titillation, and prurience caused, in part, by foreigners' inability to directly communicate with indigenous women.[52] Missionaries were also partially responsible for forming and conveying impressions that reached Westerners and the British public. Their testimony and observations about Middle Eastern women's status are monolithically negative and condemnatory, depicting women as abject and degraded, conditions they attributed to Islam.[53] The corollary to such attitudes was the assumption of the "civilizing" mission inherent in the dissemination of the tenets of a superior, modern, Western, Christian culture.[54]

British attitudes toward Arab women were strongly colored by a focus (almost an obsession) on the issue of seclusion, veiling, and women's dress, considered by Westerners "the barometer of social change in the Moslem world."[55] Descriptions of elite women invariably focused on their appearance. The implicit assumption was that wearing Western clothes somehow signified "progress," modernity, or liberation of women. The corollary was that women who dressed in traditional Arab garb were "backward," oppressed, and uncivilized. British attitudes conveyed the message that a prerequisite for entry into "modernity" was assimilation into Western culture, and the appearance of women in Western dress was a signifier of modernity and "progress." Yet an odd ambivalence over how "modern" and how quickly women should convert to modernity through dress permeated some British attitudes, which tended to waver over whether or not "native" dress among women should be eradicated. Hilda Ridler, the inspector of Girls Schools, while lamenting her students' abandonment of "native costume" in pursuit of fashion, nonetheless admitted that she allowed school girls to wear Western dress rather than uniforms because "too great insistence on this point creates a feeling that it is our wish to deny the girls the benefits of civilization."[56] A reporter for *The Star* gushed, "English women and the Arab women who live in Palestine have many ways and ideas in common.... English people... would be astonished at the amazing strides women [in Palestine] had made lately. Nowadays they wore fashionable European clothes and jewelry."[57] Surprise was expressed at Arab women's sophistication, erudition, and "European ways." Yet the above descriptions were the exception. More common were observations along the lines of Ruth Woodsmall, an American YWCA official touring the Middle East in the 1930s, who stated categorically that Palestinian Muslim women lived, worked, and studied in "harem conditions" and "practically without exception are veiled."[58]

Superficial understandings of Arab women influenced the anomalous policy of the government, producing dual, conflicting attitudes on the part of British officials toward Arab women. One was the exceptionalization—"othering"—of Arab women, an attitude based on equating "race" and culture with confessional status. Every step taken had to be weighed against what the British perceived to be "Moslem opinion." According to this mentality, Muslims—and especially Muslim women—were deviant from an unconsciously assumed, supposedly universal (but actually, Western middle-class) standard of civilization, had different desires and goals in life, and constituted an alien, coherent, and definable culture of their own. Furthermore, the British seemed unable to comprehend differentiations in status, social practice and culture *among* Muslim women, such as those of class, rural-urban distinctions, family situations, and so on, constructing a falsely homogenized entity, the "Muslim woman." Second, the British essentialized Arab women through universalizing British women as "woman." Derived from undifferentiated notions of an essential "woman," this attitude was deeply rooted in biological destiny. Thus, "women" were all mothers or potential mothers. Hygiene, "mothercraft," and modern science, conveyed via education and adapted for local conditions, were effective tools for developing all "women," regardless of whether they lived in a Palestinian village, Bombay, or an English market town. The British adapted government policies both from domestic social welfare policies in Great Britain, and ones already in place in other colonies or "Moslem" societies such as India and Egypt. The result was confusion and ambivalence, both in the actual policies pursued and in their effects. And Palestinian women did not necessarily conform to expectations. The British did not perceive the intersections between social conditions, economics, and politics as they affected women, nor did they always fully comprehend the potential social engineering effects of their policies.

Thus Palestinian women faced obstacles erected, not only by so-called tradition, but also by the colonial power, which promoted a "civilizing mission" marching toward modernity that had at its core a deculturization process. The latter involved efforts to make over the upper and middle classes, using British culture and society as the norm. From the British point of view, British womanhood was the ideal from which the construct of the new Arab woman was derived. As a British official expressed it (speaking of Africa), the goal of colonial girls' schools was "to turn out the good old-fashioned, true English type of woman who had made England what it was."[59] This attitude, which also prevailed in Palestine, contradicted government policies in Palestine against upsetting the status quo. Class attitudes infused pursuit of these conflicting, confusing policies. While remaking the middle classes, the government attempted to keep the lower classes—particularly the rural peasantry—in their place. British government officials did not seem to recognize the contradictions in their policies, and the social and economic mobility that invariably would ensue.

Furthermore, the actual incarnation of "true" English womanhood encountered by Palestinian women through their contact with British women officials or missionaries was often less than ideal from the Palestinian perspective. Palestinian women vividly recollect the condescending and even racist attitudes of some of the British women with whom they interacted. The British head of the Women's Training College (WTC), for example, in addition to requiring her teaching staff to salute her, demanded that the "natives" enter her house through the side rather than the front door.[60]

Women's Education During the British Mandate

The British government's record on female education is one of the more instructive examples of its attitudes and policies towards Arab women. Right away, the government began to expand public education, but its efforts were severely criticized throughout the entire period for their limitations and tentativeness. Analogous to other colonized peoples, Palestinians increasingly began to perceive education as a kind of "social and cultural capital" that constituted the primary and most important asset that would improve their economic and social status and enable the achievement of "reform" and progress in the modern world.[61] Hopes and aspirations of a large percentage of the population during the mandate period centered on acquiring education for their children, both male and female. A constant refrain reiterated by both British officials and Palestinian pundits writing in the press or elsewhere was the requirement that "education must precede reform."[62] This refrain epitomized government policies that dealt with women.

The "educate to reform" strategy was not inconsistent with British policy to maintain the social status quo in Palestine. Education, to the British, did not have as its goals the transformation of society. The British viewed education as "a means of both social control and individual betterment," an attitude derived from Victorian concepts of education.[63] Such concepts constituted part of the "basic tension of empire," in which "the otherness of the colonized person was neither inherent nor stable: his or her difference had to be defined and maintained; [otherwise] social boundaries that were at one point clear would not necessarily remain so."[64] Although purportedly interested in "improving" the lives of peasants and the less affluent Palestinians, the British were alarmed about the prospect and inherent "danger" of class transformations and social mobility. As part of their strategy to stall that likelihood and process, they utilized educational policy. Its keynote was the development of a two-tiered approach to the educational system in which the rural population received a distinctly different kind of education than did the people of the cities or towns. The system was geared toward keeping the social classes in their places. The British viewed with dismay the possibility that a "literary" education might give the peasant ideas above his station, causing him to "drift[] to towns," thereby disrupting the social equilibrium, and causing chaos in the more politically volatile urban areas.[65] Gender was crucial to reinforcing security and social distinctions; these attitudes were reflected in British policies toward female education. The result was an emphasis in the girls' curriculum on more practical subjects such as "hygiene," since village girls, according to the inspector of Girls Schools, Miss Ridler, did not need much training in "bookwork" but rather, in more practical subjects such as "hygiene."[66]

The government was also concerned about conveying and transmitting notions of "character"—particularly "British character"—to its students. "'Character' . . . was not derived directly from abstract and universal values, but was essentially constructed out of a cultural consensus on Europeanness" (in this case, Britishness).[67] Officials were concerned about the "unfamiliarity of Palestinians" with "British life and character," defined as "the English language . . . the English outlook and English thoughts and manners."[68] How they intended to incorporate concepts of "British character" into their agenda of producing productive peasants and peasant wives is not entirely clear. It seems that "character" training targeted the urban middle- and upper-class students, who would be future civil servants, and form a class of "interpreters" between the government and the governed, "render[ing] them fit vehicles for conveying knowledge to the great mass of the population."[69]

From the very outset, educational planning was plagued by the issue of funding, largely due to the government policy of requiring villagers to pay for most of the expense of providing rural schools, provoking the observation that "the police station on the hill rather than the school-house is the distinctive architectural landmark of British rule in Palestine."[70] Female education was explicitly accorded lower priority than male education. In 1940, boys' schools outnumbered girls' schools by a ratio of more than ten to one.[71] Furthermore, the only government-sponsored secondary school for girls from 1919 to 1935, the WTC, charged fees, which were exacted for all schooling above the primary level. Had it not been for the existence of numerous private, mostly missionary schools, many of the admittedly small number of women during this period who obtained secondary level educations would have been even more limited in their ability to do so. The government relied on them to pick up the slack.

The record of the administration in expanding and providing for female education is, by any standard, unimpressive. The government's response to the recurring and increasing demands for female education was that it could not supply enough women teachers.[72] Although the dearth of women teachers was the major motivation behind the establishment in Jerusalem in 1919 of the WTC, this hardly sufficed. The WTC could not train the teachers fast enough to keep up with the demand. In the period from 1925 to 1936 there were 1,022 applicants for 209 vacancies.[73] Furthermore, the government's policy of requiring women to quit their jobs upon marriage affected the pool of available teachers negatively.[74] In 1935, the government opened the Rural Training Center (RTC) in order to train Muslim women to teach in villages. This development came in the wake of recognition of an additional problem in rural areas: when the government assigned women teachers to villages, the families of many young women would not allow them to live away from their home village.

As with boys, the government was leery of overeducating Palestinian girls. The central goals of creating good wives and mothers dominated their concerns about curriculum; motherhood, it was believed, "needed to be taught."[75] Policies for and development of girls' education were formulated primarily in conjunction with the needs of the male population. Because Palestinian men were acquiring "modern Western" educations, it was perceived "of the highest importance that the Western education which the girls of the more well-to-do class ... acquire[d] ... should not be picked up at random, but should be acquired under wise intellectual and moral guidance."[76] "Those subjects which specially affect the lives of girls and women in a backward land"—"domestic science," "handwork," infant welfare, laundry work and "practical hygiene"—were the hallmarks of the curriculum for girls schools.[77] Academic orientation was discouraged, and the curriculum for girls was to be adapted to the "special needs" of Palestinian girls.[78] Classical Arabic was considered of "little value" educationally, and the study of subjects such as history and geography were "in many ways not suitable for Palestinian girls," whose educational goals should be to "understand the value of a good home, where cleanliness, sanitation and above all the care of children are to be regarded as the aim of every woman."[79] The director of education explicitly linked women's education to the development of the nation, which was ironic in view of the government's contradictory and ambivalent policy regarding the political future of Arab Palestinians (developing a nation without nationalism, essentially): "The future of Palestine depends ... as much upon its home life as upon its schools, and the home life of the people cannot be improved without an advance in the outlook of the mother."[80]

Although in its initial years the WTC focused on domestic science, by the mid-1930s its secondary curriculum had become more academically oriented, demonstrating confusion in view of its mission to train young, single women to teach other young women how to be good housewives and mothers. The overall number of class periods allocated to academic subjects outnumbered those of the domestic science curriculum in the 1934–35 Annual Report.[81] There is no overt discussion of this development in the archival record, but the fact that young women were taking school-leaving exams such as the Palestine Matriculation Exam and the Palestine Secondary School Certificate Exam for which all pupils, male and female, were eligible, may be a possible explanation for the change. Furthermore, young women, like young men, increasingly needed credentials to enter the Palestine civil service, which may well have been a factor in a slight increase in academic offerings at the WTC.

Academic instruction and domestic science were not the only missions of the WTC. Residence at the college for both staff and students was compulsory, in order to attain "character training."[82] This requirement also helped defray government costs, since the students performed all of the domestic labor. The fees for the school were fairly high (twenty-four Palestinian pounds per annum as of 1937), scholarships were very limited, and every student—even those on scholarships—had to pay for at least two of the four years. Fees could represent a significant percentage of a family's income: in the 1930s, teachers earned between sixty and 240 pounds per year; clerical workers between sixty and three hundred, and artisans and workers in small industries around twelve to 198 pounds. (British and foreign civil servants earned the higher levels of these scales because they had English educational credentials that were required for the upper-level positions.) The WTC thus became a select establishment for the elite.[83] A place at the WTC was highly coveted. Yusra Salah, from a prominent Nablus family, recalled that "it was the ambition of every girl at this time to enroll at the Women's Training College. They accepted only a few of the elite girls of the superior classes."[84]

When the RTC opened in Ramallah in 1935, it was with the recognition that the need existed for specially trained teachers for village schools in order to improve "child welfare, house management and general hygiene in villages where the ignorance of women so gravely retards progress." No English was taught, and only Muslim women were encouraged to apply.[85] The course of instruction consisted of the usual "domestic science" subjects, including gardening and poultry-keeping, which was rather odd, considering most village women learned such skills from their mothers or mothers-in-law without the need for special schooling.[86] The goal of this kind of training was to make village girls "realize and appreciate the importance of a clean, healthy and well conducted home."[87]

Palestinian Attitudes Toward Female Education

Palestinian interest in educating women escalated during the mandate period. A number of factors contributed to the burgeoning interest. One was economic; education increasingly came to be perceived as the avenue to material development. The mandate period witnessed severe economic pressures on the population, caused by various factors, including the devastation left in the wake of World War I and the Great Depression of the 1930s. During World War II, the situation changed. Wage labor expanded, and rural producers were able to receive higher prices for agricultural produce, enabling many peasants to get out of debt. Urban migration, a phenomenon that predated World War II, escalated during the war years, intensifying socioeconomic changes already underway.[88]

Financial benefits and work opportunities constituted part of women's motives to obtain education. A considerable number of women worked as teachers or employees for the British government after receiving their education. As a young girl, Nimra Tannus, with her mother and sister, left their father behind in their village in the north and moved to Jerusalem in order for the two girls to continue their education and seek employment. Her mother sold some of her own land to pay for the girls' education. A self-described "rebel," Nimra falsified her age in order to obtain a clerical position in the civil service. "What I wanted was to be independent," she said. "I didn't want to rely on anybody." Later, she became a telephone operator in the Department of Posts and Telegraphs. During the 1948 war, she absconded during the fighting with quite a bit of equipment and became the communications liaison for the Arab Legion, which she joined in 1951, drawing the salary of a captain. Ms. Tannus was named Nimra (tigress) because her mother had difficulty bearing live children. Out of twenty-five pregnancies, only two children survived. A soothsayer suggested she name her children fierce animal names in order to encourage their survival. Nimra's sister was named Diba (she-wolf) but she changed it later. Nimra kept her original name.[89]

Ellen Mansur taught at the Friends Girls School (FGS) in Ramallah for seven years, while her sister Nabiha commuted to Jerusalem from Ramallah to work for the police department. Ellen, a graduate of the British Syrian Training College in Beirut in 1920, taught Arabic for seven years at FGS. A British officer once asked her, incredulously, "You teach Arabic to Arabic-speaking people?!" She replied, "Don't you teach English to English-speaking people?" Nabiha was known to "fix" traffic tickets for anyone she knew. Her sister observed, "she was very popular."[90] Some graduates of the WTC ended up teaching at their alma mater, as did Nafisa Jarallah.[91] Increasingly, young women linked their ability to obtain an education with their economic welfare. One young woman from Nablus, Mazin Bint Hussein al-Masri, petitioned King Abdallah to help her gain entrance to the WTC after she had been refused admission, citing her desire to support her widowed mother and siblings. She complained that girls of the "good families" were accepted while she was not.[92]

In the early 1920s, a visiting British feminist noted that economic pressure had begun to influence Muslim parents to obtain education for their daughters: "They see educated Christian and Jewish girls obtaining posts in Government and doing well for themselves and their families by this means."[93] Some parents saw education as a way to ensure and protect their daughters' futures. Sa'ida Jarallah, one of the first Palestinian Muslim women to travel to England on her own for a higher education (in 1938), describes the attitude of her father, a prominent Muslim judge:

> My father believed in educating women. He would say that a woman should have her diploma as a bracelet in her hand. For if she did not

marry, or married but was widowed or divorced, she should be independent and have her own job and life and not depend on her father or brother to support her.[94]

Another motivation for women's education was improved chances in the marriage market. Young, educated Palestinian men of the upper classes wanted educated wives, and vice versa. This disturbed the British, who were worried about the "danger" and "lure" of the matriculation exam, which "overimpressed" young women. "It is a fact," stated the director of education, "that in the Near and Middle East wives look for men who are better educated, and men also prefer better-educated girls."[95] Trained women teachers were "specially prized" by Arab husbands.[96]

Yet another important factor that influenced families to seek education for their daughters was nationalism and competition with their Jewish adversaries. Palestinians increasingly linked development of the person, such as obtaining an education, to development of the nation, and enlisted it in the nationalist struggle. Such attitudes translated into increasing support of some men for female education, a crucial factor that affected attitudes about educating women. One "leading citizen" who "voice[d] the policy of the Supreme Muslim Council," stated:

> Zionism brought an awakening of national consciousness and a sense of the necessity for social uplift which must affect women. To oppose Zionism we have realized the necessity for the same weapons that the Zionists have. The Jews maintain a high educational level for both men and women. Hence, to bring up the Arab level, we must educate women.[97]

The few private, "national" (*ahliyya*) schools founded by Palestinians played an important role in disseminating the spirit of nationalism, and alleviating the deculturization processes and explicit attempts to dilute nationalism as pursued in the government and missionary schools. Matiel Mughannam, herself a self-proclaimed nationalist, noted, "One thing is certain in these [national] schools: they teach self-independence and imbue their students with a true national spirit. Many of their graduates have already taken their places with success in public and private life."[98]

The issue of education—for both men and women—resonated profoundly in the public consciousness in Palestine during the mandate period.[99] The Arabs had an expression for British policy on education—*siyyāsat al-tahjīl* (policy of making ignorant).[100] Palestinian assessments of the British government's record on female education were particularly critical and even bitter. The Arab Ladies Society of Jaffa highlighted government neglect of education in 1946: "Governments all over the world consider education a duty. This government has a budget of 20 million pounds and spends only 1/2 million pounds on education."[101] Hind al-Husayni, founder of Dar al-Tifl, the orphanage for children whose parents were killed in the Dayr Yassin massacre of 1948, remarked that the mandate government denied women their "rights" to receive a "proper education."[102] Her comments are indicative of an increasing tendency to see education as a fundamental right. In 1934, Khalil Totah, a prominent educator, published a scathing article in which he criticized the government for having established only seven girls' schools for the twenty-seven thousand girls of school age after its fourteen-year presence in the country. He asked, "How can the government justify this disgraceful position before God, before the association of civilized nations, and before its feelings as a civilized state [whose] stated goal is to help Palestine advance and educate her?"[103]

By the government's own admission, the record was dismal. Jerome Farrell, director of education, commented on the low attendance rate of girls in village schools, attributing it to "the almost complete standstill in girls' education in villages during the first sixteen years of the Occupation."[104] Subsequent years saw little progress; in the school year 1944–45, there were only forty-six village schools for girls, out of a total of four hundred.[105] The (to his credit) frustrated Farrell remarked almost bitterly in a letter written toward the end of the mandate, "the financial record of this Government and the Home Government in Palestine education is not very creditable. This may sound improper criticism but I am prepared to let it go on the file and to defend it vigorously before anyone."[106]

Ultimately, the significance of education for women—both symbolically and substantively—profoundly influenced Palestinians' collective consciousness, recollections, and assessments of the British Mandate government in Palestine. As A. L. Tibawi notes, education created a "new aristocracy" in Palestine—"an aristocracy that came to the foreground, not because of its wealth or birth, but chiefly because of intelligence and academic attainments. . . . The influence of this elite class was out of all proportion to the small number of its members."[107]

The Educated Woman

The significance of education to the individual women who were fortunate enough to obtain it cannot be overstated.[108] Young Palestinian women were not merely interested in learning to read and write. In school they learned to socialize with, and gained exposure to, girls from different backgrounds and religions, forming contacts and friendships that often endured through adulthood and traumatic events, such as the displacement and dispossession caused in 1948. Educated women of the mandate period shared "the same mentality" from their common school experiences.[109]

Girls were also eager for what education could offer in the way of intellectual stimulation and role models. The poet Fadwa Tuqan, who was forcibly removed from school by her father, wrote: "In school I was able to discover some parts of my lost self. There I established myself as a person, something I had not been able to do at home."[110] Teachers, perhaps the most highly respected—in some parts of the country, the only—professional women during this period, provided young girls with role models and ambitions to which they could aspire. "Teaching was the field every woman liked to enter," recalled Yvonne Kardosh, a WTC graduate who taught in her native Nazareth in the late 1940s. "During my play[] I used to close the doors at home and knock as a principal visiting classes. . . . A woman teacher was respected at that time. She had an education . . . she had a message to deliver to her community . . . to educate youngsters to have a better life."[111] Women teachers developed close relationships with students, encouraging them directly and through example to persist in what was often an uphill struggle to obtain higher education. Hind al-Husayni was inspired to become involved in social work by her teachers: "I used to try to do social work with a very good teacher of mine. She and her sister were twins, Victoria and Elizabeth Nasir . . . she used to take me with her to show me what she's doing as a social worker."[112] Yusra Salah, forty-eight years after she graduated from the American University of Beirut, recollected by name the teachers who were major influences in her life, including eminent academics such as Qustantin Zurayq.[113]

Despite the deficiencies of the government school system under the mandate, elite women at least did gain greater access to education, both public and private. Private schools picked up the slack for the government, especially at the secondary level. Some, such as the Friends' Girls School in Ramallah, became renowned for turning out the intellectual elite of Palestinian society.[114] The education in these schools and this skewed system dominated by foreigners, Western values, and culture affected women's sense of self in mixed ways that had both deculturizing and liberalizing impacts. Education promoted increased self-confidence and independence, and affected girls' sense of identity and self-worth. Attending urban or town schools provided them with exposure to cultural opportunities, politics, and the world at large—particularly for those who studied away from home at boarding schools such as the WTC or at one of the many private schools. Girls were able to take advantage of life in the city, attending movies and lectures or courses offered by the YMCA or YWCA. Female students in cities such as Jerusalem and even those in the smaller towns and villages in areas such as the Galilee region became politically active, organizing themselves in meetings, fomenting strikes, and joining in demonstrations in the turbulent years of 1936–39.[115] Despite the overt promotion of Western values and "character," young women's growing sense of nationalism was not diluted by the experience.

Educated women were also able to live independent lives abroad for the first time. A number of young women went to Beirut to attend either the British Syrian Training College or the Beirut College for Women (BCW), initially a junior college to prepare girls for entrance to the American University in Beirut (AUB), which allowed women to enroll at the sophomore level beginning in 1924.[116] Sisters Hala and Dumya Sakakini vividly recollect college life at BCW, which the AUB men dubbed "Batch of Crazy Women." Men and women students took holiday trips to Cairo together, traveling by train; went camping or hiking; participated in sports; attended jazz or classical music concerts; and entertained their "cousins"—as they called the AUB men—in their dormitory (chaperoned, of course).[117] A whole world of sociability, friendships, and cultural activities was available to women through attending college away from home. Local social norms were easier to flout for women attending colleges or universities abroad, away from their families, rather than if they remained in their own communities.[118] Women associated (carefully) with men, getting to know, befriend, socialize, and engage in intellectual exchanges with them. Yusra Salah, the first Palestinian Muslim woman to attend AUB, was a member of the debating club. She confronted one of her opponents, a young man, in a debate on the topic of the role of women in society, adopting a feminist position.[119] It should be noted that the number of women who attended universities during this period was small, however, and Christian women tended to outnumber Muslim women. This was an exceptional experience for most Palestinian women.

Despite the sometimes carefree atmosphere depicted here, women were acutely aware of being "pioneers" and behaved accordingly. "Being conscious of the critical gaze of their fellow students and of the community, they had the wisdom and the sense of responsibility to maintain high moral standards and thereby allay the fears of family and community that education would be a corrupting influence on women."[120] The judgment and potential opprobrium of men weighed heavily on women students. Yusra Salah, accordingly, was "very prim and proper," and intensely conscious of being "the daughter of the shaykh." She self-consciously sought the role of exemplar in order to encourage other fathers from Nablus to permit their daughters to attend college.[121] Her parents confronted and defied conservative Nablus society in allowing her to attend college away from home, for which she said, "I will never forget my mother's kindness and wisdom in convincing my father of the necessity to enroll me in university, and my father's conviction in sending me to university, despite the displeasure and anger of the people of the town."[122]

Another transformation in women's personal lives in which education played a role was marriage patterns. Some educated women either delayed marriage for career reasons, or did not marry at all. Women who taught did not necessarily quit their jobs (as required by the government) to marry, but, rather, married late, as did Alexandra 'Aboud, who at age thirty-five married a man younger than herself after teaching for sixteen years; Yvonne Kardosh, who taught for thirteen years; and Henriette Siksik, who taught for eleven years.[123] Wafi'a al-Duzdar, who married at age thirty, commented, "When a woman works she no longer thinks of marriage."[124]

Many of the educated women featured in this study did not marry at all. When asked about this, Hala Sakakini perceptively remarked that women were in a transition period. Educated women did not desire traditional, arranged marriages but neither were they ready to "go to the other extreme"—that is, Western-style dating. They felt they had to set an example for the next generation. "Educated women were rather special," she noted (meaning unusual). Upheavals were also an obstacle to social life, she added, referring to the political turbulence of the 1930s and 1940s.[125] Samah Nusseibeh, president of the Arab Ladies Society in Jerusalem, commented that educated women "devoted themselves to the [women's] societies, which is better than marriage."[126] Amy Aramki, active in women's groups in Bir Zeit, observed that in those days educated women were "too old" to marry by the time they completed a B.A. degree.[127]

Being "educated" in this period of time, however, did not necessarily mean having graduated from or attended college. "Being educated" had multiple meanings. For the upper classes, being educated signified familiarity with foreign languages, not wearing the *hijāb* (head scarf), and being "well informed" and "aware."[128] In Arabic, the word often used for "educated"—*muthaqqafa*—also means "cultured."

Interestingly, Palestinian notions of an "educated" woman of a certain class often corresponded closely to those of Westerners during this period. The woman of culture and education had some training in the arts—such as drawing and music—spoke foreign languages, and was well-versed in light domestic skills such as needle work, all of which were taught in the curriculum of the WTC. Yet women who attended the WTC, when asked in interviews what subjects they studied, recollected primarily the academic subjects. The private schools, which were criticized by the government for cultivating "too much the literary side of education," and neglecting "almost entirely . . . the domestic side," seem to have recognized women's desire (and possibly that of their parents) for a different kind of education.[129] The British were not entirely successful in inculcating middle-class domesticity.

In the minds of both peasant and elite women, an "educated woman" had—or took—freedoms that an uneducated woman did not. Henriette Siksik, describing the work of young women helping the Red Cross distribute aid to the indigent in Jerusalem during the 1920s, remarked, "All these St. Mary's girls were educated . . . they could go around [with] the Red Cross."[130] In commenting on women's dress during the mandate period, an older peasant woman remembered, "Christian women wore short sleeves and usually followed the new fashion. The Muslim women rarely wore short sleeves—only those who were educated did." This woman from Nazareth's largely Muslim, working-class Eastern Quarter frequently used the word "educated" ascriptively to differentiate women throughout an interview.[131]

The fact that older, elite women focused on and remembered their school days so vividly in interviews is counterposed by the above woman's bitterness and regret at not having had the same privilege: "I never went to school. There was a shaykh from Jordan who . . . used to teach the children . . . they asked him if I could sit with them and learn Arabic, math and religion but the shaykh refused because no girl was allowed to sit with the boys. Now I am against anyone who teaches his son but refuses to teach his daughter. Both boys and girls have to be treated equally."[132] This woman said that she still does not forgive her family for not allowing her an education. Other peasant women recalled the dearth of village schools as being the obstacle to their receiving an education. An older woman from the village of Zeita was asked if people would have sent their daughters to school if they had had the chance. "Yes," she replied. "Who would leave his daughter with no education? People were starting to become open-minded."[133]

Peasant women tended to view education as a door that opened up an entirely different world, one in which the acquisition of literacy equated access to knowledge and power. This door did not open easily for them. As Rosemary Sayigh notes, through their exclusion from literacy, peasant women viewed themselves as unfit to give authoritative accounts of events and thereby undervalued their own participation in such events.[134] A woman who was asked if she knew anything about nationalist hero 'Izz al-

Din al-Qassam, for example, answered "I don't know anything about him because I can't read or write," deprecating her own, nonliterate ability to remember and narrate the past. This same woman, however, ultimately became involved in the Communist Party, despite her self-deprecation. She said, "I told the man who convinced me to enter the Communist Party that I couldn't read or write and was shy. He did not listen to anything I said and told me I had to get involved and hear everything that went on."[135]

Underlying both peasant and elite women's perceptions of education were issues of power, privilege, and class. Peasant women understood that acquiring education could provide them with possibilities of economic and social mobility. Elite women could likewise improve or maintain their own positions through education, either in the marriage market or through access to employment.

Women who were a part of the elite, education-based "aristocracy" had a sense of self-worth and ability to act politically that were bound up in their identities as "educated women." Education was the catalyst that encouraged middle- and upper-class women to seek change and gave them this confidence and ability to act.[136] Their attainment of education influenced their involvement in national politics.

Women and Social Welfare

Early on, the mandate government's efforts in social welfare reform inclined toward disciplining, controlling, and punishing lower class women. Its first measures were oriented toward the "prevention or suppression of social evils." The government established homes for "wayward girls," passed legislation on prostitution and midwifery, and combated "domestic slavery" (in reality a form of patron/client relations among tribes) of girls amongst the Bedouin.[137] Concern centered on "raising the moral tone" in cities such as Jerusalem, which had experienced increased social problems as the result of World War I.[138] One aspect of this early social welfare work focused on regulating lower-class working women such as midwives, who were, according to the British point of view, a particularly contentious and resilient lot.

The government took the position that it was "impossible to provide adequate social services to meet the evils which so inevitably seem to accompany economic change." For the first twenty-two years of the mandate it did not even establish a Department of Social Services. That came in 1942, only six years before the end of the mandate.[139] Up until that time, limited government services were provided through departments such as Health and Education. As with education, private, religious, charitable organizations picked up much of the slack by providing services that the government did not adequately fund.

One matter that greatly concerned the British government was improving the overall health and "hygiene" of the population, a realm officials closely associated with women. The Western preoccupation—almost an obsession—with "hygiene" occupies a central place in the lexicon on health, education, and social welfare. One visiting Western researcher waxes eloquently on the potentially rejuvenating role of hygiene in Palestinian society:

> How, we may ask, will the teaching of hygiene ... to generations of Arab boys and girls affect the lives and customs of this Eastern people? ... The adherence to such general rules of hygiene as regular hours of sleep, ventilation of bedroom, good drinking-water, sanitary disposal of rubbish, moderation in eating and drinking, frequent baths, fresh air and sunshine in rooms—these alone could make a new people![140]

British government approaches to health and hygiene conformed to social policies at home, where "the principle aim of ... child and maternal welfare services [the major focus of the health department] was to promote a greater sense of responsibility on the part of the mother" through "educating to reform" her character, effectively divesting health issues from their broader social and economic context.[141] There was little recognition that most of the remedies advocated by the government did not take into account the severe conditions of poverty under which much of the population lived. Widespread attempts were made to teach the "virtues of cleanliness and how to attain it."[142] Few peasants had access to enough water for "frequent baths," or access to "good drinking water," however, which required more than mere "adherence to rules of hygiene." The government's entire approach was personal and individual, rather than structural, reflecting continuity in British policies on infant welfare, public health, and hygiene.[143]

In addition, some of the government's initial methods of attempting to "reform" the population were inappropriate, defeatist, and naive. In an example typifying the preferred mandate approach of relegating social services to private organizations, the Women's Council, in response to a request from the director of health to cooperate in supervising and training midwives, found itself "unable to send in any recommendations for the amelioration of conditions ... the present mentality of the women of the country was such that they do not seek professional skill on the part of the midwives. And any attempt to enforce ideal conditions would at present be unworkable."[144] The council instead disseminated pamphlets on health and hygiene, apparently ignorant of the fact that the women they were attempting to reach were mostly illiterate.

The British were wedded to their own cultural constructs of what constituted a "home" and "home life," taking great pains to communicate these to young women through training in health care, social services, and education. Through improvements in the "hygiene" of home life, they hoped to improve health conditions overall. They were also, to give them credit, genuinely concerned about containing the spread of venereal disease and lowering infant mortality rates, which were high—particularly among the majority Muslim population.[145]

Infant welfare centers were set up throughout Palestine during the mandate period, some under the direction of the Department of Health, but most privately funded by groups such as the American Colony Aid Association. By 1938, there were thirty-six infant welfare centers for Arabs, and forty-nine for Jews.[146] Their work consisted of providing both services and training to indigent village mothers, who brought their babies in to the centers or were visited by trained nurses, often young, educated Arab or Armenian women. The "rules" and requirements for proper care of infants reveal how health officials attempted to inculcate usually poor Arab women with British "middle-class ideas of responsible motherhood."[147] The mothers were lectured "again and again" about "health rules," as exemplified in the following (partial) list: "Regular hours for feeding is [sic] important . . . get doctor's advice before weaning or adding other food . . . the younger the child the more sleep it needs, always in a separate bed from the mother . . . bath [sic] the baby every day . . . when in doubt ask advice from the doctor or nurse, and not from a neighbour."[148] Most of these rules would have been impossible for poor village women to follow. Few had the resources to provide a child with its own separate bed, nor would most women have had access to (or been able to afford paying) a doctor to whom they could turn for advice on such routine matters as weaning a child. They would naturally seek counsel from other more experienced mothers.[149]

The government's narrow, culturally constructed notions about improving living conditions for the Arab population led to it locating women as the site of social welfare reform instead of targeting economic and structural improvements. British officials' attitudes reveal an inherent confusion in the government's approach to issues of culture, tradition, and religion. They constantly drew attention to the obstacles of "tradition" and widespread practices of sex segregation in the society but did not effectively utilize this information in adapting their own methods and approaches in order to solve problems. Although they encouraged the training and hiring of women doctors, nurses, and social workers in order to more effectively work with women, they nonetheless did not go far enough toward understanding the roots of social problems such as poor health.[150] They blamed the victim, citing women's superstitions (such as women's attempts to protect their babies from the "evil eye") and prejudices as the cause of their unwillingness to seek professional medical advice; they were uniformly contemptuous of the effects of so-called tradition on women's belief systems. Although officials acknowledged that women may not have sought medical aid in obstetrical or gynecological matters because of their embarrassment in dealing with a male doctor, they nonetheless continually attributed health problems to women's "ancient prejudices." It is clear from a report of a woman doctor returning to Nablus from leave who became "especially busy as the women had been *waiting* for her return," that women were perfectly willing to seek "modern" medical care when accessible and provided by a doctor with whom they felt comfortable.[151] Bertha Vester, whose family ran the American Colony's infant welfare center, recalls that women "flocked" to the center when it opened in 1927.[152]

Rather than expending money and efforts toward improving public works projects that would provide villagers access to basic services such as water, the government instead focused on targeting personal "reform" to deal with problems caused largely by poverty and lack of access to public services, not by "ignorance," "stupidity," and superstition.[153] Of course, this approach was much cheaper and more in keeping with their colonial fiscal objectives. Government expenditure for development of any kind decreased over the years. In the years 1934–39, for example, government investment on public works was 24.7 percent of total expenditures; in the years 1939–44, it dropped to 15 percent. The damning comments of a visiting team of American researchers in 1944–45 are instructive:

> The real weakness in Britain's position derives . . . from her lack of imagination and drive in development work. It is easy for the domestic upper classes of the Middle East to arouse the masses against Britain under the slogan of freedom from the foreign yoke because nothing that Britain has done for any of her wards strikes the popular imagination as reflecting a profound concern about transforming them into a literate, healthy, prosperous, self-reliant people.[154]

Women and Employment

The mandate period witnessed increased opportunities for women to work outside of the home in sectors other than the traditional one of agriculture, although Arab women's participation in the labor force was low, 9.4 percent, according to the 1931 census.[155] Although concrete data on this subject is meager, we can hazard some generalizations about women's wage work during this period. A number of women worked in family enterprises, and a not insignificant number taught or worked at private schools or for religious institutions such as charities. A limited, but increasing number of Arab women worked in industry, particularly during World War II. In 1927, only 10% percent of the personnel involved in industry were women (both Arabs and Jews combined). Like Arab men, Arab women workers received lower wages than Jewish women. In some instances, Jewish women received five times what Arab women were paid: Jewish women tobacco sorters, for example, were paid between seventy-five and ninety cents per day while Arab women received seventeen to thirty-five cents per day for the same work.[156] Figures from the 1931 census show that among Arab women who did work outside the home, the largest percentage was concentrated in the professions and domestic service.[157] Official figures for women's participation in the labor force, however, tend to be skewed because of gendered concepts of labor that do not document or take into account labor that is "unproductive," unpaid, or informal, which describes much of women's work. This includes domestic or unpaid agricultural work, housework, prostitution, peddling, and petty commodity production.[158]

Sex-based inequities were endemic to the civil service, reflecting conservative British attitudes about women in general, claims of the mandate being an "enlightened administration" notwithstanding. All women—British, Jewish, and Arab—faced official sex discrimination and informal ghettoization in government employ. Most women were employed at lower grade levels than men. In some cases, there were salary scale differentiations by sex—that is, "male" salaries for the same jobs as distinct from lower "female" salaries.[159] Even when salary distinctions by sex were not officially sanctioned, women were usually paid less than men in equivalent positions. For example, a Miss H. Hakim, who had a B.A. degree and was a teacher at the highest grade level, was paid less than every other male teacher in the same grade, regardless of her seniority. The government justified paying women teachers less than men because of their "inferior" academic qualifications. This excuse was not valid in the case of Miss Hakim, however, since a B.A. was the highest degree obtained by any teacher, male or female. Although the government did acknowledge the inequities, and recommended that women teachers with qualifications equivalent to those of men be appointed at the same salaries, in fact, the discrepancies remained.[160]

The government needed to employ Arab women in order to pursue its policy of "reforming" women to improve society. British officials' perceptions of "tradition" led to their directing Arab women—particularly through educational policies—toward certain spheres of work considered appropriate to their gender and class. As a result, government hiring practices directed upper-class women toward teaching and clerical work, and lower-class women toward more menial work such as domestic service, midwifery, and nursing. Work in an office or with other women (such as teaching) was deemed more socially acceptable and suitable than menial work for upper-middle class women.

The government employed the largest numbers of Arab women in services.[161] In the year ending December 1930, 230 Arab women were listed as junior civil servants, out of a total of 3,135. Of this total, 144 were teachers, twenty-six health workers (all but two nurses), and twenty-eight worked for the Department of Posts and Telegraphs, primarily as "telephonists" (operators). The remainder (thirty-two) were clerical workers in assorted departments such as Lands, Treasury, Police and Prisons, Agriculture and Forests, Customs and Excises, and Legal. The clerical workers' salaries ranged from a high of 168 Palestinian pounds per annum to sixty.[162] One interesting idiosyncrasy in the *Junior Service Staff List* is that the rosters record all male employees' dates of birth, but not the women's. Women's marital status was also indicated.

The situation of married women working in government reveals British government officials' conflicting attitudes about women. Writing to the chief secretary in 1929, the postmaster general displays a mixture of prudery, parsimony, and patriarchal protectiveness of domesticity. He states his strong "opinion that the retention of female officers in Government employ after their marriage is undesirable." His reasons: the greater amount of sick leave required for married women (as opposed to single women); "the embarrassment caused to other members of the staff and to members of the public by their presence in a certain condition"; and the possibility of two civil servants, husband and wife, drawing full pensions at the same time. He continues, it is unreasonable "to expect that the average female Junior Service officer in this country be able to complete a civil service career and at the same time carry out satisfactorily the normal duties of married life." One of the major anxieties was that a married woman might maintain her career long enough to earn a pension.[163]

The result of these concerns were new regulations (1933) that required a woman to resign her position upon marriage, at which time she would be paid a gratuity. No married woman could be employed, except for widows, without the approval of the chief secretary, and only in exceptional cases would one be appointed to a pensionable office.[164] An additional stipulation was that women could not accrue time to be credited to their gratuity if employed before the age of twenty.

The Department of Education, to its credit, strongly objected to this last proviso, calling it "inequitable," and drew attention to the fact that an eighteen-year-old female employee would have to defer marriage for seven years in order to accrue the five years service necessary for the gratuity. The director of education wrote, "It does not accord with Arab social customs in Palestine nor is it, in my opinion, in the public interest that female officers who do not contemplate permanent celibacy should under a species of compulsion defer matrimony until the age of 25 when, in the popular view, they are middle-aged spinsters."[165]

These regulations may explain why quite a number of educated Arab women worked for so long before marrying, or did not marry at all.[166] Annual reports on education frequently cite the numbers of women teachers lost to marriage, which set the Department of Education back in its continual demands for more trained women teachers.[167] Such policies sent mixed messages to those teachers trained and employed by the government.

If recruiting, training, and supplying teachers was a difficult task for the government, the problem of providing women health-care workers was even more acute. Regulating and training midwives, one of the first areas involving social reform in which the government became involved, provides an interesting case in point. The issue of midwife appointments became highly contentious and embroiled in local politics from the start. The government found itself caught up in a complex web of contradictions created by its own conceptual limitations as well as the resilience of the traditional autonomy and authority of midwives. Conflicts with midwives played themselves out in numerous, sometimes overlapping, power struggles: between the official, male medical establishment and the midwives; or, on an entirely different level, between different village factions competing for dominance; or, finally, between the government and villagers. One struggle represented a confrontation between two competing, gendered hierarchies of medicine, representing (male) "science" and "modernity" on the one side, and indigenous (female) authority, folk wisdom, and experience on the other.[168] The others were conflicts over who controlled resources and wielded local authority.

The battle was also generational, pitting younger midwives who enjoyed the support of the government against older midwives who fought to protect their preserve of power and source of income and status. Midwives' licenses were constantly withdrawn because of "old age" and attendant bad eyesight.

Women older than forty years were considered to be of "advanced age" for midwife training and were subsequently rejected as candidates at training centers for that reason, despite the urgent need for more midwives.[169]

The government was very concerned about taking action against midwives practicing without licenses, which were required by law as of 1918.[170] The women, however, displayed remarkable defiance of the law. For one thing, the Department of Health experienced difficulties in convincing witnesses to testify when it attempted to prosecute. In one case, a senior medical officer (SMO) wanted to suspend the license of a Miss Bahiya Afify because she practiced gynecology, gave injections at a delivery, and refused to call a doctor. Miss Afify responded that the old midwives were always submitting complaints about her and "stir[ring] up the supervisor" because they were jealous.[171] This particular case epitomizes the multiple power struggles mentioned above; Miss Afify simultaneously defied the medical establishment, while trying to protect her "turf" from the competition.

Village politics also interfered in midwifery affairs. The *mukhtars* (local leaders) in one village recommended that certain women be appointed or "trouble might follow" among the three factions into which the village was divided. In another village, the *mukhtars* replaced the superintendent's appointment with their own choice.[172] A villager wrote the SMO in Jerusalem requesting that he examine two midwives from the village of Bayt Iksa, because the one who was appointed was a relative of the *mukhtar*. (The writer clearly was from the political opposition in the village.)[173]

The position of midwife was often hereditary, which contradicted the government's attempts to regulate, control, and order the whole system of licensing and training midwives.[174] The British were challenged by the contentious and surprisingly political nature of midwife appointments, as well as the unexpectedly complex morass of issues in regulating midwives, as is illustrated by the incessantly aggrieved and exasperated tone in the superintendent's correspondence. Their naive belief that "women's affairs" were somehow divorced from their political, social, and economic milieu caused them many headaches.

The case of nurses is a different matter from the uppity midwives. No one was competing for nursing positions. Indeed, there was a dearth of Arab nurses. A special committee found that nursing was considered undesirable by Arab women (particularly those from the educated, upper-middle classes) for a variety of reasons, among them the problems of dealing with men, the "lack of protection" and gossip among men in the wards, the menial nature of the work and its low status, and its effect in lessening their chances of marriage.[175]

Furthermore, Arab nurses were afforded an explicitly inferior status in the hospital hierarchy. When not occupied with British patients, the British nurses supervised the Palestinian "sections." British patients took priority, receiving the care of the better-trained British nurses. Palestinian nurses were to remain in their own segregated space, caring for Palestinian patients and supervising their own wards only in the absence of a British nurse. In a stern memorandum indicating the existence of disciplinary problems, the chief medical officer reminds the matron of the Government Hospital in Jerusalem that her "Palestinian staff nurses must understand that British Nursing Sisters are their seniors in appointment and must behave towards them accordingly."[176] Until Arab women had control over their own nursing and imbued it with patriotic meaning during 1947–48 it held little attraction for them. In the mid-1940s, against the backdrop of military confrontations between Arabs and Jews, Arab women became increasingly involved with nursing, founding their own clinics, establishing and attending first aid classes in droves, and even forming a nursing military unit in 1947.

The Case of Doctor Charlotte Saba

An intriguing incident involving an Arab woman doctor illustrates the obstacles of sexual and racial discrimination that Arab women faced in their attempts to enter the working world in a colonial society in which the professional hierarchy consisted of European men at the top, with European women and Arab men battling over second place and Arab women occupying third.

In 1940, the Department of Health advertised a vacancy for a lady medical officer (LMO). The position required that the applicant have medical qualifications obtained in Great Britain, be single and less than thirty-five years of age, and pass an elementary Arabic exam within two years. The work involved conducting clinics in gynecological, maternity, and infant welfare care.[177] The position, as it turned out, proved difficult to fill.[178]

In 1945 Charlotte Saba, the daughter of Nicola Saba, a prominent Arab nationalist from Ramleh, applied for the position.[179] She had recently qualified as a doctor, having trained and received her degree in London, where she did postgraduate work at several British hospitals. She was interviewed by the Medical Appointment Subcommittee in England and found "eminently suitable personally and professionally for appointment." She informed the committee that she expected to be paid at the same rate at which a British LMO would be paid.[180]

The director of medical services (DMS) protested this, invoking the issue of "fairness" to other (male) Palestinian doctors, who normally served at least one year as clinical assistants at a lower rate of pay. He instead offered to appoint her as a clinical assistant with the prospect of promotion later. Then he offered the LMO position to a fifty-year-old British woman who had worked in Nigeria and retired at her own request because of illness. She declined the offer.[181]

Later that same year, a Miss McNeill applied for the post. The DMS supported her appointment, but the secretary of state for the colonies (SSC), noting that he was in a "situation which is likely to prove seriously embarrassing," stated that he was committed to a general policy of encouraging local candidates to fill appointments in their own countries, and of making no distinction between pay of similarly qualified officers performing the same work. He inquired if there were some reason why Saba's nationality would make her unsuitable for the post.[182] By this time, there was a struggle between the Colonial Office back in Britain and the local government in Palestine. The former became concerned about racial discrimination. In an attempt to defuse the race issue, the DMS continued to emphasize the question of "fairness."[183] Ultimately both Doctors McNeill and Saba were offered positions as LMOs, with the latter at a salary rate of more than two hundred pounds less than McNeill. The HC justified the lower salary on the grounds that Saba's postgraduate experience was "relatively limited." The SSC responded strongly to this:

> Doctor Saba has had as much post graduate experience as most of the present entrants to Colonial Medical Service. Had she been a European my advisor would have had no hesitation in putting her forward for post of Lady Medical Officer. If appointed at 396 in grade of Medical Officer, it will take her 12 years to reach salary of 600 which you propose for Doctor McNeill . . . I should be unable to defend such discrimination.[184]

The high commissioner, however, replied that her appointment would place her above some thirty other (primarily male) medical officers.[185] After this, the record falls silent, and it is not clear what transpired.[186]

What makes this case so interesting is how it demonstrates the convergence of gender and racial discrimination in the colonial hierarchy. The colonial authorities were willing to close ranks and defy the home government to protect two principles: European superiority and male domination. When Dr. McNeill was offered the LMO position at the rate of six hundred to eight hundred pounds per annum—above the clinical assistant level at which most Palestinian male doctors entered—there was absolutely not one word about the issue of "fairness" as it related to them. The authorities were willing to invoke patriarchal privilege in order to justify European superiority when an Arab woman was involved, but when it was a European woman, the hierarchy was reversed. Although a European woman was of the "inferior sex within the superior race," nonetheless she was equal or superior to a Palestinian man of similar qualifications.[187] A Palestinian woman was equal to neither.

Ultimately, despite British assertions about their "modernizing," reforming role in "advancing" the position of women in Palestine, their project involved attempts to replicate their own cultural and social system within a certain, elite class in Palestinian Arab society. There are striking parallels between British policies on gender in Africa with those in Palestine, as shown by Helen Callaway's observation that "colonial officers projected the gender representations of their own society on their perception of African gender relations and . . . on their shaping of the new social, economic and political order which colonialism gradually brought about."[188] British concepts about working women were infused with racial and class attitudes that projected an idea of the "professional woman" that excluded all but young, single, educated women who necessarily (in a society where most people married) would have a short working life. British concerns about interfering with "delicate matters," "Moslem sensibilities," and "traditional" gender relations restricted the opportunities of Arab women and officially sanctioned sexual and racial discrimination in employment.[189]

TRANSFORMATIONS IN PALESTINIAN WOMEN'S LIVES DURING THE BRITISH MANDATE PERIOD: THE PALESTINIAN PERSPECTIVE

Women's memories of the mandate period reflect mixed views on the nature of British rule and its impact on their society and history. Palestinians in interviews viewed the period as one of social liberalization vis-à-vis increased mobility, independence, and options in women's lives, as well as in the realm of social mores in general. The mere fact that women's presence multiplied in the public arena of work—as secretaries in the Ramallah district governor's office, such as Anisa Audi, or in the office of public health, such as her sister Najla, for example—meant that women were increasingly visible as productive members of Palestinian society.[190] Women teachers working in villages away from their natal homes experienced independence living apart from their families for the first time, and, like the Audi sisters, socialized with fellow workers, male and female, Muslim and Christian.

Palestinian women began to challenge and defy dress codes, although unveiling was not widespread before 1948 in Palestine. In 1929 a group of Muslim women in Jenin appeared at a coffeehouse unveiled and caused a "sensation."[191] Schoolgirls in 1926 wore short skirts, high heels, and shingled hair.[192] Photographs of elite women in the 1930s show them in short dresses and frequently unveiled. Even women who wore the *hijāb*, the head scarf, often wore dresses that came only to the knee.[193]

Interviews reveal diversity in experiences and opinions on the issue of dress and veiling. Some Muslim women either unveiled or never adopted the practice, while Christian women veiled in certain circumstances in order to distinguish themselves from Jews and emphasize their Arabness. This was particularly true during political upheaval, such as the Arab revolt of 1936–39 and in demonstrations. Alexandra ʿAboud and Evelyn Baramki, both Christian, practiced veiling for political reasons. Baramki said they "wanted to be like other Arabs" when they veiled during demonstrations.[194] Even Palestinian women who never veiled, such as Wafiʿa al-Duzdar, were careful to dress modestly, however. "I never put makeup on and never wore short sleeves," she recalled. She mentions that a Christian friend and coworker also "had the same mentality" about dress.[195]

Some of the changes women experienced were related to transformations in male attitudes about gender relations. Individual Palestinian men—especially male relatives such as fathers and brothers—often played seminal roles in encouraging female relatives to earn educations, engage in public activity, or discard the *hijāb*. Nahid al-Sajjadi's husband urged his wife to unveil.[196] Saʿida Jarallah described her father's beliefs in the freedom of women and the censure he experienced for allowing his daughters to go into public unveiled.

> This is a favor from my father [that] my sisters and I will never forget as long as we live. He was honest with us. He loved us and respected us and treated us like real women. . . . Once when I was riding the bus, an old woman recognized me and said to me, 'Saʿida, why are you not wearing the *hijāb*? Do you think when you get married that your husband will allow you to go out without the *hijāb*?' I answered her in front of all the men in the bus, 'If Shaykh Hussam gave me permission to go out without the *hijāb* then there is no one in the world who can force me to wear it.'[197]

Fadwa Tuqan's brother, Ibrahim, encouraged her to write poetry, and invited her to live with him in Jerusalem, where she discovered "a starting point" from which her personality "began, for the first time, to blossom," as she attended classes, went to libraries, concerts, and the cinema, nourishing her starved cultural self.[198]

There are indications that some Arab men were, in fact, more open to potential social changes in the status of women than were their British counterparts. The latter tended to have static, orientalist attitudes not only about Arab women, but also about Arab men's potential for flexibility in their relations with women; they viewed Arab men as "fanatical" and rigid, not recognizing the nuances and complexities that shaped gender relations in Palestinian society. Arab women wielded power, often from within the family, in subtle ways not easily recognizable or definable to foreigners. Describing his grandparents' relationship in his memoirs, Said Aburish depicts the complexities of how women achieved this. In recalling his grandmother, Rashedah, he asks:

> Was she the docile, obedient Arab wife of legend, or was there more to this woman than met the eye? ... she was a party to all the major decisions he took ... Rashedah had a hand in nominating Aburish's candidates for work with the British ... she determined who received *'eidiah* [presents given on the occasion of feasts] ... she warned him about his spendthrift ways and ... prevailed upon him to see al-Aref [a lawyer, about selling land to Jews].[199]

Arab men as well as women were experiencing the effects of socioeconomic transformation, and this in turn affected Arab women. Arab men were not universally resistant to change. The Supreme Muslim Council, for example, advocated raising the marriage age for girls, established schools for girls, and provided them with scholarships to study abroad.[200] Education for men could act as a liberalizing force in their attitudes. Social change incorporated changing gender attitudes about men and masculinity as well, affecting male attitudes about the role of marriage and their expectations in wives.

Another important defining aspect of identity that determined the direction, texture, and rhythm of women's lives, along with family and class status, was whether or not they lived in a village or town. Urbanization during the mandate period encouraged social change.[201] Women were able to take advantage of not only the economic but also cultural activities that a flourishing urban life had to offer. Jerusalem and Jaffa, with their religiously mixed populations and international characters, became particularly cosmopolitan compared to the more conservative, regionally oriented cities of Nablus and Hebron. Fadwa Tuqan describes Jerusalem as she knew it when living there with her brother Ibrahim in 1939:

> I was living in the midst of a free society where the modern woman's personality was not undermined by men's severity or crudeness. This was apparent in her dress, her conversation and her natural behavior in

a society where the veil separating the sexes had been lifted, a society in which the young woman had the opportunity of a better and broader education.[202]

Hala Sakakini describes Jerusalem as "something different"; people were "more open, not narrow . . . the first Muslim ladies who became free were from Jerusalem."[203] It is certainly no coincidence that the first women's organizations (not necessarily political resistance)[204] originated in the urban areas among the educated elite.

CONCLUSION

Despite the social, economic, and cultural transformations that occurred in Palestinian society in this period, tradition and innovation coexisted in an uneasy amalgam that points to an ongoing process of redefinition of Palestinian society and culture. Certainly not all—or even many— Palestinian Arab men actively promoted change in the status of women during this period. Tradition and change could coexist within one person or family and crossed gender lines. In Fadwa Tuqan's family, her father and paternal aunt were the ones who restricted her life the most while her brother encouraged her to break loose of these confines. A father might encourage and promote education of his daughter while insisting on adherence to sex segregation and wearing the *hijāb*. Mothers sometimes held more conservative attitudes than fathers. The strong grip of culture and patriarchal institutions in dictating social and behavioral norms was not pried loose, despite indications of adaptation. Most fathers, brothers, and husbands still adhered to upholding certain cultural and social practices such as gender segregation, restrictions on their female relatives' personal mobility, and the exercise of male authority over women in the family.

British government policies did not openly or directly challenge Palestinian cultural, and particularly, religious norms, yet their attempts to simultaneously maintain the Palestinian social status quo and apply their own, supposedly universal but in reality Anglocentric ideas about class, gender, and society produced confusion for both British officials and Palestinians. Palestinian Arabs responded by picking and choosing what suited them from their experiences at the hands of various British officials—as students, employees, or recipients of "reform." Yet, analogous to people in other colonial situations, a strong urge to maintain and preserve "indigenous" Palestinian culture and society against the onslaught of the European interlopers (both British and Jewish) coexisted with the development of an upper- and middle-class culture that amalgamated multiple, overlapping influences: from Islam, Arab identity, and European educations and contacts. Most of the women interviewed for this study had negative opinions about British rule for these reasons, and particularly in hindsight, when they, like most Palestinians, felt bitterly betrayed by the British role in the final outcome of their political fate.

It has become something of an adage that the *nakba* in 1948 brought about complete rupture and disruption in Palestinian society, when the responsive urge of Palestinians to maintain their culture and traditions confronted new realities and social universes in the quest for survival. Many attributed changes in the status of women and attitudes about gender to this disruption.[205] But in fact, the transformations that occurred during the mandate period were part of a process that both preceded and came in the wake of the *nakba*.

The educated, upper-, and middle-class women who came to participate in the women's movement during the mandate period reflected perhaps more than other sectors of the Palestinian population the social transformations society was experiencing. These changes, and the contradictory expectations and anxieties they aroused, increasingly caught the attention of and were discursively reflected in the Palestinian press (see Chapter 3). Often the first generation of women in their families to be educated, or to work outside of the home in offices or schools, Palestinian women in this period took part themselves in the creation and redefinition of gender roles. These conceptions were informed by their class backgrounds and experiences; their Western educations and contacts with the colonizing culture; and intellectual and cultural influences from reformist movements in the Arab world and beyond. The increased sense of self-confidence and self-worth experienced by women—particularly through opportunities for education and work—enabled them to enter the domain of politics, something that had been close to unimaginable in their mothers' generation.

3. The "Woman Question" in Palestine and the Debate in the Arabic Press

Analogous to their contemporaries in other parts of the Middle East, intellectuals, journalists, educators, reformers, and pundits in mandatory Palestine engaged in heated debate on issues related to women and gender that had begun to generate controversy among intellectuals and reformers in the late nineteenth century. In Palestine, the Arabic press was a primary vehicle through which growing alarm about gender was articulated. Some of the factors that shaped the nascent, but growing contestations about women and gender were discussed in the previous chapter. The increasing visibility of women outside the confines of their homes stimulated and fired controversy, as more of them appeared in public, attending schools, entering the work force, delivering speeches, and participating in organized activities. Articles that appeared in the Arabic press in Palestine, particularly during the 1920s and 1930s, reveal subliminal anxieties in Palestinian society that were deeply implicated in the profound social and cultural changes extending beyond the specific issues of the "woman question" on which much ink was expended.[1]

The Arabic press articulated such strong interest in the "woman question" that one can argue it became a major partisan of the women's movement. By the beginning of the mandate, the increasing numbers of women from the urban, elite strata of Palestinian society who were becoming educated and literate read newspapers and were well informed about the political and social issues of their time. The women activists who organized and led the women's movement developed a particularly symbiotic relationship with the Palestinian press, assiduously using it as transmitter, publicist, and booster for their activities. (Press coverage of the women's movement is examined in Chapter 6.)

The press reflected and engaged in intense public scrutiny and reconceptualization of attitudes about Palestinian women. Through the press, a com-

63

64 / A "New" Palestinian Woman

plex, evolving ideology of womanhood that particularly targeted middle- and upper-class women emerged in public discourse. Fermenting agitation about social and cultural issues—much of it focused on women—proliferated in the Palestinian press, which acted as a public forum for certain segments of Palestinian society. In addition to a slew of reports on women's participation in organizations and politics, speaking in public, or performance of charitable acts, a veritable barrage of editorial-style articles on issues related to the "woman question" erupted. A certain unity characterized these articles.[2] They can be roughly sorted into six major, overlapping categories that reflect the uneasiness and concern about women's changing status that began to emerge during this period: veiling, education, marriage, domestic responsibilities, women's rights, and (one overlapping, multiple category) the role of women in history, politics, culture, and religion.[3]

A major subtext in writing on the "woman question" was the complex relationship between colonizer and colonized. As Leila Ahmed notes, "From the start the discussion of women ... was embedded in considerations of the relative advancement of European societies and the need for Muslim societies to catch up."[4] The portrait of the "new woman" that emerges from the writing on women reflects the tensions generated by Western influences on elite perceptions of women, and simultaneous Palestinian attempts to preserve indigenous, traditional culture. Other, equally important but often more muted factors that contributed to changing constructs of (upper-middle class) womanhood were economic, including the entry of Palestine into the world market and the gradual evolution during the twenty-eight-year duration of the mandate of a middle-class and more consumer-oriented society.[5] The result was the development of an evolving, hybridized idealization of the elite Arab woman, articulating a new ideological construction of womanhood. This concept, however, was fluid, contradictory, multiple, and complex, allowing for simultaneous, differing interpretations that combined within them the articulation of certain common characteristics of the "new woman."

Kumari Jayawardena, describing reformist movements in other colonized Third World societies, notes a "new consciousness" about women during this period: "The new bourgeois man, himself a product of Western education or missionary influence, needed as his partner a 'new woman,' educated in the relevant foreign language, dressed in the new styles and attuned to Western ways—a woman who was 'presentable' in colonial society yet whose role was primarily in the home." At the same time, the new woman's role was to act as guardian of "national culture, indigenous religion and family traditions—in other words, to be both 'modern' and 'traditional'."[6]

These parameters and contradictions informed the debate on women in the Arab world.

Equally influential in the discourse on the "woman question" in the Palestinian press was the Islamic reform movement of the late nineteenth century and its concern with modernity, gender, and the relationship between Islam and the West. The publication of Egyptian Qasim Amin's *Tahrīr al-marʾa* (*The Liberation of Woman*, 1899) and *Al-marʾa al-jadīda* (*The New Woman*, 1901), in which he proposed modest reforms in women's education and called for gradual unveiling, provoked turmoil that sent shock waves extending far beyond Egypt throughout the Middle East. Leila Ahmed points out that "Egypt was at the forefront of the changes overtaking the Arab world over the course of the nineteenth and twentieth centuries" and led the way in formulating a new discourse on the woman question, focused primarily on the issues of the veil and education of women.[7] The dissemination of the views of other Muslim reformers such as Rifaʿah Rafiʿ al-Tahtawi and Muhammad ʿAbduh, both of whom were advocating the education of women as early as the 1870s, surely reached a segment of the population in Palestine. Historically, the intellectual boundaries of the Mashriq (Arab East) have always been porous and not delimited by arbitrary national borders that were subsequently erected after World War I.[8] Much cross-fertilization occurred, particularly in the realm of the written word and among the intellectual elite. The Arabic press played a preeminent role in this interchange. Physical boundaries were permeable as well. Journalists and writers from Syria, Lebanon, and Palestine all gravitated toward Cairo, Alexandria, and Beirut, which, with Damascus, constituted the intellectual magnets of the Mashriq in the late nineteenth and early twentieth centuries.[9] There men and women alike founded, edited, and wrote for growing numbers of journals, newspapers, and magazines that dealt with a myriad range of issues of the day, including the status, and especially, education of, women. Cairo, in particular, developed "an extremely lively and diverse journalistic press," attracting émigrés from other Arab countries.[10] From the perspective of intellectuals from Palestine's smaller, more provincial towns and cities, urban centers such as Cairo and Damascus, "the two cities whose spheres of influence overshadowed all of Palestine," provided dynamic, cosmopolitan, and stimulating climates.[11] The issues debated in their journals were followed and reflected in the pages of the newspapers in Palestine.

Women's contribution to the heady efflorescence of the Arabic press in this period was not insignificant. A unique women's press, comprising journals and magazines financed, owned, published, and edited by and for women, developed in Lebanon, Syria, and Egypt both before and after

World War I.[12] Arab women writers and intellectuals—particularly those from Syria and Lebanon—were part of the migration that contributed to Egypt's journalistic dominance. Often they accompanied parents or husbands who emigrated for business and career reasons or to escape ostensibly oppressive conditions in other parts of the Arab world.[13] Many of the founders of the earliest women's journals in Alexandria and Cairo were such émigrés, primarily from Syria and Lebanon.

THE DEVELOPMENT OF THE ARABIC PRESS IN PALESTINE

Because Palestine had no cosmopolitan centers of comparable size to Cairo, Beirut, Damascus, or Alexandria in the late nineteenth and early twentieth centuries, the Arabic press in Palestine developed at a slower pace than in much of the Mashriq.[14] Palestine, with its smaller population, had less of a potential readership than those cities; nor were literacy levels very high. Although urban life began to flourish during the mandate period, another factor that initially retarded the development of a lively and dynamic press was that the country did not have the benefit of the stimulating influence of institutions of higher education, as was the case in Egypt and Lebanon. Palestinian middle- and upper-class intellectuals received their university educations abroad throughout the entire period of the mandate. Another crucial factor, until the easing of restrictions after the restoration of the Ottoman Constitution in 1908, was censorship, which tended to be stricter in some parts of the Ottoman Empire that were still under direct control of Istanbul.

During the brief period of liberalization in the immediate aftermath of the Young Turk Revolution in 1908, the pace of development of the nascent press in Palestine dramatically accelerated, although censorship was reinstituted and the Arabic press effectively shut down during World War I. Between 1908 and 1914 alone, nineteen publications appeared.[15] The newspapers that were established—especially in Jaffa, Jerusalem, and Haifa—attracted a readership extending beyond the locality of publication. The lives of the earliest publications were tenuous and erratic, however, following a common pattern throughout the Arab world, where most of the earlier newspapers "died young, many after having published a single issue, or just a few issues." (One Palestinian journal only lasted five days).[16]

During the mandate period, the press grew rapidly due in part to technological advancements in mass communications such as the development of and improvements in the postal service, telegraph, and telephone.[17] The appearance of daily newspapers after the Wailing Wall crisis of 1929 was a turning point, according to Ami Ayalon. This development and the proliferation of new papers were responses as well to the increasing "public demand for news and opinion bred both by the intensity of current events and the rapid expansion of education, which spurred an increase in press consumption."[18] As Allison Wilke points out, "growing nationalist sentiment" was a key factor in the expansion of the press. "And the nationalist movement, in turn, spread with the help of the newspapers."[19] Although only three Arabic newspapers in Palestine survived the 1930s—*Filastīn, al-Difāʿ*, and *al-Sirāt al-Mustaqīm*—out of the constant founding or refounding of new journals and newspapers emanated a flurry of press activity that endured throughout the mandate period, resulting in the legacy of dozens of publications, albeit many of curtailed duration. Unlike their counterparts in Syria, Lebanon, and Egypt, Palestinian women did not establish a women's press. Considering the small population of Palestine, it is significant how many women did publish articles in the mainstream press or abroad, however. These included (but are not limited to) Mary Shihada, Matiel Mughannam, Sadhij Nassar, Asma Tubi, and Faʾiza ʿAbd al-Majid.

Starting in the 1920s, the Palestinian press became the vehicle for a virtual outpouring of heated, contentious articles on gender issues. We have no earlier record for the kind of "intense and furious debate" such as that which took place in Egypt upon the publication of Qasim Amin's two books in 1899 and 1901.[20] Yet in Palestine, as well as other parts of the Middle East, the issues raised by Amin and other reformers remained alive and highly charged decades after they were first broached.[21]

The extent to which the press exerted genuine influence in Palestinian society is open to question.[22] It seems clear that among "key sectors" of the elite, as Rashid Khalidi points out, the press exerted considerable intellectual influence, as it was their major "vehicle of expression" and thus a two-way means of communication among them.[23] It was not infrequent for editorial or letter writers to address each other from one newspaper to the other. Furthermore, as Marilyn Booth points out, discussing the early twentieth-century Egyptian press,

> Founding a periodical was . . . direct political action. . . . Journalism was above all a tool for activist reform and political engagement that, in depth of discussion and breadth of potential audience, could extend far beyond drawing-room debate. Socio-political change required (and would result from) a public discourse, even if it was one limited initially to a very small reading public.[24]

Many of the small, feisty newspapers founded (and foundering) during the mandate period were established for political purposes, or as "organs" of one particular political party or other. The press may well have played a socializing and politicizing role disproportionate to its size and official readership figures in the intensely political atmosphere of mandatory Palestine. Certainly, the British mandate government considered the press influential and potentially harmful. The government expended considerable effort in bribing, coopting, surveilling, censoring, and competing with the press during the course of British rule.[25] Control, censorship, and suspensions of the press by the government escalated during the 1930s during World War II, the British closed all newspapers with the exception of *Filastīn*, *al-Difāʿ*, and *al-Sirāt al-Mustaqīm*.[26]

In evaluating the role of the press, we must also take into account literacy levels and newspaper circulation figures in Palestine, for which we unfortunately have only a few isolated statistics. The indications are that literacy levels were low among the Palestinian population during the period—especially among Muslims.[27] Despite this, however, the public's keen interest in what newspapers had to offer was often remarked upon by observers, as is illustrated by this comment of members of the Commission on the Palestine Disturbances of August 1929:

> The contention that the *fellah* [peasant] takes no personal interest in politics is not supported by our experience in Palestine . . . no less than fourteen Arabic newspapers are published in Palestine and in almost every village there is someone who reads from the papers to gatherings of those villagers who are illiterate. During the long season of the year when the soil cannot be tilled, the villagers . . . discuss politics. . . . The Arab *fellaheen* and villagers are therefore probably more politically minded than many of the people of Europe.[28]

However news may have reached Palestinians in the countryside or towns, the evidence is compelling that Palestinians were well informed about current events. Reports abound in the press of demonstrations and protests in the countryside that responded to political developments.[29] The very fact that so many journals were founded during the mandate period indicates the existence of an interest in and demand for them.

Circulation figures are also elusive. Some estimates exist for a combined daily circulation figure of the four major dailies at twenty-two to twenty-three thousand in the 1930s. By 1946, the combined circulation of *al-Difāʿ* and *Filastīn* alone was around nine to fourteen thousand. Considering that papers purchased were loaned out or read aloud to others, it is safe to assume that these numbers only approximate the minimum number of people who absorbed information from the Arabic dailies. Nor were these the only dailies during this period.[30]

In the absence of reliable statistical data, we can only make educated guesses about the overall extent and influence of the Arabic press during the mandate period. Despite these difficulties, however, by examining its discourse on women we recover a rich, multivocal source of authentic Palestinian voices on the issue of gender—one of the few that exists. Clearly the press played a crucial role in provoking debate and providing a public forum for discussion on fiercely contested issues.

A Note About Filastīn and the Role of Christians in the Press

Because it provided the most extensive and frequent press coverage of women over a long period of time, the newspaper *Filastīn* deserves special mention here.[31] *Filastīn* was owned, edited and run by the Orthodox Christian al-'Isa family in Jaffa. Established in 1911, it managed to endure—with periodic closures—throughout the last decade of the Ottoman Empire until the beginning of the Israeli occupation of the West Bank in 1967. It was the only Palestinian newspaper to span the period of so many different foreign rules.

Much is made of the fact that many of the leading newspapers during the mandate were owned and run by Christians.[32] Neville Mandel suggests this explains their early support for Arab nationalism, since its unifying, secularist message had the result of diluting religious divisiveness, and thus tended to appeal to Christian intellectuals.[33] *Filastīn, although owned by a Christian family, was not necessarily identified as a "Christian" paper per se*. *Filastīn* assiduously commemorated Muslim holy days, as well as provided detailed coverage of other religious activities: for example, the presenting of gifts to prisoners by the women's groups on religious occasions such as the Prophet's birthday, or the feasts of Ramadan.[34] (In issues of *Filastīn* published during World War II, there is an increasingly defensive tone, however, in reports on Christian affairs; the activities of the Orthodox Church receive more detailed attention than previously.) The British, who categorized the subject people in Palestine by "racial" classifications—each individual was identified by religion, which was conflated with race—tended to project and overemphasize confessional grievances and conflict. In describing the owner and editor of *Filastīn*, for example, they say, "As a Christian, he finds himself increasingly out of time with the predominantly Moslem Arab Nationalism in Palestine. He feels deeply the insignificance into which the Christian Arabs have sunk."[35] From perusal of the coverage 'Isa provides in his newspaper, and the tone of the articles on issues related to religion, however, we should be cautious about accepting the British intelligence assessment at face value.

It would be misleading to assume that Christian editors and publishers were by definition any more "liberal" than Muslim colleagues. For one thing, the staffs of the Christian-owned papers included Muslim reporters and editors as well as Christians. For another, Christian opinion was not monolithically "liberal" on any given topic (nor was Muslim opinion necessarily universally "conservative"). It would be unwise to assume sharp polarities between artificial constructs such as "liberal" and "conservative." Jurji Zaydan, for example, a noted Lebanese Christian intellectual, supported veiling and also held the belief that women were inferior to men because they had smaller brains. In an article published in *Filastīn*, a Muslim writer voiced his disagreement with a Christian who had expressed admiration for the veil and criticized Christian women as being more in need of reform than Muslim women. Christian women had advanced beyond their Muslim counterparts, he wrote, because they had been "liberated from . . . that veiling which not only damages health but goes a long way in weakening the intellects of women and debilitating their morals."[36]

Palestinians of the mandate generation narrate a common, shared Arabo-Islamic culture, projecting perhaps retrospectively idealized images of Muslim-Christian harmony and cooperation. Hala Sakakini, daughter of the educator and nationalist Khalil Sakakini, explained how "even we Christians are culturally Muslim," and described Islam as "a culture which unites us."[37] Differences between Christians sometimes superseded those between Muslims and Christians, illuminating a more nuanced and complex portrait of the role of religion in Palestinian society than is often depicted.[38] Christians from Nazareth described the relationships between Muslims and Orthodox Christians as much closer than those between Orthodox and Latin Catholic Christians or Protestants. The former were depicted as "more Arab" and Eastern-oriented than the Latin Catholics and Protestants, who tended to speak Western languages, take European names, and wear Western dress such as hats rather than the traditional head coverings, the *hatta* or *iqāl*. The Western-oriented sects also were among the wealthier classes, whereas the Orthodox Christians and Muslims came from the "popular" classes and the fellahin.[39] Thus, although religious identity should be taken into account in analyzing writing in the press, we cannot assume monolithic social or political attitudes derived from religion.

Press Coverage of Women

Press coverage of Palestinian women in the 1920s and 1930s consisted primarily of two categories: articles of interest to and about (and sometimes by) women, covering the activities of both foreign and local women; and editorial-style articles, which included ones written by the newspapers' editorial staffs as well as those sent in letter form, written by readers and/or writers. The first type included coverage of topics such as the activities of Palestinian women's groups; achievements of individual notable Palestinian women (delivering lectures, receiving academic degrees); exploits of renowned foreign women (Western women aviators, royalty, scientists);[40] the activities or status of other Middle Eastern[41] and Western women;[42] "yellow" journalism or trivia such as common sayings about (usually against) women; and "women's affairs"—that is, articles offering advice about marriage, child rearing, beauty, and so forth. Many of these articles appeared in the special women's columns that began to appear in 1926 in *al-Karmil*'s "*Sahīfat al-nisā'*,"(women's page), edited by Sadhij Nassar, the owner/publisher's wife,[43] and later, in *Filastīn*'s "*Nisā'iyyāt*" (women's affairs), edited by Asma Tubi, a renowned journalist and writer. Initially rather sketchy and sometimes superficial, coverage of women in papers such as *Filastīn*, *Mirāt al-Sharq*, and *al-Karmil* began in the mid-1920s to comprise more substantive thematic and analytical articles.

The editorial-style articles that are examined below cover a diverse range of subjects, including historical topics such as "The Arab Woman Before and After Islam," "The Muslim Woman Today and Yesterday," "Woman in History," "The Impact of Woman Among the Arabs, Past and Present," and "Women's Freedom in Islam." Photographs of Arab women rarely appeared in the Palestinian press until the mid-1940s, although there were quite a few of European women.[44]

Although the majority of contributors to the press were men, a number of educated, middle-class women participated in the gender debate. They began to write in the mainstream press, and a few became eminent professional writers and journalists. Both Mary Shihada and Sadhij Nassar were married to editors of newspapers, Boulos Shihada of *Mirāt al-Sharq* (Jerusalem) and Najib Nassar of *al-Karmil* (Haifa), respectively. Nassar, besides being editor of the women's page, was also director of administration and editor, according to the journal's masthead.[45] Asma Tubi, who wrote for a number of newspapers in and outside of Palestine, became an acclaimed writer and journalist during this period, and later published a book on Arab women. Quite a few women who were not professional journalists contributed pieces or letters to the editor, voicing their opinions on the issues of the day. The fact that women wrote indicates that there was a female readership, however small.

The absence of a women's press or the publication of a women's magazine in Palestine during this period merits special comment. Women in Iran,

Turkey, Egypt, Syria, and Lebanon all founded newspapers, journals, or magazines beginning as early as the late nineteenth century. Indeed, the Palestinian press often heralded the establishment of a new women's magazine in these countries.[46] The interesting corollary to this dearth is the extent to which Palestinian male voices, along with (fewer) female voices, articulated positive—sometimes even militant—positions on raising the status of women, female education, and the like. It would be irresponsible to extrapolate from this and the related discussion below that Palestinian men were more "progressive" than other men in the region; Palestine had its own conservatives. However, there is a striking difference between Palestine and, for example, Iran and Syria, where the opening of girls' schools and unveiling provoked physical assaults against women;[47] there is less evidence of analogous violent reactions in Palestine against women's contraventions of social norms.[48]

The question remains, however: Why was Palestine different from other Arab countries in not establishing a women's press? Possible explanations might be demographic. Palestine's population was smaller, more rural, and less literate than those of Syria, Egypt, and Lebanon.[49] Starting a newspaper or journal required a certain amount of resources, financial and otherwise. Palestinian women possibly did not have the wherewithal and may have realized the limitations of potential readership among Palestine's smaller towns and cities. Furthermore, because of Palestine's geographical position between Greater Syria and Egypt, women may have considered the idea of starting their own journals redundant when they had relatively easy access, both as contributors and consumers, to those published in Beirut, Damascus, and Cairo.

As a caveat of sorts to the dearth of a women's press, one could argue that Sadhij Nassar's contributions as editor of *al-Karmil*'s women's page constituted a kind of one-woman press. Between 1926 and c. 1933, she wrote extensively in the paper, commenting on a wide range of topics and reporting on women's activities locally, regionally, and internationally. The sheer energy and output of these articles is striking. She chastised, praised, criticized, encouraged, blamed, and sometimes hectored women to become involved in politics, to raise their female and male children in equality, to unify themselves and avoid factionalism, and to liberate themselves by becoming economically independent through work, among other things.[50] The range of her opinions is complex, contradictory, radical, and conservative all at the same time—much like the male and other female pundits analyzed below.

Despite the absence of a women's press, however, the amount of press coverage on gender issues provided in the mainstream press is striking. Some of the more influential and longer-lasting newspapers during the mandate period—*Filastīn, al-Difā'*, and *al-Karmil*, as well as *Mirāt al-sharq*—published diverse and fairly secular opinions, providing contributions written by both "modernist" liberals and conservatives.[51] In contrast, the more religiously identified newspapers, such as *al-Jāmi'a al-'Arabiyya* (the mouthpiece of the Supreme Muslim Council), *al-Sirāt al-Mustaqīm*, and *al-Jāmi'a al-Islāmiyya* tended to highlight religious topics and publish mostly conservative writers and articles, the tones of which were sometimes alarmist or defensive regarding Muslim affairs.[52]

VOICES IN THE PRESS
A Debate Begins

In the May 21, 1927, issue of *Filastīn*, Wasfi Basisu, a student from the American University of Beirut, issued a call for "harmony and solidarity," expressing his concerns about a debate over veiling and unveiling that, he said, seemed to be dividing society and its intellectuals. The debate to which Basisu was referring had commenced approximately a month previously. Our first inkling of it appears in *Filastīn* on April 19, when Ghalib al-Sa'id wrote the first article—entitled "The Veil and the Duty to Lift It"—in a series on "Unveiling and Veiling" (*al-sufūr wa al-hijāb*). Thus commenced a heated series of articles on this subject that continued through the spring and into the summer.[53] Although the majority of the articles were part of the series in *Filastīn*, the debate spread beyond the pages of one newspaper; writers referred and responded to articles written in other papers.[54] A total of at least fifteen articles, written by ten authors, was published between April 19 and June 7, 1927. Nine of the articles advocated unveiling, giving the "unveilers" a definite edge. (This could well have been due to editors' biases in providing more space to the unveilers.)[55]

In the course of the debate, writers traded insults, engaged in heated rhetoric and polemic, or pleaded for compromise and harmony. They utilized loaded references to religion, tradition, and history to buttress their various arguments.[56] But the articles that ostensibly focus on veiling ultimately examine and discuss much broader issues. Embedded in the discourse on women was the formulation of a public dialogue in which intellectuals thought out loud about, and fought in print over, the compelling question of how to redefine Palestinian Arab culture and society. The site upon which these redefinitions were constructed was the nexus between gender, modernity, and social and economic change.

The threat posed by the Zionist movement to Palestinian Arab national identity underscored the urgency of the issue and involved complexities that distinguished it from other colonized Middle Eastern countries. Unlike Egypt, where by the 1920s there was a nominally sovereign government, and Syria, Lebanon, and Iraq, whose mandates explicitly promised eventual independence, Palestine faced a much more ambivalent future. Furthermore, it was threatened by two external sources: an imperial power that controlled it; and a rival, colonial political movement that had formal recognition from, and support of, that power. The nature of Zionist settler-colonialism endangered Palestinian culture and the very existence of Palestinian society in a way that differentiated Palestine from states under other types of mandate or indirect colonial rule. Although, interestingly, most of the articles on women do not directly refer to the Zionist threat, it was indeed a subtext to much of the discourse on gender, as is revealed in debate on changing attitudes and behavior of young *men*.

More obvious is writers' concern with the West, and gender issues perceived as relating to Western culture and influence. Mata Lani, writing about the debate on *sati* (the Hindu practice of burning widows on their husbands' funeral pyres) in British colonial India, observes that "what we have here is not a discourse in which pre-existing traditions are challenged by an emergent modern consciousness, but one in which both 'tradition' and 'modernity' as we know them are contemporaneously produced."[57] Palestinians were engaged in analogous discursive contestations, yet in the Palestinian situation the debate articulated in the press was not between the colonizer and colonized so much as *among* the colonized. The nature of a distinct colonization project was the true focus of the debate. On the surface—initially, at least—it seems that the terms of the challenge amongst Palestinians involved either acceptance or rejection of westernization.

Frequent references to history resonate in the articles on gender. It is striking how history is utilized to defend and buttress each particular writer's point of view and construct new concepts of gender, including understandings of veiling that, for the most part, call for its demise. In invoking and reconstructing history, the authors projected their own contemporary ideas and values into the past, claiming it as "the origin of [their] own contemporary culture."[58] This process involved a re-creation of Palestinian Arab culture and tradition as well as history, utilizing gender as the site upon which these new elaborations were constructed. The debates were "not primarily about women but about what constitutes authentic cultural tradition."[59] This involved constructing new meanings and interpretations of history in service to an evolving ideology of modernity. Writers in the press were "salvaging modernity by asserting its indigenous pedigree" through history.[60] The diffusion of references, invocations, and allusions to history in the press are utilized not only to provide lessons and sound warnings, but also to articulate a hybridized culture that synthesized the best of both East and West.

Writers drew widely upon both Islamic and Western history, quoting not only the Qur'an and the Prophet, but also invoking figures such as Voltaire, Napoleon, Edison, Madame Curie, and Alexander the Great. Islamic history was reinterpreted from almost a feminist slant. "In Muslim history the woman has enjoyed full rights and done many great things," wrote "a son of Jaffa." "Anyone who reads the history of the Arab nation and its wars would quickly realize the great impact of women," Sadhij Nassar asserts.[61] Christians as well as Muslims took inspiration from Islamic history, as exemplified by Mary Shihada, whose 1931 speech at the Orthodox Youth Club in Jaffa on "Woman and Her Impact on the Social Structure," was reported in three installments in *Filastīn*:

> The Arab woman has spurred the Arab man to all his great historical deeds. . . . In war, the Arab woman performed valuable functions, like bearing water, caring for the wounded, and encouraging weary troops. The sacrifice of women who send their sons into certain death while encouraging them cannot be underestimated. [Lists several examples from medieval chronicles of female bravery on battlefields.] I would not mention these examples except to strike fear into the stronger sex [*al-jins al-nashīt*] which always accuses us of cowardice. . . . Women have enjoyed greater freedom. . . . Islamic history is full of stories like these . . .[62]

Another article quotes Matiel Mughannam, also Christian, who proudly states, "we're the daughters of those ladies who took part in *jihād* [holy war] with their men in past history."[63] Muslims as well as Christians held up female role models from Western cultures to inform their points of view. Muhammad Isma'il, writing on "The Necessity to Liberate Women," admiringly tells the tale of the wife of an English colonial official who offered to go to work and take care of their five children so the husband could fight in the "Great War" (World War I). "It is people like that who made England what it is; don't we want to be great like England?"[64]

Palestinian intellectuals debating "modernism" and "reform" in the 1920s and 1930s did not reject their own culture out of hand. Instead, they reinscribed history and tradition, infusing them in retrospect (and not necessarily through wishful thinking) with the qualities that articulated their collective, contemporary construction of ideal womanhood. Writers' invocation of history was a common device for expostulating that the veil was not intrinsically Islamic but had been imported and borrowed from other cultures, thus invalidating its cultural authenticity and allowing them to call for its demise. 'Abd al-Ghani al-Karami, one of the biggest opponents of veiling,[65] asserts that the veil originated in predemocratic Greece and pre-Islamic Persia, and disappeared in both places with the enlightenment of democracy and Islam, respectively.[66] Others, including a "son of Jaffa," claimed veiling was un-Islamic and not a part of heritage to which one should cling. "The veil has nothing to do with religion" *(Al-hijāb laysa min al-dīn fī shay)*, he states emphatically.[67]

Yet others used history to claim that Islam does not, in fact, call for veiling. Ghalib al-Sa'id states that "the Quranic strictures on the veil are directed only at the Prophet's wives. Further, women in early Islam played a prominent public role. . . . Only in the Dark Ages did men impose authority upon women, and force them to live enclosed within four walls, even though many enlightened men know that women are pure, tender angels with minds as capable as those of men."[68] Karami points out that in accounts of the Four Righteous Caliphs and Mu'awiya (one of the early caliphs in Islam), women were uncovered.[69]

A whole new concept of womanhood was painstakingly constructed from the logic that flowed from these arguments. The battle over definition was fought issue by issue. The ideal "new woman" as portrayed by the press was unveiled, but still modestly attired; educated—her thoughts enlightened with "science"—in order to raise well-brought up (especially male) children who would lead the nation and uplift it; a good companion to her husband; and capable of supporting herself by working if absolutely necessary.

Unveilers Versus Veilers: Sin, the Nation, and Westernization

Chronologically, the first battle in the press took place in the veiling-unveiling series in 1927. The unveilers poured forth passionate invective against veiling, ascribing to it all evils of society.[70] "The veil is not among the reasons for a woman's purity," wrote Ghalib al-Sa'id. "Witness how many veiled women are really devils cursed by the wickedness they hide under the cover of that veil, and how many unveiled women keep watch over their honor."[71] Another writer goes so far as to claim that the veil was the biggest incentive for adultery and sin, and that most of the bawdy houses were staffed by Muslim prostitutes, citing health reports that stated the incidence of sexually transmitted diseases was higher among Muslims because veiled prostitutes spread them to men. "What do the champions of the veil say to that???" he asks. "Won't they say with me that unveiling invites protection of morals and health???"[72] Saʿid concurs that the veil was a health hazard, since it was "an ideal repository for microbes and fatal germs transmitted through the air by idle spitting or the sick."[73]

The writer who fired the initial salvo in the debate over the veil concludes his opening challenge by contending that "the veil is the cause of our deterioration and a source of regression of our homeland."[74] As illustrated by this and Basisu's article, one of the unveilers' major tropes was conflation of the demise of the veil with determining the entire future of the nation, the corollary being that women were the saviors of the nation. This placed high hopes and burdens upon them. Basisu asks an opponent:

> Why do you support stagnation over change? . . . Those who are trying to liberate woman have made very clear—and Qasim Amin's voice can still be heard—that they want to liberate woman not because they are imitating the West, but because unveiling will result in a woman who is able to raise a generation capable of fixing the shortcomings of society and the nation.[75]

The nationalist imperative and building "national life" in fact infused the debate as much as religious discourse. One writer, noting somewhat irritatedly that the debate over the veil is unimportant and trivial, states: "What is unveiling and the hat other than a symbol? . . . the core of the matter is for woman to take part with men in practical, national life as she does in other aspects of life . . . if this is the case, there's no difference to me if a man wears a tarbush or if a woman is veiled or unveiled."[76] Another fires off: "We, the young champions of the new and the useful, the revolutionaries against servitude, colonialism and ignorance, are absolutely right that this country will never break its enslavement unless its better half—as the Europeans say—is better educated and refined. . . . We call for unveiling that the woman may join with us in public action."[77]

The whole dialectical process of defining and redefining Palestinian Arab culture was profoundly informed by the seeping cultural hegemony of European colonialism, and the ensuing conflict between ruler and ruled. The self-consciously acknowledged tension is a frequent referent in the discourse on women, providing subtext and dialogue in many of the articles. The references to "the West" (*al-gharb*) and "westernization" (*tafarnaja*) are striking throughout; writers frequently compare their own civilization or culture to that of the West, even directly addressing "the West" at times.[78]

The wife of Mamduh Effendi al-Nablusi, delivering a speech during heated nationalist demonstrations in Nablus in 1931, tells the Arab woman to raise her head high because she has entered the battle of her political life. She adopts a simultaneously defensive and aggressive stance vis-à-vis Westerners. She thunders:

> This is an unequivocal answer when Westerners accuse us of apathy and say of us . . . that we stay in our houses and have no part in national life . . . they say that we're dependent upon our fathers and husbands and that we don't extend a helping hand in their national struggle against the enemy . . . they say that we don't concern ourselves with anything but cooking and fooling around and do not share with our men in their troubles defending the beloved nation. All this is said about us, and the aware among us listen . . . we wait patiently for the sun of the women's revival to rise.[79]

Two distinct trends of thought emerge from the pages of the newspapers in this period: one attributes all of the various social ills (such as the "marriage crisis," or "women's ignorance," for example) to Arab backwardness vis-à-vis the West; the other places the blame for these problems on "blind imitation" of the West.[80] The undercurrent to the first is that the Arab woman needed to adopt some modern "Western" ways in order to play a role in the nationalist struggle. The question of "westernization," "westernizing," and "the West" was highly contentious. For those anti-Western writers, westernization denoted bars, dancing, night clubs, excessive freedom and sex, as this author illustrates in his impassioned argument on "The Harm of Unveiling":

> The advocates of the veil want us to continue adherence to old principles and the advocates of unveiling want precisely the opposite. They want us to 'become civilized' and 'advance' as per their opinions; in short, they want us to be Westernized. . . . They . . . don't want to know that 'becoming civilized' is the root of all chaos and error. . . . If you westernize—God forbid—and go with your wife to a party where there is dancing, and a young man approaches and asks your wife to dance with him . . . and there she is before your eyes pressing her body into his, wrapping her arms about his waist as his are about hers . . . how will you feel then?[81]

Numerous writers blamed the "marriage crisis" on the "westernization of our women," or young men who attended bars and clubs in an effort to westernize and imitate the "fake ways" of the West.[82]

For those advocating change, however, the "advanced" nature of Western culture and its supposed "progress" came to epitomize what reformers wished to attain for Arab society. In *al-Difāʿ*, Suʿad Khuri discusses how "the West has taken the place of the East as the source of civilization and scientific discoveries." She (incorrectly) claims "one of the most important accomplishments of the West in the Renaissance period was granting women their rights, and allowing them to join men in all aspects of life." The Eastern woman, Khuri continues, although she has taken steps in the right direction, has been "outstripped by the Western woman in the speed of progress."[83] This theme of "catching up" to the West was a subtext to much of the debate. "Our country today is different than yesterday," writes Yusuf Haykal, a contributor to the debate on the veil. "We need to adapt woman in a new way that corresponds to the modern spirit of the present time, and to make her keep pace with the Western girls of her sex."[84] There are frequent comparisons and references to stages of development of Western and "Eastern" women. "I believe that woman was not created uselessly next to the man, but to work with him for what is best for them. The West did not reach this stage without its women taking their role and duties. As for us Arabs, we are backward because of our upbringing and woman's ignorance of her duties."[85] One writer flatly states, "we should give woman back her stolen rights if we want to progress like the West."[86]

Palestinians' positions on "westernization" also came to be fraught with inconsistencies. Some writers who advocated change could not easily be categorized as "pro-West" or not, reflecting the ambivalence and the contradictions with which Palestinian society viewed the increasingly visible transformations in women's roles. They encouraged change, but not too much and not too fast. Wasfi Basisu, after calling for "harmony" in the debate, and "change" over "stagnation," hastens to add that the unveiling he is calling for is compatible with the *sharīa* (Islamic law). Those advocating unveiling have taken into consideration the Qur'an and the hadith, and do not want a Western-style liberalism where women are given too much freedom, he assures the reader.[87] A number of writers who identify with the unveilers and reformers advocate partial or gradual unveiling, rather than "sudden unveiling."[88] Yet another position adopted was more synthetic; Arab society should consciously decide what to adopt and reject from the West, as well as what to preserve from the East.[89]

The contradictory feelings experienced among Palestinians about these issues are graphically illustrated in an article by "a Muslim woman" who describes a gathering of Muslim and Christian women in which the majority opine that they approved of "moral unveiling" (*al-sufūr al-adabī*). A dissident then says that she would prefer the Muslim woman to "remain veiled and ignorant" rather than unveil and "expose her forearms in the road and such things." At that, the rest of the group's "anger would have boiled over" if the writer had not intervened to speak to the young lady "gently" and discuss the issue of the veil.[90] It seems that the women were more strongly supportive of unveiling than it at first seemed from the writer's initial, tepid description.

The pro-Western and anti-Western camps did not necessarily connote "liberal" or "conservative" on social and political issues. Many ostensibly "westernized" Arabs expressed ambivalence and/or outright hostility to Western culture, recognizing it as a threat to national (authentic) culture. Mary Shihada demonstrates this in a blistering speech she delivered at the Orthodox Youth Club in Jaffa in 1931, in which she describes the sorry state of today's women. Echoing other writers' criticism, she says the only topics women talk about are fashion and problems with the hired help. The reasons for this "miserable situation" are the imperialist enslavement of the Palestinian people; Palestinian men, "who fear the awakening of woman and [who] have begun to place obstacles in the path of her awakening and resist it"; and the "superficial adoption of Western civilized ways."[91] The writing of many who advocated reform, education of women, and unveiling, be it gradual or not, exhibit this paradox of being westernized (seemingly) themselves, yet hostile to certain elements of it. There are distinct nationalist undertones to this ostensible contradiction.

"Liberate Women in Order That the Nation Be Liberated":[92] The Role of the "New" Woman

One of the major loci of hostility towards Western civilization's influence on women centered on nationalism and culture. Often the concern about these issues was embedded within articles ostensibly about other topics, such as education of women. An intricate web of meaning permeated discussions of the role of women as mothers, educators of the young, and, ultimately, those responsible for imparting values, culture, and tradition to the entire upcoming generation. In this function of women, upon whose centrality both modernists and conservatives alike seemed to agree, the question of education came to be loaded as well, encompassing more than a discussion over whether or not to allow women to be educated, but also a debate about the future of the nation.

The trope of mothers as "repositories of national identity, as well as markers of national progress or backwardness" was one that resonated in many colonized societies and was closely bound to concepts of a "new woman."[93] The new woman—as mother, educated woman, wife—constituted the "savior" of the nation, albeit within a clearly circumscribed role. The rhetoric wavers between extolling woman's virtue and blaming her for the current catastrophe facing the nation. One writer, opining that the liberation of the country is dependent upon the liberation of woman, laments the poor education of women "for it is inconceivable that Palestinian children born of educated mothers would have allowed such calamities [as the Balfour Declaration and subsequent British occupation] to occur and entrench themselves as easily, as has happened."[94] Writers consistently warned women that "sav[ing] Palestine from humiliation depends on you and your actions."[95] An increasingly urgent tone came to infuse much of this gendered discourse as the national situation intruded and insinuated itself into every issue, with the escalation of crises beginning in the late 1920s.[96] "You [women] are responsible," intoned Sadhij Nassar, writing in al-Karmil. "Yes, you Palestinian Arab ladies, Muslim and Christian, you are responsible for the integrity of the nation [watan] and keeping Palestine Arab as it was until now. Every woman will spread the spirit of cooperation among the sons of the Arabs in the souls of her children."[97]

Su'ad Khuri attributed Western women's presumed advantage over Eastern women to education in their own "national" schools (al-madāris al-wataniyya), in which they learned love of their country, courage, and nationalism, and subsequently imparted these to their children, "the builders of the future." "As for the Eastern woman, where are her national schools?" she asks. She questions the character and goals of the education received by women at missionary schools run by foreigners. Girls do not learn about their own history, national heroes, or language, "the epitome and symbol of the honor of the Arabs." She concludes the article by calling upon girls to demand their rights to an education that includes learning about Arabic culture and language, and upon parents to support national schools.[98]

What, exactly, was an "educated" woman, according to the press pundits? It is here, in particular, that we see the tense intersections between British and Palestinian cultures. British officials in the Education Department and Palestinian intellectuals concurred that the major goal of educating women was to train them in the "complex art" of child rearing in order to create "expert mothers who can prepare the child to go into the world as a courageous, able man."[99]

A very real tension was generated, however, over what kind of mothers women were educated to become. In the Palestinian lexicon of ideal mothers, it is striking how the concept of "home life" takes on nationalist connotations linked to culture, history, and nation. While British Mandate educational policies were oriented toward creating docile, proper, middle-class housewives for male civil servants, Palestinian pundits in the press advocated educating women in order to produce men—and women—to serve the nation. This notion extended beyond the confident male voices that debated the issue, and included "average" citizens, demonstrating the extent to which almost all Palestinians began to conceive of so many aspects of their lives in nationalist terms. One young woman, describing her education in an English school in Bethlehem, wrote an article advising parents to educate their daughters to enable them to "fulfill their duties toward their home and country."[100] Clearly, the British Mandate educational system was not attaining its goals with women but rather, letting a genie out of the bottle. Both women and men used their educations to contribute to the debate over national identity and culture, and women's role in promoting them. Out of this process emerged a construct of an educated woman citizen whose major contribution to society was as a mother of sons of the nation. Thus education, motherhood, and nationalism became fused.

It is revealing how closely so many writers' views corresponded with those of Qasim Amin in *Tahrīr al-mar'a*, in which he identifies women's most important function to be mothers who prepare men to be successful in life, declaring this to be "the worthwhile goal that civilization has entrusted to the women of our era."[101] Thus "the only way that the woman will be able to produce scientists, intellectuals, leaders and fighters is by being educated and unveiled," claims Basisu, echoing Amin.[102] This sometimes militantly articulated vision of Arab mothers raising future Palestinian "fighters" contrasts markedly with British concepts about adapting education to "suit the needs of the peasant wife and mother-to-be."[103]

Amin closely links the issue of veiling to the education of future mothers, whose own upbringing, he states, "cannot be effective unless there is a change in the present use of the veil."[104] The unveilers in the Palestine debate concurred, declaring that the act of veiling was an impediment to a girl's education. "If we veil the girl, then we cut off the road between her and real knowledge," warns Yusuf Haykal of Jaffa (whose writing follows Amin's line of argument so closely that it borders on plagiarism). "If we pledge education to a girl and plant in her blessed morals, and then imprison her in the home and prohibit her from contact with men and entrance into higher education then she will forget what she has learned . . . until she becomes exactly like the girl who was never educated."[105] One experienced female educator, who supports gradual unveiling, states that girls must be educated first before unveiling.[106] This idea that a girl needed to be educated before she unveiled seems to have had credence even among the unveilers. One writer suggests that girls should be sent to boys' schools when young in order to prepare them to leave school unveiled and accustomed to mixing with men.[107]

The new Palestinian woman was not only to be trained to be the consummate mother, however, but also to be a helpmate to her husband, and this, too, required education. The lexicon of companionate marriage seeped into the discourse on marriage and education, inextricably linking them. In another eerie echo of Amin, Subhiyya Miqdadi, writing on " woman's education and upbringing," expounds at some length on the subject, expressing concern that

> the wife be compatible with the husband. . . . In this day and age, when the man of the house is likely to be more educated than the woman, cases of marital incompatibility are common and lead to broken homes, as a man's love for someone with whom he cannot hold a serious conversation must be temporary.[108]

An educated man wants an educated wife to share with him in both personal and public affairs—not just someone to perform housework.[109] The responsibilities of running a home that is to be a "shelter from the world" rather than "a catalyst for corruption," however, "require a great deal of variegated knowledge." The woman "cannot run her household unless she has obtained an adequate amount of rational and literary knowledge." This requires that the woman/wife "comprehend[] something of the study of social structure and the natural sciences" in order to reject the superstitions and legends that "cripple the minds" of women and are then imparted to their children.[110]

This discourse—or "cult"—of domesticity that was articulated in the press and other texts written in the Middle East in the early decades of the twentieth century has been critiqued in recent feminist scholarship.[111] Afsaneh Najmabadi, however, objects that this categorization is a "misnomer that prevents us from understanding why women"—and I would add, some men—"embraced these notions." She argues that, on the contrary, "Women's assuming the position of the learned manager and head of the household . . . far from frustrating the dynamics of women's movement into public life and national recognition provided the empowering basis for it."[112] Palestinian women were to be the ultimate helpmates, constituting sympathetic, intelligent—not merely domestic—assistants to their husbands and conveying the best in Arab culture to their children in order to make them brave, strong, and intelligent enough to provide for the future of the nation. In order to achieve this goal, women had to be educated in the "arts" of motherhood and wifehood, subjects that, in the discourse of the press, became imbued with nationalist meaning. One can claim, as does Najmabadi, that the nationalization of domesticity created an outlet and justification for women and men to argue for increased educational opportunities for women and discarding the veil in the name of the nation.

The "Marriage Crisis"

Changing expectations of marriage, along with the economic problems associated with providing for the *mahr* loomed large in yet another debate in the press—the "marriage crisis"—that was carried on in the pages of *Filastīn* beginning in August 1931 in an eight-part series, after a number of isolated articles on the subject began to appear in late 1927.[113] The "crisis" consisted of a "strike on marriage" in which young men were either delaying marriage or balking at marrying at all. The writers in this series spread the blame for the crisis fairly equally among parents, prospective brides, and the young men themselves.

From the type and tone of the criticisms, it is evident that the depression was hitting Palestinian society hard, as reflected in the overwhelming emphasis on the economic constraints against getting married. The two major complaints were the high costs of marrying—either to pay for the dowry or for luxury items and a lifestyle the man could not afford—and the "westernization" of the young people. "The blame for the marriage crisis falls primarily on the parents of single women, and secondly on men themselves," writes ʿAbd al-Fattah Jabr. "When parents ask for high *mahr* for their daughters and put conditions that the house must contain luxuries and unnecessary items that exceed logic and religious texts, it makes it very hard for men to meet these requirements."[114] Although, as often as not, it was the parents' greed that was the focus of writers' ire, young women also came in for their fair share of criticism for being demanding and acquisitive. "I think that the whole problem lies with the single women who are asking men to offer them much more than what they could afford," asserts one anonymous (probably male) writer. "I know of a good man who is doing relatively well financially, and when he proposed to a girl she refused because he does not look 'chic.' Who would dare propose to such girls? The blame is on our westernized single women who only care about appearance."[115] In one article, the author addresses the fathers of prospective brides, the president of the Islamic Legal Association, and the government, calling upon the latter to interfere to reduce the dowry and make it affordable.[116]

The economic issue, underlain by increased consumerism, is directly linked to westernization. Numerous articles in the press discuss and criticize women's love of fashion and luxuries and interest in new forms of entertainment like dancing (with men) and attending the cinema. Men's reluctance to marry is blamed on westernization of women, who "rush to follow the fake civilization of Europe and imitate the habits that the wise in Europe themselves despise" (for example, acquiring excessive material goods); or on young men who go to bars and clubs and waste their money on "club girls" in a desire to be westernized.[117] A number of writers point to a number of reasons for men not marrying, including men's (not women's) lack of choice in a marriage partner; bad exemplars in the form of parents' and friends' unhappy marriages; or marriage without love. The major focus of criticism, however, was westernization and its effects, primarily financial—promoting acquisitiveness among young women—but also cultural.

Interestingly, the series on marriage demonstrates a more conservative orientation than that on veiling. Although virtually all writers called for some "remedy" to the marriage crisis, their proposals were hardly innovative: compelling young men to behave in a respectable manner in sexual and family matters, lowering the *mahr*, and educating women to be virtuous and modest.[118] Indeed, there were sexual undercurrents to the debate on marriage that articulated anxiety about both female and male gender roles; one can perhaps identify similar attempts at "taming ... unruly forms of male sexuality" that Deniz Kandiyoti sees in modernizing Turkish society.[119] Male and female writers used the marriage crisis to both criticize and excuse men's sexuality. 'Abd al-Fattah Jabr (cited above criticizing parents' excessive dowry demands) adds that "when this happens, the single men think that they have no choice but to resort to mistresses and bars and bad magazines, not realizing that this money could be enough to raise a family. . . . the single men must . . . stop attending bars where women are sold because this will make them forget marriage and its benefits."[120] An added aspect to this anxiety in the Palestinian case was the presence of another kind of "unruly" (Jewish) female sexuality available in the bars and establishments of more Europeanized places such as Tel Aviv.

The signs of something coming apart at the seams is evinced in the plaintive tone in the series on marriage. Clearly, the entire concept and meaning of marriage was undergoing transformation.[121] The discussion of marriage portends profound transformations in other domains such as the encroaching effects of an increasingly consumer-oriented economy and generational conflict; a number of articles resonate with considerable bitterness against parental control over youth in making marriage decisions. Young men were clearly not acquiescent about accepting parental choice of brides. One writer in the "marriage crisis" series complains that "the ignorance of the majority of parents makes them believe that they should treat their sons and daughters the way they themselves were treated, forgetting the tremendous differences between the two generations. Not getting married is the only way for youngsters to show resistance against their parents' control over their lives. I know a lot of men who decided to leave the country just to be free of their parents' control."[122]

Recovering Women's Lost Rights

Scattered articles on "women's rights" began to appear in the press in the 1920s. These, like so many of the articles on women, also drew upon Islamic history and compared women of various Eastern countries to each other and to Western women. Writers were clearly aware of debate on the issue and feminist gains and activity in Turkey, Iraq, Egypt, and other Arab countries. They extolled prominent women writers and intellectuals such as Munira Thabit and May Ziyada for their roles in the women's revival or awakening (*al-nahda al-nisā'iyya*). Characteristically, most of the articles in *Filastīn* were encouraging and sympathetic to women's increased involvement in the public domain. Some were even provocative at times, urging Palestinian women to become more politically active and berating them for trailing behind their sisters in Egypt and Syria in fostering a women's "awakening." A letter writer in 1926 to *al-Karmil*, Qass ibn Sa'ida from Acre, demands, "Where's the awakening? Where are the haters of indifference? Where are the women reformers and demanders of rights?"[123] Muhammad Isma'il from Jaffa went beyond being merely supportive of women's rights, mincing no words on the subject. "The right of woman to live in equality with men is not subject to discussion," he states categorically.

> To all Muslim women . . . I say . . . today you have the most difficult role [in the struggle], for you must step forward with a steady, fearless foot, because demanding rights requires that you not fear anything or anyone. Indeed if you freeze up or retreat from your demands, you will lose all of your position and hope . . . and become entirely dependent upon others, sentenced to death in the dark prison of tradition. Form women's organizations and light up the way for other girls in whose eyes the light of the civilization of the twentieth century does not shine. . . . O Muslim woman, tear up that insulting veil whose chains [*sic*] bind you . . . God and the spirit of youth and the norms of progress are behind you.[124]

Despite numerous calls for "rights" and "equality," these concepts are never precisely clarified; "women's rights" is used rather loosely in most texts. Matiel Mughannam, reviewing Arab women's recent participation in nationalist politics in 1935, comments on the International Women's Union's promotion of the "rights of women everywhere," asking, "what rights are these when Zionism and imperialism hold sway?"[125] Her notion of "rights" and the attainment of them is linked to political, rather than social, change in patriarchal institutions such as marriage and the family. One author, a supporter of "rights," calls on the one hand for woman to work toward equality with man; on the other, he cautions against women becoming "extremist like what has happened to some women in America in a way that does not correspond with oriental values."[126]

Extrapolating from its discursive context in the press, one can interpret "women's rights" to connote women's participation in the public, political domain, and, increasingly, in the nationalist struggle. "Rights" in general, in this discourse, seemed to denote individual autonomy in order to enable women to participate in public life and make choices in their personal life, but primarily in order to serve a collectivity, the nation, rather than the individual herself. This collective and somewhat abstract concept seemed to correspond with the general understanding of "rights" as articulated in articles about the political situation in Palestine, in which the word explicitly and clearly signified national sovereignty and was coupled with the adjectives "democratic," "constitutional," or "representational." Renowned Egyptian feminist Huda Sha'rawi, in an article published in the Palestinian press, implies that women's rights constitute the "right to participate in any national or religious movement." She complains about the Islamic Council meeting held in Jerusalem in 1931, to which only male representatives were invited, "as if Islam was a religion for men only."[127]

Another connotation of "rights" for women in the press refers to those provided in Islam. A number of writers contend that "rights" in Islam are equal for men and women, and deplore their absence or weakness in contemporary society. A "son of Jaffa" echoes the trend of thought of Muslim reformers such as Muhammad 'Abduh, implying that a return to the true path of Islam will restore to women the full rights they previously enjoyed in Islamic history, and blaming men's oppression of women on the "recent deterioration of Islam, [which] has blinded the eyes of men with ignorance and ruined their morals."[128] Papers such as *al-Sirat al-Mustaqim* tended to be conservative on social issues but staunch advocates of upholding women's rights under Islam. The paper published a strongly worded article defending women's rights under *shari'a* and criticizing guardians or relatives who deprived women of their dowry and property, husbands who forced wives to work, and fathers who sold their land in order to avoid leaving it to daughters as inheritance. "A woman's right to inheritance is written in the Qur'an and no one can deprive her of that right," the writer firmly asserts.[129]

Paralleling the discussion about women's historical rights under Islam was a conceptual framework formulated as a "restoration" of "lost," previously existent rights or freedoms. An assumption of something gone awry results in different analyses of the situation. One writer sees hope in a "great movement underway to educate woman and restore her rights," whereas another deplores the "disappearance of the Palestinian woman from the public arena discussing her cause."[130] Mary Shihada also mentions the "loss" of the modern woman's courage and freedom, partially blaming men for this change.[131] All of these writers share the assumption that Arab (or "Eastern") women had somehow "lost" something they had in the past, be it attributable to the rights granted to women by Islam, or to some other, unidentified phenomenon. They linked the loss of women's historic rights under Islam to foreign domination undermining Arab-Islamic culture. In this, writers in the Palestinian press echoed Egyptian discourse on "lost rights"; at the International Women Suffrage Alliance Congress in Rome in 1923, Sha'rawi delivered a speech in which she declared that "Egyptian women were calling for a restoration of their lost rights," which were lost "when the country fell under foreign domination." Twenty-one years later she reiterated the same theme at the Arab Women's Conference in Cairo, demanding that the Arab woman "regain her political rights, which have been granted to her by the *sharī'a*."[132] It is interesting that she considered the *sharī'a* a source of *political* rights. Also interesting is that the refrain of "lost rights" resounds in British feminist history. British "feminists . . . liked to argue that female emancipation was really just the recovery of lost rights implicit in the constitution." It seems that attempting to reclaim lost rights somehow appeared more legitimate than demanding new ones.[133]

Yet there was opposition to the "great movement" as well. Writers deployed the idiom of ridicule—historically, a familiar and popular tactic in discourses resistant to changes in the status of women—to demean and deride any potential gains by women. An author wonders sarcastically if the great leader necessary for the Palestinian cause—"the like of Hitler, Mustafa Kamal or Reza Shah"—could come from Palestine's women. Answering his own question, he proceeds to derogate women in three equally disparaged "classes," concluding that the possibility of a woman leader emerging from such a milieu constitutes "empty talk."[134] Women were frequently criticized for their idle chatter, indolence, and concern for frivolous matters such as fashion. An anonymous woman writer claims that, unlike other women, the Palestinian woman does not want to participate with men and be equal economically, but is happy to stay at home doing her "natural work," since she is a "mother and housewife above all else."[135] Even Mary Shihada, who herself defied tradition and deplored women's lack of an active role in public life, echoes this view, presenting a somewhat muted version of what that role should be. Lamenting the "feeble voice of women" in the "revolution," she states, "we women" have a "different perspective in life" and cannot join men in their political activities, clubs, and associations. She describes women's duties as standing beside men, doing without, and saving by not spending money on luxury goods.[136]

Clearly, the articulation of women's rights and indeed, new responsibility, to participate in the nationalist arena was somewhat abstract at times, due to the lack of common definitions of these rights and how women were to exercise them. The pundits in the press expressed confusion over the distinction between rights and responsibilities.

CONCLUSION

In trying to make sense of the contradictions in the debates on gender in Palestine during the mandate period, it is important to note that the discourse that raged around these issues tended to shine the spotlight upon a small segment of the women of Palestine: the elite. It was this group of women who were at the core of the debate; the situation of peasant women was hardly ever addressed, except to compare them (usually favorably for their simplicity and hard work) with urban, elite women. Indeed, the discourse on women and gender reveals as much about the writers as it does about the issues they addressed. The writers and debaters who participated in and shaped the discourse in the press were articulating their own experience as members of groups that were experiencing more social and cultural upheaval during the 1920s and 1930s than the peasantry, whose major struggles centered on economic difficulties. The elite had increasing contact with Westerners and foreign ideas and cultures. Furthermore, economic changes tended to affect social positions and class status.[137]

As can be seen from the highly personal nature of many of these articles, they were cries from the heart; the writers were essentially writing about themselves—be they man or woman. Although much of the discourse focused on women, gender was at the core of the matter, since the discussions were as much about men.[138] These writers, many if not most of whom were men, were testing the waters of their own desires for and fears of change, which coexisted uncomfortably within their own psyches. Deniz Kandiyoti, referring to newly republican Turkey of the 1920s and 1930s, states that male reformers "found the plight of women a powerful vehicle for the expression of their own restiveness with social conventions they found particularly stultifying and archaic."[139] This observation seems particularly apt as well in describing the situation of Palestinian men, as revealed in the discourse of the press. Thomas Phillipp highlights how

> the issue of feminism [in the Middle East] touched perhaps more directly than any other aspect of the modernist movement upon the personal life of people and upon the strongest traditional sentiments. One could proclaim oneself in favor of ... nationalism, constitutional rule, or the validity of modern sciences without necessarily having to change one's private life very much. But new ideas about the role of woman in society had direct bearing on the private life of each individual.[140]

Throughout history, feminists everywhere have confronted this situation; resistance to change within the personal realm—how one lives one's private life, organizes one's domestic and interior mental space—has proven impervious to lofty declarations of support for "equality," or women's "rights," and contributed to confusion and contradiction between political ideals and the reality of lived lives.[141] Although many reformers and seeming feminists supported expanding women's access to education and encouraging them to do their part in building the nation, the voices for change were muted when it came to altering the status and role of women within the traditional, patriarchal family. This domain was perceived as connected to religious and cultural life in a way that employment or education for women were not; attempts to change its structures were practically nonexistent. Women "still had to act as the guardians of national culture, indigenous religion and family traditions."[142]

In fact, the East-West dichotomy was not so sharp as all participants in the rhetorical battle believed. As Lila Abu-Lughod notes, the notions of "separate cultures have themselves been produced by the colonial encounter."[143] Proponents of Western culture, for example, completely concurred with the agenda of a domestic curriculum for women (see Chapter 2). Indeed, one could almost portray this kind of education as characteristic of Western civilization. Notions of companionate marriage and the utilization of "scientific" methods to manage homes infiltrated the press debate from Western discourse on women's "new" role. No one on either side of the divide seemed to question the merits of educating women for a role that they had effectively fulfilled for the length of human history. One would assume that women's own experience passed on from one generation to the next; modified over time, it constituted pretty effective training for "mothercraft" and the like.

The fact that quite a number of writers on women identified themselves as university students indicates that writers' educations influenced and perhaps changed their concepts about the role and status of Palestinian women.[144] It also suggests that the idealism and openness of youth played a significant role in constructing concepts of the new, "modern" woman. After all, it was young peoples' lives that were most affected by the social and attitudinal changes Palestinian society was experiencing around the issues of veiling, marriage, education, and so forth. That women themselves wrote and contributed to the debate demonstrates that a not insignificant number of women did indeed read the newspapers and utilize it as a means of personal expression and public forum. Yet another dimension worth noting is the varied opinions expressed by these women writers on the range of issues of the day, demonstrating the heterogeneity among women—even elite, educated, presumably westernized women. As we have seen, women variously, and even simultaneously, defended "tradition," supported notions of women's domestic role, railed against social mores, and advocated change.

The discourse in the press reflected changing class configurations in Palestinian society, and of course, women were members of different social classes as well. Interestingly, there are few direct references to the British mandate as one agent of these changes, yet the social and economic effects of its rule are omnipresent in analysis of both what was written about and what was not. The period of 1920–39 was a pivotal time—one of distinct uneasiness with the various transformations Palestine was experiencing. It is difficult to assess the degree of polarization that developed in Palestinian society over the issues addressed in the press. The overall impression one receives is of a liberalizing tendency, albeit over the protests of more conservative or religiously minded segments of the literate population. This characterization, I hasten to add, of course elides the heterogeneity of opinion and individuals within these broad categories. Clearly the discourse signified true debate that covered important topics, and the press played a major role in igniting the debate as well as mediating the various forms of contestations within it. But missing is the village and peasant perspective; after all, the majority of Palestinians were from the rural areas. Newspapers also had their own political, social, and religious agendas, as well as restrictions caused by censorship. A newspaper such as *Filastīn*, despite its sheer superiority in output and longevity, may not have necessarily reflected the views of significant numbers of people. Through combining the press accounts with oral history and documents, however, one can state unequivocally that changes in women's status and condition were observed, fiercely contested, and irrevocably under way. Out of this polemic emerged an image of the "new (middle-class) woman" who combined the best of "East" and "West," and upon whose influence the future of the nation would depend.[145] 'Aziza Taybi, writing in *Filastīn*, eloquently expresses the hopes and burdens placed on this new woman by the press and Palestinian society: "Woman is the lamp that nations use to light their path to perfection. Pity the nation that has a dark lamp."[146]

PART II

The "New" Woman in Politics
The Palestinian Women's Movement, 1929–1948

4 The Roots of Movement

Charity and the Nation

Palestinian women self-consciously and deliberately founded a movement at the Palestine Arab Women's Congress of 1929. Yet one could argue that the "movement" predated this event. Many of the limited but growing number of women's organizations—primarily charitable—that were established before 1929 became part of the nation-wide network that eventually established coordination and cooperation among women's groups.

Palestinian women's organizations evolved from a complex matrix of charitable, reformist, feminist, and nationalist impetuses, which overlapped and informed the nature of women's initial organizational endeavors. It is thus difficult to characterize them as "charitable," as opposed to "political." The nationalist discourse about preserving a way of life, a culture, and society against the threat of Zionism increasingly permeated all segments of Palestinian society. Women participated in this idea through their involvement, initially, in charitable associations. Over time, and from the effects of constant crises that led to heightened politicization and tension in the country, women's experiences in charitable societies were transformed with their increasing public and collective activity into a movement. But Palestinian women's initial organizing efforts and the eventual movement were part of broader historical patterns as well.

THE GLOBAL CONTEXT

In the early years of the twentieth century, Palestinian women, like their counterparts in the rest of the Middle East, established women's associations and charitable societies.[1] In doing so, the women became part of a global phenomenon spanning the late nineteenth and early twentieth centuries, when educated women throughout the world started to become involved in a multitude of reform, social and, ultimately, political movements, usually by founding women's associations separate from men's.[2] The establishment of indigenous women's organizations by women of colonized Third World societies was a relatively recent development that differed from previous reform movements. The latter had aimed at improving the status of women, or raised social concerns related to gender issues, but were often led by men or Western women from the metropolitan countries.[3]

This widespread, new phenomenon occurred in different parts of the world, and in societies with disparate social, cultural, economic, and political structures; the women's organizations that were established reflected this rich diversity, varying in goals, structures, and forms. Despite these differences, it is possible to make a few generalizations about women's organizing endeavors. The primary, initial motivations for establishing these associations tended to be charitable and reformist. Most of the women participating in benevolent societies, women's groups, and the like were from the educated, wealthier urban classes. One of the major transformations that occurred in many such women's lives around the turn of the century was expansion of women's education. Middle- and upper-class women became more cognizant about the needs of their own societies and more analytical about the potential for change. Particularly in Third World societies, where colonialist governmental priorities were not necessarily oriented toward providing social services to the indigenous population, women began to perceive that these needs and privation required action. In many respects, women's and men's charitable organizations fulfilled the functions of the modern state, providing such services as medical care and education, which colonial states, in particular, did not adequately provide. Also, with the increase in industrialization that accompanied the growth of capitalist relations of production and the decline of the family as an economic unit in the late nineteenth century, some women from the upper classes experienced an increase in leisure time and attendant desires to fill it.[4] Finally, the emergence of indigenous nationalist movements and in various places, the intensification of anticolonial conflicts, also brought many of these overlapping and intersecting issues to the fore. These factors combined with religious ones in propelling women toward activism derived from initially benevolent impulses. In Palestine, where the Arab population was primarily Muslim with a (then) significant Christian minority, the doctrine of obligatory charity inherent in both faiths was part of Arab culture, with a historical legacy. There developed among the elite a tradition of noblesse oblige toward their more indigent coreligionists.[5]

Yet although women's new activism may have been clothed in the garb of charity and "reform," it also constituted tacit political protest and social critique. By stepping in to fill perceived gaps (in services, for example), women were also implicitly criticizing those responsible for not fulfilling the function. Indeed, ultimately the criticism was not necessarily implicit and muted but openly directed against the government for its neglect of the population. Although this criticism may not have been articulated in an explicitly political way, such as calling for representative government or arguing for political change, it constituted a form of politics nonetheless. As Guida West and Rhoda Lois Blumberg point out, "women participate politically in ways that are rarely recognized or documented as political behavior or social protest."[6] This lack of recognition speaks to the need to redefine "politics," detaching it from the restricted and gendered realm of formal "political" activities that constituted a segregated male domain, such as holding government office, engagement in diplomacy, fighting wars—of resistance or state-sanctioned—and forming political parties and the like. Inasmuch as social and economic issues addressed by women's work in charitable and religious associations derived from the politics that shaped these issues' very contours, women's involvement in such groups was in and of itself a political statement.

HELPING THE NATION

During the course of the early twentieth century, nationalism was a—perhaps the—major motivation for women's entry into organizational work. Although the existence, date, and origins of Palestinian nationalism before the onset of Zionism are still being debated,[7] a sense of social and civic responsibility linked to protonationalist stirrings reached middle- and upper-class women even before the British Mandate and Zionism brought Palestinian nationalist sentiment into relief. As Palestinian writer/journalist Asma Tubi put it, ultimately, "in the welfare of the community [lay] the welfare of the homeland."[8] Helping one another signified helping the nation.

The sheer proliferation of women's organizations in Palestine in the first four decades of the twentieth century is striking. Between 1910 and 1947, women founded groups ranging from charitable, religious societies to women's unions, sports, and literary clubs, Girl Scout troops, [female] student unions, and a women's labor union. Although the diverse and eclectic women's organizations focused on ostensibly different objectives, women of the mandate period would have likely agreed that their overarching goal was national survival. Of course, "women's movements do not occur in a vacuum but correspond to, and to some extent are determined by, the wider social [and one should add, political] movements of which they form part."⁹ The primacy and ultimate urgency of the national issue over all others in Palestinian society determined that each association came to labor on disparate causes within a nationalist framework. This may not have been the case in the very earliest years of "organized womanhood" at the turn of the century, but was certainly so during the course of the mandate period (and indeed, up until the present).¹⁰ The inexorable intensification of the political conflict with Zionism ultimately affected—either directly or indirectly—every aspect of life in mandatory Palestine, coloring the work of each women's organization. Thus it was ultimately the national issue that united the women's movement in Palestine and conferred on it a distinct character during this period. As Ruth Woodsmall observed, commenting on Muslim women "of the East" during her travels to the Middle East in 1936, "in this awakening of national consciousness women have become deeply imbued with the sense of their relationship to national life."¹¹ The nationalist character of the women's movement helped Palestinian women forge a new sense of identity as members in a collectivity with common purpose.

Considering the diversity in purposes and activities of these groups, one may well interrogate use of the term "women's movement" to characterize Palestinian women's entry into organizational activity. "Movement" usually connotes a certain level of popular support, dynamism, organization, and coordinated activity directed toward a common objective by its constituent parts (organizations) and individuals. Until 1929, when women self-consciously launched and began to orchestrate the "women's movement" (al-haraka al-nisā'iyya), explicitly using this phrase, the women's movement did not entirely conform to this definition. Yet, Palestinian women's associations, although working severally in different groups, supported the common goal of "uplifting the nation" through raising the level of women and the poor in this initial period. But Palestinian women were also aware of being members of another, broader movement. They—and men writing about them as well—used the terms "women's revival" or "awakening" (al-nahda al-nisā'iyya) to characterize their organizational efforts.¹² Even before the national issue came to determine and dictate the trajectory of the women's movement in Palestine, women saw themselves as part of the regional women's awakening that was underway in Egypt, Turkey, Iran, and other Arab countries. They never lost sight of this greater movement in which they participated. And indeed, the pan-Arab women's movement became involved in issues that defied externally imposed, arbitrary national boundaries. It self-consciously correlated local concerns with regional and international issues (see Chapter 7). Arab women activists, of whom the

Palestinian women were a constituent part, early on articulated regionalist and internationalist perspectives. The Palestinian women's movement was inspired and nurtured by contact with and the support of other Arab women's groups.

Early women's organizations, however, also developed a strong sense of gender identity through focusing much of their efforts on improving the status of women through education and charity. This work cultivated a "feeling of a mutuality of interest with other women."[13] This sense of gender identity may partially explain why (mostly from 1929 on) Palestinian women thought of themselves as a *women's* movement, and rarely referred to themselves as the Palestinian women's *national* movement.[14] Another possible explanation of their use of this nomenclature is that women perceived the formation of their own movement as a legitimizing device to carve out their own niche within the nationalist movement without threatening men's primacy. They did not identify themselves as an "auxiliary" of the (male-led) national movement, instead asserting their own explicit political identity.[15]

The less explicitly political women's organizations that sprang up during the first decades of British rule were also part of an overall evolution toward the establishment of a Palestinian civil society. These women's associations did not necessarily conform to the overtly nationalist, more political agenda of the women's movement as *the* women's movement per se; yet they were a constituent element of the broader umbrella of "movement" under which the Arab Women's Association (AWA) and Arab Women's Union (AWU), the organizations that led the movement, operated. As such, they also played a significant part in many women's lives, influencing both their personal and political development, and cultivating new loyalties that transcended older ones of family, religion, and *hamūla* (clan).

GENDER AND CHARITY

The genesis of women's organizations in Palestine comprised two levels. First, on the local level, it was "part of an evolving social tendency [in Palestinian society] to form societies and clubs as voluntary associations."[16] But it was also part of a global trend of middle-class women's establishing benevolent organizations, whose foundations were built upon the universal ideology, seemingly shared by most societies, that posited women's "inherent goodness" and "natural disposition[] "for "doing good."[17] Benevolence was perceived as "natural to the merciful heart of woman," part of her "special domain," or, as Asma Tubi poetically put it (quoting an unnamed source), "woman's heart is the door to the house of humanity."[18] Diverse historical circumstances and specific events propelled women in various parts of the world to form benevolent associations, but some shared characteristics and ideology among the different organizations are striking.

Women in Arab and Islamic societies had been involved in benevolence long before the period under discussion, through the foundation of charitable *awqāf,* and the endowment of schools, mosques, and hospitals.[19] As Afaf Lutfi al-Sayyid Marsot points out, philanthropic donation was part of the Islamic tradition: "Among the powerful and rich it was a noblesse oblige sentiment throughout the ages that part of one's wealth be expended on charitable works. . . . there was a definite tradition of public service on the part of the rich, both men and women."[20] Some of the magnificent Islamic monuments and buildings still standing today in the Arab world are visible testimony to wealthy women's acts of benevolence. But the phenomenon of Arab women actively founding and actually administering benevolent organizations of their own was something new and distinct from endowment and financial management. For one thing, it signaled the entry of middle-class women into charitable work, since they did not have the wealth of women from the richer classes to be able to fund schools or hospitals from their own personal capital. For another, it signified increasing social acceptance of women's admission into public life and active engagement with social, as opposed to family and domestic, affairs. This opening derived in part from the evolution of civic life in Palestine during the early decades of the twentieth century and from the proliferation of various cultural, educational, and other kinds of organizations in Palestinian society. During the 1920s–1940s, the announcement of the establishment of yet another women's charitable association invariably came to be heralded in the Palestinian press as a "blessed" event and the women's moral virtue and goodness extolled.[21] Indeed, women were urged to form women's charitable organizations, and on one occasion, criticized for not doing so sooner.[22]

Increasing approbation and acceptance of women's involvement in organizations accompanied a process in which the articulation of concepts of womanhood and woman's proper sphere made benevolence work an extension of woman's domestic role. The types of work in which the early women's groups engaged, such as providing for the poor and ill, were seen as part and parcel of their innately feminine "ethic of care." The domestic nature of women's charitable work did not challenge patriarchal institutions in Palestine. In discussing the articulation between domesticity and the development of liberalism in the United States, Joan Williams notes, "domesticity . . . intimates that anyone who rejects self-interest in favor of more 'humane' values is . . . choosing to be relegated to the margins of economic and political life." She demonstrates how, historically, women's selflessness has been set up against men's selfishness in a dichotomy that has political implications: "virtue" over time became dissociated from male (public) activity and instead "belonged in the private spheres of the home, the church, and voluntary associations," which became increasingly the domains of women.[23] The corollary to this process was that virtuous activity became devalued and feminized, even while at the same time women were praised for their "innate" compassion. In the case of Palestine, the feminization of benevolence was mitigated by the politicization of charity as a nationalist act, making it attractive to a certain extent to men as well. Thus this dichotomy, although it existed and was built upon the same gendered assumptions about women's "nature" and the link between it and domesticity, developed along a somewhat different trajectory than in the West, since Mashriq societies underwent their own processes of liberalization that had both parallels to and distinct differences from Western types of liberalization. In the Mashriq, the influences of Islamist reformers, the *nahda* (Arabic literary and cultural renaissance), and constitutional movements all commingled. Furthermore, the forms these took in each society (Palestinian, Syrian, and so on), despite many common characteristics, were colored by disparate local realities.

In Palestinian society, virtue had its rewards, and acting out of womanly virtue was given a cautious nod of approval. Furthermore, other factors helped ease women's transition into "discreet public activism"[24] in the early years of women's organized activity: women organized separately from men, maintaining proper sex segregation; initially, more often than not, they worked within the context of religion and among their own coreligionists;[25] many of the women were from upper- and middle-class backgrounds and had servants to perform their household tasks, giving them the freedom to become involved in organizational work without upsetting their families' domestic order; and finally, women were fulfilling a needed function in societies that had few civic institutions to provide social services, particularly on the governmental level. These factors and the fact that charitable work did not initially contest or challenge the patriarchal institutions that upheld the social, political, and cultural status quo eased women's entry into the public sphere.[26] The question arises, Why didn't the women challenge patriarchal institutions? Like women elsewhere, Palestinian women, gauging the realities of the power differentials between men and women, realistically calibrated their own objectives and initial organizing strategies commensurate with the social and political realities of their society at that time.[27] They realized they needed male support, and as we have seen, support of men, particularly male relatives, was crucial to women's defying social norms. Thus they were circumspect in initially challenging cultural and social norms, although this would change later on.

And yet, despite somewhat limited social acceptance of women's charitable organizations, and the noncontroversial nature of the enterprise, Palestinian women's work in this domain also signified the creation of a subtle, potentially subversive means to personal empowerment. Women discovered strength in collective action, and experienced "self-discovery" through their organizational work; "working towards collective goals tapped wellsprings of creativity that had been quiescent . . . [women] were exposed to a wider range of social experience than would have been common in family life."[28] Women learned they could wield authority and influence from within a group, whereas as individuals they received little notice unless they were somehow exceptional.[29] They had to develop and use organizational skills, exercise control over resources, and manage their own organizations. Unlike their counterparts in Egypt, most of the women who worked in charitable organizations in Palestine did not come from large, wealthy households, although most of the women involved in women's organizations during this period were urban and educated—that is, those who had the "freedom to organize."[30] Doing voluntary work in these organizations also provided an outlet for them to use many of the skills they had acquired through education.

Rural, peasant women, burdened with heavy physical labor and domestic responsibilities certainly were limited in their ability to participate in women's groups, both because of isolation resulting from their social and economic conditions, and because the organized women's activities tended to take place in towns and cities. The towns and cities provided models of organization through other, largely urban institutions such as religious charities, governmental agencies and schools. The work of these organizations relied on the types of skills (such as literacy, managing finances, and delegating authority) mentioned above, which also precluded poorer women's active involvement. Furthermore, the very character, identity, and foundations of the earlier women's societies derived from a class-based concept of benevolence that excluded the participation of poorer women except as passive recipients of charity.

A further explanation as to why the early women's groups did not arouse controversy was women's initial, seeming acceptance that "politics occupied a wholly separate realm from morality," and therefore, men and women moved in two separate but complementary spheres.[31] Henriette Siksik, whose mother founded the Orthodox Society for the Destitute Sick in Jerusalem in 1924, commented that the bylaws of the organization explicitly stated "no intervention—no interest in politics."[32] Women worked within a framework of appropriate female behavior that did not deviate from cultural norms. As 'Anbara Sallam al-Khalidi wrote, they "undertook their national duty without noise and turmoil," performing tasks that were ostensibly nonpolitical.[33] However, as Scott points out, women's style of "ladylike behavior" could be a "convenient mask[] for innovation, or possibly even subversive ideas." Some women "had so internalized the ideology of domesticity that they took [it] for granted and operated within its framework."[34] This seems to have been the case in Palestine, where women such as Khalidi struck an almost defensive tone in describing their selflessness and motives in becoming organizationally involved.

Distinctions among "political," "charitable," and "social" in Palestinian society, it should be noted, are fluid. Both organizations that defined themselves as political and those that defined themselves as charitable often engaged in similar activities with identical goals. Wadi'a Khartabil, who was active during the mandate period in women's organizations in Tulkarm, told an interviewer that "social work was a cover for political work," a theme that was reiterated many times by others as well.[35] Certainly Palestinian women came to imbue their work—be it "social" or charitable—with political meaning. Women used concepts of womanhood and "sacred tradition" to manipulate the British and serve their own political agendas. Furthermore, a point was reached where the political crisis in Palestine spilled over to include all segments of society, and women were actively encouraged (by men) to enter the political arena.

A major dichotomy in the early women's charitable organizations existed in their maintaining gender subordination through support of the tradition of woman's work in a "separate sphere," while simultaneously creating power for themselves through collective action that ultimately had social and political implications extending beyond "helping the poor." This contradiction continued to infuse the more explicitly political women's organizations as well, ultimately creating internal tension.

WOMEN GET ORGANIZED: 1900–1930S

Indigenous Palestinian women's organizations—that is, ones directly established by Palestinian women—appeared in the first decade of the twentieth century.[36] Not surprisingly, these groups were founded in the major cities, particularly in those with significant Christian populations: Jaffa, Jerusalem,

Haifa, and Acre. The Orthodox women's societies, which tended initially to serve primarily their own communities, were prominent among the first women's groups to form.[37]

The first Palestinian women's organization on record, established in 1903, was the Orthodox Aid Society for the Poor in Acre.[38] Its goals were to help provide clothes and trousseau items for poor young girls "to prevent them from remaining unmarried." One of its members commented, "We helped the girl feel equal to her peers from the middle class status." It also attempted to support families from the Orthodox sect by giving them money, and sending delegations to visit them on special occasions, such as the birth of a child.[39]

A similar group was the Jaffa Orthodox Ladies Society, founded on February 15, 1910. In a rare first person account, one of its founders and long-term president, Adele 'Azar, describes its establishment:

> In 1910 the educational and social conditions were different from what they are today, in terms of progress . . . and the majority of girls were not able to enter school because of economic hardships, so at that time a group of Orthodox (Christian) ladies from Jaffa, including myself, decided to found a national women's association [*jam'iyya nisā'iyya wataniyya*] to bring up and educate orphan girls and those in need. And this organization was the first national women's organization to be founded in Palestine. The aim of this organization and its main objective was to open a school to educate girls.[40]

It is interesting to note 'Azar's language here: her emphasis (writing in 1966) on claiming the group was the first national women's organization as well as her repeated use of the word "national" could be interpreted as either a retrospective endowment of the group with a nationalist orientation or an indication of an incipient expression of nationalism among middle-class women during the late-Ottoman period—or both.[41]

Although initially the group provided funding to send indigent girls to other schools, it eventually founded and ran the girls' section of the National Orthodox School, which also had a boys' section run by the Orthodox Charitable Society. At the time of its opening, the school employed three teachers, with one hundred girls in attendance, both Christian and Muslim. Mrs. 'Azar was principal of the girls' school from 1924 until 1948. After the girls left school, she attempted to find employment for them:

> It wasn't customary at the time when we opened our school, for girls to work in public after their graduation, even though they might be in great need for a job to help their needy families. They were only allowed to work as teachers. After the girls' graduation I used to look

for jobs for them, after persuading their parents that nothing was shameful about educated and well-mannered girls working, but they must be a good example for other educated women in neighboring countries such as Egypt, Lebanon, Syria and others. So I used to find them jobs in the government circles, the Post Office and Telephone Company and in trade, and as nurses in hospitals. I was known as the "leader" [al-za'īma] and "mother of the poor" [umm al-fuqarā'], because of all my charity work and all I tried to do to help the suffering of humans.[42]

'Azar's descriptions of the need for young girls newly out of school to work to help support their families confirm that economic factors played a major role in contributing to changing attitudes about women entering the workforce (see Chapter 2). The latent expression of identification with other Arab women also points to the bonds that existed between middle-class women across local boundaries, indicating the early development of a pan-Arab cultural consciousness among women.

Adele 'Azar exemplifies the intersection of Palestinian women's religious, professional, and political identities: she was concurrently the president of the Orthodox Ladies Society, the principal of its school, and a member of the Arab Ladies Association in Jaffa, which was founded in her home sometime in the 1930s. Her pride and sense of achievement and self-worth in her organizational activities is evident:

Whenever any scholars [udabā'] or notables came to our city of Jaffa, I used to be visited by the clubs and organizations to participate with them by hosting welcoming parties and delivering speeches, for which I became well-known. Many times I used to invite these scholars and notables to my home. . . . In 1944 I was invited to Cairo by the leader Huda Hanim Sha'rawi to attend the Arab Women's Conference that was held on the 7th of December 1944. I went to Cairo as the president of the Women's Orthodox Society and vice president of the Arab Women's Association in Jaffa. My speech at this conference called for Arab unity and strengthening the Arabic language and educating village women. After the conference was over, which took eight days, many grand parties were held for us. [She describes them all.] . . . We were invited to many places, from clubs to media parties, etc. So we spent twenty days in Egypt, which we enjoyed thoroughly, and we are grateful for the generosity and care we received from the great leader Huda Hanim Sha'rawi.[43]

As Asma Tubi notes (somewhat rhapsodically), "There were no women's activities in which she did not take part, no conference she did not attend, and no nationalist demonstration at the head of which she did not march."[44]

Quite a number of Palestinian women were publicly involved at multiple, overlapping levels in charitable societies, political organizations, and cultural or literary clubs. Nahid ʿAbduh al-Sajjadi, originally from Nablus, for example, was a member of the Arab Women's Union, the Women's Solidarity Association, and the Society of the Wounded Fighter, and a founder of the Red Crescent Society in Jerusalem. She describes how she became active:

> I was very active in Jerusalem. When I was young in Nablus, my mother used to take me with her to visit her friend, Miryam Hashim,[45] who was the first woman to establish the women's union in all of Palestine. . . . This was in the twenties. My mother would help her friend care for the poor. . . . If my mother passed in the street and saw children playing with their eyes dirty and irritated, she would send me with cotton and eye drops and soothing cream to their mothers to clean and cure their eyes. My mother could only read. She couldn't write.[46]

Mrs. al-Sajjadi attended the WTC in Jerusalem, where she became involved in the Jerusalem Arab Women's Union (AWU) in the early 1930s, after her marriage. "There were a lot of demonstrations in Jerusalem. The women used to participate in demonstrations . . . one day the head of the Women's Union came to visit me and I became an active member of the union. . . . We used to participate in demonstrations out in the streets of Jerusalem and write protest letters to the different governments." Asked whether her father or husband objected to her working outside the house, she responded, "No, they used to encourage me to work outside. In the first few years we used to wear a head cover [*hijāb*] but after that we stopped wearing the head cover and went outside without them. We were from the liberated class. Neither my father nor my husband stood in my way."[47]

Women such as ʿAzar and Sajjadi were very active and involved in their local communities. The kinds of personal ties and connections they developed through charitable work were easily transferable to their political work. Although the women's societies were not mass-based constituency organizations, ʿAzar, Sajjadi, and their peers became acquainted with a diverse circle of people, both wealthy and poor, young and old, Christian and Muslim. Sajjadi explains, "I hate to see anyone suffer. The human factor was always behind my activities . . . . We used to help the poor, give them money, and help them to buy flour. I also helped the poor students who passed their *tawjīhi* [matriculation] exam."[48] In Jerusalem in particular, Christian and Muslim women worked together in charitable, political, and social welfare endeavors, some of them becoming intimate friends across religious lines in the process, as did Melia Sakakini, an Orthodox Christian, and Zlikha al-

Shihabi, a Muslim.[49] Through their charitable work with poor urban and town dwellers and the *fellahin* (peasants), the women developed intimate knowledge of their problems, and in later political work tended to focus on their situation and particularly their economic difficulties and concerns.

Elite women involved in organizations ultimately politicized their noblesse oblige sentiments, targeting the British colonial government for criticism and solutions rather than developing an internal critique of class relations and the socioeconomic inequities within their own society. Nuha Abu Daleb attributes this to the unlikelihood "that the consciousness of the women was developed enough for them to question their status" and (by implication) to develop this kind of critique. Elite women were not unique in this, however; the national issue loomed larger than any other. At this particular historical juncture (class) "consciousness" and analyses of internal sources of inequity in Palestinian society were rare, other than among the small numbers of Arab communists and some trade unionists.[50] Consciousness is constructed through experience, and the overwhelming experience that determined the political reactions of these elite classes was the national situation and how it threatened their lives and those of their society in every aspect.

Jerusalem also had its Orthodox women's society, which, like the others, provided for the education of intelligent, needy girls by sending them to institutions with higher levels of instruction, such as the English College and Schmidt Girls' School. Its long-term, "permanent president" from its establishment in 1918 until the *nakba* was Kathryn Dib, who was also a member of many other women's organizations.[51]

Other than the Orthodox ladies societies, the record on Palestinian women's organizing activity prior to the mandate remains rather obscure. The effects of World War I, however, stimulated a proliferation of women's organizations; Asma Tubi comments that the country was "filled" with them as the year 1920 drew to a close.[52] The war had devastated the country, resulting in a depletion of the population, famine, locust plagues, deforestation, currency devaluation, and a complete disruption of the economy.[53] Poverty was pervasive in many of the cities, where living conditions were conducive to outbreaks of disease. The military administration that took over from December 1917 to June 1920 was forced to deal with grave social and economic problems. Groups such as the Red Cross and the American Colony (an American mission that provided social services) helped ameliorate conditions in the immediate aftermath of the war. Women of different communities worked in organizations such as the Palestine Women's Council or the Social Service Association, a voluntary society founded in 1918 by three women, Arab, Jewish, and American, to deal with the many "social problems which arose at the end of the War." The Arab women who participated in these organizations, however, tended to be primarily Christian. These two groups focused on providing relief, founding a girls home, and working to "clean the city up morally."[54] Katherine Siksik, a Christian Arab from Jerusalem, worked with the Red Cross units in postwar Palestine. After their departure, she founded the Orthodox Society for the Destitute Sick, one of the few groups that provided care for the handicapped.[55]

The history of other organizations that existed in these early years is unrecorded, lost, or fragmented. Activity may have been temporary, spontaneous, or short-lived. Palestinian women did begin in a somewhat disjointed and sporadic fashion to participate on the overtly political level as well during this period, however. There is evidence that some had reached a level of awareness of, and organized efforts against, British policy and politics as early as did men, despite Westerners' claims to the contrary that they were "politically unborn," "unorganized," and "inarticulate." (In the words of feminist delegations from the International Alliance of Women visiting Palestine in 1920 and 1921.)[56] There are reports that, as early as the late nineteenth century, women joined with men in strongly and even violently resisting Zionist settlement, participating in protests against Jewish immigration in the countryside in 1884 in Affula.[57] In March 1920, twenty-nine women from northern Palestine sent a letter to the chief administrator of the region expressing their concern about and awareness of the implications of the Balfour Declaration. "We have read your declarations concerning the Jewish settlement in our country and making it their national home," they wrote. "As this right is detrimental to us in every way . . . we Moslem and Christian ladies who represent other ladies of Palestine protest vigorously against these declarations that cause the sub-division of our country."[58] They may have been reacting to an incident that took place earlier that month, when a leader of a Jewish colony in the north opened fire on Arab bands who subsequently attacked other northern Jewish colonies.[59] Women also participated in violent disturbances in Jaffa in May 1921. Disorders broke out when police, attempting to disperse a May Day demonstration of Jewish Marxists, shot into the air, causing Arabs in the area to believe it was the Jews firing at them. In the subsequent outbreak, which lasted several days, forty Jews were killed by mobs.[60]

In late 1921 women were actively involved in raising money for the delegation sent to London by the major nationalist organization, the Arab Executive, to present demands for the abolition of the Balfour Declaration, a halt to Jewish immigration, and the formation of a representative government directly to the British government. Women formed committees and held meetings in all the major cities to collect funds, for which they received praise and recognition in the press.[61] In 1922, women began to hold meetings at which they directly confronted the government, echoing the demands of the nationalist movement: "To the Prime Minister, Colonial Minister: Muslim ladies of Haifa protest the Balfour Declaration. We declare an end to Jewish immigration, and independence."[62]

The apparent precursor to the Arab Women's Association, which evolved into the preeminent women's political organization in the 1930s, was founded sometime during these turbulent events, around 1919–20. Accounts of this group are muddled. Common belief—history retrospectively inscribed[63]—has it that the Palestinian Women's Union (called the Arab Women's Association until the late 1930s) was established in Jerusalem in 1921, but the information upon which this is based is sketchy.[64] A 1921 publication of the Palestine Women's Council mentions a "Mohammedan Ladies Society" headed by Mrs. Jamal Husayni; Matiel Mughannam, who was the major chronicler of the women's movement, also refers to an "Arab ladies association," also headed by Mrs. Husayni, founded in 1919. The AWU, in its Golden Jubilee pamphlet (1983) says that an "Arab Ladies Club" formed in 1921 in Jerusalem.[65] These three sources possibly refer to the same group, which was established to provide relief to the poor and "raise the standard of woman" by working in the field of education. According to the AWU, the organization only lasted two years.[66] However and whenever it was established, clearly some kind of women's organization was briefly formed in the early 1920s, but we know little of its actual activities or founders. Similarly, the Society of the Arab Women's Union of Nablus was founded in 1921 but the history of its early years is also somewhat obscure. From its inception, its goals were charitable, although it developed in political directions as well over time, sending delegates to the 1938 Eastern Women's Conference in Cairo. Early on, it focused on providing health services, eventually founding its own hospital in 1948.[67]

Despite the beginning of women's political activities described above, most of women's organized efforts throughout the early 1920s focused primarily on social and charitable work. Yet their "one goal," according to chronicler Asma Tubi, was "to be of benefit to the nation"; they increasingly began to politicize and situate their work within a nationalist framework.[68] Although nationalism was a strong motivating force in their involvement, one can also argue that the reverse perhaps played a role as well: their politicization and nationalism arose *from* their charitable and social work, as they became increasingly aware of and frustrated with the limitations and restrictions on economic, social, and educational development inherent in an imperial (under the Ottomans) or colonial (under the mandate) context. All of these different strands overlapped and influenced their work and organizing activities to the extent that one cannot accurately say that groups were necessarily "political" or "social" or "charitable" but rather, all three simultaneously.

On a different level, Palestinian women also became involved in international women's organizations, initially through the YWCA, which established itself in Palestine in the late nineteenth century.[69] Not much is known about its early years; it formed branches affiliated with the World YWCA in Palestinian towns and cities with significant Christian populations, although both Muslim and Christian girls and women eventually participated in many of its activities, which were educational, vocational, and cultural.[70] Julia 'Awad, who was involved in the YWCA from the time she was fourteen years old in the early years of the twentieth century, remarked in an interview that the YWCA in Jerusalem was the "only outlet for girls" during the Turkish regime. "The whole environment of the YW was to develop girls."[71] During the mandate, both the YWCA and YMCA evolved into important cultural institutions and gathering places for young people. Young women attended classes and lectures at both the YWCA and YMCA in Jerusalem, in subjects such as English, biology, typing ,and secretarial training.[72] The two Ys shared facilities (since the YMCA, not surprisingly, had "greatly superior equipment") and often collaborated in events, picnics, social evenings, and piano recitals.[73] They also provided rare opportunities for girls to engage in sports. The Ys were not above criticism on the issue of cultural imperialism, however, and the establishment of new branches was often viewed with alarm. An article in the newspaper *al-Jāmi'a al-'Arabiyya*, an organ of the Supreme Muslim Council, warned that the YWCA was a "stronghold" of missionary activity aimed at Muslim women. Its goals were to weaken the Islamic creed, and it had strong links with Western imperialism—observations that were, in fact, impossible to refute.[74] One (Christian) Palestinian woman, looking back, remarked that the ideas promoted by the Ys were "imported" and "not from us."[75] The institutions attracted groups of active young people disseminating radical political as well as cultural ideas. Samira Khuri of Nazareth, while a student at the Women's Training College, first became politicized through attending YMCA lectures where the Communist Party (which she later joined) passed out pamphlets on the Partition Plan in the 1940s.[76]

In the course of the 1920s and 1930s, Palestinian women's organizations steadily multiplied. Religious groups such as the Society of Saint Teresa,

Charity and the Nation / 111

founded in 1922, continued to proliferate, but worked primarily on a confessional basis.[77] Some groups that included women from the three major religions continued to exist, such as the Palestine Association of University Women, founded in 1932. Most of its members were Jewish or European, not surprisingly, considering the difference in women's access to education; to be a member, one had to have a college degree. Yet there were a few Arab women, such as educator Olga Wahbi, a Miss Deeb, B.A., and Nahil Habub Dajani (a dentist) on its roster of officers and committee members. During the 1936–39 revolt, its annual report shows the effects of the strain politics exerted on this mixed-member group. "Our meetings and activities this year were perforce under the shadow of disturbances in the country and were inevitably shorn of some of their customary brightness," the secretary notes rather elliptically.[78] For the most part, however, Palestinian women started to form and belong to their own organizations, which were increasingly tinged with the nationalist tenor that had already taken roots earlier. Significantly, the women's organizations began to expand beyond their initial communal bases, organizing for wider communities than their coreligionists, including Muslim and Christian women as members, and forging bonds of Arab womanhood. Indeed, this intercommunal spirit was emphasized in the press and by all Arab sources on this period. Articles about the various groups took pains to mention that activities included Muslims and Christians together, and that there was no difference between them, "for the sake of land and country."[79]

In their establishment of new and different organizations, Palestinian women were part of an overall trend in Palestinian society during this period to form clubs, societies, and organizations that began to diffuse and in some cases replace traditional, more narrowly defined loyalties based upon clan or religious affiliation. A perusal of the Arabic press from the 1920s throughout the 1940s yields numerous articles announcing the founding of infant welfare centers, new branches of the women's union, Girl Scout troops, ladies associations, women's revival societies, student groups, and women's labor unions. The focus of most of these organizations was on developing girls through education or by providing them with cultural opportunities; on extending direct relief to the more indigent urban population during crises; and on setting up programs to train poorer women in vocational skills, particularly sewing.

Girls, too, became involved in organizations.[80] Another international organization that catered to young women was the Girl Guides, which was established in Palestine in 1919, in association with the Girl Guides Association in England. In 1927, a visitor reported that the "movement," which was "widely popular," had 260 guides and ten rangers, most of them Arabs.[81] The director of education, Humphrey Bowman, described the association as "side by side with the Boy Scouts but under an independent body and organized under strictly 'harim' conditions." Like the Boy Scouts, it was confined to the Arab community, where it was "extremely popular" among the girls. The "Guiders" (presumably the adult leaders) were recruited from among teachers in the government and private schools.[82] Although not much is known about the various Girl Guide troops, some participated in demonstrations during the 1930s, paralleling the activities of the Palestinian Boy Scouts, a highly politicized group in the 1930s.[83]

CONCLUSION

The ostensibly charitable endeavors in which Palestinian women engaged in the first three decades of the twentieth century became increasingly imbued with political and nationalist content to the extent that these concepts became almost inextricable in the nationalist discourse on women.[84] On the socioeconomic level, it is true, as contemporary Palestinian feminist scholars have pointed out, that to a great extent, the work of the women's organizations tended to buttress and sustain patriarchal social and cultural institutions, such as the family, uncritically, resulting in their exhibiting a certain conservative character.[85] Their efforts were geared toward preserving a way of life under threat from socioeconomic and political transformations whose root causes they initially did not examine or attribute to internal political, economic, or social dynamics in their society. Over time, they linked these directly to the Zionist threat and the lack of Palestinian national sovereignty.

Nonetheless, the existence of the women's organizations indicated a new, assertive, outward effort both by and, to a great degree, on behalf of women, who began to perceive themselves "not merely as member [sic] of a family, but as units in society."[86] Despite Palestinian women's initial tentativeness in challenging the internal status quo in their society, one must not underestimate the obstacles women still faced in even appearing on the street during the first decades of the twentieth century. The proliferation of women's associations signified a true movement of women outside the confines of previously restricted and limited domains of activity.

This having been said, it is true, however, that the majority of Palestinian women were barely affected by the activities of the women's organizations whose founding impulses were directly connected to the problems that affected the urban poor in particular. Peasant women for the most part remained beyond the scope of organized women's activity. They were aware of the consequences of the threatening political changes taking place in their society, and they were not quiescent when opportunities arose for them to act. But at the most elemental level, peasant and poor townswomen simply did not have the time or inclination to become involved in women's associations, nor were they invited or expected to do so by the elite women who founded and controlled these groups.

Yet the initial impulses of the elite women in the first decades of the century in founding religious charitable groups indicate their awareness of socioeconomic disparities or, at the least, problems caused by them in Palestinian society and desires to alleviate distress. Many of the concerns upon which women's groups ultimately focused—providing sports and cultural lectures at the YWCA, for example—were not concerns shared by most women in Palestine. Yet, participation in some of the organizations described above enabled elite Palestinian women to acquire valuable skills and develop a burgeoning, more profound awareness of social conditions in their society. Women's involvement also signified the beginning of attempts to deal with the social chasm that yawned between rural village women and urban, educated women. An example of such was a project of girls from the Ramallah branch of the YWCA, who made an informal survey of the health and welfare conditions for women and children in their home districts, inspecting the "cleanliness of the place, and the food, milk and water supplies, and [looking into] the question of employment for women and girls, and what agencies were responsible for all these services."[87] Providing village schools for girls, particularly since the government's record in doing so was abysmal, was a real service to rural communities by women's groups.

Observers such as Woodsmall wrote (in 1936) that there were no "voluntary Palestinian welfare agencies" other than those founded by Europeans, and that Palestinian women were unaware of "new conflicting currents of thought" and "simply reflect[ed] the prevailing religious conservatism" of Palestinian society.[88] This is simply inaccurate. The record of women's activities in this period indicates the development of social and political consciousness and the entry of Palestinian women into national life. Educated middle- and upper-class Palestinian women, analogous to women in other societies during this time, experienced their own "women's awakening," commencing with the establishment of the earliest women's benevolent associations at the turn of the twentieth century.

The gradual and steady proliferation of women's organizations reflected needs in Palestinian society that were not fulfilled by the state, be it the Ottoman Empire on its last legs, or the British Mandate government. Middle- and upper-class Palestinian women, with growing but still few opportunities to channel their energies and utilize their educations in the workplace, put them to use for charity and the nation. Along the way they developed skills and gained confidence to mobilize on the political level as well. Their linking of socioeconomic issues solely to the national issue ultimately limited their ability to develop a critical understanding of some of the sources of internal problems in Palestinian society while at the same time, their focus on the national situation provided an opening for their more overt political involvement.

5. Woman Is All the Nation

The Palestinian Women's Movement, 1929–1939

> They said that woman is half the nation, but they only say that when they want to give woman the utmost of her rights or to compliment her. I say that woman is all the nation; without her this worldly heaven would not have existed.[1]

The Arab Women's Association (AWA; later, Arab Women's Union), the single, most active women's group in Palestine, epitomized the Palestinian women's movement.[2] The founding of the AWA in 1929 signified a transformation in women's organizing strategies, manifested by their self-consciousness in launching an actual women's movement in Palestine. In organizing the First Arab Women's Congress in 1929, the AWA established a national framework for the women's movement by creating local chapters and national committees. The agenda of the women's movement was fluid, which permitted flexibility in navigating both within and around the dictates of nationalist categories. The way that women initiated the movement allowed them to seamlessly appropriate nationalism and "politicize" their experiences of working within the framework of charitable societies and other associational structures. Their flexibility allowed them to both utilize (for their own political purposes) and transcend the gendered dichotomies and artificially constructed boundaries between the "social" and "political." After 1929 elite women consolidated their forces and built a movement characterized by considerable organizational acumen.

The 1930s was a definitive period and a distinctive time of "unprecedented mobilization" in the history of the Palestinian national struggle.[3] The repercussions of the 1929 Wailing Wall riots, which resulted in the deaths of 133 Jews and 116 Arabs, had a profound effect on the national movement and Palestinian society. The rioting broke out in August 1929 over possession of the Western Wall (the Wailing Wall) of the Haram al-Sharif (the compound housing the Dome of the Rock and al-Aqsa Mosque), and spread throughout the country. Around 1,300 people, mostly Arabs, were arrested, and ultimately, three death sentences were upheld; the men

115

116 / The "New" Woman in Politics

(all Arabs) were hanged in June 1930. These death sentences aroused powerful responses among the Arab population. A Commission of Inquiry was appointed to investigate the causes of the riot and means by which to avoid a recurrence.[4] The almost moribund Arab Executive (AE), which had constituted the principal leadership of the nationalist movement in the early 1920s, was galvanized and resuscitated in the wake of the riots, leading the country in a resurgence of activity that endured throughout much of the first half of the decade.[5] The nationalist movement became increasingly militant, perceiving Zionism as "totally dependent upon" British imperialism, the "principal enemy of the Palestinian Arabs."[6] The movement targeted the British government and public opinion for the airing of grievances and proposals for self-government, initially through persuasive means such as sending delegations and written missives to London (and elsewhere), but ultimately, by resorting to militant tactics, resulting in the 1936–39 strike and revolt.

It was within this political atmosphere of escalating crisis that Palestinian women decided to act. Rosemary Sayigh observes that the "national crisis acted directly on women rather than through the mediation of men's organizations." The creation of a women's movement was one of women's responses to the crisis, which increasingly disrupted and affected their lives. This act highlighted women's perception of themselves as actors representing at least half, if not "all the nation," in Mary Shihada's resonant words.

THE BIRTH OF THE ARAB WOMEN'S MOVEMENT

The First Arab Women's Congress

On October 26, 1929, Sir John Chancellor, the high commissioner of Palestine, remarked on the significance of the First Arab Women's Congress, which was attended by more than two hundred Arab women who converged on Jerusalem from all over Palestine.[8] Reporting privately to the secretary of state for the colonies, he sententiously intoned, "I have the honor to report that the Arab women have now entered the field of political agitation."[9]

Contrary to Chancellor's solemn pronouncement, this event represented less an entry into political activity than a continuation of movement already under way. But the fact that the government paid a considerable amount of attention to the congress indicated that officials were aware of an intensification of the politicizing process in effect among the Palestinian population.[10] The congress did not emerge from a vacuum; as we have already seen, "political agitation" among women predated the congress. The inauguration of the congress was, in fact, the result of considerable orchestration, the outcome of which was a highly publicized event, organized by a core group of politically savvy women primarily from notable families in Jerusalem—many of them married to men involved in the nationalist movement. Organized activity among a nucleus of women had already begun earlier in 1929 when they collected donations through the formation of an "Aid Committee" to support Palestinian nationalist delegations' trips abroad to explain the Palestinian cause.[11] Their efforts in organizing the congress demonstrated foresight, vision, and sophistication, particularly in the way they mounted a type of public relations campaign by utilizing the press and manipulating tradition and gender to draw attention to their acts.

Matiel Mughannam, one of the organizers of the congress, notes that it sought to concentrate and "consolidate the endeavors of all forces, individual and collective."[12] Although women had mobilized politically before this point, their actions had not constituted the building of a movement. The women who planned the congress recognized that collective, sustained, organized efforts were required for effective action, and they approached the task armed with specific strategies and tactics.

The commonly accepted scenario of how the congress was organized is as follows: Palestinian women from all over the country convened a large general meeting at which they passed resolutions dealing with the national problem. A delegation from this congress then presented the resolutions to the high commissioner, who received them at Government House. Upon the delegation's return to the general congress, participants decided to hold a demonstration and were then driven in a convoy of cars throughout the city, visiting various foreign consuls to whom they presented their resolutions. Finally, the women returned to convene a concluding session, where an Arab Women's Executive Committee (AWE) was elected to execute and administer the congress's resolutions.[13]

The confusion that results when one attempts to reconcile divergent historical accounts of the early women's movement is instructive in accenting certain features of its early leadership. I highlight discrepancies because they demonstrate the political sophistication of the congress organizers, who recognized the importance of public perceptions of their political behavior. Significantly, this "public" included the colonial community. Most versions of the congress stress both fervent, nationalist-inspired spontaneity, and organized democracy. In fact, the AWE was formed before the congress at a preliminary meeting at which it drafted the resolutions of the congress in advance. Thus the ratification of the resolutions at the congress was primarily a rubber stamp for decisions that had already been made by the core group that constituted the Executive Committee. From the conflicting accounts of the "election" of the Executive Committee, it is clear that the committee elected at the preliminary meeting was presented as a slate at the congress, which, in electing it, merely confirmed and bestowed additional legitimacy on a previously constituted group.[14] These accounts demonstrate the control over the formation and outcome of the congress that was exerted by the nucleus of women who organized it.

Another contradictory detail concerns the demonstration, which was not spontaneously proposed at the congress but rather, previously negotiated between Chancellor and Arab men. The week before the conference, the women announced their intention to demonstrate at Government House, where they planned to present the congress's resolutions to the high commissioner's wife. Matiel Mughannam, one of those present, states that the women thought they should see Lady Chancellor, "as Moslem members of the delegation could not properly appear before the High Commissioner." But the women were informed that Lady Chancellor could not "receive ladies proposing to submit resolutions of political character," so they "had no other alternative but to wait upon the High Commissioner ... and to ignore all traditional restrictions."[15] It is worth noting how punctilious the British themselves were in maintaining the boundaries between their own gendered "separate spheres." Chancellor agreed to see a delegation himself, but attempted to "induce some of the Moslem leaders to dissuade the women from holding the demonstration." The men "declined to intervene" at first, but after Chancellor threatened to stop the demonstration by force, they arranged to have it take place in cars in certain parts of the city. The women were forbidden by the government to deliver speeches or go near the Wailing Wall.[16] They rode through the city in cars, horns honking, accompanied by watchful police officers and soldiers.[17]

The resolutions that the congress presented to Chancellor dealt primarily with national issues, and specifically addressed concerns that arose from the mounting tension in the country that preceded and followed the Wailing Wall incident. Among them were protests against the Balfour Declaration and Jewish immigration; the mistreatment of Arab prisoners by police; and the enforcement of the collective punishment ordinance. The women also pledged to "support all resolutions, decisions and demands of the Arab Executive."[18]

The convening of the Arab Women's Congress acted as a catalyst for women all over Palestine to organize. In addition to formulating nationalist demands, the congress resolved to participate in an "Arab women's national revival" like other countries; consider the congress to be the foundation of the women's movement in Palestine; link up with other women's organizations in Syria, Egypt, and Iraq; unify the women's movement in Palestine through the establishment of Arab women's associations; encourage national trade and industry; and attempt to spread Arabic culture in Palestine, demanding that girls schools adopt this position.[19]

These resolutions reveal that the organizers perceived political, economic, social, and cultural concerns as interconnected and overlapping. As Guida West and Rhoda Blumberg note, "analysis of 'reform' issues, 'women's' issues, and 'feminist' issues reveals that the boundaries shift, not only over different periods of time, but also in different parts of the world."[20] The fluidity of issues addressed by the women at the congress allowed the Palestinian women's movement a great deal of latitude to become involved in and act on multiple social and political levels, defying linear descriptions or characterizations that reduce their movement to simplistic categorizations such as "nationalist," "feminist," or "reformist." Although the resolutions of the congress, and, more importantly, the activities the women engaged in during the 1920s and 1930s focused primarily on the national issue, the movement clearly situated gender at the forefront of its political consciousness. The articulation of this consciousness was muted, often inconsistent, and subtly subversive rather than explicitly "feminist," as contemporary Western discourse would define this term. Its gender critique was often hidden within a manipulation of traditional gender norms.

Shortly after the convening of the congress, the AWE called a meeting to organize the Jerusalem Women's Association. Branches of the AWA[21] were eventually established in Acre, Ramla, Haifa, Jaffa, Nablus, Nazareth, and Gaza; the Jerusalem branch, although not necessarily founded first, rapidly became the dominant chapter and "official center" from which the AWE operated.[22] The president of the Supreme Muslim Council donated a building for the Jerusalem Executive Committee to meet in, and at a meeting on November 16, the AWA was established.[23] The aims of the AWA, as articulated in its founding by-laws, suggest ambitions for it to be everything to everybody. They were to "elevate the standing of women" by working for their social, economic, and educational development; and to assist "national institutions," supporting any "enterprise" that would benefit the country economically, socially, and politically. The AWA was to be directed by the AWE, which was also responsible for assembling the other women's associations around the country.[24]

THE EARLY YEARS: 1930–1935

The AWE/AWA[25] quickly became embroiled in nationalist activities during the early 1930s. They first focused on the political and social repercussions of the Wailing Wall incident. Among the major concerns of the women's movement throughout the mandate period were the problems confronting prisoners and their families. The massive arrests and wide-scale imprisonments that resulted from the 1929 riots signaled the beginning of a phenomenon that was to become part of the Palestinian political landscape for the rest of the mandate period (and indeed, up until the present) and a common experience affecting most Arab families. This experience traversed class boundaries. Palestinians were arrested for participating in riots, for fighting in rebel bands during the revolt, for weapons possession or arms smuggling, or merely for political activity.[26]

The AWA/AWE held an extraordinary session in May 1930 over the impending executions of the three men sentenced to death for their role in the Wailing Wall riots, sending a flood of telegrams of protest to the Arab delegation in London, the Colonial Office, and the House of Commons and Lords. In February 1931, they visited Hebron, distributed aid, and bought land for the families of those executed, recognizing that one of the prisoners' major problems was financial; men arrested and detained were often the sole support of large families.[27] In June 1931, the AWE called on women to strike on the anniversary of the executions, even after the male-led national movement had abandoned the plan.[28] The women's tireless efforts on behalf of detainees, prisoners, and their families continued up through the 1940s.

Consistent with the concern to support the national economy as articulated in the congress's resolutions, in 1932 the women's movement turned its attention directly to agriculture, trade, and industry. The AWA was "the first national institution to publicize the plight of the fellahin,"[29] sending a detailed memorandum to the Permanent Mandates Commission, in which they called for abolition of the tithe (recognizing that the peasantry "contribute[d] the greater part of the revenue") and reinstitution of the Ottoman Agricultural Bank, which had been disbanded in 1925. This long memorandum demonstrated sophisticated, technical knowledge of the workings of the government. Besides the situation of the fellah, it dealt at length with issues such as education, discrimination against Arab officials in the civil service, and the rights of the Arabs to a national government.[30] As part of a pan-Arab effort in the 1930s to boycott "non-national" goods and promote local (that is, Arab) products through agricultural and economic fairs, the women's organizations participated in the Arab exhibition held in 1932 and helped enforce the boycott of "non-national" goods through "propaganda" and visits to shops, where they threatened to publicize the names of noncompliant merchants who sold foreign-produced goods. They also donated generously to the National Fund, an endeavor initiated by the AE in 1930 to organize local committees from the major towns in order to solicit contributions from Palestinian households and individuals to help support its work. The project's success was mixed, however.[31]

The early 1930s witnessed increased participation by the women in demonstrations. In 1931, at a massive demonstration held in Nablus in response to press reports and nationalist agitation about sealed armories in Jewish settlements, the women recited nationalist verses as they marched between middle-aged men in front and young men in back.[32] When the police attempted to separate the men from the women, the young men threw stones, and the police fired on the crowd. Four people were wounded by bullets, and eleven by batons. One of the women, according to a Zionist intelligence report, killed a policeman.[33] This incident and the behavior of the police provoked outrage in the Arab community and galvanized protests and expressions of solidarity with Nabulsis, setting the tone for future militancy among the women.

The year 1933 was a significant one for the AWA which began to adopt more combative tactics commensurate with the heightened tension in the country. In April 1933, on the occasion of General Allenby's visit to Palestine to dedicate the new YMCA building, the AWA, joining a nation-wide boycott of the event, marched in a highly symbolic and emotionally charged procession in a "heavy downpour and intense cold" from Damascus Gate in the Old City of Jerusalem to the Mosque of 'Umar in the Haram al-Sharif, where a Christian (Matiel Mughannam) delivered a speech in which she announced that "the Arab nation" would not accept the "injustice of this imperialist administration." Then the women marched to the Holy Sepulchre, where a Muslim (Tarab 'Abd al-Hadi) did the same before Christ's tomb. "The Arab ladies ask Lord Allenby to remember and tell this to his government," she said. "The mothers, daughters, sisters of the Arab victims are gathered here to make the world witness the betrayal of the British. We want all the Arabs to remember that the British are the cause of our suffering and they should learn from the lesson."[34] Police noted the unusual presence at this protest of peasant women, who generally did not participate in the urban women's demonstrations during this time.[35]

In October 1933, the AE called for a general strike and demonstration in Jerusalem as the first in a series in a nationwide campaign to protest Jewish immigration. Heated demonstrations took place in Jerusalem on October 13, and then in Jaffa, Nablus, Haifa, and again in Jerusalem October 27–29, accompanying a merchants' strike. The Jaffa demonstrations resulted in twenty-six deaths, largely due to shooting by police. The high commissioner, Arthur Wauchope, noted that "a new and disquieting feature" of the first Jerusalem demonstration was "the prominent part taken by women of good family as well as others."[36] According to *Filastīn* (whose reliability, like most newspapers reporting demonstration figures, is somewhat suspect on this account), five hundred women took part in the Jerusalem demonstrations.[37] Part of the reasons for Wauchope's "disquiet" derived from the protests provoked by police behavior toward the women, as well as reports of the women's unruly conduct during the demonstration. The police complained that the women had to be forced aside in order to allow police to charge the main body of the demonstration; that the women "did all they could to urge the male members of the demonstration to defy Police orders"; that they assaulted the police; and that they screamed at police and kicked at the gate of government offices.[38]

Undeterred by the rough behavior of police in the Jerusalem demonstration, a delegation of Jerusalem women traveled to the Jaffa demonstration on October 27, "at the instance [sic] of the Arab Women's Executive at Jerusalem."[39] Matiel Mughannam, one of the delegation, delivered an "inflammatory" speech from a balcony, "excit[ing] the crowd" and heightening the "considerable tension in the air."[40] The women "formed themselves into a special procession" and, according to Mughannam, "were made the subject of a baton charge and firing by the police."[41]

The Jaffa demonstrations resulted in the arrests of those considered by the government to be the organizers of the demonstrations, including several members of the AE. The women held several interviews with the high commissioner, one in Jerusalem, and one in Nablus, at which they excoriated the government's policies and the behavior of the troops, demanding that those arrested during the incidents be released. They also attended the trials of the prisoners. (Undoubtedly, one factor that motivated the women to attend the trials was that two of those arrested were husbands of AWE members: 'Auni 'Abd al-Hadi, the husband of Tarab, and Jamal al-Husayni, married to Na'imati.)[42]

The October 1933 demonstrations were "milestones in the history of the Palestinian-Arab nationalist movement," revealing the growing readiness of Palestinians to confront the government and sacrifice for the struggle.[43] After 1933, tension in the country intensified as Jewish immigration increased rapidly, due in large part to the deteriorating political situation in Europe. The last months of 1935 were particularly tense. Two events had a "catalytic effect." In October 1935, a secret cache of illegal weapons smuggled into the country by the Jews was discovered in the port in Jaffa, provoking angry responses from the Arabs.[44] The AWA of Jerusalem presented a protest to the High Commissioner, demanding an investigation of Jewish settlements, confiscation of weapons and a halt to immigration.[45] During this period, a general strike, widely adhered to, was declared. Sadhij Nassar, one of the most active members of the Haifa AWA, prowled the city of Haifa, "convincing" (*qana'*) the shopkeepers and street vendors to observe the strike, according to the press. (The British version of this activity described it as "intimidating" the vendors.)[46]

The second seminal incident was the killing of Shaykh 'Izz al-Din al-Qassam in a surprise skirmish between his band of armed rebels and police on November 21. Al-Qassam, of Syrian origin, was a well-respected, al-Azhar-educated *'ālim* (learned religious man) of high moral caliber and "magnetic character" who had begun to create an underground movement to fight the mandate government and resist the imposition of the Jewish National Home.[47] He developed close ties with villagers and the growing numbers of poor working class laborers who swelled the shanty towns in the Haifa area, where he was the marriage registrar *(ma'dhūn)* of the *sharī'a* court, a position that enabled him to become well acquainted with the people in the region. In the late 1920s and early 1930s al-Qassam began secretly to recruit young men, organizing cells that engaged in military training. The "premature attempt at Revolt echoed within the Arab community"; the clash that abruptly put an end to al-Qassam's life is generally considered the spark that ignited the 1936 strike and revolt.[48] Al-Qassam's "organization was a complete novelty," in that he was among the first to organize peasants and the working classes in Palestine, commingling religious with nationalist discourse on a populist level. His underground network was the "first clear indication that the basic tenets of Palestinian-Arab nationalism ... overcame the barriers between the higher and educated strata and the lower classes," although the revolt that it spawned ultimately brought into sharp relief class tensions that had been evolving before its outset.[49]

THE 1936–1939 STRIKE AND REVOLT

The 1936 strike that broke out following al-Qassam's death was the culmination of the tension that had been building in the latter part of 1935. As Yehoshua Porath describes it:

> This atmosphere of tension and resentment caused by growing Jewish immigration, land purchases and 'Hebrew labor' was the foundation

from which the idea gradually evolved that in order to preserve the Arab character of Palestine and to prevent its transformation into a country with a Jewish majority, the Arabs had to resort to violence.[50]

These factors created economic pressure on the Arab working classes, resulting in growing unemployment and landlessness. The climate of war in Europe and effects of the depression further contributed to the worsening economic situation. Political developments played a role as well in convincing the Arabs that peaceful means had become ineffectual as a strategy to change British policy in Palestine.[51] Even before al-Qassam's death, other clandestine, paramilitary organizations had been forming, and the mood in the country became increasingly combative.

During the revolt, women's militancy reached new heights, and their participation in the nationalist movement underwent a transformation and radicalization commensurate with that of the rest of the country. Some women were cognizant of what was stirring in the countryside even before the call for the general strike. In late 1935, the Central Intelligence Department (CID) reported that, in the north, "certain Moslem ladies of the upper class ... were discussing the situation when one made a statement that a secret plan was afoot whereby in the near future sudden and simultaneous disorders would occur."[52] In fact, this prediction was prescient. In early April 1936, a series of intercommunal killings in the Jaffa region inflamed the already heightened tension. Shortly afterward, on April 20, a general strike was called by the national committees that had sprung up throughout the country. On April 25 the Arab Higher Committee (AHC) was formed to coordinate strike activity. Headed by Hajj Amin al-Husayni, the mufti of Jerusalem, the AHC initially included men from most of the major political parties.[53] By May, organized, armed bands were operating in the country, attacking and sabotaging railroads, telephone lines, and other communication infrastructures. Adherence to the strike was surprisingly cohesive throughout its six-month duration, revealing the depth of Arab feeling against the Zionist project. Hind al-Husayni, who was a schoolgirl during the strike, described it as "stricter than now [referring to the ongoing merchants' strike of the intifada]. It was a real strike. Not a shop was open for six months. No schools were open ... and nothing else at all. No transportation unless you can have a donkey or a horse ... it was a real strike to show the whole world what [was] happening in Palestine."[54]

The strike and initial stage of the revolt lasted until October, when it was called off through the intercession of Arab leaders from outside the country, but without disarming the rebels. Then there came a lull in activity from November 1936 until July 1937, followed by an escalation in July 1937, which lasted until the autumn of 1938. From autumn 1938 until the summer of 1939, the British made a concerted effort to repress the insurrection, utilizing methods such as collective punishment, deportations, mass arrests, house demolitions, night raids on villages, air strikes, restrictions on movement, and martial law. By the winter of 1939, these measures, combined with the imploding effects of internecine conflicts, assassinations, and new political developments, had ground the revolt to a halt.

Peasant Women and the Revolt: Stones and Ammunition

Both AWA members and unorganized women mobilized immediately during the revolt. The conspicuous involvement of peasant and village women in the revolt was one of its distinctive elements, highlighting the class-based, urban character of the organized women's movement, as exemplified by the AWA, and underscoring differences between its members and village or peasant women. Palestinian peasant women had been active before the revolt, albeit on a lesser (or perhaps more accurately, less remarked upon) scale. As noted, "Palestinian women were among the peasants who acted against the first [Zionist] agricultural settlement" near Affula in 1884. When the Commission of Inquiry after the 1929 disturbances traveled throughout the country, "what impressed the Commissioners most" was a group of more than two hundred peasant women who waved their shawls as the cars passed, shouting, "Down with the Balfour Declaration."[55]

Rosemary Sayigh notes that "a great deal of women's political action is spontaneous and individual, taking place outside of an organization."[56] This was particularly the case with peasant women, whose more physically active involvement in resistance was in many respects a response to the fact that "it was their communities that were coming under physical attack."[57] The major military activities of the revolt moved fairly quickly to the countryside, once the British had pacified the more easily controlled cities. The rebels tended to flee to and hide near the hill and mountain villages between battles, relying upon the villagers to provide food, water, concealment, and information, functions in which peasant women played a prominent role. As Ted Swedenburg remarks, "Women were central to the rebels' amazing ability to blend in with the rural population, to sustain the armed resistance, and to escape detection and capture."[58] The rebels' presence drew British troops, who conducted searches and raids, and engaged the rebel bands in battles. Women were often caught in crossfire either as innocent bystanders or while carrying water, warning rebel fighters of imminent attack or conveying information over the hills.

One of rural women's primary functions was to incite and motivate men to enter battle, a role that has historical and cultural roots.[59] In village and tribal battles during the late nineteenth and early twentieth centuries, women manipulated traditional concepts of shame and honor in order to encourage combatants by flinging "epithet[s] of contempt or scorn" at men who hesitated in battle. An observer remarked, "We always found that the women took the keenest interest in warfare, that they acted as scouts and conveyed intelligence with great rapidity and accuracy over the hills, and that they were quick in detecting plots or secret movements of the enemy."[60] These comments foreshadowed the multiple roles women played in the revolt. In a report on the revolt distinguished by its irritated tone, the British characterized women as "bellicose" agitators who instigated the young men to become combatants.[61] Police reports warned that "women are taking an active part in village affairs and are constantly urging the men to take definite action for the safety of their homeland."[62]

From the start, peasant women were not hesitant to resort to violence to defend their villages or menfolk, resisting searches, raids, and arrests in the villages. Clashes occurred between police and women who stoned them from rooftops, such as one incident in the village of Kafr Kanna, where a young girl was shot dead and a British constable seriously injured.[63] In other villages, women assaulted police, who had come to make arrests for possession of weapons, and attempted to kill police, critically wounding one.[64] Women's violent acts were not limited to targeting the British troops. One woman in the Galilee region, 'A'isha al-Mayat, beat up and attempted to kill Fayaz Fahum, a collaborator with the British forces who had slain her husband.[65]

Unlike urban women, some peasant women actually joined the revolt in a military capacity. Their numbers were seemingly few, as evinced by the elusiveness of sources of information about them, which tend to be obscure, anecdotal, secondary, or inferential. One woman who is cited in a number of sources is Fatma Ghazzal, who was killed in the battle of Wadi Azzoun in 1936. One can only guess at the nature of women's involvement from numerous British reports of women who were killed in village incidents; it is possible that they were combatants. In their accounts of incidents, the British seemed to assume that women would not be involved in military activity.[66] In interviews with elders, people remembered women's actions but in vague terms, recalling their male relatives' names rather than their own. Villagers in the Galilee region, for example, recollected 'Abdallah al-Hanut's sister, who supposedly killed a Captain Brandt and subsequently had her hand cut off (by whom was not mentioned). Another villager remembered Muhammad Bashir al-Safuri's female relative, who worked with the rebels, bore arms, wore a uniform, and ultimately died of a disease.[67]

Stories about women's military involvement circulated beyond the villages. In a letter to the high commissioner protesting government atrocities in the villages, the AWA mentions an Arab woman "who was compelled, under the pressure of Government's policy and the acts of oppression, to join the bands in the mountains, in order to avoid the barbarous acts which are committed by British troops and was shot dead, as many other women were, by the troops." Similarly, in a telegram to a British sympathizer to the Arab cause, Miss Farquharson, the Arab Women's Committee (probably the AWA) states, "Tyranny forced women to join revolutionists on hills."[68] The acting district commissioner in the Galilee mentions a "favorite story" that was being disseminated in the countryside about "a follower of Abu Durra [a prominent rebel leader] who was killed and whose wife then took his rifle and ammunition and joined the 'jihad.'" He adds, "this propaganda is having a disturbing effect."[69]

The frequency with which peasant women were arrested for arms smuggling or possession of weapons suggests that women had a greater military role than has been assumed or recorded.[70] The women (and men) manipulated "tradition" and British distaste for violating it, by thrusting women into roles that overturned assumptions about gender. One such tactic was to have women conceal and convey weapons. The British complained about this stratagem:

> The sanctity of Moslem womenfolk, whom British troops and police were forbidden to touch, was . . . exploited to the full . . . their voluminous clothing was a great asset in which to conceal weapons and to hide the tell-tale marks of recent digging, while for hiding arms on the move the village woman in her shapeless bundle was an extremely useful carrier.[71]

In many cases, women used their children as shields, concealing weapons or ammunition behind infants in arms or among the folds of children's clothing. Villagers often buried weapons to conceal them. A group of peasant women resting on a rug during work in the fields was arrested after buried arms and ammunition were discovered under the rug.[72] Ruqiya Huri, while traveling to the mountains with a doctor to dispense medical aid and deliver arms, hid weapons under her clothes, groaning and pretending to be in labor when at a British checkpoint.[73] Tharwa ʿAbd al-Karam Hassan, of Safuriyya, smuggled her uncle's gun in a haystack.[74] Another woman smuggled guns over the border from Lebanon.[75]

In a number of trials in which women were prosecuted on weapons charges, they were sentenced to heavy prison terms of seven to ten years, while men in the family indicted with them were acquitted. Women sacrificed themselves to protect men, probably because their sentences were less severe, and tended to get reduced, although not necessarily. A number of those convicted for weapons violations were middle-aged or older women. Sabha 'Ali Gallad, of Tulkarm, sentenced to five years imprisonment for possession of a rifle, was "judged to be" sixty years old.[76] Certainly peasant women were willing to take substantial risks that courted severe penalties. Sayigh reports the comments of a Palestinian who described the "bourgeois woman" as "educated, free, she has more time to give but she works cautiously" whereas "women of the oppressed classes are more ready to sacrifice, [and] capable of moving towards nationalist goals by leaps."[77]

Women's more subversive activities were not limited to weapons infringements. Munira Khalidi of Qalunya, a member of a secret society called the "Black Hand," was arrested and convicted for writing threatening letters to police.[78] One woman hid a wounded fighter in an ancient, hollow olive tree in her garden during a search by British troops, who interrupted their operations to eat lunch under the tree while the man was concealed inside it.[79] Peasant women also "relied on secrecy, a fundamental principle of clan solidarity," to protect their villages. Peteet reports that they would withhold recognition of the bodies of male relatives killed in clashes to protect the villages from collective punishment.[80]

Even though many peasant women provided so-called support, their militancy and commitment equaled that of men. One woman, who carried water for the rebels, encountered the District Officer (DO) after her son had been killed in battle near the village of Arrabi. The DO expressed condolences over her loss and handed her five pounds. She "refused the money and suggested that it would be better to give the money to the Brigands for ammunition."[81]

Elite Women and the Revolt

Urban, elite women, whose participation in the revolt has been described as more "passive" than peasant women's,[82] took part in demonstrations, collected significant amounts of money to fund the revolt, formed new women's committees in villages in an effort to coordinate resources, enforced the strike, held secret meetings to support the militants, and barraged the government with written protests and condemnation. These missives, which often produced meetings or interviews with government officials, repeated certain themes tirelessly: demands for the release of detainees and the return of deportees (many of whom were husbands of AWA members); denunciation of partition;[83] expressions of outrage over civilian bomb attacks and demands for the disarming of the Jews; and condemnation of government measures such as searches, house demolitions, internment camps, death sentences, bombardment, and other methods of repressing the revolt.[84]

One of the first major acts of the women's movement at the outbreak of the strike was to organize and participate in a series of massive meetings, condolence visits, and demonstrations in May 1936. On May 2, a delegation of the Jerusalem AWA, accompanied by a car full of young men, traveled to Jaffa to commemorate the martyrs of the Jaffa incidents that had ignited the revolt. There they visited the hospitals and cemeteries (both Islamic and Orthodox Christian), where they delivered short speeches, presented the wounded with gifts, scattered flowers on graves, and were welcomed by a member of the National Committee. All along their route to and from Jaffa, the women were greeted by huge crowds cheering them on; the throng was so dense that they had to curtail their trip.[85]

In the early stages of the revolt, women's committees sprang up in regions of the country that had seen little previous organized activity among women; in Tulkarm one hundred women participated in a big meeting and demonstration on May 4, billed by the press as "the first time ladies have gone out on a demonstration." Women of Jenin, Qalqilya, Hebron, and Beersheba also convened meetings (many with over one hundred in attendance), raised money, sent telegrams and demonstrated.[86] The Jerusalem, Jaffa, and Haifa branches of the AWA, its most active chapters, took the lead in convening massive assemblies of four to five hundred women.

A new phenomenon witnessed and remarked upon during the revolt was the organization and mobilization of female students. Although there is scant evidence that schoolgirls were politicized before the revolt, apparently al-Qassam had recognized early the activist potential of young women during his underground activities in the 1930s. He provided educational and religious instruction to schoolgirls, establishing a women's organization called *Rifaqāt al-Qassam* (Comrades of al-Qassam).[87]

Both male and female students became caught up in the revolt. Girls speaking at the mosque in the Haram al-Sharif were noted with alarm in police reports that recorded the crowd's having been stirred by their "political and inciting" speeches. This was "a most unusual development," the police commented.[88] In the Galilee region, schoolgirls went out on strike, prevented other students from attending school, and demonstrated throughout late April and early May, causing the police such problems that they threatened to close down schools and took the step of informing fathers "that they would be liable to fines if their daughters committed offenses."[89]

In Jerusalem, the AWA asked the [female] students to attend a big meeting and "do their share," but the students went a step further, demonstrating their own organizing abilities. On May 5, 1936, according to the press, they convened a meeting of six hundred girls at the home of Ishaq al-Budayri; elected their own executive committee with representatives from different girls' schools (including private, missionary schools); and decided to strike school, boycott foreign goods, and hold a peaceful demonstration several days later.[90] The day after this meeting, the AWA convened its own massive assembly that carried over into the next day. During this event, the "young ladies," in an apparent disagreement with the main body of the meeting, decided to go against its decision not to hold a peaceful demonstration. On May 8, the students marched through the streets of Jerusalem, surrounded by a Girl Scout troop carrying the Arab flag, and accompanied by youths who marched at the back as guards. The young men were blocked, separated, and beaten by the police, but the women marched undisturbed. The women students subsequently presented their resolutions to a government official.[91]

Even very young girls participated in the political activities of the strike and revolt. At a big women's meeting convened in Jaffa that ended in a demonstration of more than five hundred people (according to the newspaper *Filastin*), nine-year-old May al-Safri delivered a speech in which she highlighted the special role of the young in defending the homeland, saying, "The future is ours, and we will be the ones that taste its sweetness or bitterness." Another young girl, ten-year-old Hafiza Subhi Khurshid, also delivered a speech at the meeting.[92]

The strike and revolt inspired and politicized individual schoolgirls, some of whom experienced political initiation through their involvement. Now elderly women in interviews recall the enthusiasm and pride that the revolt aroused in them as students. Salma al-Husayni emphasized that the students held their own demonstrations and convened secret meetings, although she also mentioned that they cooperated with and were recruited by the women's associations. The students would strew nails in the streets to puncture the tires of British vehicles (a tactic also used during the intifada in the 1980s and 1990s). The British threw water at the students in demonstrations.[93]

Hala and Dumya Sakakini, teenaged students at the time, were excited and stirred by the strike and revolt. They imposed strict discipline on themselves by adhering to the strike's boycott of nonnational goods and merchants to the extent that they denied themselves a major pleasure—attending the (Jewish-owned) cinema. "When you're fifteen and sixteen this is hard," they commented more than fifty-five years later. They recall wanting desperately to see *Gone With the Wind*, but, infused with the idealism of youth, maintained the strike long after it was over, until 1942–43. Their friend Salma al-Khadra (whose mother was a founding member of the AWE/AWA) also observed the strike way beyond its cessation.[94] The students at Friends Girls School in Ramallah went without dinner, donating the money allocated for it to the rebels.[95]

The revolt found urban, elite women and students engaged in militant activities that often resulted in confrontations and arrests by the authorities. In Acre, while men prayed, women demonstrated; police attacked a peaceful demonstration held by women, students, and young girls in July 1936, wounding some of the latter who had been carrying the flag. A Mrs. Hasun was arrested and detained, while Anisa al-Khadra (mother of Salma and of one of the young girls marching in front), confronted police, upbraiding them for "attack[ing] women and children in this way." The women then marched to the mosque where the men were praying; a delegation of notables subsequently negotiated the release of Mrs. Hasun at the police station.[96] As in the 1929 demonstrations, the British and Arab men colluded in exercising patriarchal control over the women: the British in policing them, the Arab men in mediating on their behalf.

Elite, urban women were also arrested for other infractions during the revolt. Women and children in Jaffa were detained for curfew violations.[97] The women of Haifa were distinguished for their militancy in enforcing the strike. Often accompanied by "street Arabs," they were arrested for "intimidating" shopkeepers. In one incident, a procession of women, which included Sadhij Nassar, smashed the windows of a nonstriking bakery and the office of a British official. Three women were arrested, and others were "interviewed" by the acting district commissioner. Disturbances broke out after the women's arrest, resulting in the wounding of two people. This seems not to have deterred the Haifa women, however, who continued the same activities several days later.[98]

Like their peasant counterparts, elite women also participated in weapons smuggling and other subversive activity. Wajiha al-Husayni, the independently wealthy wife of 'Abd al-Qadir al-Husayni, one of the fighters in the revolt (and a major military leader in 1947–48), helped pay for ammunition and arms herself. She would ride in the car with her future husband, weapons and dynamite concealed under her seat, which the British did not dare to search because of their respect for the "sanctity" of Muslim women.[99] Hind al-Husayni traveled from Jerusalem to Ramallah disguised as a peasant woman and pretended to be the sister of a man imprisoned in a well in order to visit him to reassure his family and deliver blankets to him.[100]

One of the more militant members of the AWU paid a high price for her activities during the revolt. On March 23, 1939, Sadhij Nassar, the wife of Najib Nassar, the editor of the respected newspaper, *al-Karmil*, was arrested by police and detained at the women's prison in Bethlehem under the Emergency Defense Regulations No. 15B, which allowed the police to detain people without bringing charges.[101] Although Mrs. Nassar was never formally charged, the British described her as a "very dangerous woman," a "menace to public security," and "a prominent agitator" who had "organized a number of demonstrations attended by violence." She was detained because her "activities [had] become more virulent and dangerous," and "she was actively engaged in subversive propaganda." Upon her arrest, which aroused a storm of protest both locally and internationally, Sir Thomas Scrivenor, assistant district commissioner in the Galilee region, commented, "a sojourn of three months in a detention camp would be excellent. . . . Mrs. Nassar is an unmitigated nuisance and she should have been dealt with long ago."[102] Nassar subsequently had her detention renewed; she was finally released on February 23, 1940.

Sadhij Nassar was one of the more unusual activists in the women's movement, a woman of strong character and conviction. The granddaughter of the Grand Baha'i, the founder of the Baha'i religion, she was of Iranian descent and married to an Orthodox Christian (who converted to Protestantism).[103] Fluent in four languages, she was "'ahead' [of her fellow AWU members] in the sense that she knew how to organize and how to conduct meetings."[104] Unlike most of the other urban-based AWU members, she actively attempted to recruit peasant women in the Bisan region, spending time living among them, although she admitted to failure, attributing it to "backwardness" and the lack of schools in the area.[105] She was constantly in the news, delivering fiery speeches, writing for *al-Karmil* (which she edited from 1941 until 1944, when the authorities refused to renew its permit), "inciting revolution," leading demonstrations, and intimidating merchants to observe the strike.[106] According to people who still remember her, she and her husband, whose difference in age was vast, had some sort of estrangement towards the end of his life. (He died in 1948.) Najib Nassar had been previously married to a woman who ran off with a Turkish officer, leaving Najib and ultimately, Sadhij, to raise his four children, along with their one son, Faruq, whom she used to bring with her while leading demonstrations.[107] The Haifa branch of the AWU reflected Nassar's radical character.

Most women involved in the AWA/AWU did not engage in openly subversive activities; one of elite women's most important tasks was collecting funds for the revolt. The AWA, under the strike's Central Relief Committee, was responsible for raising money for the relief of indigent families whose men were in custody, and for medical assistance to people wounded in attacks.[108] The sums women gathered were substantial, sometimes reaching as much as one hundred pounds (almost five hundred dollars, a large sum of money in those days) in one collection. Women also sold their jewelry to donate its proceeds, a not insignificant act in a society where jewelry was a major source of security and financial independence for women.[109] In the cities, women went house to house gathering donations and encouraging the buying of national products; urban women also went out to villages to collect funds. In addition to monetary donations, one ladies committee (in Qalqilya) collected a chicken donated by "two poor ladies who do not own a dirham each." A fair amount of money funneled through the AWA came from other Arab countries.[110]

The End of the Revolt

Several scholars have suggested that women's activity began to wane in 1938, due to a "reactionary current" and "concerted campaign of intimidation . . . launched against urban women activists."[111] A much-discussed aspect of the revolt was the rebel enforcement of conservative social norms, particularly concerning behavior, movement, and dress (the last were addressed to men as well as women). Men were commanded to "doff the *tarbush* and don the *kufiya*," ostensibly as a gesture of support and solidarity for the revolt.[112] The rebels issued "quasi-ethical edicts forbidding Arab women to follow European modes, to go to hairdressers or sell commodities" and ordered them to veil.[113] The rebels did not merely attempt to control women's behavior, but also to enforce a certain level of morality on the population at large, issuing decrees that forbade "strong language" and "invite[d] the wives of faithless husbands to seek redress in the rebel courts."[114] British sources stress the coercion of Christian women, who had to "fall[] into line" and begin to veil along with Muslim women,[115] whereas Palestinian sources reveal that a more complex, ambiguous admixture of nationalism and pragmatic strategy informed these edicts, and women's compliance with them. Christian Palestinian women, in remembering the revolt, stated that they veiled to avoid "look[ing] like Jews," to "show they were Arabs," and to "be like other Arabs."[116]

Toward 1938, there could well have been a certain element of fear as a result of increasingly violent internecine conflict, which began to limit women's enthusiasm—particularly among those women with Nashashibi ties.[117] Sayigh quotes a popular poem, recited by young boys who ran after women in the street, harassing them:

Umm al-bunya, al-raqqāsa
Biddha bumba wa rasāsa
[The woman who wears a hat, the dancer
Deserves a bomb and a bullet][118]

As Swedenburg notes, this "couplet contained both a threat and an insult." The woman wearing the hat indicates a Westernized woman, whereas the dancer sobriquet implies a loose woman, "a virtual prostitute." The bomb and the bullet are self-explanatory.[119]

Attempting to answer the question why (some) men attacked women who were in fact supporting the national struggle in a moment of intense crisis is a difficult task. In fact, as Ted Swedenburg suggests, it seems that gender became a site upon which the internal contradictions and class tensions of the nationalist movement were played out. Women interviewed by Rosemary Sayigh attributed "campaigns of moral censure and physical threats solely to Islamic ultraconservatives and British conspirators."[120] But as Swedenburg points out, the mainstream nationalist leadership also called upon (urban) women to dress modestly like their "sisters the warriors of the villages."[121] These kinds of edicts and invocations need to be juxtaposed against two things: the internecine struggles of the revolt, in which the competing factions in the nationalist movement began to violently turn against each other, resulting in assassinations, threats and campaigns of intimidation and harassment; and the internal class and rural-urban conflict between the notables, who constituted the mainstream national leadership, and the largely peasant rebels, who were the actual combatants in the revolt. Women—certain ones in particular—became caught in these swirling conflicts. Because the women in the movement, by and large, tended to be urban, upper and middle class, and, in many cases, westernized through education and/or dress, they became symbols of, or guilty by association with, the enemy, the British, while at the same time, their male counterparts in the nationalist movement were themselves under similar attack (for wearing Western hats instead of the *kufiya*) by the rebels in the countryside. In many respects the dress issue was emblematic of class tensions. Although Swedenburg finds evidence that the mainstream male leadership issued a mildly worded admonition to women regarding Western dress (in 1931, before the revolt), I found no evidence that they supported the edicts emanating from the rebel leadership.[122] The dress issue here foregrounds class and cultural tensions within Palestinian society.

Despite the repressive efforts to control women's dress and limit their behavior and the increased internal violence of the revolt, however, elite women did not "retire[] ... from nationalist work."[123] The results of the intimidation and harassment were ambiguous. I found no concrete evidence of a decrease in involvement—in fact, the women were extraordinarily active during this period. A rough count of articles in only two newspapers, *Filastīn* and *al-Difāʿ*, yields at least 130 reports of women's demonstrations, weapons infractions, meetings, telegrams or memoranda of protest, fundraising, and other activities from the period 1938–39 (out of a total of 360 from 1936 to 1939). Furthermore, the press coverage was generally enthusiastic and supportive. What did change was the form women's activity took; during the 1938–39 period, elite women increasingly turned to less public and controversial types of protest activity and instead wrote hundreds of telegrams, statements, and memoranda of protest to the outside world, the British government and public, and the press. In the Central Zionist Archives alone, there are twenty documents for the period 1938–39, comprising letters of protest from the women, minutes of their meetings with government officials, or police reports about their other activities.

In attempting to assess the role of Palestinian women in the revolt, the historian is confronted with gendered perceptions of "active" or "passive" forms of resistance that have contributed to obscuring the nature of this role. The implication is that women's "support" work is somehow less significant than the "real" work of participation in actual armed struggle.[124] Even older Palestinian women reveal internalized notions of their own marginality in their memories of the revolt. One woman in the village of Zeita, when asked about women's involvement, commented that "the women of Zeita did not help any rebel" while saying virtually in the next breath that they used to hide rebels in their houses and conceal and smuggle food and ammunition for them.[125] For these acts, they could have been punished by having their houses demolished. Because few women took part in actual battles, their more subtle, less visible subversive activities tend to be dismissed by most as peripheral to the (male-defined) national historical narrative of the revolt. Furthermore, most of their acts are perceived as being within the usual discursive norms of female behavior and the culture. Notions of what constitutes an "active" person are entirely gendered; women were not by and large visible as fighters in rebel bands, heroes of renowned battles, or famous military leaders, thus many if not most women who participated in the revolt are anonymous and not remembered as individuals.

CONCLUSION

The revolt exhausted both the Palestinians and the British while enabling the Jews to "make important steps towards the fulfillment of their aim of achieving economic self-sufficiency."[126] The possibilities inherent in the White Paper (see Chapter 7), combined with the entry of Great Britain into World War II, temporarily blunted the adversarial relationship between the British and the Palestinians.

The activities of the organized women's movement in the ten-year period that began with the Wailing Wall incidents and culminated in the end of the revolt reflected the vicissitudes of this decade. As the pressures created from increased, intensified Jewish immigration during the 1930s escalated, so did the involvement and activity of the women's movement. During the heady, active years of the revolt, the rhetoric in the AWA's correspondence with the government became sterner and more impassioned. The AWA held demonstrations, was active in villages, and intervened on behalf of women arrested for weapons and arms violations, often getting their sentences reduced. They kept the issue of deportees and detainees alive way beyond the life of the revolt itself.

During the first decade of its existence, the Palestinian women's movement had proven itself to be "political," as opposed to "merely" social and charitable, by entering the nationalist fray; it was only through this nationalist involvement that the women's movement, whose work often *was* socially oriented, was perceived as "political." Samira Khuri, describing women's activity during the 1930s, said that the women's organizations "weren't pure political organizations. They were social, charity. They used to help the revolutionaries."[127] Her comment demonstrates Palestinians' blurring of the ostensible dichotomy between the political and the social. This ambiguity is highlighted in when one examines its organizational structures, strategies, and internal and external dynamics.

6 The Politics of the Women's Movement

The Question of Feminism, Nationalism, and the "New" Woman

From its inception, the Palestinian women's movement's feminist agenda, which was not explicitly articulated, was located within a nationalist framework. One of the first resolutions and subsequent by-laws published during the establishment of the movement in 1929 included a clause that stated the goals of undertaking a "women's awakening" and elevating the standing of Arab women in Palestine.[1] The movement's work toward these goals, however, was inconsistent and unprogrammatic, and usually the feminist content of its agenda took second place to the national issue. This was because the women's vision of how to elevate Arab women's status was embedded in their concepts of the role of the nation-state. This view was not premised upon a direct reconceptualization or critique of gender roles; nor did it usually locate sources of oppression internally. Rather, the women perceived both the means and end result of social change as "reform," the achievement of which was intimately linked to the struggle for and building of the nation-state. When nationhood was achieved, reform would follow. The only barrier to necessary changes in Palestine was the nation's dependent status.

> These women's movements... which swept most of the Moslem or Arab countries with anything like an independent form of government, did not have a corresponding effect in countries under British or French mandate. The reason is simple: such measures of reform can only be introduced by National Governments, or by persons deriving their authority from the people.[2]

Matiel Mughannam (who constitutes the movement's main spokesperson on this subject by virtue of having left a written record), illustrates the point by recounting how the mandatory government could not enact legislation to raise the minimum legal age of marriage for a girl (to fourteen) because it did not have "a legislative council elected by the people, [which] could introduce any such reformatory measure without making itself liable to or risking any criticism or attack." This analysis does not take into account the fact that the very people most apt to resist changes, or reforms, were those most likely to be elected to such a body.[3]

The women's movement adhered to liberal bourgeois notions about the nation-state by basing its gender agenda on the belief that social change is effected through legislation in a representative government. It is perhaps significant that the major mouthpiece of this political theory, Mughannam, was raised in the United States where women did, in fact, make social as well as political gains in the 1920s and 1930s through legislation. Undoubtedly, women in the Palestinian women's movement were cognizant of the achievements and reforms made by other women through parliamentary democracy. Yet ultimately, this faith that resolution of the national problem would ipso facto result in progressive social reforms led to the incipient "two-stage liberation theory" ("national liberation now and women's liberation later"), a doctrine that would come to haunt later generations of Palestinian women activists.[4] This theory is grounded on the assumption that "rights" somehow automatically flow from membership in the citizenry of a nation-state. For the women in the movement, this concept of rights had a narrow, political connotation linked to suffrage and nationhood. When asked about whether the women's movement worked for women's rights, activists from this period frequently responded by asking, as in the words of Wadi'a Khartabil, the former president of the Tulkarm women's union, "How could women demand rights when the men did not have any?"[5] This view of rights has been tenacious up until recently; a noted, older woman activist in Gaza commented in the early 1990s, "When we have an independent state we can fight for our rights as women. But to fight for women's rights when men do not even have their political rights is nonsense."[6]

This concept of women's rights was embedded in and inextricably interwoven with a legalistic notion of citizenship that could only be conferred by a national government, and that did not address internal, gendered structures and sources of inequities in Palestinian society such as the family or even the national movement itself. The women's notions of rights, democracy, and citizenship precluded the realization that, historically, disenfranchised groups such as women had to actually fight for these rights. As Anne McClintock points out, "No nationalism in the world has granted women and men the same privileged access to the resources of the nation-state."[7] Mere establishment of a sovereign state did not automatically bestow "rights" on women; "the notion of citizenship focuses on the way the *state* acts upon the *individual* and does not address the problem of the way in which the state itself forms its political project."[8] But as we shall see below, the women also manipulated the concept of rights in a novel way as a tactic against the British government, converting ostensibly repressive social practices into rights to be protected.

Perhaps it was only natural and even rational, considering their situation, that Palestinian women took the position they did (or, to be more accurate, did *not*) on women's rights. Khartabil's words resonate, describing the undeniable political reality of statelessness and lack of any kind of political or civil rights, under which (had she but known it at the time) Palestinians would continue to live for decades to come (if not forever, as seems the case as of this writing).

Women in the movement furthermore did not construct themselves solely by gender, but, rather, incorporated notions of their subordination along nationally defined lines, analogous to other women living under colonial hegemonies.[9] Thus, their work for "elevating the status of women" was closely connected to their struggle against the colonizer, the embodiment and usurper of (their) state which, in their view, should have been the agent of change.

One way for Palestinian women to earn their (future) rights as women citizens was through their involvement in the movement, which worked consciously at rehabilitating the image of Arab women. Despite the focus on the national issue, the Arab Women's Association (AWA) continually asserted its identity as a *women's* movement. In doing so, it necessarily grappled with changing definitions of gender that were being discursively constructed via the press, by way of education, through contact with colonialist mentalities and culture, and in women's own expanding experiences in new spheres of activity. Like the British government, the women's movement believed that Arab women must be "reformed," but its goals were diametrically opposed to those of the government, which sought, paradoxically, to "reform" women in order to improve upon and maintain, not transform, the status quo. The status quo that Palestinian women sought to overturn, however, was not sociocultural but rather political, as they defined this term. Clearly, for them "politics" had a distinctive, very explicit connotation—of nationalist politics—divorced from internal socioeconomic politics. "Politics" equated "nationalism," as is illustrated by the response by the president of the Arab Ladies Society when I asked if the organization had engaged in nationalist work as well as social work: "National work—what do you mean? In politics, you mean."[10]

The women's movement reflected the discourse and understandings of a "new woman" paradigm in desiring the creation of a "new," nationally defined Arab woman, who would play her part in helping to preserve the threatened national culture. A major role for this new Palestinian woman was to save the nation through inculcating her children, "the builders of the future," with love of country, courage, and nationalism.[11] Women's traditional domesticity thus was assigned value, reinscribed and imbued with new meaning.[12] Although the term "new woman" was infrequently used by Palestinian women or others (such as the press), the concept was implicit in the way the women expressed themselves through participation in the movement. Their actions, organizational style, writing, and relationships with other groups articulated a new Palestinian Arab woman which syncretized traditional, modern, and reformist attributes. Thus, the Arab woman could simultaneously be "an enlightened and free citizen enjoying equal rights and privileges as her mate," "a faithful wife," "a born mother," and "a loyal patriot to her people and her country."[13]

Significantly, the new woman construct was entirely class-based, reinscribing the roles and functions of a small, elite minority of Palestinian women, while leaving intact those of the majority, the peasant women. Despite accelerating processes of urbanization and industrialization during the course of the mandate in Palestine, by its end, two thirds of its Arab population was still rural.[14] Most peasant women living in Palestine's villages did not receive an education, or participate in the debates over new meanings of womanhood.

But although the primacy of the national problem relegated feminist issues to the background, the women's movement nonetheless developed its own form of indigenous feminism. Elite Palestinian women active in the women's movement interpreted and redefined the new woman to suit their own political and personal agendas. Located within this discourse and their activities in the movement was a subtle, muted, or implicit critique of both internal patriarchal structures (Palestinian Arab) and an externally imposed, colonialist patriarchal structure (British). Sometimes this critique was explicit; when criticized by the press for not allowing newspaper owners to sit in at one of their meetings, the women responded, "The mixing of Muslim women with men depends on men's will. If men accept it . . . to have more usefulness for our country, you'll find us ready and we'll not refuse to meet with them."[15] As one observer remarked, "the spirit of nationalism" helped women develop a "sane and constructive interest in national life," which seemed to point toward gains for women.[16] Yet this spirit of nationalism also limited concepts of emancipation, linking it inextricably to women's ability to work for the nation.

The women's concept of nationalism was nebulous and not clearly defined. This is hardly surprising; the movement was actively involved with, and responding to, continual, escalating crisis, and one has to assume the leadership did not have the time or inclination to sit around theorizing about nationalism when it was demonstrating, participating in strikes and revolts, assisting prisoners, following and challenging diplomatic positions on the Palestine problem, garnering regional and international support, and so on. Furthermore, because the women's movement was marginalized by the mainstream, male-led national movement, the women internalized a gendered division of labor between the two, amorphous, yet sometimes overlapping, movements. (In the 1940s, the mainstream movement acted to incorporate, include, and even issue directives to the women's movement as a constituent part of the overall national movement. See Chapter 7.) Thus, the leaders in the women's movement possibly felt it was not really their role to articulate a specific vision of the future state, although Mughannam's ideas were undoubtedly shared by many of her colleagues. However, there were also major differences in political visions among the women that were not much discussed, revealed, or initially recognized because of the almost constant state of emergency under which the movement operated, as well as the need for unity during the first decade of the movement's existence. James Gelvin has shown how a united "essentialized 'Arab nationalism'" did not really exist after World War I in the Arab Middle East. Different experiences of individuals and groups resulted in disparate articulations of national aspirations. Some of these were complex and seemingly contradictory ideologies that combined expressions of political concepts from the European Enlightenment with more "traditional" social values, for example.[17] These kinds of complexities informed the thinking within the women's movement, as we can only infer from the fragmented record that exists. The answer to the question what kind of nation were the women fighting for? may be unanswerable because of the multiple, disparate, competing, and even overlapping visions of "nation" that they expressed.

The use of competing and conflicting definitions of "the nation" and the "new woman" within the women's movement reflected the tensions in Palestinian society over these issues. These tensions manifested themselves in the movement's leadership, strategies, tactics, internal organization, and public activities, which were in turn influenced by the women's concepts of nationalism, their ideas and use of differing definitions of gender, their links to the male-led nationalist movement, and their relationship to the colonizer.

INTERNAL ORGANIZATION
Leadership: The Arab Women's Executive

The Jerusalem-dominated Arab Women's Executive (AWE) formed at the 1929 congress was the central force in the women's movement in the first years of its existence. (See Appendix II). According to Mughannam, it was "entrusted with the execution of its [the congress's] resolutions and the administration of the Arab Women's Movement."[18] Originally it was supposed to be elected for only the six-month period following the congress, but new elections were held in July 1930. It apparently disappeared as a separate group after about five years,[19] although the distinction between the AWE and the Jerusalem Arab Women's Association (AWA) was nebulous from the start.[20] The identities of the two groups are often indistinguishable in the early 1930s, since the AWE constituted the leadership of both the women's *movement* in Palestine, and the Jerusalem AWA. The government, probably the public, and even the women themselves apparently conflated the two.

The members of the Arab Women's Executive Committee represented an interesting cross-section of women from some prominent and not-so-prominent families, the majority from Jerusalem. During the mandate, Jerusalem dominated the political scene. It was not only the seat of government but also the stronghold of the major nationalist leaders—in particular, the Hajj Amin al-Husayni, who was Mufti of Jerusalem, head of the Supreme Muslim Council, and president of the Arab Higher Committee (established in 1935). The centralization and unity of the administrative system established by the mandate government, with Jerusalem as its center, "enhanced the power and influence of the Jerusalem families who dominated these structures."[21] Some of this rubbed off on the women from these families. The AWA (and, later, Arab Women's Union, or AWU) was also dominated by the Jerusalem leadership and affiliate, although other cities' chapters were active, and developed their own distinct characters.

Most of the women involved in the women's movement were primarily from the urban, educated, middle and wealthier classes that constituted the elite in Palestine. I use the term "elite" advisedly. My definition of "elite" comprises women from family backgrounds whose social and political status derived from wealth, position, or education. This included women from families whose men were merchants, landowners, *'ulamā',* or professionals, the last including a range of occupations: for example, teachers, lawyers, medical doctors and civil servants in the mandate government.[22] A number of women on the AWE were working women or had some professional experience: Melia Sakakini, for example, had a long career as a teacher and school headmistress, and Mary Shihada wrote for her husband's newspaper, *Mirāt al-Sharq*.

There was a common perception (then and now) that the women who could participate in "any basic way" in political organizations were limited to those who were educated, "cultured," and urban, and thus "could run a movement."[23] Nahid al-Sajjadi, who joined the AWA in the 1920s, describes her fellow activist women as educated and well informed; they read newspapers, listened to the news, and "were completely aware of the situation. At that time if you interviewed women from Europe and women from Jerusalem, you would find that women in Jerusalem were better aware of our situation."[24] It is clear from the substance, language, and subject of their numerous memoranda and letters to, and interviews with, the government that the women were extremely well informed about daily political developments, the internal machinations of British diplomacy and mandate politics, and even the latter's legal, economic, and bureaucratic workings.

The social and economic backgrounds of the women's leadership were not necessarily homogeneous and undifferentiated. Women's motivations for, and extent of, involvement could vary according to age, religion, and political consciousness.[25] It is difficult to gauge women's incentive to join the women's groups during the mandate in the absence of direct testimony from the women themselves.[26] Evidence tends to be anecdotal; according to Zlikha al-Shihabi's niece, for example, "political activities were born in her."[27] In interviews, a number of women stressed the desire to "help" as their major impetus. But use of this word is misleading; different women stressed helping "everyone," the "poor," or "the men," thus revealing the multiple social and political meanings inherent in their diverging concepts of "helping."[28] Some women understood the women's organizations as purely voluntary associations whose major objective was to provide services to the poor, whereas others perceived them as a "means by which women mobilized and exerted political pressures," albeit within the framework and structure of traditional benevolent institutions.[29] The 1929 congress, with its call for local chapters and self-conscious articulation of itself as a movement, situated these associations in an explicitly political framework. A certain amount of tension between the two orientations (charitable and political) eventually evolved and caused conflict later on in the movement's history. A number of women—particularly founding members of the movement—

were clearly politically inspired. One gets the impression that some of the leaders lived and breathed their work, and indeed, were merely waiting for an opening to engage in political activity. Matiel Mughannam, referring to the 1929 disturbances, commented, "There are times when you can't do anything except just go out and do something. We had to do something to help the men."[30] It is interesting that the women felt that they *could* "help" the men. This unobjectionable motive, modestly phrased and continually reiterated in the press and interviews, cleverly articulates a rather disguised, collective self-confidence and assertiveness. "Helping the men" provided a convenient pretext for political mobilization.

Clearly, women's impetuses for involvement in the AWA/AWE and their level of political consciousness varied widely. Some AWE members were more comfortable playing inconspicuous roles, such as lending their names to efforts rather than committing their personal time or appearing frequently in public. When the delegation met Chancellor in 1929 after the women's congress, quite a number were still veiled and, as noted earlier, ill-at-ease at attending an interview in mixed company (albeit consisting of one man).

The issues of sectarian tension[31] and religious identity within the women's movement were muted and consciously dismissed both by producers of nationalist discourse (the press and the women's movement itself in its written statements) and by elders remembering the past in interviews.[32] It is clear that common class and educational experiences united women. Sa'ida Jarallah's innocent use of "we" in discussing this issue obviously signified a select group: "We were all the same. We were educated and never felt any difference. . . . We used to live together in boarding schools and . . . [were] members of the same associations. . . . we used to love each other."[33] The Muslim-Christian tie was repeatedly evoked and stressed by nationalists, men and women alike; the women's movement emphasized that the "Muslim women share[d] . . . with their sisters, the Christian women" in the "national women's renaissance."[34]

Women paid deference and attention to religious traditions. The women's movement always commemorated important religious observances; for example, during the feasts after Ramadan, AWA members of both religions would serve meals to the prisoners and provide gifts for their families.[35] However, religious traditions were also evoked to manipulate British reaction. But at the leadership level, religion was a nonissue, and there is little evidence that sectarian tension, to the extent that it existed in the upper echelons of Palestinian society, was reflected within the women's leadership. The AWE counted four Christians among its ten to fourteen members.[36]

A significant number of the women who were most prominent in leadership positions were either youngish and single, or young, married women.[37] The writer of a newspaper article expressed the belief (and indeed, reality) that young, unmarried women were the ones with time to work in women's organizations when, after directly calling upon women to form women's committees, he offers a word of advice: ensure that the majority are formed by young, educated ladies "who don't have a house from which to take flight and a spouse with whom to fight" *(laysa warā'hin lā bayt yahrab wa lā zawj yadrab)*.[38] Single, educated elite women "were young and idealist, and they had the leisure to think, question and discuss the issues of the day."[39] As one woman commented, these women "devoted themselves to the societies, which is better than marriage."[40]

The differences in the roles played by these two groups of women are interesting. The married women tended to be most visible as the official spokeswomen in the earlier years of the movement, chairing big meetings or conferences, speaking at demonstrations, and signing (as officers) tens of memoranda and telegrams. For example, the Arab Women's Congress was chaired by Mrs. Musa Kadhim al-Husayni, wife of the chair of the Arab Executive Committee. It was married women, Mrs. Mamduh al-Nablusi and Mrs. 'Aziz al-Masri, who delivered fiery speeches during a solidarity visit from the women of Jaffa to Nablus after the 1931 demonstration.[41] Married women Matiel Mughannam and Tarab 'Abd al-Hadi delivered the provocative speeches in the Mosque of 'Umar and the Holy Sepulchre in 1933. But the single women ended up remaining in the movement for longer periods of time and dominating the leadership positions to a large degree, holding lengthy tenures in administrative or executive positions. Zlikha al-Shihabi, for example, whose prominence in the movement became more pronounced toward the end of the 1930s, was president of the AWU from 1937 until her death in 1992.[42] Similarly, Zahiya Nashashibi, who became head of the AWA upon the death of Shahinda Duzdar (who also never married) in 1946, held the position until her own death in 1977.[43] Both married and single women attended and participated in meetings held with government officials; these events were less public than demonstrations or speeches. Initially, it seems, the women's leaders were careful to protect the reputations of single women who would have been more vulnerable to censure for maintaining high public profiles, but they also recognized single women's ability to spend extended time performing the work of the organizations by appointing or electing them the groups' officials.[44]

Starting around 1936, during the revolt (and when women students began to organize), single women became more visible as political actors. The fact that such movement stalwarts as Zlikha al-Shihabi, Shahinda Duzdar, Zahiya Nashashibi, and Melia Sakakini would all have been older and more experienced by then suggests that, over time and with age, they were less susceptible to social norms, and/or that these norms were also becoming more elastic for some single, elite women. The support of male relatives also probably helped protect the reputations of many single activist women. Their prominence seems to indicate increasing public (and, importantly, male) sanction of women's activity within the nationalist framework.[45]

Both single and married women discovered in their work in the movement a respectable channel for their energies. Despite the fact that increasing numbers of women began to work outside the home during the mandate, there were nonetheless still few professions open that were considered appropriate for women in the middle and upper classes. Involvement in the organizations contributed meaning and purpose to their lives. Supportive male family members were crucial to most women's ability to become involved. As Ghazi al-Khalili points out, it was primarily women whose family situations allowed them freedom of movement who could participate in women's organizations.[46] Through their involvement, these young women developed leadership skills such as public speaking, negotiating, writing, fund-raising, and organizing. Furthermore, the work was exciting; the leaders of the movement were in the forefront of important political issues and rapidly breaking events, particularly throughout the 1930s.[47] That some women labored decades for the women's organizations attests to the fact that the women received more than just altruistic satisfaction from the work.

Although married women's motivations for involvement paralleled those of single women, marriage itself was an additional factor. The leadership belonged to overlapping, multiple and interrelating networks, some of them based on consanguinity. Many activist women were married to renowned nationalists or men from notable families (often one and the same), from whom they acquired the legitimacy, prestige, and power derived from their husbands' political and social status. The movement's most prominent, married women activists tended to come from or married into the "big" families such as the Husaynis, Khalidis, and Nashashibis, for the most part, whereas the unmarried ones came from less distinguished branches of the notable families. For example, Zlikha al-Shihabi, Shahinda Duzdar, and Melia Sakakini (all single) did not come from big notable families, whereas married AWE members Wahida al-Khalidi, Naʻimati al-Husayni, Tarab ʻAbd al-Hadi, and Anisa al-Khadra did—or married into one. (Matiel Mughannam, notably, did not come from a prominent family.

For some reason, the Christian women who became involved in the movement tended to belong to the less wealthy middle class of professionals.) Interestingly, some of the women who are now remembered as the founders and leaders of the movement came from the "lesser notable" group. It is also interesting to note that, regardless of marital status, the women who were most active on a sustained basis were from less notable families.[48]

Through their marriages and family affiliations, women activists moved in social circles that were inextricably bound up in politics, and their interest in the political situation undoubtedly derived in some measure from its relationship to their personal circumstances. For them, the personal was political. Some women's husbands were government officials who had access to power and information, but were at the same time vulnerable to governmental policies that affected their positions, status, and incomes.[49] Later, during the revolt, some of the women's husbands were imprisoned and/or exiled by the British, which certainly influenced their political involvement. Clearly AWA/AWE members discussed politics with their husbands and were informed and apprised of what was going on within the nationalist movement through their affiliations to the male leadership. Single women had contacts with the male leadership as well, through family connections and friendships.[50]

This communication, knowledge, and influence traveled in both directions. After the AWA wrote a letter to the high commissioner (HC) protesting a series of vicious bomb attacks that killed scores of people in Haifa, Jerusalem, and Jaffa in 1938, Mughannam Mughannam, a member of the National Defense Party and the husband of AWE member Matiel, suggested to its president, Raghib Nashashibi, that they should emulate the women and submit a protest "similar to that submitted by the Women's Association." When Nashashibi refused to "take any such course," Mughannam resigned from the party.[51]

But for women of the elite classes, regardless of marital status, activity in the women's movement also bestowed upon them a sense of power and self-worth, strengthening their individual and collective identities. Zlikha al-Shihabi was, according to those who knew her, "outgoing and brave with a strong personality," "outspoken," and "always in love with her work." The women's work meant so much to many of them that they "forgot about themselves" in it.[52] Their names and that of their organization became known to the public through the press, and to the government through numerous meetings and written communications. The attention they received must have been gratifying, signifying a form of recognition and legitimation of their efforts. There are literally hundreds of articles in the press between 1920 and 1948, for example, in which the main body of the text comprises lists of women who donated money (with amounts included) and reports of their elections, meetings or conferences, and so forth. Sometimes the women are identified only as "the wife of so-and-so," bestowing recognition and credit upon the husbands for the nationalist contributions of their wives. Indeed, one receives a distinct impression that certain leaders, by their very ubiquity in press accounts, may have sought the limelight, or at the least, did not discourage and even enjoyed it.

The class-based aspect of the AWA women's identity resulted in attitudes of both condescension and social responsibility toward village, peasant and poorer women. The organization was not membership-based with a clearly defined constituency, and the democratic procedures were rather limited.[53] Matiel Mughannam revealed elite women's sense of political as well as social hegemony[54] when she responded thus to questions about how the AWA organized rural chapters in the villages: "They brought the poor women to us and we would tell them you should do this or that to better yourself, your children."[55] Zahiya al-Nashashibi described the AWA's work with village women as "spreading nationalist principles among the villagers [and] working toward raising their morale."[56] The sense of distance, superiority, and "othering"—"them" versus "us"—resonates in the very language of such statements. Excluded by gender from the realms of political power available to Palestinian men, AWA members asserted class hegemony over their social subordinates, peasant, village, and poor women, assuming their own leadership role as a given. In their inability to draw in the poorer classes, the women leaders ultimately diluted their own effectiveness. Although they did work with and for the poorer classes more directly than almost any other group, their efforts fell short at including them as constituent, active members or leaders in the movement, reinforcing the class divisions that separated women.

One of the most distinctive attributes of the AWE was the consanguinity between it and the (male) Arab Executive Committee (AE). Five women on the AWE were married to members of the AE: Tarab ʻAbd al-Hadi (ʻAuni), Naʻimati al-Husayni (Jamal), Anisa al-Khadra (Subhi), Mary Shihada (Boulos), and Matiel Mughannam (Mughannam).[57] Melia Sakakini,[58] who was unmarried, was the sister of Khalil Sakakini, also a member of the AE.[59] The president of the AWE, Wahida al-Khalidi,[60] was the wife of Husayn Fakhri al-Khalidi, the mayor of Jerusalem (elected in 1934), a physician and member of the Reform Party (founded in 1935) and the Arab Higher Committee in 1936.

Throughout the early 1930s, the women's movement transcended for the most part the severe factional divisions that fractured the Palestinian nationalist movement as a whole. AWE members came from both of the *hamūlas* (clans) of, or were married or related to, men from competing political factions. Na'imati al-Husayni's husband, Jamal, for example, was president of the Palestine Arab Party, aligned with the Husayni faction, while Matiel Mughannam's husband was secretary of the Nashashibi-dominated National Defense Party.[61] These were the two major political cleavages in Palestinian Arab society for most of the mandate period. The head of the Supreme Muslim Council and the Palestine Arab Party, Hajj Amin al-Husayni, and the head of the National Defense Party, former mayor of Jerusalem Raghib Nashashibi, were bitter rivals for dominance of the national movement. In an interview, Matiel Mughannam said that members of the AWE were "like sisters," and although many of their husbands were from these opposing factions, they were able to maintain unity on the political front. Some women tended to ally with their fellow AWE members, taking different political positions from those of their husbands.[62] Indeed, the women were elevated in the press as exemplars for their unity, as described in an admiring article in *al-Karmil:* "The best thing the women are doing is declaring at every opportunity their desire to distance themselves from factionalism and quarreling and to work for unity. . . . Perhaps this may influence men and dampen if only a little their factional and clannish ardor."[63] Women of Haifa went so far as to publish a pamphlet inciting the men in the national movement to unite and overcome their differences.[64] Comparisons with the men may have created some tensions between the women's and the male-led national movement. But in fact, the women's movement was not as impervious to factionalism as has been commonly believed or stated;[65] conflicts and strains appeared within the movement early on. These did not paralyze it or render it ineffectual, however; the women's movement was more capable of containing and working with dissensions among its ranks, unlike the national movement, whose factionalism ultimately undermined its every effort.

Affiliates of the AWA/AWU

The different affiliates of the AWA (and later, AWU) were organizationally fluid and eclectic; for this reason, their relationship to the movement's Jerusalem center of power is difficult to determine. It is usually impossible to ascertain the branches' founding dates and often, names, which tended to fluctuate, depending upon the source.[66] Many of the chapters of the AWA were probably local women's organizations that predated the 1929 congress.[67] But the momentum of the congress resulted in conscious attempts to either affiliate these groups with the AWA, or help found chapters where they did not exist, particularly in the early 1930s. The Jerusalem women, for example, dispatched a delegation to Nazareth in 1930 to help establish a group there, and similarly, the Haifa AWU traveled to Nablus, Jenin, and Tulkarm in 1935 to do the same.[68] The chapters did not necessarily have uniform, fixed, or corresponding names that explicitly linked them to the "mother" AWA; for example, the Acre women's association was called at one point the Society of the Ladies' Awakening [*jam'iyyat nahdat al-sayyidāt*].[69]

Relations between the different associations were both cooperative and competitive. From the start, groups from one city would demonstrate solidarity and provide mutual aid with those of another, particularly after an incident took place. For example, after the turbulent Nablus demonstrations of 1931, delegations from both Jerusalem and Jaffa visited Nablus, where they delivered speeches and visited the wounded with the Nablus AWA.[70] Quite often, the AWA from one town would join forces with another, as when the women of Jerusalem decided to participate with the Jaffa women in the October 1933 demonstrations.[71] Competition tended to arise over the prominent, indeed dominant, role played by the Jerusalem AWA/AWU, which often took the lead in responding to national crises. In one article, *al-Sirāt al-Mustaqīm* chides the Jaffa women for not working for the benefit of the country like their Jerusalem counterparts; in another, the author extols the exemplary work of the women's union in Acre, noting rather defensively that it "is not inferior to the Jerusalem Union in its level of activity."[72]

Local chapters developed their own distinct characteristics, leadership, and identities, which contributed to some rivalry between them and Jerusalem. The impression received from various sources is that the Jerusalem AWA/AWU, as the center, dictated to the periphery, a portrayal that needs to be modified when one examines the level and type of activity engaged in by other, dynamic affiliates. The Jerusalem AWA/AWU played a more diplomatic and even statesmanlike role in the overall activities of the movement. It was the group that met most frequently with government officials and visiting dignitaries, and had a web of contacts with international organizations, such as other women's associations and nationalist groups such as the Indian National Congress. It was only natural that the Jerusalem organizations played a prominent role, considering their proximity to the seat of government, and their access to information from the corridors of mandatory power. Although it is unclear to what extent the Jerusalem AWA and initially, AWE, directed and centralized the activities of

The Politics of the Women's Movement / 151

the other groups in the 1930s, it certainly dominated the national scene in this period—particularly in representing the movement externally.

The other branches, however, were often more original and militant in style, tone, and tactics. This was particularly true of the Haifa AWU, which was led by the dynamic Sadhij Nassar.[73] This organization was distinguished for its radicalism—particularly in its demonstrations—that resulted on more than one occasion in the arrests of its leadership.[74] The Haifa AWU openly defied not only the British, but also the male-led national movement. In 1933, for example, both the Islamic Society in Haifa and Musa Kadhim, head of the AE, bowed to government pressure, and called for a day of silence to commemorate Balfour Day, canceling previous plans for demonstrations. The Haifa AWU went ahead and demonstrated on their own, however, carrying their children with them (one of their favorite tactics) and taking them around to government offices and various international consulates.[75]

All of the major cities and towns had fairly active chapters of the AWA/AWU, although the ones that received the most publicity were the Jerusalem, Haifa, Jaffa, Acre, and Nablus branches. There is very little information about Hebron and Gaza, although these regions did have women's associations that, apparently infrequently, participated in the women's movement.[76] The women in the coastal areas were particularly energetic in their work on behalf of the detainees whose numbers began to swell during the revolt. The major detention camp for those arrested was in Acre, and women from Jaffa, Haifa, Acre, and Ramla exerted constant efforts to provide food and clothing to prisoners, demand releases and family visits, and protest death sentences. The coastal chapters of the AWA/AWU also tended to be among the most militant. Women in Jaffa were arrested for curfew violations and sparked massive demonstrations of five thousand people more than once when they sent delegations to visit British officials.[77] The Acre group, which frequently coordinated its activities with, and seems to have been colored by, the militancy of the Haifa branch, held lively, massive demonstrations, particularly during the revolt. In response to the high commissioner's appeal to the women of Palestine to cooperate in the restoration of peace to the countryside during the revolt, the Acre women turned around and blamed the government for the situation, stoutly rejecting the role of feminine peacemaker. "The usurpation of the rights of the people is liable to inflame the feelings, and tyranny engenders rebellion," they wrote. "Peace could only be achieved through the administration of justice."[78]

Local leaders developed their own followings and reputations, receiving press coverage and achieving prominence that extended beyond their specific regions. Agitation and competition over local offices developed, particularly when elections were held; these rivalries sometimes were related to the factionalism of the national movement or could be contests for power between leading women. The latter was the case when Wadi'a Khartabil, a new bride arriving from Lebanon, was invited to be the chairwoman of the Tulkarm branch of the AWA in order to defuse the power struggle between two local leading women.[79] The competition between two young women (also in Tulkarm) spilled over into the press in 1935, when the two bandied accusations about each other in letters published in *al-Difā'*.[80] At issue was which one was the rightful secretary of the association; in the course of the vitriolic exchange, one accused the other of "disgusting factionalism," indicating that the national movement's divisiveness did indeed infect the women's movement before its split into two factions itself.[81] However, the prolonged and sustained commitment, involvement, and tenures of certain local leaders indicate the stability of many of these local chapters, and the movement as a whole. Leaders such as Haifa's Sadhij Nassar and Miryam al-Khalil;[82] Acre's Anisa al-Khadra and Asma Tubi; Jaffa's Adele 'Azar; Nablus' Miryam Hashim; and Jerusalem's coterie of stalwarts—Mughannam, Shihabi, Duzdar, Nashashibi, Sakakini—were distinguished for their activity over many years. Yet this stability may have been at the expense of democratic structures within the affiliates and the movement overall; the fact that so many of the leaders were constantly reelected to or held their offices for so long hints that their dominance of the organizations left little room for other women to advance to leadership positions. The response of Layla Mughannam, Matiel's daughter, to questions about this subject, are revealing and somewhat contradictory. She stated: "It was almost like a monarchy. There were two or three people that were up there, that were acknowledged. Nobody tried and nobody cared to be in these positions. Everybody wanted to help and do things, and they knew there were two or three leaders." In the same interview, Matiel commented that, although elections were held, "not much" changed; she herself remained president of the Ramallah women's union for forty years.[83]

The Split

One casualty of the revolt was the united front previously maintained by the AWA. As mentioned, the women had been, for the most part, exemplary in their ability to transcend the divisiveness that characterized the male-led national movement. But the seams of harmony had already been strained before the revolt, and sometime toward its conclusion, the AWA became affected by the factionalism that had intensified to the point of internecine assassination within the national movement. Around late 1938–early 1939, the AWA-Jerusalem split into two groups: the Arab Women's (or Ladies') Association and the Arab Women's Union.[84] Details about the split are elusive, and informants were reluctant to discuss it even almost sixty years after the event, indicating the power the myth of national unity still exerts within Palestinian national memory.[85] However, most agreed on two points: that the fracture into two groups was indeed the result of the Husayni-Nashashibi rivalry (one informant commented that the reason for the split was competition between Zahiya Nashashibi and Zlikha al-Shihabi over the presidency of the AWA); and that the AWU, aligned with the Husayni faction, evolved into the more "political" of the two groups.[86] After the breach, Shihabi, as president of the AWU, played an increasingly prominent leadership role in the movement. Another point of difference was over whether the movement should focus on politics or "social work," with the AWU choosing the former and the AWA the latter.[87]

A third question that has arisen is whether or not the split was the result of a "profound divergence between conservative and progressive tendencies within the women's movement." Rosemary Sayigh suggests that conflict within AWA ranks surfaced over the feminist/nationalist content of the movement, as manifested by disagreement over whether or not women should wear "modern" (Western) dress.[88] The dress issue may not have been necessarily over the conservative or progressive nature of the movement, however, but rather, over culture. Matiel Mughannam, in an interview in the press, equated "culture" with Western dress, implicitly negating Arab cultural traditions:

> All English women think Arab women are uncultured. They believe they speak only Arabic, that they all wear veils and rush away at the sight of a man. How I wish I could take English women around to see my cultured Arab friends. How surprised they would be—European clothes, silk stockings, highheeled shoes, permanently waved hair, manicured hands.[89]

Other women in the movement must have been alienated by the attitude expressed here, and Mughannam was not necessarily representative of most of her colleagues. Certainly some women activists maintained modest dress and continued to veil. In historical photographs of the leadership, women wearing a head covering are a distinct minority, however. Zlikha al-Shihabi, for example, sometimes wore a head scarf but did not veil her face, and photographs of her usually show her without even the scarf.[90] On this issue, there was differentiation within the women's movement by region and sometimes age; women in areas such as Nablus and Tulkarm were more limited in their behavior and dress than women from Jerusalem.[91] Wadi'a Khartabil sent her daughter dressed like a nurse to greet 'Abd al-Qadir al-Husayni, the renowned military hero in the war of 1947–48, when he visited Tulkarm to open the hospital she established in her house. "I couldn't greet him . . . otherwise no one would work with us."[92]

Yet another possible explanation for the internal dissension and the split may have been related to competing and contested visions of nationalism. Disparate notions of nation might have become imbricated with cultural issues as well. The dress issue was clearly about much more than dress. A more conservative, "traditional" nationalism aligned with the male-led national movement may have been the articulation of an ostensibly more "authentic" and indigenous nationalism, which opposed an "alien" and imported Western, liberal democratic style of nationalism that was laced with Enlightenment assumptions about progress and modernity (with Western dress epitomizing an expression of these).[93]

One would infer that those women active in the very political AWU would express a more "progressive" tendency, but in fact, Zlikha al-Shihabi, AWU president from 1937 until her death in 1992, declared at the 1944 Cairo Arab women's conference that "demanding women's rights was before its time."[94] As discussed earlier, "politics" in the Palestinian nationalist lexicon exclusively signified the nationalist issue, and social issues were discursively (but perhaps not substantively) divested of "political" context. This leads one to conjecture that groups such as the AWA and the Women's Solidarity Society (see Chapter 7), which engaged in activities such as founding girls schools in villages, where the need was great, were every bit as "feminist" as the AWU. But despite its ambivalence about the woman issue, its inarticulateness of an ostensibly feminist agenda, and some dissension within its ranks, the women's movement overall increasingly expressed its own form of indigenous feminism.

Another factor that played a role in the split was the formation of an all-Arab Women's Union at the Eastern Women's Conference in Cairo in 1938 (see Chapter 7). One informant suggested that Huda Sha'rawi, the renowned and influential president of the Egyptian Arab Women's Union, actually founded the AWU on a visit to Palestine in 1937, and that the reason for the split was that the "Mufti wanted Palestinian women to mix with other [pan-Arab] women's unions"—perhaps as part of an effort to bolster pan-Arab support for the Palestinian cause, which, in fact, was the major focus of the 1938 conference.[95] This move to become more involved and identified on a pan-Arab level parallels similar developments in the male-led movement in this period. It also takes us back to the issue of nationalism, the nature of national loyalty, and the complexities of women's overlapping, sometimes conflicting identities along the lines of gender, family, religion, and politics. As the political fabric of Palestinian society was straining at the seams, women would inevitably become embroiled in the sometimes deadly internecine struggles. (At least one woman in the movement, in fact, lost her husband as a result of the factionalism.) Clearly the AWA, which had always been engaged on the political level in confronting the British, became enmeshed on the intrapolitical level, and it was this feature that caused the bifurcation into two groups.

The impact the division had on the other AWA branches throughout the country is difficult to ascertain. One source claims that the other groups "went with the Arab Women's Society," while another states that, with the exception of the Jerusalem chapter, the AWA branches all transformed into women's unions in 1938.[96] The AWU apparently became the dominant political force, loosely sanctioned by the main party of the national movement, and most organizations operated loosely under its bailiwick. The use of the word "union" to designate the women's groups became more pronounced, and well-coordinated national activities multiplied.[97] For a period, the AWU increasingly dominated the news, whereas reporting of the activities of the AWA waned. Despite the breach that resulted in two major women's organizations in Jerusalem, actual enmity and hostility was muted, at least publicly. Women from both groups continued to work together at times. A letter to the high commissioner protesting death sentences of men active in the revolt contains the signatures of women from both associations.[98] Interviews and other sources yielded comments such as "it was better to have two groups," "they had mutual respect," and they "worked alongside each other."[99] Still, evidence of resentment and competition does surface. In a 1939 letter to the HC (about Sadhij Nassar's arrest), Shahinda Duzdar and Matiel Mughannam pointedly assert that their committee had "representative capacity on behalf of the different women organizations [sic]."[100] An article about the 1944 Arab Women's Conference in Cairo mentioned that, since one of the two organizations "was allotted more seats at the Conference than the other the latter refused to attend."[101] Several members of the Husayni/AWU faction commented that the AWA was "weak."[102]

"We Women are Not Less Nationalistic Than Men"[103]*:*
The Relationship with the National Movement

The precise nature of the relationship between the Palestinian women's movement and the male-led nationalist movement is a surprisingly elusive and undocumented topic.[104] This contrasts markedly with the fairly extensive record of the women's interaction with the colonial government. Interestingly, historical memory of the mandate generation on this topic differs according to gender. Men who were questioned about interaction between the men and women stated rather categorically that there was "no contact whatsoever" between the groups.[105] Some men even claimed that the women never organized at all or demonstrated during this period. Women, however, contended that the men encouraged the women, and that the women combined forces and coordinated with the men, and there is evidence that supports this.[106] Certainly, by the mid-1940s, the male nationalist leadership began to incorporate the women's movement into the overall national movement (see Chapter 7). Jamal al-Husayni, a member of the AE, praised the women in a letter to the 1929 congress for their "national spirit. ... which [had] changed the common belief that the Arab women were a dead limb of the population." He wrote, "Your voice will prove a source of inspiration to every noble heart."[107] The Supreme Muslim Council welcomed a delegation presenting the resolutions of the congress and donated a meeting place to the newly formed Jerusalem AWA in 1929.[108] As'ad Shuqayri, a prominent member of the Nashashibi-led Opposition, both defended and thanked the women for their participation in the big nationalist demonstrations of 1933 in two newspaper articles, addressing the women directly, and responding to an editorial in which the women (unusually) had been attacked and criticized for their activities.[109] It is apparent from other sources that cooperation, encouragement, and collaboration coexisted with contradictory elements of mutual uneasiness, competition, support, compliance, and defiance (on the part of the women). There is no evidence that the male-led national movement ever envisioned direct participation of women in its own leadership or organizations, other than in supporting roles, such as raising funds for the men's activity.

The women's movement had its own actions, meetings, demonstrations, and subsidiary institutions such as clinics and schools; it maintained a distinct and separate identity and sometimes fought to protect it. Elements of struggle and rivalry between the women and men arose in contests over the women's role in the overall national movement, control of such a role, and how to differentiate the women's groups from constituting the women's "auxiliary" of the nationalist movement.[110] When the Nablus women organized their first follow-up meeting after the 1929 congress to form a local chapter, for example, men intervened in the meeting, attempting to take control of the funds collected by the women. The women decided on the spot that their organization should be independent; they would "never allow men to join," but would "only accept their useful suggestions and their valuable advice, as they would accept the same from the ladies."[111]

There were also tensions and contradictions within the women's movement over the issue of their own organizational and political identity vis-à-vis the larger, male-led nationalist movement. From the very start, women stressed their desire to "be of help to," "share with," and "work side by side with" men.[112] Women's activities were often in support of decisions taken by the male nationalist leadership. (The 1929 congress came in the wake of calls by the AE to organize countrywide meetings of protest.)[113] Numerous statements and speeches from the women's leadership emphasized this point. On the eve of the congress, Mary Shihada, a member of the AWE, wrote an article entitled "We Women Are Not Less Nationalistic Than Men," in which she articulated that "women's duty at this critical stage [is] to stand by our men" and advocated economic activities (economizing, boycotting foreign goods, and being "satisfied with what we have") within a nationalist discourse.[114] The defiant title curiously contradicts the tame content of this article. Despite their declarations of support for the national movement, it is significant that the women's activities were perceived by both them and others not as a "branch" of the national movement, but as a "women's movement," as attested to by the use of this term in numerous articles in the press.[115]

Explicit comparisons by commentators in the press between the women's and men's nationalist activities indicate a certain tension between the two movements. The press tended to extol the women while criticizing the men. One writer noted during the 1936–39 revolt that Arab women sent more telegrams of protest over British policies than the men. Another described how a women's demonstration in Haifa went to Government House "just as the ladies planned for it to, unlike the men's demonstration which never oversteps the government's boundaries." In a third article, the author mentions a pamphlet sent out by the Haifa women calling upon the men to unite. One of the men was so incensed that he demanded the women be punished; the author then adds, "It should be noted that these women were the only ones who raised their voices against the government when some of the men were meeting with the district governor." The women's movement was described by one man as "more organized than the men."[116] There were even external perceptions that the women were more active than the men. One of the British officials at a session of the Permanent Mandate Commission, describing his own encounters with the Arab women, stated that that they "had put forward their views with more emphasis and vigor than their menfolk."[117] For their part, the women responded testily to accusations that they did not "share with the men in their pain and take part with them in public works."[118] In a letter responding to the 1937 Peel Commission's recommendation to partition the country, the women noted defensively that "the Arab ladies are not less concerned than the man with the Arab cause," responding, one infers, to previous criticism.[119] Usually, however, it was the male-led national movement that came in for the greater share of public criticism.

The formalization of the rivalry between the Husayni and Nashashibi factions, with the formation of their respective political parties, the Palestine Arab Party (March 1935) and the National Defense Party (December 1934) intensified the divisiveness that fractured and weakened the nationalist movement during the 1930s. This factionalism disrupted the women's movement from within; it also threatened the relationship between the national movement and the women's movement. An article in *al- Karmil* mentions a "war" between the two movements and hints at a more intense enmity and contentiousness than one is led to believe existed from other sources:

> It appears that the men of the parties who cannot live or breathe except in the choking atmosphere of factionalism exerted their energies against the activity of the women's movement; whereas the gentle sex calls for harmony and concord, the strong sex set screams of divisiveness and discord even among the ranks of the women. There's no doubt that ... the gentle sex declares a war absent of all clemency against the strong. No one but God and those familiar with the ways of women can say which side will emerge victorious.[120]

Clearly, despite memories to the contrary, there *was* coordination and joint actions among the women and men even before the 1940s. Matiel Mughannam, in describing how the women combined forces with the AE, said, "For example, if we were to send a memorandum to His Majesty the King in Britain we wouldn't do it without having the Executive Committee look it over to see if it's alright."[121] Sometimes the coordination among the men and women consisted of the men determining the actions of the women. After the 1931 demonstration in Nablus, the young men of the city held a meeting during which they agreed upon only one decision: a group of women was delegated to present the district commissioner with a protest over arrests of demonstrators.[122] It is unclear to what extent the men may have directed the women during this early period in the women's political activity, although the women's behavior during incidents such as the 1933 speeches and demonstrations was hardly subordinate. A police report claims that the national movement coordinated the women's associations, students, and other groups in spreading propaganda and enforcing the economic boycott as part of the nationalist strategy in the aftermath of the 1933 demonstrations.[123] It becomes more apparent later on when and how the women correlated their actions with, or responded to, the male-led nationalist leadership's calls for specific action. *The Palestinian Encyclopedia*, for example, describes the role of the women's movement in 1936 as one that explained and carried out the decisions of the Arab Higher Committee to other women's groups, despite evidence of women's additional, autonomous action.[124]

Although they cooperated with and even "took orders" from the men to an extent, the women primarily focused on pursuing their own strategies, as deemed appropriate by them, resisting the notion that the men were their "bosses."[125] As demonstrated above, they were sometimes sharply critical of the men's tactics, inaction, and attempts to dominate. What is most interesting is the almost total absence of coeval, male, insider accounts of the links between the national and women's movement. The only "official" historiography that explicitly includes women as active members within the male-led nationalist movement, *The Palestinian Encyclopedia*, is somewhat suspect as a source.[126] In fact, it was the (primarily male) press that provided the major, most positive source of information about the women's movement rather than the male actors from within the nationalist movement.

PUBLIC ACTIVITIES, TACTICS, AND STRATEGIES

Much of the AWA's activity on a variety of fronts during the 1930s was responsive to the national crisis—or, as the women themselves repeatedly called it, "the current situation."[127] Their acts were not merely reactive, however, but were also often "creative" and original, as Sayigh has pointed out.[128] They utilized widely eclectic strategies and tactics, which could be interpreted either as reflective of ambivalence about their identity as new women and actors within the larger nationalist movement, or as indicative of their organizational inventiveness and unpredictability (or a combination of both).

Underlying the tactics and strategies of the women's movement was a complex dynamic that was colored by the movement's relationship to three entities: Palestinian society, the male-led nationalist movement, and the British colonial government. In their public activities—demonstrations, fund-raisers, or declarations in the press—the women were conscious of how they presented both their cause and themselves as its champions. These representations were elaborated within an intricate web constructed of their cultural assumptions about the mentality and attitudes of the colonizer, the Palestinian public, and the international community. They very consciously played upon these assumptions, manipulating and subverting sexual, religious, and class prejudices for their own political purposes. They could be "traditional" when it suited their purposes, yet they also projected a positive self-image constructed of their identity as new women and bourgeois citizens of a future "modern" state. Not surprisingly, their use of these different discourses varied depending upon the audience. When addressing Western and Arab public opinion, they projected the active "faithful" woman citizen, whereas in their interactions with government authorities, they reverted to invoking an essentialized womanhood and "tradition." In a speech before a mixed audience of British and Arab women, Matiel Mughannam, for example, states:

> I feel it incumbent upon me to refer at the outset, to an assumption which, unfortunately, gained grounds in the minds of many people. It has been assumed that the Arab woman was, to say the least, unprepared to share with the man the actual discharge of his duties towards home and country.... History has numerous illustrations which certify to the perseverance, courage and loyalty of the Arab woman. As a loyal wife, a devoted mother and a faithful citizen, she has always fulfilled the role which fell to her in society.[129]

Demonstrations

During the early 1930s, women's increasing participation in mixed demonstrations and later, organization of their own women's demonstrations, signified their willingness to engage in "unladylike" and even violent behavior. In doing so, they defied cultural norms that prescribed limited mobility and visibility of women in the streets. The British government's response to the women's demonstration after the congress in 1929 reveals interesting aspects of the government's approaches toward, and notions of, gender—specifically gender in Arab society. Curiously, the British feared a women's demonstration—which was well organized and rather tame by some standards—to the extent that they threatened to use force against it. Their strategy to suppress it involved coercing the Arab men into a patriarchal collusion that assumed definitions of gender that precluded the concept of Arab women's independent agency. Rather than deal directly with the women themselves, the British government chose to assert and maintain colonial hegemony by suppressing any unseemly, gendered expressions of defiance such as street demonstrations through resorting to involving Arab men in controlling and diluting the women's militancy. Rigid, official British notions of Arab womanhood and Arab gender constructions collided with the potential reality of disorderly, demonstrating Arab women whose public behavior deviated from British normative preconceptions of how women in a "traditional" society should behave. In order to elide this disjuncture, the British government deferred to patriarchal notions (both their own and their assumptions about those of Arab men) about both Arab manhood and womanhood. At issue was who actually wielded authority over the women's actions. Interestingly, the Arab men were reluctant participants in this collusion, unlike in other colonial situations.[130] (It will be remembered that in the 1929 demonstrations the men intervened only after being threatened. See Chapter 5.)

The British government also clearly feared "infringement of certain 'moral' borders" associated with women as "moral symbols." As Rema Hammami and Eileen Kuttab point out, discussing the contemporary Palestinian women's movement, "physical attacks on women pose a moral challenge to the occupiers' sense of their own moral superiority. As such, occupiers are loathe to physically attack women.... At the same time the reason women challenging borders is so symbolically powerful is precisely because it breaks down a notion that women are controlled by their men."[131] One can see the historical roots of these dynamics during the 1933 demonstrations in Jerusalem and Jaffa when the British government's worst fears were realized: they were perceived as attacking defenseless women. This act delegitimized them in the eyes of both the Palestinian and international community. The government interpreted its own actions as having provoked male outrage, and upset "tradition." The AE complained to the government about women being struck by police, who compiled a special report in response to their grievances. (Interestingly, the AWA sent a delegation to the high commissioner to demand the release of *men* who had been arrested in the demonstrations and protest the British "atrocities" in firing upon the crowd. They did not complain about their own mistreatment.)[132]

The 1931 and 1933 demonstrations illustrate the working of the multiple dynamics among the British authorities, Palestinian men, and Palestinian women. It was the practice of the British authorities to separate women and men during demonstrations in order to deal with the men by force while avoiding physically harming the women. The police had orders at the 1933 Jaffa demonstrations to "endeavor to get women and children away before action, and on no account strike them" unless their own lives were endangered. The Palestinians, for their part, in marching with the women enclosed by the men, or merely by having women involved in the demonstrations at all, were able in some degree to protect both women and men: the women were out of range of the clubs of the police, yet their very presence in the midst of the men acted as a deterrent to police violence, or, as the police bitterly observed, "as a buffer between the mob and the Police." The police, all too aware of the Palestinians' strategic intentions in including women in demonstrations, complained in their report, "the women are brought into the plan of campaign solely for the purpose of embarrassing the Police." This was a common tactic in mixed demonstrations, as used in Nablus in 1931.[133] However, young men or Boy Scouts frequently accompanied the women to "look after" them or prevent the crowd from mixing with them and presumably, protect them from harm from both the British and/or the roughness of the street.[134]

Women's actions in the early 1930s demonstrate an increasing awareness among both the nationalist and women's movements of an important and positive role women could play as foils to British brutality. By exploiting British fears and timidity about upsetting patriarchal "tradition," the women could exercise a certain amount of power and control, both by restraining the violence of troops and police and also by affecting how such incidents were presented to and perceived by the public.

Starting in 1935–36, as the strength and autonomy of the women's movement developed, women began increasingly to hold their own, segregated women's demonstrations, unlike the years 1931–33. Men—especially young men—often continued to participate in these protests primarily as guards. This change suggests that women's aims in demonstrations may have shifted to focusing primarily on the attraction of as much publicity as possible, an endeavor for which the women's movement was well equipped. They also may have become aware that they could attract larger crowds of women to sex-segregated demonstrations, thus dramatizing the events and increasing their impact by organizing massive groups of women. (Many of their demonstrations from 1936 on were very large.) A third explanation for these demonstrations could be that, with the heady upheaval of the 1930s and the greater mobilization of women (as with the overall Palestinian Arab population), the movement's leadership reacted logistically and strategically by staging women's demonstrations. It is unclear from the record whether they were responding to events or initiating an explicit organizational strategy. Finally, yet another possible explanation for this phenomenon could be related to the beginnings of a conservative backlash during the revolt, as discussed in Chapter 5. The women may have adapted their demonstrating strategies in order to fend off criticism and attack from some critics. None of these potential explanations is mutually exclusive; the fluidity of the situation and the women's increasing organizational experience argue for a number of possibilities.

The Press

The 1929 First Arab Women's Congress received much fanfare and press coverage. The three major Arabic papers of the 1920s, *Filastīn*, *Mirāt al-Sharq*, and *al-Karmil* all covered it, as did *Filastin*-English and the *Palestine Bulletin*. This was not purely serendipitous. Early on in its history, the AWA drew attention to gender, manipulating its normative meanings in Palestinian society to dramatize women's acts and produce effect. One method by which they attempted to achieve this was to draw attention to, embellish, and emphasize the novelty and historical significance of women engaged in certain activities for the first time; for example, one of the delegates who attended the 1929 meeting with the high commissioner stated self-consciously in her speech, "This is the first time in history that Arab women indulge in political activities." The women continued this strategy of signification by counting, emphasizing gender and the singularity of their actions by stressing, for example, that "this is the *second* time in our awakening that we have announced that the Arab nation would not accept this injustice." These enumerative litanies were used, almost as a method of recording, as well as a means of gaining attention. They appeared not only in the press but also, repeatedly, in protest meetings with the high commissioner, where women intoned, for example, that it was the "third or fourth time only in the history of the Arab Women [sic] Movement" that women "interfere[d] in politics."[135]

The press colluded in this counting strategy, also utilizing these phrases in their coverage of the women's activities.[136] Press reports of the 1929 congress all heralded the event as "the first time in history" Arab women had organized a women's congress, or entered the world of politics.[137] Such phrasing became a signature that distinguished discourse about women, used for any and everything; whenever the word "first" or the phrase "for the first time" appeared in a headline, it acted as a coded signifier, practically guaranteeing that the article that followed was about women. Articles appeared about the "first Muslim woman dentist," the "first Arab woman to be conferred with the honor of arrest in Palestine," "the first time an Arab lady addressed [a particular] club," "the first time that Tulkarm ladies demonstrated," "the first time that Arab women in this district (Beersheba) shared men's struggle," and so forth.[138] In fact, the Arab Women's Congress was explicitly called the *First* Arab Women's Congress, and the Executive Committee was named the Executive Committee of the First Arab Women's

Congress. The mnemonic use of this word indicates a high level of self-consciousness on the part of the women. They intended to be noticed. Furthermore, the evidence strongly indicates that the women fed the press "inside" news about the congress. Matiel Mughannam and her husband were close friends of the al-'Isa family which owned both *Filastīns*.[139] The detailed article that *Filastin*-English published about the congress on the very day during which it took place demonstrates insider knowledge.[140]

Women's participation with men in demonstrations was also part of the strategy to ensure publicity for their actions and the Palestinian nationalist cause. They deliberately exploited normative gender proscriptions in order to dramatize and propagandize. Women's demonstrations received more extensive and sensational press coverage than mixed ones, grabbing big headlines.[141] Use of the words "women" or "ladies" in headlines, analogous to the "first time" phrase, also acted as coded signifiers, alerting the reader to novel and noteworthy events.[142] The women even enlisted their children to dramatize these happenings, bringing them along to demonstrations. At one such demonstration in Haifa, the children presented a banner that read "We want to know our fate!" to the district governor.[143]

The press was a constant, enthusiastic partisan of the women's movement, regardless of the particular political orientation of the newspaper. A remarkable, mutually cozy relationship developed, whereby the press assiduously reported every little activity engaged in by the women's movement, be it a tea party or a donation to charity by one of its leaders.[144] Its statements, telegrams, and other missives were often quoted verbatim. When asked why the press provided so much positive coverage of the women, one of the surviving members of the al-'Isa family responded that it was "because the women's activities were part of the national activities, and the women were very vocal and very strong in the national movement."[145]

But the complicity and cordiality between the press and the women also derive from a common discursive agenda involving the construction of a positive, active image of the "modern" (elite) Arab woman. This agenda involved targeting both the Arab world—in attempts to garner sympathy and solidarity abroad—and the West, including the colonizer. Both the journalists who covered them, and the women themselves, were acutely aware of Western, negative portrayals of Arab women as backward and degraded. This is evidenced by articles that engaged in a one-sided, imagined dialogue with the West, such as the one in which women provided "answers" to Western "accusations" of their apathy and nonparticipation in "national life."[146] It was crucial that they projected a countervailing, positive image—particularly to the British public, which could influence their adversary, the

British government—that depicted a "civilized" and "enlightened" woman who was capable and deserving of representing her society as worthy of independence. The following excerpt from a newspaper article expresses this most eloquently (Significantly, it was reported in the English-language version of *Filastin*).:

> It is gratifying to be able to inform the West and Westerners that an end is being put to their misconceptions of the Arab woman and her alleged slavish status. The Arab woman is not, as most Westerners think, a veiled creature hidden behind screens in voluptuous Hareems [sic] of wealthy Pashas and Beys. She is an enlightened and free citizen enjoying equal rights and privileges as her mate, and participating in his political activities.[147]

The contrast is striking between the silence of the male nationalist leadership about the women's movement and the effusive male discourse on the subject as articulated in the press. This dichotomy points to differences among the male elite; intellectuals (if one can so designate the press) expressed, by and large, more progressive views on the women's actions and the overall issue of gender, whereas the male nationalist leadership was rather mute on these subjects. Underscoring the silence on the one hand and support for the women on the other, were tensions within the male-led nationalist movement itself. Although the evidence on the attitude of the male leadership toward the women's movement is regrettably scanty, indications from the press point to tensions between conservative (and perhaps older) men and more radical (younger) men within the movement.[148] This leads one to believe that the women's activism, and the positive notice it received, constituted a potential threat to male hegemony of the national movement—particularly the more established and traditional leadership. Myriad newspapers that criticized the mainstream Husayni-dominated national movement simultaneously praised and encouraged the women's activities—many if not most of which were in explicit support of the former, reflecting some of the complicated political contradictions within Palestinian society over gender and nationalism.[149]

Defiance and Deference: The Weapon of the Word

Although women were active in demonstrations and actions that attracted attention in the press, they were more comfortable engaging in a form of protest that was less controversial and upsetting to the patriarchal social order, that is, use of the written word. The AWA sent virtually hundreds of telegrams, letters, and memoranda—practically daily—to the British government, sympathizers in the British press and public, the League of

Nations Permanent Mandates Commission (PMC), Arab kings and heads of state, and other women's organizations throughout the world. Written protests allowed women to attract maximum publicity via the press without actually being visible in the streets. One factor that contributed to the women's penchant for written protest was their educations, which had inculcated in them a belief in the power of the written word. An indication of the significance they ascribed to this form of communication is the fact that the AWE had two secretaries, one in Arabic (Katrin Dib) and one in English (Matiel Mughannam). Often the AWA/AWE would send appeals outside the country, as exemplified by a pamphlet entitled "An Appeal to Every British Woman Wherever She May Be," which outlined the Arab position on the "causes which brought about . . . the present critical situation" during the 1936 revolt.[150] The class base of the movement's leadership also undoubtedly was a factor in the women's feeling a greater sense of ease deploying this more genteel form of political activity. Despite the fact that many of the leaders of the movement were "exempt" to an extent from some of the more restrictive social norms of Palestinian society, due to the support of male relatives and the "cover" of their nationalist work, nonetheless this remained a society where upper-class women did not normally mix freely with unrelated men, or regularly appear in public engaged in nontraditional or physical activity, such as defying curfews, demonstrating in the streets, and battling with police. For many upper-class women, challenging society's norms engendered intense discomfort and provoked criticism from conservative elements, although, as we have seen, a number of the movement's leaders courageously flouted these norms.

The AWA's focus on wielding the weapon of the word reveals inherent complexities and contradictions in the nature of the women's relationship to the colonialist ruler. Their use of certain styles of writing and repeated references to particular themes also reflected their ambivalence about their own identity as new women in the political order. The discursive style of the AWA wavered between two diametrically opposed characteristics: deference and defiance. One articulated notions of their own responsibilities as bourgeois citizens engaged in state-building (however hopefully, under colonial rule) within the formal sphere of official and diplomatic politics and organizations; the other comprised the language of protest and even rebellion.

In the first, they were correct, legalistic, and formal, which robbed their indignation of its moral power, sting, and outrage. In their salutations, for example, no matter how heated the rhetoric of protest and accusation in the text, they invariably addressed the high commissioner as "Your [or His] Excellency" (*fakhāma*), used the royal plural, and signed off with such phrases as "please accept this with highest respect" (*wa tafaddalū bi-qabūl fā'iq al-ihtirām*).[151] Although one must take into account the formal and ornate style of written Arabic (particularly in salutations), the contrast between the message and the medium often disconcerts.[152] After lambasting the government for atrocities, the women would make conciliatory, self-deprecating statements, such as "we do not of course profess competence to give any advice on such an intricate problem" (which they then proceeded to do) or disclaimers like "no one doubts the good intentions of the government towards the people" (which were already negated by their forceful condemnations).[153]

In their second, defiant incarnation, they used strong, condemnatory language that bordered on menacing. In one letter, they accuse the government of being "a hired tool" in the hands of the Jews:

> They order and you obey. They make suggestions and you carry out their suggestions. They demand and you grant. . . . You deport no one of their men and impose no fines on them. . . . You apply to us the most drastic measures and treat them with the maximum measure of leniency and kindness . . . we protest against your discriminative [*sic*] and unwise policy and hold you responsible for all consequences. Let it be known to you and the Jews that the country is ours and that we are neither weak nor cowards.[154]

Often, letters or proclamations (*bayānāt*) would combine elements of both styles, producing an ambiguous and confusing effect. In one letter in which the women express outrage at the "deplorable conditions" in the country and government's measures of "intimidating" and "compelling" the Arabs, they nonetheless mention they find this surprising, considering that the British government has "played the leading part in defending weak nations against . . . aggression."[155] They played two roles simultaneously: those of woman citizen and nationalist rebel. Perhaps this was a deliberate "good cop, bad cop" strategy on their part. Indeed the contradictory tones may have been a shrewd tactic on their part, deliberately calculated to put the British off guard and confuse their assumptions about Arab women.

The fervor and frequency with which the women's movement resorted to the tactic of the written word reflect a certain trust in the British government and institutions, however, that seems unwarranted in retrospect. Palestinian Arabs of a certain class had the notion that the British were somehow responsive to notions of "British justice," which was evoked mnemonically in correspondence. Throughout the mandate period, surprisingly, the Arabs thought of the British character as "the incarnation of honesty, justice, courage and integrity."[156] (These idealizations, needless to say, were inculcated via the educational system in Palestine.) Fa'iza 'Abd al-Majid, appealing for the release of prisoners in the 1940s, transformed the myth of Britain's "world famous sense of justice" into "democratic justice, which was and still remains, the fundamental British generous character."[157] The AWA, by entreating repeatedly (and vainly) to "British justice" in its correspondence, tried to shame the British into living up to this high-minded concept, as is illustrated by a desperate-sounding telegram sent during the Arab revolt to a British sympathizer. It says in part: "Traditional British justice nowhere, confidence lost; hopes frustrated . . . entreat you in the name of humanity to put an end to Chaos and Tyranny; protect British honor; don't break Arab Moslem friendship forever."[158]

The women were careful to differentiate between the "British public" or "nation" and the government in a kind of propaganda war, attempting to drive a wedge between the government and public opinion. Matiel Mughannam, for example, in a speech delivered in 1929, stated, "When I say, the British Nation, I do not mean the Colonial Office, I mean the British public which cannot but feel with oppressed people, who ache for, and are entitled to liberty, and freedom!"[159] Ultimately, despite expressions of adversity, the women did not express outright, sustained expressions of hostility toward the British in their writings, revealing an ambiguous relationship with the colonizers and all that they represented.

COLONIZED AND COLONIZER: THE WOMEN'S MOVEMENT AND THE BRITISH GOVERNMENT

The Palestinian women's movement developed a complex relationship with the British Mandate government, resulting in their pursuit of tactics and strategies that were often riddled with contradictions. These contradictions reflected women's—and Palestinian society's—ambivalence about changing definitions of gender, and expressed concrete notions of class. These two constituent elements of their identity frequently clashed, creating further inconsistencies in the discourse and actions of the women's movement. Palestinian middle- and upper-class women were also caught between the sometimes competing, sometimes compatible ideologies of womanhood constructed through multiple cultural referents. Education at the hands of and exposure to the British sometimes came into confrontation with the values and divergent, overlapping cultures which constituted Palestinian society.

The women were crafty and perceptive in their understanding of the British government and its self-image of embodying "British character," referring to the latter in order to hoist the government by its own petard. Playing upon British attitudes about gender, class, "tradition," and justice, the women exploited these for their own purposes. They perceived contradictions between the government's policies and the British "world famous" sense of justice—contradictions to which some British officials were not impervious.

Manipulating Tradition

The women's movement was cognizant of British sensitivity to upsetting the religious, cultural, and social status quo in Palestine, and they were aware of how they, as Arab women, were viewed. They exploited this sensitivity at every turn. One of their major weapons was thus to resort to "tradition" and "religion," using them in both a "calculated and creative" manner.[160] Palestinian women invoked transgressions against "tradition" and "religion" constantly in an effort both to affect British policies and measures to enforce them (particularly during the revolt) and to shame and alarm the British. The British were very susceptible to such attacks, issuing cautionary communications to troops during the revolt, for example, about respecting "both mosques and women," thereby conflating and/or equating the two as metonyms for religion.[161] The women repeatedly brought up incidents in which "sacred Arab traditions [were] violated, mosques desecrated and [the] Holy Quran trodden upon."[162] One can only infer, through the women's continual deployment and reiteration of such phrases—strategically publicized in letters, telegrams, and the press—that they knew full well the consternation such complaints would arouse in the government.

Not only did the AWA prey upon British sensitivity to Muslim affairs, they also slyly played the Christian card as well, deflecting the issue of religion back toward the British, appealing to their Christian identity while at the same time implicitly (or even explicitly) comparing British rule—negatively—with previous, non-Christian authorities. In the meeting with the high commissioner in the wake of the 1933 disturbances, Melia Sakakini attempted to shame the "Christian government":

> I feel very reluctant as a Christian to express my deep indignation. . . . The Government of Palestine is said to be a Christian government and as such should govern the country with Christian tolerance. We lived under the Turks for 1300 years and we were not molested. No such atrocities were committed then as are committed now.[163]

A letter from the AWA to London uses a well-placed reference to Christmas by concluding with the request for a "Christmas gift" from the government in the form of release of detainees and cessation of searches in the villages during the revolt.[164]

The most frequent issues raised by the movement, however, were transgressions against the "traditions" of seclusion and sexual segregation, practices they as a group rarely engaged in.[165] Leaders constantly referred to the "Muslim women" among them, and drew attention to the novelty of their appearing in public. Ladies who had kicked the gates of government office, "done all they could to urge the male members of the demonstrations to defy Police orders," and stood on a balcony "inflaming" the (male) crowd during the 1933 Jaffa disturbances, turned around and attended a meeting with the High Commissioner at which they demurely declared that "the traditions of Arab women, especially the Moslems among them . . . would normally prevent them from calling on Your Excellency or any officer of Government."[166] This particular line was used over and over again to excoriate the government and turn accusations around; thus women could blame the government for "forcing" them to engage in protest activities that sometimes turned violent. After the 1933 Nablus demonstrations, the women's delegation that met with the governor of the city opened their meeting with the statement:

> It is not the custom of Nablus women to leave their houses and interfere in the sphere of politics . . . and it is not part of the Islamic social tradition for them to surpass men and interfere in their affairs, but the incidents in Nablus and the tribulation that has fallen upon them due to the government's behavior and policies had made the Nablus women leave their houses and depart from their sacred tradition to join their voices to the voices of the men. . . . Muslim women are not allowed to have interviews with men, but they were forced to that to protest the behavior of the police and the government's policy.[167]

At the same time the women referred to the "traditional rights" of Arab women "to live in dignity and away from the mixing with men" (a phrase that, ironically, comes from a statement by Matiel Mughannam, a Christian).[168] By implying that tradition conferred upon them special rights, the women were able to subversively convert the ostensibly oppressive practice of sexual segregation into a "right" that made British abrogations of this practice seem heinous and called into question "British justice" and the moral authority that ostensibly legitimized colonial rule. Women's innovation in departing from "tradition," and the dichotomy between their actions and public discourse were justified by nationalism, allowing them to subvert and manipulate gender limitations, turning them upside down, and converting them into a tactical weapon.[169] They appropriated "tradition" to suit their own political agenda.

During the revolt, in particular, one issue about which the women constantly complained was body searches of Arab women,[170] which "offend[ed] their womanly sanctity" and were "a contempt for the traditions and religions of this country and inconsistent with chivalry and honour."[171] Indeed, the British were acutely sensitive to this issue, paying particular attention not only to recruiting women inspectors, but also to suppressing information about some of the more controversial aspects of these inspectors, such as the fact that most of them were Jewish.[172] In a communication to the censors, the district commissioner directs that one matter that "should *not* be mentioned in telegrams" was "the fact that Jewesses search Arab women."[173] During the revolt, the British even went so far as to establish specific hours when only women could enter certain gates to the Old City in Jerusalem.[174]

Both the women and the British invoked essentialist concepts of womanhood in their dealings with each other, albeit maneuvering these for different purposes. The women claimed special sensibilities and authority as interlocutors in the conflicts between the national movement and the government, based upon gendered stereotypes such as women's innate tenderness and the sanctity and moral symbology of motherhood.[175] Speaking as mothers, rather than mere women, resonated with universal appeal and special authority. The women were cognizant of the effectiveness of this trope since "no one wants to be seen as attacking mothers."[176] Thus their tactic of bringing their children to demonstrations was calculated to invoke their moral, maternal authority. In the meeting between the high commissioner and the AWA after the 1933 demonstrations, the women stated, "We as mothers and wives seek peace . . . we as ladies suffer more than anyone else when we see such misery as exists."[177] In his response, however, the high commissioner opines that the women should use these special qualities for moral policing in order to rein in the men: "Ladies have much influence . . . in this country," he notes. "I beg you to use your powerful influence towards the restoration of peace and good order in Palestine."[178]

British Responses: Man to Man

Despite politely worded professions of respect for the "ladies," the British authorities took pains to ensure that the women did not step out of line by utilizing their own manipulation of tradition in order to facilitate administration, mediate conflict, and impose control. Patriarchal collusion was their favorite tactic to both suppress and control women's demonstrations. When a demonstration of women and girls in Safad was planned during the revolt, government officials enlisted the assistance of "notables and elders" to prevent it, much like they had in the Jerusalem demonstration in 1929.[179]

The British government not only engaged in patriarchal collusion, but also, ironically, coerced the men into upholding and enforcing not only traditional, ostensibly Arab gender norms but also its own restrictions on women. In 1936, when the Jaffa AWA attempted to hold a meeting, they were informed by the government that their association was not legal because it did not have a permit. Instead of dealing directly with the women, the government delegated two Arab male officials to negotiate with the (male) national committee and imposed upon it the condition that it prevent the public from mixing with the women when they entered and exited the meeting.[180]

The British reaction to the AWA, as revealed in the discursive style of their own writing, mixed perplexity, caution, contempt, and paternalistic condescension. The following diary entry of an official, reporting on an incident mentioned above involving Sadhij Nassar, is worth quoting at length for its tone, which provides a subtle illustration of this condescension:

> The police reported at 9 o'clock that a procession of women (the same ones that serenade these officers periodically) was forming in the Suq and that they and various 'street Arabs' were intimidating shopkeepers. [Skirmishes then took place between the police and the youths] ... The women left the Suq and returned to their usual post under the District Commissioner's office and did not disperse until the three ringleaders were removed in a prison van and released at a sufficiently great distance from Haifa to keep them busily occupied for some time walking back.[181]

(Less than a year later, this same officer defended the arrest and detention without trial of Sadhij Nassar, whom he described as "actively engaged in subversive propaganda," and who "should have been dealt with long ago," demonstrating that a year's time had transformed flippant contempt into repressive action.[182])

The British maintained a superior and remote public posture in their numerous meetings with the women, uttering unctuous expressions of "great sorrow" and "sympathy" with them, while rarely promising specific action that addressed their grievances.[183] Despite its ostensible composure (as exemplified usually in the person of the High Commissioner) the British government nonetheless engaged in surveillance against, and compiled many intelligence reports about, the women's movement. It took some care in responding to the women's litany of complaints, and noted their reactions in meetings. When Chancellor met with the delegation in 1929, he described in some detail an incident whereby several of the women refused to take coffee with him because they said it was the custom of the Arabs to eat and drink only in houses of their friends, and therefore they would not touch the refreshments offered to them.[184] He remarks: "Such a breach with the Arab traditions of the courtesy due to a host in his own house is significant of the bitterness of the hostility now felt towards the Government in certain quarters."[185]

The British government also found itself compelled to respond to international pressure produced by the publicity efforts of the women's movement. Voluminous correspondence resulted from outrage over Sadhij Nassar's arrest in 1939, for example; Mrs. Corbett-Ashby, president of the International Alliance of Women for Suffrage and Equal Citizenship, wrote about Nassar's detention.[186] Government files are replete with letters from different groups responding to appeals and complaints by the women's movement over various government measures. The government often replied defensively to this correspondence, sometimes issuing special reports, as in the case of the 1933 incidents and Sadhij Nassar.

In fact, the relationship between the women leaders in the movement and British government officials was more ambivalent than one should assume by merely reading the correspondence between them. Some of the Palestinian women lived the contradiction of targeting government officials for criticism while simultaneously socializing with their wives at charity events or tea parties. These women clearly had more in common and could better identify with British women of a certain social class than they could with their own countrywomen in villages. Mughannam's idea of "culture" illuminates how certain Palestinian women felt bonds of class and culture with the colonizer. Others, however, felt British exclusiveness and condescension; class played a role in differentiating women's experiences. Julia 'Awad, who came from a modest background and worked for many years for the YWCA in Jerusalem, said that the British were "horrid," "looked down on us," and "felt superior."[187] The close relationship between some elements of the Palestinian population and the British is a touchy topic and not often discussed in the sources, but the traces of its existence are unmistakable in the utterances of women such as Mughannam, who constantly appealed to the West for support. Her pro-British sympathies may well have been one of the underlying sources of tension that led to the split in the women's movement, as well as contributed to the deferential discourse in the AWA's correspondence with the government.[188]

CONCLUSION

The evolution of the women's movement during the first decade of its existence reflected its ambivalence about changing gender definitions and new constructions of Arab middle-class womanhood; the relationship between the women's and the male-led nationalist movement; middle-class women's role as "modern," future citizens in a nation-state; and even about the role of the colonial government. But although the mechanisms and dynamics of the movement were in some respects expressions of ambiguity, its position on the issues of nationalism and the preservation of Palestinian society was unequivocal.

Although its narrow class base limited its effectiveness, the women's movement played an important role in the nationalist struggle. The women were often among the most militant groups in Palestinian society to oppose the British government's policies. They did not engage in the backroom negotiating and factional backstabbing that rendered the male-led nationalist movement ultimately ineffective, despite experiencing their own internal divisions. Unlike the men, they were usually able to transcend the paralysis born of factionalism, despite its existence in their own movement.

The Palestinian women's movement in this period was not "feminist" in the sense that it did not strive for political, legal, social, and economic equality with men. Yet the women in the movement demonstrated their own indigenous kind of feminism, whereby they manipulated and exploited gender norms in order to subvert and challenge power structures. Gender and an implicit critique of gender relations were major elements in their oppositional strategies and tactics. They pushed against the boundaries within which gendered social practices confined them, yet they calibrated their own militancy to the particular times of crisis to which they responded. Afsaneh Najmabadi, studying Iranian women in the early twentieth century, has suggested that women's ostensibly conservative discourses were actually both "disciplinary and emancipatory" at the same time. Women accepted—and in some cases even embraced—seemingly repressive ideas and practices, transforming them in the process and converting them for their own liberatory purposes.[189] Palestinian women, in simultaneously articulating support for "tradition" while transgressing its norms, chose to utilize it as a tool that, ironically, empowered them to behave radically in the name of its defense. When it seemed relevant, they invoked "tradition" and religion; when it seemed significant, they situated themselves as modern women citizens in the emerging Palestinian polity. This very duality and flexibility, however, left them open and vulnerable to shifting social winds, including conservative backlashes.

Toward the end of the 1930s, as the revolt wound down, the conciliatory element in the women's discourse became more pronounced. Shortly after Great Britain entered World War II, there is a curious reference in *al-Difāʿ* to a decision by the women's union to "stop its work for an indefinite period" due to the "influence of the international circumstances."[190] Yet, several weeks after this announcement, articles reappear about the group's activities.

The ten-year period from the movement's inception in 1929 until the end of the revolt in 1939 was a turbulent, energetic and, in many ways, heady era for the women's movement. After the revolt, the women's movement changed directions and began to focus its efforts increasingly on service-oriented activities, reflecting a kind of institutionalization of itself, and a deepening response, not just to the national crisis, but also to the effects this crisis produced on Palestinian society.

7   Pan-Arabism and the 1940s

After the tumult of the revolt, the onset of World War II paradoxically initiated a period of deceptive calm and even stability during the first half of the 1940s in Palestine. In 1939, the British unilaterally published the White Paper, after intense negotiations in London between various Palestinian, Jewish, and Arab state delegations. It provided for the establishment of a Palestinian state within ten years, with the proviso that Arab-Jewish relations at that point "'would make good government possible' "; tighter restrictions on land sales to Jews; limitations on Jewish immigration to seventy-five thousand over the next five years; and the appointment of "some Palestinians to head certain departments [in the government], once peace was restored."[1] Although officially the Arab Higher Committee (AHC) rejected the White Paper, public reaction was less negative, and the early years of the war "saw a quiet, low key dialogue between the government and Palestinians who were ready to accept the White Paper."[2]

Despite the lack of a settlement to the national conflict, a certain political quiescence and (in retrospect, precarious) social stability prevailed in the early 1940s. Overall economic conditions improved due to the demands of the war, which produced a "tremendous expansion of wage labor," employment in the public sector, and a "psychology of growth."[3] "Prosperity was everywhere in evidence," and a kind of lull in hostilities ensued among the battle-weary British, Palestinian Arabs, and Jews, resulting in "a peaceful period of coexistence.... Both sides to the strife seemed to forget their enmity of over twenty years and to relax."[4] Palestinians focused their efforts on seizing the opportunities offered by the improved and rapidly developing economy. Urbanization and labor union organizing intensified, particularly in the coastal areas, where heavy industry and shipping were located; agricultural wages rose as well, injecting new prosperity into the rural economy.⁵ "Even the villagers in the forties were well off, living on their own land and planting it."⁶

The first half of the 1940s also witnessed a cultural and social efflorescence in Palestinian Arab society, particularly among the educated elite in the towns and urban localities, but also spreading into villages and rural areas. Sports and literary clubs were founded, and Palestinians increasingly attended lectures, concerts, poetry readings, and theater presentations. The Palestine Broadcasting Service, established in 1936, developed special programs for women and girls, such as the "Talk to Women" series and the eight-part series in 1941 on "The Modern Arab Home."⁷ Prominent women renowned for their political, charitable, or literary endeavors often broadcast on the radio.⁸ The bigger cities in Palestine hosted traveling theatrical and musical productions featuring much-beloved and acclaimed Arab artists such as the Egyptians Umm Kulthum, Najib Rihani, and Yusuf Wahba.⁹

The period witnessed mounting pan-Arab sentiments and involvement throughout the Mashriq, as politicians from the other Arab states increasingly played an active role in attempts to resolve the Arab-Jewish conflict. The disjuncture between the "crescendo of nationalist cries that Palestine . . . arous[ed] in the general public," divisions among Arab leaders, and fears about confronting Western interests, resulted in confusion and the diffusion of real unity, professions of the same notwithstanding.¹⁰ "By 1945 Palestine had become firmly embedded in the emotions and consciousness of a young generation of educated Arab nationalists and the generally aware populaces of the urban centers."¹¹ Arab women of this generation shared this consciousness, articulating their concern through pan-Arab social and political organization and an extensive network of contacts with one another. Some of these contacts were facilitated by intermarriage; a number of "Palestinian" notable women were, in fact, Palestinian by marriage only. Matiel Mughannam, Katy Antonius, and ʿAnbara Sallam al-Khalidi were all Lebanese by birth. Wahida al-Khalidi was from Iraq.

The halcyon period in the early 1940s was short-lived and illusive, however. Lurking beneath the seemingly untroubled surface were the unresolved problems that had made the 1930s so turbulent in Palestine. World War II provided a temporary respite and even distraction for some, but ultimately effected acceleration and escalation of Arab-Jewish tensions, due in part to the large waves of Jewish immigration resulting from the Nazi regime's "final solution," the Zionist movement's well-organized plans and responses to the post–World War situation, and the Palestinian national movement's paralysis born of factionalism and disunity. The movement's disarray resulted in its inability "to unite or at least evolve a common program" during this period.[12] Ultimately, this fragmentation proved to be its undoing.

The trajectory of the Palestinian women's movement corresponded to the vicissitudes of the 1940s. In the early 1940s, the movement deflected its attention from confrontations with and accusations against the British Mandate government, and concentrated on social and development issues, focusing increasingly on the specific concerns of Arab women. The organizations that had expended most of their efforts in the 1930s in demonstrations and antigovernment denunciations turned to establishing literary and sports clubs and founding schools for girls. Despite the ostensibly "social" nature of these activities, nationalism remained deeply embedded in the work. Militant activities rose once again to the fore in the mid to late 1940s, when armed conflict between Jews and Arabs intensified and culminated in the *nakba*, the disaster of 1947–48.

The 1940s witnessed the evolution of a pan-Arab feminist movement whose roots can be traced to the convening of a number of regional women's conferences in the 1930s and 1940s. Responding to these developments as well as others mentioned above, the women's movement adopted new forms of organizing in the 1940s that changed its character and activities. Yet the intersections between its constituent elements of feminism and nationalism remained an enduring and sometimes tense and contradictory dynamic within the movement. Around the beginning of the 1940s, the Palestinian women's movement had come of age; after an initially hesitant involvement in pan-Arab and Middle Eastern women's conferences (which occurred during the Palestinian women's movement's infancy, it should be noted), the movement worked at attracting regional and international support. It was less successful in building a mass movement that included the majority of Arab women within the borders of mandate Palestine. These issues are explored below.

PAN-ARAB WOMEN'S ACTIVITY

Margot Badran states that "when Arab women came together to deal with the nationalist issue of Palestine [in 1938], they unintentionally set [sic] the groundwork for Pan-Arab feminism."[13] But, in fact, the roots of pan-Arab feminism reach further back in time and extend beyond Egypt, the acknowledged vanguard of Arab feminism; women's "awakenings" were underway in Lebanon, Syria, and Iraq before 1938.[14] Affinity between Arab women of Lebanon, Syria, Iraq, Trans-Jordan, Egypt, and Palestine transcended individual national identities linked to a state. The threats from Zionism and colonialist hegemonies—be they embodied in French or British mandates, or indirect rule—heightened and brought into relief perceptions of the unity of Arab culture in the Mashriq, particularly among the educated elite. Mrs. Munir Khuri expressed this notion of Arab oneness in her speech at the 1944 women's conference: "I'm the daughter of one nation, one language, one upbringing, one set of customs, one system of mores and one set of goals."[15] Arabs from the Mashriq, as has been mentioned, considered political borders imposed by European powers artificial. They intermarried, owned land and property, engaged in business, and moved relatively freely across these boundaries up until 1948.[16] This was particularly true of, although not limited to, the middle- and upper-class elite—landed notables, merchants, and professionals. This cultural homogeneity was more a desire and myth than reality, however. Most Mashriq societies experienced deep internal divisions along various fault lines: rural versus urban, nomadic versus sedentary, and among different class, *hamūla* (clan), and religious groups. Common threats such as colonialism and Zionism united people around a relatively new, imagined national construct, but, as history has demonstrated, this unity proved to be fragmented, temporary, and ultimately elusive. These internal fragmentations were reflected in relations among the different, emerging Arab national identities.

During the late 1930s and 1940s the women's movements in neighboring Arab countries became increasingly concerned about the situation in Palestine. Activity on behalf of Palestine by solidarity networks of Arab and "Eastern" women (as they sometimes referred to themselves) multiplied during the 1930s—particularly during the 1936–39 revolt—reminding Palestinian women that they were not struggling in isolation but were part of a larger women's movement. Women's organizations in Syria, Iraq, Lebanon, and Egypt all seized initiative in supporting the Palestinian national struggle on multiple levels. These groups provided tangible assistance in the form of financial aid, and important emotional support through solidarity actions.

The Early 1930s: Regional Cooperation

In the early 1930s, Arab (and Eastern) women began to cooperate on the regional level, convening local women's conferences. In late March of 1930, an Eastern Arab Women's Assembly met in Beirut to organize a general conference, issuing a call to women's groups in the region to attend. The Arab Women's Executive Committee in Jerusalem sent a delegation of eight women.[17] The conference convened two sessions: the first in Beirut, in late April, and the second, called the "Eastern Women's Conference," in Damascus in July. The Beirut conference was to have been headed by Huda Sha'rawi, but due to illness, she could not attend, so Labiba Thabit took her place.[18] Speakers at the conference discussed the "natural duties" of women, protecting women's rights, limiting child marriage, raising the literary level of written culture—novels, plays, and articles. The focus was "family values": the conference adopted resolutions "for happiness in marriage and the family and for compulsory, primary education, and against ostentatious consumerism, drugs, alcohol and public prostitution." It also demanded censorship of films to protect children.[19] The Damascus session, presided over by Nur Hamada, a Lebanese activist, was attended by women from Iran, Iraq, Afghanistan, and the Hijaz, as well as Syria and Lebanon, "all of them . . . concerned with the history of the women's awakening in the East."[20]

In October 1932, another two-part women's conference was held, the objective of which was "to raise the Arab and Eastern woman to higher levels of freedom and participation."[21] Convened first in Damascus and then Baghdad, it was sponsored by the General Syrian Women's Union, and received support (at least verbally) from the Syrian and Iraqi governments.[22] A number of high officials (and other men) attended and delivered speeches, including the Syrian prime minister (in Damascus). A representative from the International Women's Union was also present, and spoke about Western women's efforts to achieve "full rights."[23] The conference resolutions dealt primarily with women's legal status, proposing that the age of marriage—of both spouses—be raised; the dowry and trousseau be reduced; spouses become acquainted with one another before marriage; polygyny be prevented; women obtain the right to divorce; and women's guardians be invalidated for not upholding women's inheritance rights. Despite such strong reformatory positions, ambivalence remained over certain sensitive, cultural issues; for example, it was resolved to leave the cause of the veil to be solved by time, "because going into it now would only muddle things and electrify the atmosphere."[24] This resolution may well have reflected Lebanese and Syrian women's recent, unsuccessful attempts to unveil, which aroused such violent reactions "that by the early 1930s they had dropped the issue like a hot potato," according to Elizabeth Thompson.[25] Indeed, women's acknowledgment of the controversial nature of such a resolution was perhaps a tactical and political move to calibrate their demands in order to maximize potential "transgender alliances" (and male support) for future demands.[26] Nur Hamada's speech at the 1930 Beirut conference seems to indicate this kind of political strategy, paralleling Palestinian women's deferral of raising the issue of female suffrage, as discussed in

Chapter 6. Hamada called for educating women so that "when women know how to raise children, they can demand from men their rights and take them in hand."[27]

One interesting development revealed in these conferences was the emerging Arab states' articulation of support for social change among women, however circumspect their actual implementation of somewhat vague goals.[28] It is difficult to ascertain how much of this was rhetoric. The deputy prime minister of Iraq, Sami Shawkat, welcomed the women to the Baghdad conference, bringing to their attention the fact that "part of the reason why Western countries have prospered is because women have taken their proper roles, something we still lack in the East."[29] The states' motivations to "raise the level of woman" (the common phrase of the times) were intricately intertwined with anticolonialist political legacies, and the project of constructing the "modern" nation in order to compete with and struggle against Western political domination. A state could not be "modern" when its women were "backward."

Controversy seems to have arisen over the lack of participation of Palestinian women at these conferences; a Fatima Murad delivered a speech on "The Situation of the Palestinian Woman" only because she happened to be in Damascus while the conference was convened (as noted irritatedly by a Palestinian newspaper reporter). One article in the Palestinian press asked, "Why didn't Palestine send a representative?"[30] In an interview, the chairwoman of the conference, Nur Hamada, stated that many attempts were made to invite Palestinian women, even to the extent of sending a request to the high commissioner, but they were all rejected or ignored.[31] Subhiyya Miqdadi spoke on women in Palestine at the Baghdad conference.[32]

The third General Eastern Women's Conference, intriguingly, was held in Tehran in December 1932. In addition to expressing support for the resolutions of the previous conferences, the 1,300 conferees drew up additional ones that included the right to vote for Eastern women in kingdoms where educated women were "more than half"; the establishment of schools for "ignorant" women to be educated to raise children in the "modern" system; the retention of sound morals (*ikhlāq*) by Eastern women, and avoidance of "evil Western customs and morals"; and the establishment of factories and workshops to employ repentant prostitutes.[33]

It is difficult to know what to make of these conferences. Very little has been written about them in secondary sources, and it does not seem as though they were very influential in achieving their objectives. The contradictory and simultaneous articulations of defense of "Eastern" identity and culture, emulation of Western "progress," and demands for concrete, feminist-oriented social and legal reforms reveal the complexities of the cultural, social, economic, and political atmosphere in the Middle East in the 1930s. Gender and the position and status of women—particularly middle-class women—were clearly at the forefront in the "imagining" of the newly emerging "modern" state, both in women's and men's minds, although there were differences both among and within the two sexes. Women articulated feminist concerns, albeit in carefully worded phrases designed not to raise issues of power, but rather to refer to "rights" and "responsibilities." Although the women who attended the conferences came from heterogeneous and diverse societies, clearly they felt strong, common cultural bonds, identifying similar threats to problems confronting their societies and culture, and proposing analogous solutions for them.

On the political level, Arab women in the region were highly conscious of one another's struggles; women sent numerous expressions of solidarity and support back and forth, raised funds, and demonstrated on behalf of one another's causes, particularly on the Palestine question. During the 1931 Nablus demonstrations, the Egyptian Sa'adist Ladies Committee sent greetings to the women of Nablus congratulating them for their "sacrifice" and exemplariness in the face of oppression; the women of Damascus, Beirut, and Irbid protested British measures for repressing the 1936–39 revolt and against the partition plan of 1937; the Egyptian Feminist Union designated June 3, 1938 "Palestine Day," calling on Egyptians to donate to the Palestinian cause; the Iraqi Women's Union protested the 1946 Anglo-American Commission of Inquiry.[34] Palestinian women reciprocated, sending telegrams of congratulation to the Syrian *"mujāhidāt"* (female strugglers) in 1933 when they demonstrated against the proposed treaty between Syria and France over the terms of Syria's entry into the League of Nations, for example, and protesting the ceding of Alexandretta to Turkey by the French in 1939.[35]

Arab women also engaged in social and cultural exchanges. Renowned educators, writers, poets, and leaders of the women's organizations traveled to one another's countries on lecture tours or to visit schools and other women's associations. In 1944, for example, the Egyptian writer Amina al-Sa'id was celebrated and fêted during a visit to Palestine, where she delivered lectures on the public duties of the modern Arab woman and the women's awakening in Egypt at the YMCA, the Haifa Orthodox Club, and on the Palestine Broadcasting Service.[36]

Literate, elite Arab women were cognizant of and attentive to one another's political, cultural, and social endeavors, due in large part to the diffusion of the Arabic press and its role in facilitating communication between

Arab women in the region. The telegram wires virtually buzzed from the amount of news transmitted back and forth between the women's groups, much of which was duly reported in the newspapers. The Palestinian press assiduously conveyed news and information about the pan-Arab women's movement, reporting other Arab women's struggles, and detailing their feminist and nationalist activities.[37] Similarly, the women's press, particularly in Egypt, covered the activities of the Palestinian women's movement in detail, stirring up nationalist emotion and drumming up support for the Palestinian cause.[38]

The Cairo Women's Conferences

The revolt in Palestine galvanized the Mashriq communities on behalf of Palestine. Women in neighboring Arab states formed ladies committees to defend Palestine, engaging in the same kinds of actions as the Palestinian women's movement: demonstrating, fund-raising, and sending letters and telegrams of protest to foreign diplomats and governments.[39]

Arab women had championed the Palestinian cause in the international arena before the revolt, activity which highlighted the tensions between them and Western-dominated international women's organizations. In 1935, the International Alliance of Women (IAW) requested the support and solidarity of the Beirut Arab Women's Union in joining the International Committee of Peace's boycott of Japan for its invasion of China.[40] The Arab women responded by concurring, but also raised the issue of Palestine in their letter, chiding the IAW for not presenting their cause to the committee. A series of letters went back and forth on the matter; ultimately the committee stated that such an issue was outside of the range of their four basic articles, one of which stipulated that they could not interfere in the domestic affairs of any country. The Arab women of Beirut responded bitterly:

> The eyes of the Arabs have been opened to the painful reality ... that the League of Nations and its numerous committees, and the Western countries and their committees and conferences held in the name of peace, disarmament and assistance to the helpless, are only dust stirred up in the eyes of the weak, and means by which to implement their imperialist plans under legal pretexts.[41]

This interchange hinted at the problems and divergent points of view that were to develop between Arab and Western women over issues of peace and justice, due to their widely disparate experiences and positions on opposite sides of the colonial divide.[42]

By the time the revolt was a fully fledged armed insurrection, Arab women were prepared to stand with their Palestinian sisters in bringing the

Palestinian cause to the forefront in regional and international arenas. The idea of a women's conference on behalf of Palestine gestated from within a circle of Syrian, Palestinian, Iraqi, and Lebanese nationalists (both men and women). Akram Zuʻaytir claims in his memoirs that the idea originated with men, although British officials reported that "discussions have been proceeding between the Moslem Women's Societies in Egypt, Palestine and Syria for the holding of a 'Women's Congress' in Syria."[43] (Originally the women attempted to convene the conference in Syria but the prime minister, after a private meeting with the British consul in Damascus, forbade it.)[44] There does seem to have been, at the least, a high level of involvement of male nationalist leaders in its planning and organization, particularly among some of the Palestinians in exile.[45] After a flurry of organizational activity and negotiations among various individuals, Huda Shaʻrawi, deemed by all the appropriate leader for the conference, was given "power of attorney" to represent the Arab women in the international arena by the Ladies Committee to Defend Palestine, in the name of, and signed by, the women's organizations in Iraq, Syria, Lebanon, and Palestine.[46] She subsequently issued a call to the Eastern Women's Conference, to be held in Cairo October 15–18, 1938.[47]

In early October, various women's delegations began to arrive in Cairo to prepare for the conference, organize the program and elect officers. Zuʻaytir graphically describes the chaos and humming of activity in breathless prose; women bustled in and out, arriving by plane and train, and the house of the Egyptian Women's Union, where this all occurred, was "teeming" with delegates.[48] A preliminary election of officers took place; to the surprise of no one, Shaʻrawi was elected president, along with a roster of seven vice presidents and eleven assistant secretaries, representing each attending Arab country.

On October 13, news arrived from Jerusalem of the assassination (presumably by agents of the Mufti Hajj Amin al-Husayni) of former National Defense Party (NDP) loyalist Hassan Sidqi al-Dajani, whose wife was attending the conference.[49] Matiel Mughannam approached Akram Zuʻaytir, "terrified and breathless" about the assassination, saying she had received a threat warning her not to speak at the conference because her husband was not a partisan of the Mufti's party. She wanted to excuse herself from delivering her speech, but Zuʻaytir reassured her that he would personally guarantee her safety.[50] This incident indicates how the underlying factional tensions in the national movement had begun to permeate the women's movement and ultimately led to the creation of the Arab Women's Union (AWU) out of the split within the Arab Women's Association (AWA) (see

Chapter 6). However, the presence of women with NDP associations working alongside Husayni loyalists at the conference signifies the Palestinian women's recognition of the importance of maintaining public unity for this momentous event.[51] The strain, however, must have been great. Maymana al-Qassam, daughter of the revered martyr, 'Izz al-Din al-Qassam, delivered a fiery speech alluding indirectly to the factionalism, invoking unity:

> I am not the first young woman to lose her father to martyrdom for the cause of the Arabs. . . . aren't the martyrs 'Arif al-Husayni, the mufti of Gaza, Doctor 'Ali al-Nashashibi and Kamil al-Budayri uncles of the noble Palestine delegates at this conference from the Husayni, Nashashibi and Budayri clans?[52]

The conference, attended by delegations from Syria, Lebanon, Iraq, Palestine, and a lone Iranian representative, opened with great fanfare and attention. The women who attended were "socially liberated, and politically smart"; none was accompanied by male relatives, as noted pointedly in the conference's official publication.[53] Nationalist hymns were sung, telegrams of support were read, and moments of silence observed for the martyrs of Palestine. Then the speeches began; these were the major activities at the conference, in addition to various social functions held for the delegates. The overwhelming themes of the conference were the innate, historical "Arabness" of Palestine; the necessity to maintain and develop Arab unity in the face of the Zionist threat to Palestine; and identification of European imperialism as the major source of the problem. The first of the twenty-two resolutions stated that the Palestine problem was a creation of Europe for which the Europeans must take responsibility and find a just solution. The rest of the decisions consisted primarily of proposals for action on the Palestine issue. The major demands were for abolition of the mandate, abrogation of the Balfour Declaration, and prohibitions on Jewish immigration and land sales to Jews. The conference condemned the partition plan and protested British measures for repressing the revolt. The women denounced the foreign press for its bias in attacking the "righteous *mujāhidīn*" and calling the Jews "noble ones defending their country." They proposed to send telegrams and petitions to major world leaders protesting Great Britain's tyranny; to encourage Arab national products and boycott foreign goods; and to form ladies committees to defend Palestine in Arab countries in order to implement the decisions of the conference and continue in the defense of the Palestinian cause. A central committee under the auspices of the Egyptian Women's Union was to coordinate communications.[54]

The pan-Arab support on prominent display at this conference injected adrenaline into the Palestinian women's movement, and perhaps, the national movement as well. Arab unity and support on the Palestine issue boosted the Palestinian women's morale, reduced their isolation, and bestowed international standing upon their movement. At the closing of the conference, Zlikha al-Shihabi expressed this when she stated,

> Each one of us is completely convinced that the Palestine cause has become the subject of concern for all of the Eastern people; that the people of Palestine are not alone in the holy war to liberate our country; and that the Arab and Eastern ladies are behind their Palestinian sisters.[55]

The Palestinian women had heretofore not participated as fully in international and regional women's affairs as had the other Arab women's associations.[56] The 1938 conference ultimately effected a strengthening of their bonds to other Arab women's organizations, and a gradual expansion of their interests beyond their major nationalist concerns. On the other hand, the conference, coming as it did in the midst of the great revolt, also played a role in bringing to the fore the tensions within the movement that resulted in its bifurcation into two main groups.

The conference generated a great deal of publicity. The Arabic press coverage was effusive, extensive, and favorable, extolling the "historic" nature of the event.[57] Western reaction was mixed; the British government, having kept close watch on the development of the conference, was irritated at its "intemperance of language" and "strong anti-British" overtones, and decided not to acknowledge receipt of its resolutions.[58] The British press noted admiringly, "one of the most interesting features of the Women's Congress is the revelation of the degree of social emancipation and political enlightenment to which leading Oriental women have already attained."[59]

It is not clear whether the Arab women actually implemented their plan to centralize and coordinate among themselves. It seems that the onset of World War II intervened to temporarily quash this development. The idea, however, kept simmering in the mind of Huda Sha'rawi, at least, for the next five or so years. In the summer of 1944, she, Hawa Idris, and Amina al-Sa'id set off to visit women's organizations in Lebanon, Syria, Palestine, and Trans-Jordan to explore the "idea of a confederation of Arab feminist unions," and discuss the plan for another major women's conference in Cairo.[60] In early September, the Egyptian women arrived in Palestine where they were treated like royalty, hosted and fêted in every city they visited, drawing crowds and entertained by both male and female dignitaries. The AWU convened a mass meeting with the Egyptian delegation in Jerusalem, issuing invitations to all of the women's organizations in the country. The conference under discussion was to "be an exploration of subjects concerning women and women's affairs," but, as Palestinian journalist Asma Tubi warned, "the Palestinian Arab woman adds to her sister a vital, different claim . . . which is to keep her country alive, and to demand her Arab country for her children."[61]

The idea for the Arab women's conference derived from Shaʿrawi's dissatisfaction with the European-dominated International Alliance of Women, on whose board she sat, for their biased Western political orientation which did not allow criticism of Western democratic governments for their imperialistic policies and support of Zionism.[62] The divisions within the international women's movement during this period were a precursor to those that intensified between First World–Third World feminist movements in the latter part of the twentieth century. At issue, then and now, was Western feminists' inability to perceive the contradictions between their support for imperialist projects of certain Western democracies and their selectivity in upholding in international arenas so-called democratic principles for some nations and not for others.[63] While priding themselves on their internationalism, they perceived Arab women's nationalist expression as some kind of aberrant extremism, yet, as Leila Rupp points out, when internationalism and nationalism "came into conflict . . . [their own] nationalism took precedence."[64] Shaʿrawi originally conceived of forming an Eastern women's union to constitute an "Eastern front" that would represent the East at international conferences and provide for balance, but due to the changing circumstances during the war, she instead worked toward establishment of a general Arab women's union.[65]

The 1944 Arab Women's Conference, which was held December 12–16 in Cairo, was markedly different from the 1938 conference. In contrast to the latter, its very name stressed its Arabness, and it received "highly visible state support." The Egyptian queen was president of the conference, and the Minister of Education addressed its opening session.[66] Its goals were mostly oriented toward specifically gendered issues: to research women's political and civil rights and work toward providing educational, literary, social, humanitarian, and economic services for women in Arab countries. But, of course, it also addressed the "defense" of Palestine.[67] It had a tighter organizational apparatus and focus than the 1938 conference, formulating in its resolutions specific, concrete calls for legal and other changes. Some of its demands were quite radical for the time: resolutions included advocacy of suffrage for women, equal pay for equal work between men and women with commensurate qualifications, and elimination of the feminine endings in the Arabic language. Many of the resolutions dealt with the sensitive issue of changing personal status laws under the *sharīʿa*, recommending restriction of polygyny to cases where the wife was infertile or ill; allowing divorced mothers to retain custody of both male and female children until puberty, after which a judge would decide which parent was the better guardian; raising and enforcing the minimum marriage age for girls from fourteen to sixteen; and restraining men from using divorce to harm women. Other, less controversial resolutions dealt with improving and standardizing educational systems and providing health care to women. The issue of "morals" was also addressed, mostly in the context of prostitution, which the conference proposed to outlaw; it also recommended finding alternative "honorable" means for young women to support themselves.[68]

Palestine was one issue among many, unlike at the 1938 conference. The resolutions included practical proposals to save Palestinian land by setting up a committee to oversee the collection of funds for this purpose.[69] The Palestine problem was uppermost on the Palestinian delegation's minds, however. Mrs. Shukri Dib delivered a stirring speech in which she advocated fighting the Jews with their own weapons: money, propaganda, and the inculcation of nationalism in the schools and other institutions.[70]

The particular situation in Palestine—the extreme and very real danger of complete social, cultural, and political annihilation—distinguished Palestinian feminism from that of countries such as Egypt, Syria, and Lebanon. Because the Mashriq countries were explicitly slated to become, or were, independent (whereas Palestine was not), they could concentrate a more focused effort on feminist issues.[71] The resolutions of the conferences that took place in the early 1930s indicate that some Arab women of the Mashriq had begun to formulate explicit feminist agendas, demanding concrete legal and social changes. Demands were often articulated in the name of making the nation "modern" or reforming family life, via women, in order to strengthen the nation. At the 1944 conference, "embattled," veteran women's activists from Lebanon and Syria, whose unsuccessful suffrage struggle in the 1920s had inflicted some heavy wounds, reopened demands for suffrage, albeit limited and in a more subdued way than previously. Their own nationalist struggles against the French in 1943 had mitigated their feminist agenda.[72] Yet some Arab women were expressing a more militant feminism than the less threatening social welfare feminism which generally dominated much of the pan-Arab feminist movement. Widad (Mrs. 'Arif) Hajjar, a member of the Syrian delegation, delivered a speech in which she declared that, "Arab women should boycott every man who places obstacles in the face of the advancement of women."[73]

The Palestinian women's efforts, however, continued to be pulled into the orbit of the national struggle, often at the expense of women's issues. Maintaining national unity was perceived as a survival issue, and feminist concerns were considered divisive. Furthermore, Palestinian women perceived the nationalist issue to be their one, overriding concern, which was more "important" than feminism. Leila Mughannam compared the women of Egypt to those of Palestine:

> I'm not saying the Palestinian women were not interested in the improvement in the status of women as women . . . the women of Palestine had a more important role to play, as they saw it . . . the people in Egypt, like Huda [Sha'rawi] and the others, were happily sitting in Cairo and at that time they didn't have an issue that was very important like the Palestine issue.[74]

The preoccupation with the nationalist issue ultimately produced a conservatizing effect on the Palestinian women's movement.[75] Zlikha al-Shihabi, who by 1944 was considered the major leader of the movement, stated in an interview before the Cairo conference that "women in Palestine and Trans-Jordan will not demand more rights than what is allowed under Islamic law and the holy Qur'an. Demanding political rights for women is before its time."[76]

THE PALESTINIAN WOMEN'S MOVEMENT IN THE 1940S

The Early 1940s

In the early 1940s, the Palestinian women's movement became more institutionalized, coordinated, and organized. There is increased mention of individual branches of the AWU and other women's organizations electing officers and forming special administrative boards and committees.[77] The AWU formally nationalized its structure shortly before the 1944 Cairo conference by establishing a "higher committee" of the boards of the Arab women's unions in Palestine, with Shihabi as president.[78] The American consul viewed its existence as "an indication that the Arabs are seeking to become more united in their external political front."[79] At the nationwide meeting where the committee was formed, the different representatives from around the country also resolved to establish an Arab college for girls and a monthly magazine in the name of the AWU.[80] The AWU began taking upon itself a stronger coordinating and centralizing role. After receiving notification of the dates of the 1944 Cairo conference from Huda Sha'rawi, the Jerusalem AWU informed the other women's committees that it would get in touch with them about electing representatives to attend.[81] Journalist Asma Tubi, in her column *Nisā'iyyāt*, called the move to establish the higher committee a "blessed step" toward uniting the ranks of the "women's front" and "getting organized." She praised women's work but added that their efforts needed organization since "a number of societies only work in one sphere where others are neglected." These veiled references to divisiveness and implicit criticism of certain unnamed groups hint at still unresolved internal struggles within the movement.[82]

New language and terminology began to emerge in writings on the movement in the press, articulating a self-conscious *Palestinian* Arab identity for women: in 1944, the AWU began to call itself the Palestinian Arab Women's Union (PAWU).[83] Previously, the women felt little need to highlight the Palestinian part of their Arab identity. In part, these new discursive constructions reflected pan-Arab politics and new terminology that began to permeate political discourse. The Lebanese and Syrian women's unions, interestingly, changed their names in 1944 to the Lebanese-Arab Women's Union and the Syrian-Arab Women's Union.[84] Language was used to specify both particularist nationalist structures and institutions, and to connote broader, more inclusive political entities. There was increasing use of the word "front" (*jabha*), for example, to refer to women's activities during this period. The AWU, or PAWU, attached the word "general" to its appellation, becoming the General (Palestinian) Arab Women's Union; it also began to issue directives from its "bureau" or "office" (*maktab*). One sees the word "association" (*jam'iyya*) sometimes replaced or accompanied by "league" (*rābita*).[85]

The women's movement also expanded its activities into cultural, social, educational, and economic spheres.[86] Cinema and theater parties, major sources of fund-raising among the women's organizations, proliferated during the 1940s, fulfilling a dual function of providing entertainment and accomplishing serious national, charitable work.[87] There is increased mention of specialized, ancillary committees with specific functions and tasks, such as the Jerusalem First Aid Committee (founded in 1940), and the Sports Committee, founded in 1945. The latter developed its own identity as a separate club, called the Sports and Literary Club, and built its own athletic field and tennis courts.[88] The women's movement used this athletic field to hold nationwide conferences and mass meetings during the 1940s. The AWU also developed special projects, such as the clinic founded by the Jerusalem branch in 1946, with its own staff of doctors.[89] These committees took on lives of their own; the members of the first aid committee sent delegations to prisons and raised funds in its own name.

In the early 1940s, the women's movement did not participate in politically oriented activities to the extent that it did in the 1930s, due to this period of quiet and lull before the storm. Indeed, there is evidence of the development of a certain amount of Anglo-Palestinian amity. British

Institutes sprang up in various towns and cities, sponsoring English classes, literary lectures, libraries, and sewing and first aid lessons. One sponsored a debate between "mind" and "beauty." (Mind won.)[90]

Although, in contrast to the 1930s, the women did not frequently meet with the high commissioner, demonstrate, and barrage the British government with protests, they nonetheless continued to work on residual problems from the revolt. Their work on behalf of prisoners continued unabated; they visited them, provided aid to them and their families, and petitioned the government for their release.[91] They also spent much of their time working on behalf of orphans of the revolt, sponsoring their education and fund-raising on their behalf.

In shifting its focus back toward social issues, the movement reflected developments in Palestinian society. Several interesting incidents illustrate some of the changes that were occurring in the country. In 1940, women voted in some village elections for *mukhtar*. In January, in the village of Brir in the Gaza district, they justified their participation on the basis that they paid taxes. According to *Filastīn*, the men "accepted" it, and the women's candidate won.[92] Women also participated in elections for *mukhtars* in the villages of Ijseir and Hamama in March and July of 1940.[93] In April, 1941, the district commissioner for the Lydda district reported that "a movement of certain Moslem women in Jaffa to do away with the veil began early in the fortnight, and, to make it effective, they alleged that they had secured a *fatwa* [legal opinion] from the Qadi. The Qadi, who of course had never given such a *fatwa*, was heckled in the mosque at the midday prayer in Friday and had to issue a *dementi* from the pulpit."[94]

These incidents, and the reactions they provoked, indicate the shifting social and political ground upon which gender categories stood. The 1940s was a period of confusing and conflicting social tendencies. The war, in particular, effected transformations in Palestinian society. Economic opportunities for women opened up; indeed, women's labor was actively courted by the government in some rather unusual ways. These developments upset patriarchal structures and norms. Women were occasionally more assertive, even militant, in challenging these norms, which in turn produced contradictory responses to women's increased role in public and political spheres. During this period there were reports of attacks against women who appeared unveiled in the streets of Jaffa,[95] while there were also accounts (beginning in 1946) of women's organizations holding cultural functions in which both sexes participated.[96] Women and men increasingly worked together, as in the AWU's clinic, which was staffed by volunteer male doctors, but which was directed by the AWU, and included female staff as well.

Partly as a result of some of the changes Palestinian society was experiencing, and partly because of the maturity of women's organizational and educational experiences, the 1940s witnessed new innovations and deviations from the earlier, more familiar charitable-style societies which were the foremothers, so to speak, of the women's movement. A number of different women's organizations were established in the 1940s; interestingly, the impetus for their establishment came from external sources, not Palestinian women themselves. Yet they obviously struck a chord.

Different Forms of Organizing

In 1942, a group called the Women's Volunteer Auxiliary Army was formed, dispatching Miryam Za'rour of Ramallah, accompanied by (male) Arab and English army officers, to primarily Christian areas to recruit Arab women to "volunteer" (yet be paid good salaries) to perform such work as stenography, accounting, cooking, driving, transmitting, and switchboard operation.[97] The "army" had a camp in an "unidentified place," complete with dormitories and kitchens, where women from Damascus, Beirut, and Palestine engaged in sports and participated in their "national duty."[98]

This curious group apparently was the result of a war effort by the British to bolster the wartime economy and workforce in Palestine by appealing to Arab women's notions about democracy and "defending the free world" (rhetoric Za'rour utilized in her speeches). Significantly, it only recruited in towns such as Nazareth, Bethlehem, and Beit Jala, where the Christian population was concentrated. The endeavor does not seem to have elicited overwhelming response. One report mentions that a special troop of ladies would be formed when there were enough of the required number of volunteers; there are no indications that significant numbers of women ever joined, although evidently some did.[99] It is curious that the British adopted the strategy of recruiting women into a special military unit, considering that women could well have been induced to work simply for financial reasons, as was the case in the later 1940s. Obviously, the British assumed that Christian Arab women (and their families) would have fewer objections to this kind of endeavor, since the recruitment effort centered only on Christian villages. Since the British considered Muslim women more traditional and restricted than their Christian counterparts, the authorities did not make a very serious attempt to enlist them, although they put announcements in newspapers calling for volunteers without distinction of religion or "race."[100] This also reflected British essentialist notions about the "character" differences between the "races" (read: religious communities) in Palestine. The British, conflating religion with culture and nation, perceived

Muslim women to be more nationalistic and thus less likely to join such an endeavor than Christian women, who, according to this attitude, were culturally more "Western" and thus identified more closely with "Western" concepts such as democracy. The fact that the recruiters continually used nationalist rhetoric in their speeches indicates that they were straining for a motivating force to induce (any) women to join. Considering the British government's recent history of often very hostile confrontations with nationalist women's organizations that included outspoken Christian leaders, it is odd that the British thought Palestinian women of either religion would join the war effort on their behalf.

The existence of this group, however insignificant the number of its members, indicates that some Arab women saw membership in such an association as offering opportunities. Women were clearly motivated (and willing) to join certain groups not only out of charitable or nationalist impulses but also for personal development or self-interest, and to pursue interests denied them through other outlets.

Asia Halabi, a Christian Arab woman from Jerusalem, is a case in point.[101] When Asia was a young girl, her brother taught her to drive, something that immediately appealed to her and evolved into a serious vocation. As an adult, she enlisted in the British army (not the women's auxiliary) during World War II, becoming a driver for the Royal Military Police.[102] Eventually she became a junior commander in the Army Transport Service, in charge of examining, driving, and supervising all repairs on all types of transport, including light vehicles, four-wheel drive vehicles and three-ton trucks. During 1948 she was a liaison officer between the Jordanian army and the United Nations. Ms. Halabi was a unique woman for her time and place, impressing others of her generation who still recollect her unusual character and exploits. Raja al-'Isa (the son of 'Isa al-'Isa, the owner of the newspaper *Filastīn*), commented, "Asia is a tough guy . . . she's two men in one woman."[103] Her story illustrates how women used organizational or associational structures, even within the mandate government itself, in order to seek fulfillment in nontraditional roles. Such organizations could provide legitimacy or shield women from overt public censure. Belonging to an organized group could help women deflect unwanted attention from themselves as individuals, affording them security to pursue interests considered unorthodox.[104] Some women, however, sought the limelight through their involvement with organizations, as press coverage demonstrates.

One of the more intriguing and well-documented women's organizations of this period, founded in 1944, was the Women's Social Endeavor

Society, called in Arabic *al-jam'iyya al- tadāmun al-nisā'ī* (literally, The Women's Solidarity Society).[105] Although the group's work corresponded to women's traditional charitable work, the history of the founding of this society is rather unusual. It initially originated from a secret British public relations scheme developed and supervised by the Middle East Bureau of Information out of Cairo during World War II.[106] Originally, the organization was to consist of cells called "The Brotherhood of Freedom" (*ikhwān al-huriyya*) or, later, "Sisterhood of Freedom," targeting Arab government officials for membership.[107] The purpose of these groups was twofold:

> To foster a realistic conception of the post-war world and with it the idea that the future prosperity of the Arabs depends on their being able to develop a healthy society of a modern type, and that this can be done successfully only in cooperation with ... Great Britain in particular. ... [and] to form an unofficial channel of communication between Government and the Arab population.[108]

Interestingly, the officer chosen to organize the cells was a young, Oxford-educated woman of Trans-Jordanian origin, Luli Abu al-Huda, the daughter of a former prime minister of Trans-Jordan, and assistant to a British officer who was to "control the operations of the Brotherhood."[109] Although Abu al-Huda apparently had some success in organizing men in the Hebron area—an extraordinary feat, considering the traditionally conservative character of this region—she ultimately confronted problems in dealing with "explanations" demanded from them about land sales to Jews, lower salaries for Arab officials performing the same work as British ones, and so forth. The bureau subsequently decided, upon her recommendation, to work with women "on the basis of social work" and "home-building," since they would be "'easier' to deal with" and Abu al-Huda would be "less pressed for explanations and less inundated with politics!"[110] Thereafter, Abu al-Huda, with generous government funding from the Social Welfare Department, established the Women's Social Endeavor Society.[111] The society was described by one British official in 1947 as "one of the factors making for social advance among the Arabs in a quiet way without any left wing, or at least, communist inspiration."[112] This comment reflected the increasing Cold War fears and politics of the postwar period among the British, revealing their motivation to found such organizations was to preempt and preclude potential "left-wing" influence on Arab society. What is particularly remarkable about all of this is the fact that the British perceived Arab women as an important target for their propaganda efforts. Through focusing on those most closely concerned with "home building" the British hoped to influence and reach the young through their primary educators, mothers, in order to develop a "modern" nation that would be loyal to British interests.[113] The explicitly political agenda of the British which accompanied this "modernization" scheme of targeting women via formation of the Solidarity Society is striking.

The society ultimately formed nineteen branches in most of the major cities and some towns and villages, performing social work. It established the first day-care center for working mothers in the country (in Jerusalem).[114] Founding schools for girls in villages was one of its major projects. Much of its work was quite valuable in providing services for women in villages—such as education—a responsibility the British themselves abrogated. It is highly unlikely that many—if any—of the Palestinian women who ultimately became involved in the society had a clear idea of its origins, since it attracted a considerable number of women from prominent, nationalist families. Asma Tubi, in describing its social work, adds that this was "in addition to [its work in] other national matters."[115] It is also quite telling that its name in Arabic uses the word "solidarity"(*tadāmun*), and in fact, Arabic sources and speakers, when referring to it, shortened the name simply to "solidarity."[116]

The society participated in nationalist demonstrations in the late 1940s, taking particular care to draw attention to this through use of the press.[117] The articles it provided to the press adopted a defensive tone. In one notice, it mentions a "lack of understanding" and concern to set the record straight, saying that it had no relationship with the government and was purely charitable, only "taking help" from the Social Welfare Department. Many "national" charitable societies get "help," it continues. "Does this mean that these are governmental associations?"[118] This particular article appeared shortly after the Anglo-American Committee issued its report in 1946, which aroused a storm of protest among the Palestinian Arab population. It is clear that the society feared being associated with the increasingly unpopular British government and its hated policies. Reports on the society's activities in the Arabic press in the 1940s indicate that it did compete with the AWU-sponsored women's groups. A correction notice in the newspaper reveals vying for credit, jealousy, and rivalry over nationalist credentials; it notes: "We stated in yesterday's edition that the demonstration of the Arab Ladies Association in Jaffa took place from the site of the Women's Solidarity Society, and the truth is that it took place from the Association of the Women's League."[119] British financial support for an organization that duplicated already well-established groups' efforts suggests that suspicions that it was part of "a [British-originated] stratagem to divide the nationalist movement," may have been accurate, and that the government intended to use it in part to undermine and dilute the influence of the more militant women's movement.[120] It is suggestive that the year of the founding of the Women's Social Endeavor Society (1944) coincided with the establishment of the higher committee of the Arab Women's Union, the change of name to the Palestinian Arab Women's Union, and the Cairo Arab Women's Conference.

A third unusual organizing effort involving Arab women occurred in the 1940s when attempts were made to establish women's labor unions. The first indications of women's union involvement occurred in 1943 in Haifa, when a meeting was held at the Catholic Club where women from the Labor Department spoke about the need for forming unions of Arab women workers. Sultana Halabi "urged those present to enroll in the proposed union and asked them to interest their friends in it." Sadhij Nassar, who seems to have been among the vanguard in every political effort involving women, attended this meeting.[121]

An effort was made in 1946—again, in Haifa—to organize women workers. This endeavor was sponsored by the Palestine Arab Workers Society (PAWS) led by Sami Taha. Both of these organizing drives probably derived in part from changes in government policy toward labor unions. In the early 1940s the government began to encourage the formation of Arab labor unions in order "to combat their position of inferiority in relation to Jewish workers and employees in general." A little later, as the contours of the Cold War began to take shape, the government's motivation in encouraging unions was also part of its attempts—analogous to its formation of the Women's Solidarity Society—to mitigate the feared left-wing influence on Arab society, which was increasingly a factor in post–World War II British colonial policy.[122] From the Arab perspective, PAWS might have had its own motivations for cultivating the formation of a women's labor union. In 1946, in conjunction with the International Union of Railway, Telegraph, and Postal Workers, it organized an initially limited strike that evolved into a broader general strike including white-collar government employees.[123] Organizing women's unions in 1946 may have been part of an attempt to broaden the base of union members in the heat of the strike. Furthermore, as the predominant Arab labor union in the 1940s, PAWS had become increasingly politically oriented in 1946 as a result of the restoration of municipal elections (which had been suspended since the revolt of 1936–39). Viewing the elections as "an avenue of gaining support and strength," the union engaged in a big membership recruitment drive, although it did not elect any candidates to municipal office.[124] Its efforts to organize women were possibly part of this organizing drive as well.

Meetings of the Arab women employees in the Haifa area were convened beginning in late January 1946 when PAWS invited the women workers in the Royal Navy to form a women's workers union. (Women were not asked to join PAWS directly, but their labor union was to be affiliated with it.) A preparatory committee was subsequently established, which requested women from different departments of government, the banks, and foreign and national companies to attend a general meeting where they would discuss the "special needs" and concerns of women, one of which was "favoritism toward English women."[125] In addition to women speakers, men from PAWS attended and spoke at all of the meetings. Most of the women speakers apparently were Christian.[126] A permanent administrative board was to be elected and undertake the rental of a building for the union. The results of their efforts are unknown, however, since the record curiously falls silent after the reports of the initial meetings.

Through their union organizing experiences, some Palestinian women received a taste of a new kind of organizational endeavor—one that was based upon membership, a clearly defined constituency, goals and a distinct agenda, and was more consciously mass-based than the AWA, AWU, and the charitable organizations. Arab women, like their counterparts in Europe and the United States, were drawn into wartime employment, which created new types of work for women besides the more customary teacher, service, and clerical positions in education and government offices. Haifa, in particular, was an area where these new opportunities existed, since oil refineries, banks, industry, and the recently completed harbor were all located there. Women worked in all of these sectors, which were targeted for recruitment by the preparatory committee of the women's labor union.[127] In 1942 there was a drastic increase in women requesting work identity cards in the Haifa area (particularly for sewing work); six thousand Arab women were employed in the Haifa area alone in 1946.[128] That Arab women entered new domains in the workforce during World War II is an interesting development, considering that the reasons for them to do so would have differed from their Western counterparts, who for the most part were filling the gaps in male employment created by the conscription and enlistment of men. (Very few Palestinian Arabs served in the British army during the war as soldiers.) But clearly, there was a need for women's labor in Palestine during and after the war years, as evinced by the peculiar army recruitment effort described above, and by the other scant documentary evidence. Indeed, during the war years women were lured away from other sectors of employment in which they had traditionally participated, such as agriculture.[129] By the 1940s, Palestinian women had begun to enter the industrial work force, albeit to a modest degree. Through this experience, they were exposed to forms of organization distinctly different from the other women's associations. This type of experience may have played a role in the internal organizational developments of the women's movement in the later 1940s.

The Late 1940s

The respite of the war years was short-lived. After World War II, Britain was paralyzed by "conflicting pressures that it could not reconcile, [which were], on the one hand, Zionist demands backed by American pressure and growing Jewish terrorism in Palestine and, on the other, growing Arab nationalism."[130] One of the major, far-reaching effects of the war was the increase in the Middle East of American interest and influence, which began to play a role in affecting policy in Palestine for the first time since the imposition of the mandate. In 1946, under American pressure, the joint Anglo-American Commission (AAC) was formed, and dispatched to Palestine, like so many previous commissions, to formulate recommendations for solving the conflict. The resultant proposals, as was always the case with these commissions, pleased none of the conflicting parties, and did not provide for a long-term solution. The proposals were that Palestine should be neither an Arab nor Jewish state; the mandate should continue pending a trusteeship agreement at the United Nations; Britain would grant entry to 100,000 Jews; and Britain would rescind the prohibitions against land sales to Jews as promulgated in the 1939 White Paper.[131]

The recommendations of the AAC acted like a match set to fire on the Palestinian and Arab public. Response was quick, and overwhelmingly negative. The AAC's report was a catalyst that galvanized and reenergized the women's movement, instigating a return to its previous militancy and solidifying its opposition to British policies. The movement's leadership had developed and learned from its experiences during the almost twenty years of its existence. In the postwar period, it intensified its efforts toward tighter internal organization, delegating tasks to specific committees, and centralizing and coordinating communications. Yet its external political strategies and tactics appear to have remained relatively unchanged. It began, once again, to send condemnations to British officials and to demonstrate. It also increasingly drew in a wider assortment of women's groups, uniting such disparate organizations as the AWA, Women's Solidarity Society, Ladies Anglican Society, Orthodox Girls Association, and the Ladies Arabic Club, to name a few.[132] An atmosphere of intense urgency and emergency that pervaded the country was a factor in facilitating women's unity, as the Arab population came to realize it was preparing for an all-out armed confrontation against the Jews. Ironically, just when the women's movement self-consciously had striven toward unity and female solidarity by solidifying its branches and working with groups outside of its organizational framework, the male-led national movement was fractured and fragmented as never before.[133]

In the wake of the AAC's arrival and subsequent findings, demonstrations and protests erupted not only in Palestine but all over the region.[134] The women's associations in Palestine called for a boycott of the commission, sent telegrams of protest to the government, and held massive demonstrations in Jerusalem, Jaffa, Gaza, Tulkarm, Jenin, Acre, and Haifa. In Jerusalem, the AWU repeated a version of its 1933 stunt; Zlikha al-Shihabi presented a speech from the *minbar* (pulpit) of the Dome of the Rock in the Haram al-Sharif compound, and Matiel Mughannam spoke at the Holy Sepulcher. Interestingly, they did not repeat the symbolic crossing of religious lines as they had in 1933; here, a Muslim woman spoke at the mosque, and a Christian woman at the church.[135] Christian clergy were actively involved in many of the demonstrations, ringing church bells and presenting fiery nationalist speeches from the pulpit.[136]

Shortly after the AAC's failed mission, in late 1946 and early 1947, the British decided to hold a conference in London to attempt to come up with proposals satisfactory to both Arabs and Jews. The British government was itself divided over strategies and plans for Palestine. The Foreign Office, supported by High Commissioner Alan Cunningham, favored partition; the Colonial Office supported a unitary, binational state (the Palestinian position); and various individuals offered a third, compromise interim "provincial autonomy" plan, which could either ultimately result in a unitary state or a partitioned one. The provincial autonomy plan was based upon the concept of a type of cantonization that would comprise two provinces, Arab and Jewish, each controlling local affairs (education, health, public works, general administration), with a central government, controlled by the British, in charge of foreign affairs, defense, communications, and so forth. The London conference went nowhere; before it was over, the British decided to refer the Palestine problem to the United Nations, a decision it announced in February 1947. The United Nations Special Committee on Palestine, formed in May 1947, made its recommendation for partition in September. On November 29, 1947, the United Nations formally voted to partition Palestine.

The women's movement spent the rest of the years 1946 and 1947 in intense activity and involvement, responding to the escalating domestic tension and international intervention in the affairs of Palestine. "Outrage over

Western, particularly American, interference, reached vociferous heights," inflaming Palestinian and Arab nationalism. Furthermore, by September 1947, "clouds of war gathered" over the country, which began to brace itself for more violence.[137] The PAWU began to hold frequent meetings of its different branches to prepare and organize on a national level. In 1946, the PAWU chapters stepped up efforts to gain the release of prisoners and detainees still in detention because of their activities during the revolt, deluging the government, the Arab League, and Arab governments with protests. They also requested a review of the expulsion orders of a number of Arab leaders, among them Jamal al-Husayni and Akram Zuʻaytir.[138] Reviving their appeals to "British justice," the women once again attempted to shame the government by invoking (its own) high-minded political ideologies. "Where are the torches of liberty which you kindled with your hearts to secure justice for everybody?" wrote Faiza ʻAbd al-Majid in a letter to the high commissioner demanding the release of prisoners. "What happened to those doctrines of democracy and those promises which were long heralded as relieving necks of yokes, and defending nations against the calamity of aggression?"[139]

In June 1947, women met all over the country to prepare for a big conference to be held by the PAWU in Jerusalem on July 17, 1947, as part of a large-scale program announced by the reconstituted AHC to strengthen and enforce a boycott of "Zionist goods" which had been instigated in 1945 and was now formally under the direction of the Central Economic Committee for the Boycott; and to effect "the complete stoppage of land sales."[140] Three conferences were to be held: one by "all chambers of commerce, political and social institutions and organizations," one by youth, and one by Arab women. The AHC, at a press conference announcing the campaign, also directed that three members be elected by each conference "to implement their decisions in cooperation with the AHE (Arab Higher Executive) and its national committees."[141] It is interesting to note the high level of coordination between the women's movement, now considered part of the body politic, and the male-led national movement, faulty male memories notwithstanding. (See Chapter 6.) In fact, in its directives, the AHC mentioned that the women's conference was to be supervised and prepared by the AWU, and "other women [sic] societies."[142] The conference was convened at the PAWU's athletic field in Jerusalem. Most of its resolutions were recommendations for action by the AHC or local national committees (which were supposed to be forming throughout the country). In order to save the land, the conference proposed that a committee be formed to "look into the reasons persuading those of little faith to sell land"; research ways to protect landowners in order for them to hold onto their land; develop projects to revive and improve Arab villages; and establish agricultural and economic training schools. The resolutions on the economic boycott dealt with the formation of a committee composed of economists and merchants who would oversee provision of needed commodities, publishing of merchant's prices, and ensuring that Arab prices were equal to or lower than Jewish prices.[143] Khalaf remarks that "the only practical call" of the national conferences held in the summer of 1947 came from the women, but none achieved "any concrete results beyond the momentary heightening of nationalist fervor and consciousness."[144] The vanguard and creative women's union of Haifa, which actually bought land in the Bisan area in order to "save" it, was a rare example of an organization actually acting on, rather than meeting and talking about, a nationalist issue.[145]

Throughout the autumn of 1947, the women's movement was active in promoting the boycott, supporting the efforts of the AHC, and encouraging national industry and an Arab economic exhibition—all activities they had engaged in during the 1930s. They published the names of people who sold land to Jews in an effort to shame them. In October, attention shifted to preparation for the impending conflict. First-aid committees sprang up all over the country. Women's organizations set up training sessions led by volunteer doctors, solicited donations and supplies, and readied themselves for the confrontations to come.

After the UN vote on partition on November 29, fighting broke out immediately in the wake of the decision, and the AHC called a general strike. "December was marked by a spiral of violence" between Arab and Jewish militias.[146] On December 5, the women's movement held massive demonstrations in all the major towns, joined in some cases by scouts, students, the Muslim brothers, shaykhs, and "religious young men." In Jaffa, Nariman Nihad Khurshid expressed the increasingly militant mood in a speech, stating "Independence is taken not given," invoking the early Islamic historical heroines 'A'isha and Hind.[147] One interesting new development in the demonstrations of the latter 1940s was the carrying of the flags of the Arab states and pictures of various Arab rulers, signifying an increasing tendency on the part of the national and women's movement to invoke pan-Arab themes and sentiments. The women also began to manipulate religion and tradition in a different way than in their previous dealings with the British. Now they used historical and religious symbology, such as equating the selling of land with being of "little faith," and invoking Islamic historical figures in order to shame or inspire fellow Arabs rather than rebuke the British.

Throughout December, the women's movement found itself preoccupied with the needs created by the escalating military conflict for financial aid and medical care to both the armed fighters and an increasingly embattled Palestinian society. The women's unions were busy signing up volunteers for first-aid centers and collecting donations. In Jerusalem they divided the city into six different sectors, and enlisted more than one thousand women volunteers. On December 19, all of the different women's groups met in Jaffa and decided to establish a special committee comprising two members from each group to form the "sole line of communication" between the women's groups and the National Committee (that is, the Arab Higher Committee).[148] From December 1947 and throughout the war of 1948, the women's movement continued their emergency services, setting up makeshift hospitals, transporting and healing the wounded, and preparing food for the fighters. A special women's unit called *zahrāt al-uquhān* (camomile flowers) accompanied armed fighters, going behind the lines to treat the wounded.[149] As the security situation worsened, the PAWU sent telegrams of protest against Jewish terrorism, asking the increasingly ineffective British government for protection of the Arab civilian population.[150] Some individual women actually fought with the *Jaysh al-Inqādh* (rescue army), and were decorated later by the Syrian government.[151] Women became increasingly involved in dealing with casualties from front-line situations, such as the survivors of the Dayr Yassin massacre of April 1948. Hind al-Husayni, a former student activist and president of the Jerusalem Solidarity Society, caught in the crisis in Jerusalem, found herself taking care of the children whose parents had been killed in the Dayr Yassin massacre. She ultimately founded the renowned orphanage Dār al-tifl al-'Arabī.[152] "It was the worst of times," she recalled. "It was the end of the mandate."[153]

The end of the mandate signified the end of Palestine, which ceased to exist by May 1948. Here the chronicle of the women's movement changes directions. With the scattering and expulsion of the Palestinian population and the partitioning of Mandatory Palestine into the new Jewish state and the Arab-controlled West Bank and Gaza came the fragmentation of the women's movement. But that is another story for future investigation and research.

CONCLUSION

The Palestinian women's movement matured in the 1940s, demonstrating potential to build upon the foundations it had already laid in the 1920s and 1930s for promoting greater participation of Palestinian Arab women in new spheres of social, political, cultural, and economic life. Its leaders exemplified this process; many had long experience in the movement and were public figures in their own right, with national stature. The structure of the movement, its organizational development, methods of protest, and political discourse reveal much about its vitality and politics. Its formation of specialized committees, delegation of tasks, and elections for officers all signified that new, democratic, mass-oriented political techniques and ideologies were permeating groups that had formerly relied upon a more informal, associational structure based upon kinship, friendship, and clientelism. These developments that took place in the 1940s contrast with the loosely organized, Jerusalem-dominated movement of the 1930s, which often seemed more reactive to crises and less oriented toward organization building. One result of the changes was that the militant character of the movement in the 1930s gave way to a more institutionalized, almost bureaucratic quality in the 1940s. This was exemplified by the new terminologies used by the movement, demonstrating the significance it attached to the discursive meanings of new organizational structures such as the central "bureau," or *maktab,* of the PAWU. In the course of this process, the women's movement became more politically sophisticated, which did not, ironically, necessarily mean it was more effective and activist. Accompanying these changes were, paradoxically, latent expressions of a conservative social and religious discourse that had not been as noticeable during the 1930s. Although the movement had established itself as a permanent and seemingly noncontroversial presence on the Palestinian political landscape, nonetheless a certain cautiousness entered its political vocabulary, perhaps as a result of some of the articulations of a conservative backlash mentioned above.[154] Furthermore, despite the evolution of a more cohesive and organized internal structure, the movement continued to rely on time-honored, albeit not necessarily successful, tactics from the 1930s. It had deepened its structure, but not necessarily evolved in its social ideology.

Although the movement may have adopted new organizing techniques more conducive to building mass-based organizations, it did not achieve this goal. One of its major failures was its inability to broaden its narrow class base beyond Palestinian women of the elite classes. In this, it mirrored the male-led national movement. It is not clear that the women's leadership even attempted to alleviate this problem, or entirely realized the full import of this failure, since most of the women involved were products of their personal class backgrounds and Palestinian social practices of clientelism and patronage. Attempts to organize greater numbers of women may not have included a vision of including them as active, fresh new leaders, but rather, as warm bodies to direct and recruit as volunteers for increasingly needed services. Some of the women leaders suffered from fears of the potential power of the lower orders. Mughannam expresses this cogently in her description of how Zionism imported "Bolshevik principles" into the country, producing "an effect on the population, not by its propaganda only, but by the genuine uneasiness which it inspired amongst the Arabs, especially amongst the poorer classes."[155] The clientelism and patronage practices of Palestinian society were easily grafted onto the women's organizations. One of the few women who did realize the importance of developing a broader, grassroots base was Sadhij Nassar, who also had a more explicitly feminist sense of what was needed, maintaining that "if women were really to liberate themselves . . . it could never be achieved by a few upper class women doing social work."[156] She actively attempted to recruit poorer women as active members, rather than recipients of largesse, yet ultimately even she gave up in defeat, overwhelmed by the problems involved in breaching the distances between elite and peasant women.

Contemporary Palestinian feminists continue to believe that "women's interest in women's rights is a recent phenomenon dating back to the late 1970s," but the evidence indicates otherwise: another interesting development in Palestine in the 1940s was a newly articulated feminist consciousness that expressed rumblings of "gender trouble."[157] During the AAC's tour of the country in 1946, the women of Jaffa expressed their dissatisfaction that the commission had "only been listening to male witnesses but the cause of Palestine . . . is not limited in importance . . . to men only but is important to Arabs of both sexes."[158] There were stirrings of a decoupling of women's rights from nationalism, the signature of Palestinian feminism. In a debate entitled "Should Women Have Equal Rights with Men" between a women's and a men's club at the YWCA in 1946, the women received more votes than the men.[159]

It is perhaps revealing that these feminist expressions usually came not from within the officially organized women's movement, but from within Palestinian society at large. The timing of PAWU president Zlikha al-Shihabi's statement that demanding political rights for women was before its time is significant. Although this declaration came right before her participation in the explicitly feminist 1944 women's conference, Shihabi's public announcement seemed designed to reassure male nationalist opinion that Palestinian women would maintain and uphold the implicit political pact of Palestinian society that nationalism take priority above all other political ideologies.

Yet embedded in the actions, statements, discourse, and strategies of the

Palestinian women's movement was an indigenous feminism that did demonstrate awareness of gender inequality and desires to mitigate it. This is a complex issue, however. The unprecedented nature, and indeed, continuation of, the peril confronting the Palestinian people has had an extraordinary effect on Palestinian politics since the mandate period. Few colonization projects in history explicitly resolved to transform the indigenous majority population into a subjugated minority under the political control of the colonists in a newly constituted independent state.[160] In addition to desiring a dominated minority, the Zionist movement equally aimed to displace as much of the indigenous population as possible. The Palestinian women's movement was founded in response to a particular crisis, one that sometimes receded in intensity but always recurred and, within the first two decades of the movement's existence, culminated in the realization of Palestinians' worst fears. Shihabi gave poignant and prescient expression to these fears in a letter to the high commissioner in which she said, "The Arabs at every hour sense their dark future and dismal fate."[161]

Survival—of a people living on its land, maintaining its culture and way of life, and directing its future development—had to be the paramount issue facing every Palestinian, man or woman. The Palestinian women's movement became inextricably caught up in the contradictions of a nationalist feminism that implied preservation of a culture and nation under attack, while simultaneously, subtly (even unconsciously at times) deconstructing the patriarchal institutions that formed the very pillars of that culture and nation. At its core, Palestinian patriarchal nationalism was atavistic and inherently conservative in the literal meaning of the word. Although it was ostensibly intercommunal and secular, the national movement sometimes invoked religious symbols, manipulating religious sentiment on behalf of, and linking it to, nationalist concerns. A "leading citizen of Jerusalem who voice[d] the policy" of the Supreme Muslim Council explained this to a visitor:

> The Mandate power in giving protection to the Jews has made it necessary for us to safeguard Moslem traditions. The awakening of Arab interest has led us to re-examine the Arab religious sources and to keep the true idea of the veil.[162]

The very existence of women's dynamic activism defied the definitional foundations of Palestinian nationalism. In becoming publicly active and involved, the women were not conserving culture, traditions, and religion, but challenging them. They did this not defiantly, however, but almost unconsciously. The leadership of the movement, in particular, embraced the characteristics of the new, modern woman—a construct that was widespread in this period in other colonized societies struggling to liberate themselves from imperialism—without entirely rejecting the "old" woman who represented authentic national culture.

These contradictions profoundly informed the feminist content of the Palestinian women's movement during the British Mandate period. In assessing their feminism, it is important to remember that its leaders and participants were products of their own time, and to avoid castigating them for what they were not. As Sharon Sievers points out, historians have tended to

> judge historical feminism and its advocates by contemporary expressions of both feminism and feminist theory. Our problem is to define in the broadest sense (consistent with time and place) the entire complex of issues specific to women and their concerns—issues that fit our historic sense of what might constitute feminism.[163]

As important, historians also need to allow women from the past, who were historical agents in their own right, to define their own historical sense of feminism. Older Palestinian women, when asked about feminism in the women's movement, sometimes responded that it was not "very important like the Palestine issue."[164] But as often, women struggled to explain it. There was a certain inarticulateness on the issue; women clearly were wary of Western notions of a feminism that posited individual ("selfish"), as opposed to communal rights. Lydia 'Arraj said:

> [Women] weren't after their rights so much as community rights . . . her rights . . . you have to be very careful how you put it. We have a more Islamic attitude. Why? Because we're influenced by society. Her rights . . . they have it in the Qur'an. She doesn't have the same rights as man. The condition of the country forced her to take other steps.[165]

Palestinian women, Muslim and Christian, had a concept of "rights" that corresponded to Temma Kaplan's notion of "female consciousness," which I consider a form of historical feminism. As Kaplan points out, "women's movements follow common patterns: they focus on consumer and peace issues and they oppose outside aggressors." Female consciousness was predicated upon a "vision of society" in which "social cohesion rises above individual rights."[166] Palestinian women linked all of these in their organizational strategies; in efforts to conserve a community under the most extreme attack of all—denial or even obliteration of its peoplehood as a nation—they used such tactics as consumer boycotts, and explicitly gendered their promotion of peace through claiming special status as women.

'Arraj's comments also reveal the ambivalence of Palestinian women about Islam and how it shaped their culture and their feminism. It is not incidental that 'Arraj, a Christian, includes herself when mentioning Palestinian society's "Islamic attitude[s]."[167] Both Muslim and Christian women realized that Islam provided both rights and restrictions, and that it also signified a potentially unifying force in Palestinian society. But, generally, activist women tended to avoid exploring this sensitive subject. Mughannam's book is a fascinating example of how they delicately participated in a contradictory exercise of exceptionalizing themselves based upon their "Eastern" identity while simultaneously, proudly proclaiming themselves as "cultured" as Western women. One of their major strategies, as we have seen, was to manipulate religious and "traditional" discourse to suit their own political agenda, while quietly abiding by a common culture that they sometimes defined as "Islamic," or at other times, Arab. Mughannam describes how the Arab woman could "promote the welfare of her sex without trespassing on her traditions and customs."[168] Women's ideas about what constituted these "traditions and customs," however, were not monolithic, and thus the emphasis, or not, they placed on issues such as dress or veiling, varied widely from individual to individual. As I have mentioned, the issue of veiling does not appear to have been of paramount importance. Photographs of elite women at conferences and signal events, particularly in the late 1930s and the 1940s, show that many were unveiled, and, as Nahid al-Sajjadi commented, in certain places such as Jerusalem, "if the woman wanted to take the veil off, she just did. Men did not bother her."[169] The point is, however, that, despite their sensitivities to, and proclamations in support of, maintaining culture and traditions, their acts often implicitly negated their discourse on the issue.

Another way in which Palestinian women's feminism deviated from and distinguished itself from Kaplan's female consciousness model is that they did not necessarily place "quality of life over access to institutional power."[170] Palestinian women clearly perceived access to institutional, political power as crucial to their aims. But their demands were implicitly for male access. It is not so clear whether or not these demands were part of a gradual strategy to introduce female suffrage or other measures for sexual equality; over time, as the national struggle remained bogged down at an elemental level, women had to deal with a reality in which no one had rights, as they frequently pointed out, and as has been mentioned. But Palestinian women did discuss women's rights and were aware of the intellectual antecedents of, and debate over, this issue that was being contested throughout the Middle East. Nahid al-Sajjadi comments:

> The idea of feminism existed in these groups. We used to talk about women. Mostly Huda Sha'rawi and Amina Sa'id would talk to us. . . . Huda Sha'rawi came from Italy and she took off the veil in front of everybody. . . . At that time there was Muhammad 'Abduh and Jamal al-din al-Afghani who formed what we would now call the fundamentalist movement. At that time the fundamentalists weren't military, they were more informative.[171]

Ultimately, in attempting to grapple with Palestinian women's feminism versus their nationalism, perhaps it is more useful to see these two seemingly contradictory political interests as the natural expression of two overlapping and sometimes conflicting identities that were both sites of attack--at times one more so than another, at other times both simultaneously. It was and still is easy for Western feminists to criticize Third World women's nationalism as somehow nonfeminist or politically regressive, without realizing that "national identities are as salient for women as they are for men."[172] An Algerian feminist, in remarks to an international gathering, could have been speaking directly about Palestine: "Probably most of the women at this Symposium take for granted that they belong to a country, a nation, which does not have to prove its existence; it allows for transcending the concept of nation, and criticizing it."[173] Such a luxury did not and still does not exist for Palestinian women, who have always had to deal with the issue of a national existence that is constantly questioned.[174] That Palestinian women necessarily had to make accommodations and negotiations between the two ostensibly contradictory interests/identities demonstrates the way that "gender and nation rub up against each other."[175]

West and Blumberg identify a "common theme" among the different ways that women have been drawn into protest activities, which is that "at least for a critical mass within the group the situation has become intolerable and those in power have to be challenged."[176] In the Palestinian case, it was the national situation that became "intolerable," and the major threat to existence.

During this period in history, Palestinian women did not perceive the "threats" that conservatives posed as deep seated and insurmountable.[177] They held a positivist, linear view of history that centered the nation-state as the pinnacle of nationalist achievement, the site of power and the granter of "rights." "Time" was a crucial component in this view; over time, women would win the rights that naturally came with the evolution of the nation-state and the inevitable progress that accompanied this process. From these attitudes came Shihabi's statement that demanding women's rights was "before its time," and Matiel Mughannam's comments about the necessity for authority derived from "the people" and its representative institutions—institutions that would arrive in time with the achievement of the nation-state.

Examining what Palestinian women did, as opposed to what they said, or how they articulated their political ideologies—be they feminist or nationalist—is key to understanding both. Their very acts of participating publicly, sometimes even violently, in the major issue of their day, and transgressing gendered norms of behavior constitute feminism. All of their actions, whether or not they were explicitly nationalist, indicate awareness of female solidarity and potential for female empowerment. If they did not advocate "feminism" as we define it, they acted it in a way that conformed to their own notions of how far they could go and effect changes. But perhaps their most feminist act was the building of a movement of their own, as opposed to reacting to events, then retiring back into private life between crises. They actively nurtured, developed, paid for, and maintained their own movement over the course of almost twenty turbulent years. And one of the goals of the movement was advancing or "raising the level" of the Arab woman, which involved a change in gender consciousness on the practical level, and an implicit critique of gender relations, whether the movement explicitly articulated this or not. Through their movement, Palestinian women of the mandate years provided a training ground for women to enter public activity, including nationalist and feminist politics. Najjar says that "the old methods of women's charitable organizations would *not* have led to substantial gains in women's status in the long run."[178] I would respectfully argue the opposite: it is *precisely* the legacy of the women's movement born of the charitable organizations that has set a precedent for and enabled contemporary Palestinian women's activists to mark a place for themselves in nationalist and feminist politics.

Postscript

The events of the *nakba*, and the transformation of hundreds of thousands of Palestinians into refugees resulted in immense upheaval in Palestinian society. Now Palestinians who had been peasant farmers were transformed into urban dwellers in camps on the outskirts of cities such as Beirut, Amman, and Damascus, or clustered in camps near larger towns that had not been conquered and incorporated into the new Jewish state. This process presaged the decline in importance and innovation of upper-class women's role in the nationalist movement. Palestinian women in the diaspora became caught up in family and communal survival, and the women who remained in the remnants of historical Palestine were overwhelmed by the humanitarian problems created by the *nakba*. Ironically, women who had placed great hopes in the transformational possibilities inherent in their own state now "performed the crucial function of substituting for state services" by setting up soup kitchens, first-aid clinics, orphanages, and the like.[179] In the 1960s, women's participation in the nationalist movement took a radical departure from the mandate period, with the founding of the Palestine Liberation Organization in the heady revolutionary atmosphere of national liberation politics which swept many still colonized Third World societies.[180] In the diaspora, some Palestinian women became guerrillas and fighters; in the Occupied Territories, they developed a new women's movement that was part of the evolution of a civil society that nonviolently resisted Israeli occupation. Palestinian women played a major role in the intifada that erupted in 1987. In the period preceding and after the Oslo Accords (1994), the Palestinian women's movement continued to deepen its efforts, establishing research and legal centers that deal with women's issues; and founding a women's studies program at Bir Zeit University, the major Palestinian university in the West Bank. In light of the current tense and uncertain political situation, the direction women's present and future participation in a Palestinian national entity will take is a tale yet to unfold.

APPENDIX I

Sources from the Palestinian Press

Of all the newspapers and journals published during the mandate, most were marginal and short-lived; unfortunately, not all are extant. In the 1920s alone, forty-eight different journals were published, and most did not survive into the 1930s. (See Chapter 3.) I consulted the collections at Hebrew University in Jerusalem, Jordan University in Amman, Bir Zeit University, and the Library of Congress. Hebrew University, to my knowledge, has the largest compilation of the Palestinian Arabic press in the world. Even this collection, however, has incomplete runs of the journals, many gaps, and damaged, illegible editions. Nonetheless, among these institutions there are solid holdings for two major newspapers, *Filastīn* (publication dates: 1911–68), and *al- Difā'* (1934–67). *Al-Karmil* and *Mirāt al-Sharq* have many issues missing. The library also has some years of *al-Sirāt al-Mustaqīm*, *al-Jām'ia al-'Arabiyya*, *al-Jām'ia al-Islāmiyya*, and *al-Hayyāt*. The latter were shorter-lived papers. The Library of Congress has much of *Filastīn*. Doing a comprehensive survey of all years of the mandate proved to be impossible, due to limited resources of travel, time, and availability; some runs were not all in the same place, and numerous years and fragments of years are missing of many of the mandate-era newspapers. Furthermore, during World War II the papers that had survived into the 1940s were heavily curtailed in their production, and many issues are missing for those years.

The rough breakdown of articles I found on women in the years surveyed: *Filastīn*: 1,109 (1921–39, 1942, 1944, 1946–47); *al-Difā'*: 360 (1934–39, with twenty-three months missing; 1945–46); *al-Karmil*: 239 (1920–39); *Mirāt al-Sharq*: 43 (Oct. 1926–38); *al-Sirāt al-Mustaqīm*: 65 (Nov. 1929–38); *al-Jām'ia al-'Arabiyya*: 47 (1929–33); and *Al-Jām'ia al-Islamiyya*: 24 (Jan.–Apr. 1933). This comes to a total of 1,887 articles.

Considering that not all extant newspapers were surveyed, and that significant numbers of issues of those that were examined are missing and not included in these figures, this is a considerable amount of reporting on this topic for a country the size of Palestine. Ela Greenberg generously shared her work from *al-Karmil*, on the years 1920–31, which constituted around 200 of the articles or headlines.

APPENDIX II
Members of the Arab Women's Executive Committee

The sources that listed rosters of members of the AWE were Matiel Moghannam's *The Arab Woman and the Palestine Problem* and articles in *Filastīn, Mirāt al-Sharq,* and *Filastin*-English.[1] The other sources were consulted for background information on the members or their families (usually husbands).

1. Mrs. Wahida al-Khalidi[a,d,e,f] Of Iraqi origin, Mrs. Khalidi was married to Husayn Fakhri al-Khalidi (1894–1962), mayor of Jerusalem (1934), member of the Administrative Board of the Reform Party (f. 1935), the Arab Higher Committee (AHC) in 1936, and the Arab delegation to the London Conference in 1939. He represented the Reform Party in the AHC and the Higher Arab Front in 1945. A physician, he was deputy director of health under the British, but was deported in 1937. Mrs. Khalidi was the first president of the Arab Women's Executive Committee. Her name was on numerous petitions and telegrams of protest in the early 1930s, but she seems to have faded into obscurity, although she attended and spoke at the 1938 Eastern Women's Conference in Cairo. She did not attend the 1944 conference.

2. Miss Shahinda Duzdar[a,b,c,d,g] Born 1906 in Jerusalem; died 1946, also in Jerusalem. Miss Duzdar studied at the Islamic Girls School in Jerusalem, "completed university studies in Cairo",[g] and was the first president of the Arab Women's Association. She was very active in the 1930s, attending and speaking at numerous meetings with the high commissioner, visiting other women's organizations, and writing and signing protests. The press reported she attended the 1938 Cairo conference, but she is not in the conference publication as a speaker; she did not attend the 1944 conference. She is listed as a founder of both the Arab Women's Association and the Arab Women's Union. She became prominent in the AWA when the two groups split.

3. *Mrs. Naʿimiti ʿAlami al-Husayni*[a,b,c,d,h]   Born 1895 to the al-ʿAlami family, her brother was the well-known nationalist Musa al-ʿAlami. She was the first female in her family sent to school, where she learned Italian, French, and English. She married Jamal al-Husayni in 1919, helping out with the family finances since she was wealthier than he. Jamal was secretary of the Supreme Muslim Council, 1928–30; president of the Arab Executive (AE) in 1934; president of the Palestine Arab Party, elected March 1935; a member of the AHC, the Central Committee of the Jihad and the 1939 delegation to London. In 1937 he fled the country to avoid arrest and deportation. The family lived in Iraq during 1939–41. Naʿimiti and Jamal separated after World War II. It is not clear if she attended the 1938 conference; she did attend the 1944 conference. She does not appear to have been consistently active (possibly due to family circumstances and living in exile).

4. *Mrs. Tarab ʿAuni ʿAbd al-Hadi*[a,b,c,d]   Not much has been written about her. She married the prominent nationalist ʿAuni ʿAbd al-Hadi. He was a member of numerous groups: al-Fatat, Central Relief Committee to Aid Syrian Victims in 1925; Central Relief Committee to Aid Victims of Palestine in 1929; Arab delegation to London in 1930; Islamic Conference in 1931; founding member of both the Jerusalem Branch of the Islamic Conference, 1927–30, and the Istiqlal Party, 1932; Arab Higher Committee in 1936. He was deported to Sarafand in 1936. Tarab attended and spoke at the Eastern Women's Conference in 1938, and attended the 1944 Arab Women's Conference.

5. *Mrs. Katrin Shukri Dib*[a,b,c,e,i,j]   Mrs. Dib, a Christian, was active in Orthodox affairs in Jerusalem, and was president of the Orthodox Girls Educational Society. She attended and spoke at both the 1938 and 1944 women's conferences in Cairo. Her husband, Shukri, was also active in Orthodox affairs, as president of the St. Yaʿqub Orthodox Church; signer of the Call of Christians of Palestine to the Christian World to Save the Holy Places From Zionist Danger; member of the Orthodox Board of Jerusalem; and the Executive Committee sent to the Orthodox Conference of 1931. He was also on the National Committee of Jerusalem in 1936 (on the treasury committee).

6. *Mrs. Mary Boulos Shihada*[a,b,c,d,k,l]   Christian, born December 28, 1901, in Jaffa; died 1994. Mrs. Shihada's father was a teacher of foreign languages in

Jaffa. She began to write at an early age and met her future husband, Boulos, through her writing. They married in 1923. She contributed articles to his newspaper, *Mirāt al-Sharq* in the 1920s and early 1930s, lectured at various clubs in the 1930s, and broadcast on the radio in the early 1940s. Her husband was a member of the Third Palestine Arab Conference, a member of the AE (elected 1928), and a representative of the Arabic Club.

7. *Mrs. Anisa Subhi al-Khadra*[a,b,c,d,e,m] Born circa 1897, in Shwayfat, Lebanon, of the Salim family; died 1955 in Damascus. Mrs. Khadra, whose father was Druze and mother was Muslim, was educated at an English school in Shwayfat. Her brother, Fu'ad, and future husband, Subhi, were active together in the Arab revolt of 1918 and as members of Faysal's government in Syria. She became engaged to Subhi in 1920. After the battle of Maysalun, they moved to Palestine (she with her brother). She and Subhi married in 1925. They lived first in Jerusalem, where she became active in the women's movement, then moved to Acre, where she was a leader in the Acre AWU. She did not attend the 1938 and 1944 conferences. She and her family moved back to Jerusalem in 1940. They left for Damascus in 1947 when fighting broke out. (Her husband was on the military committee.) Subhi, originally from Safad, was a founding member of the Istiqlal Party in 1932. He was also a member of the Arab Executive Committee, and the 1931 Islamic Conference. He was deported to Sarafand in 1936 and imprisoned from 1937 to 1940. The Mufti appointed him legal advisor to the Supreme Muslim Council. He died in 1958.

8. *Miss Khadija 'Arif al-Husayni*[b,c] No information.

9. *Miss Diya Nashashibi*[b,c] No information.

10. *Miss Melia Sakakini*[a,c,n,o] Christian, born 1890 on Orthodox Christmas Day, in Jerusalem; died 1966. Miss Sakakini was educated at the Arab Orthodox School in the Old City of Jerusalem, then studied at the Training College in Beit Jala run by Russian missionaries. She taught at various government schools during the mandate and was headmistress of a school in Jaffa. She was very active in the early years of the women's movement, and was a close friend of Na'imiti 'Alami al-Husayni. She lived with the family of her brother, Khalil. Twelve years her senior, he had been responsible for her since the death of her father when she was young. Khalil Sakakini, born 1878, was a renowned nationalist and educator, and a member of the AE. He was assistant inspector of schools for the government in Jerusalem, director

of the Teachers College and general inspector for the Arabic language. The Sakakini family fled to Cairo in 1948, where Khalil died in 1953, three months after the death of his son, Sari. Miss Sakakini and her two nieces, Hala and Dumya, moved to Ramallah shortly after Khalil's death. Hala Sakakini died in January 2002.

11. *Mrs. Matiel Mughannam*[a,b,c,d,e,k,q] The chief chronicler of the early women's movement, Mrs. Mughannam, a Christian, was born in Lebanon around the turn of the century. She died in the United States in 1992. She immigrated with her family when young to the United States, where she met and married Mughannam Mughannam, a Jerusalemite who was studying law there. They moved back to Jerusalem around 1921–22 after spending their honeymoon there and discovering there were opportunities for men with law degrees and English language proficiency. Mrs. Mughannam was very active in the movement in the 1930s, and wrote numerous articles for the press as well as her book. She was a founder of the Cultural Club in Jerusalem, and attended the Cairo conference in 1938, but not in 1944. Her husband was secretary of the central committee of the National Defense Party, and a member of the AE. In 1938–39, the Mughannams moved to Ramallah, where Matiel was a founder and president of the Ramallah Women's Union until she moved to the United States in the 1950s.

12. *Miss Zlikha Ishaq al-Shihabi*[a,b,c,d,r,s] Miss Shihabi was born and died in Jerusalem, in 1903 and 1992, respectively. She attended the Sisters of Zion School, run by nuns in Jerusalem, supplemented by private lessons in religion and languages. She was a founder of the Arab Women's Association in 1929, and was elected president of the Arab Women's Union in 1937, a position she held until her death. Very active and involved throughout her life, she helped establish a permanent building for the union, and was a founder of the Sports and Literary Club. She attended and spoke at both the 1938 and 1944 women's conferences. She was deported by the Israelis in 1968, but the United Nations interfered, helping her to return.

13. *Mrs. Kamil Budayri*[2c] No information.

14. *Mrs. Saadiya Musa al-'Alami*[b,p] Little information about her. She was Na'imiti al-Husayni's sister-in-law. Apparently her marriage to Musa was rocky; they eventually divorced.

15. *Miss Fatima al-Husayni*[b,c] No information.

16. *Miss Zahiya Nashashibi*[bc]   Not much information about her. She graduated from the Sisters of Zion. Miss Nashashibi was a founding member of the AWA, and its president (after Duzdar's death in 1946) until her own death in 1977.

SOURCES FOR APPENDIX II

[a] *Filastīn*, Oct. 29, 1929.

[b] Matiel Mogannam, *The Arab Woman and the Palestine Problem* (London: Herbert Joseph, 1937).

[c] *Mirāt al-Sharq*, Oct. 28, 1929.

[d] *Filastin*-English, Oct. 26, 1929.

[e] Bayan Nuwayhid al-Hut, *Al-qīyādāt wa al-mu'assasāt al-sīyāsiyya fī Filastīn, 1917–1948*, (Beirut: dār al-huda, 1986, third printing).

[f] Ya'qub 'Awdat, *Min 'ālam al-fikr wa al-ādab fī Filastīn* (Amman: wakala al-tawzi' al-Urduniyya, 1987).

[g] Ya'qub al-'Ansari and Ibrahim al-Husayni, *Jam'iyyat al-sayyidāt al-'Arabiyyāt al-Quds* (Jerusalem: 1985).

[h] Sarah Graham-Brown, *Images of Women*, (London: Quartet Books, 1988).

[i] *Al-mar'a al-'Arabiyya wa qadiyyat Filastīn* (Cairo: 1938).

[j] *Al-mu'tamar al-nisā'ī al-'Arabī* (Cairo: dār al-ma'rif, 1944).

[k] Asma Tubi. *Abīr wa majd* (Beirut: Matba'at qalalat, 1966).

[l] Orayb Najjar with Kitty Warnock, *Portraits of Palestinian Women* (Salt Lake City: University of Utah Press, 1992).

[m] Salma Khadra Jayyusi, interview with the author, July 1, 1996.

[n] Hala and Dumya Sakakini, interviews with the author, 1992–94.

[o] Sakakini, Hala, *Jerusalem and I: A Personal Record* (Amman: Economic Press, 1990).

[p] Sir Geoffrey Furlonge, *Palestine is My Country: The Story of Musa Alami* (New York: Praeger Publishers, 1969).

[q] Theodore Mogannam, interview with the author, Sep. 28, 1995.

[r] Sharaf, Randa, "Zlikha al-Shihabi fī dhimmat al-tārīkh: rā'idat al-haraka al-nisā'iyya fī Filastīn, mu'assasa al-ittihād al-nisā'ī al-'Arabī," *Al-mar'a* 13 (June 1992): 8–10.

[s] Zlikha Shihabi, unpublished paper (N.d., probably 1980s).

Notes

The following abbreviations are used in the notes and bibliography:

AUB	American University of Beirut
CID	Central Intelligence Department
CMO	Chief Medical Officer
CO	Colonial Office, Great Britain
CS	Chief Secretary
CZA	Central Zionists Archives, Jerusalem
DMS	Director of Medical Services
FO	Foreign Office, Great Britain
HC	High Commissioner
ISA	Israel State Archives
JSS	*Junior Service Staff List*
LMO	Lady Medical Officer
MAQF	*Al-mar'a al-'Arabiyya wa qadiyyat Filastīn*
MEC	Middle East Centre, St. Antony's College, Oxford
MNA	*al-Mu'tamar al-nisā'ī al-'Arabī*
OETA	Occupied Enemy Territory A
OAG	Officer Administering Government
PRO	Public Records Office, London
RG	Record Group
RH	Rhodes House, Bodleian Library, Oxford

SMO   Senior Medical Officer
SSC   Secretary of State for the Colonies
USNA United States National Archives
WO   War Office, London

CHAPTER 1. INTRODUCTION

1. The pronouncement of Samah Nusseibeh, president of the Arab Women's Association (AWA). While gesturing to a pamphlet, the "official" history of the AWA, she rejected any information not written in its pages. Interview with the author, Nov. 23, 1993.

2. *Mirāt al-Sharq*, Oct. 15, 1929; *al-Jām'ia al-'Arabiyya*, Aug. 27, 1931; *al-Difā'*, Mar. 25, 1935; *Filastīn*, June 23, 1944; and Dec. 4, 1947. (Throughout this book, the article titles are translations from Arabic into English.)

3. Throughout the course of this project, when I informed people that I was researching the Palestinian women's movement, the most common response of non-Palestinians was, "I didn't know there *was* one." A frequent reaction of Palestinians was, "The women didn't do anything." When I asked for names of women to interview, they invariably referred me to men instead.

4. Rosemary Sayigh, "Femmes palestiniennes: une histoire en quête d'historiens," *Revue d'études palestiniennes* 23 (spring 1987): 13.

5. Technically, the mandate formally began in 1922, after the completion of the World War I negotiations, but the British actually began to rule in 1918, when they captured Palestine during the war. I thus date the years included in this study somewhat arbitrarily. I begin roughly with 1920 because this signaled the laying of the groundwork of more formal administrative structures to come, as the British government was confident it would obtain the mandate over Palestine.

6. There is a long, complex, theoretical, and historically based argument here, which I am going to resist entering into, insofar as the subject is outside of the scope of this book. I am not arguing that anticolonial struggles and nation-building are inherently separate processes; many national liberation struggles have been characterized by strong, dynamic, and even in some cases successful nation-building strategies, institutions, and leadership. One need only look at a few cases, such as South Africa, to recognize the blurring of certain of these elements. However, in examining other postcolonial, independent states, and particularly upon analyzing the politics of the Palestinian National Authority (a separate category in and of itself), one can only come to the conclusion that the two processes are not always one and the same, each requiring different political strategies and, often, leadership.

7. There is much confusion over the name of this group, which was also referred to variously as the Arab Women's Committee, the Arab Ladies Committee, the Arab Ladies Society, the Arab Women's Society, the Arab Women's

Union (AWU), and others. For the sake of clarity I will use the name Arab Women's Association (AWA). Until 1938, all of these names referred to one group. After that time, the organization split into two groups, the Arab Women's Society and the Arab Women's Union. (See Chapter 6 for discussion of this split.) Part of the problem in untangling the various names used for one or two groups stems from inconsistencies in the sources' interchangeable usage of "ladies" and "women" in both English and Arabic. For example, the Arab Ladies Society sometimes translates its name into English as "women," although it always uses "ladies" in Arabic. On the other hand, the AWU never uses either the Arabic or English word for ladies in its name. Matiel Mughannam, the only participant chronicler of the women's movement in this period, refers to the "Arab ladies association" on one page, then later calls it the "Arab Women's Association." Matiel Mogannam, *The Arab Woman and the Palestine Problem* (London: Herbert Joseph, Ltd., 1937), 55, 57. In British government documents, the women and the government often refer to the AWA as the Arab Women's Committee.

8. I concur with Anne McClintock, who warns of the "pitfalls" of the term "postcolonial," which "reorients the globe . . . around a single, binary opposition: colonial-postcolonial. . . . The term confers on colonialism the prestige of history proper; colonialism is the determining marker of history." The term tends to define the histories of countries that experienced diverse types of colonizations solely by their "'common' experiences of European colonization." Although she does not reject the use of the concept altogether, she calls for using it "judiciously in appropriate circumstances, in the context of other terms." Anne McClintock, *Imperial Leather: Race, Gender and Sexuality in the Colonial Contest* (New York and London: Routledge, 1995), 11–13.

9. Rita Giacaman and Muna Odeh, "Palestinian Women's Movement in the Israeli-Occupied West Bank and Gaza Strip," in *Women of the Arab World*, edited by Nahid Toubia (London: Zed Books, 1988), 61; Anne McClintock, "'No Longer In a Future Heaven': Women and Nationalism in South Africa," *Transitions* 51 (1991): 122.

10. For a thoughtful assessment of the critique, see Frances S. Hasso, "The 'Women's Front': Nationalism, Feminism, and Modernity in Palestine," *Gender and Society* 12, no. 4 (1998): 441–65.

11. Rosemary Sayigh, "Women in Struggle—Palestine," *Third World Quarterly* 5, no. 4 (Oct. 1983): 881.

12. Orayb Aref Najjar, "Between Nationalism and Feminism: the Palestinian Answer," in *Women Transforming Politics: Worldwide Strategies for Empowerment*, edited by Jill Bystydzienski (Bloomington: Indiana University Press, 1992), 158.

13. Didar Fawzy, "Palestinian Women in Palestine," in *Women of the Mediterranean*, edited by Monique Gadant (London: Zed Press, 1986), 80. The author is quoting activist Samira Khoury.

14. Ruth Woodsmall, *Moslem Women Enter a New World* (New York: Round Table Press, 1936), 363.

15. Yusra Berberi, "Active in Politics and Women's Affairs in Gaza," in

Palestinian Women: Identity and Experience, edited by Ebba Augustin (London: Zed Press, 1993), 52.

16. A particularly incisive critique is Rima [sic] Hammami and Eileen Kuttab, "The Palestinian Women's Movement: Strategies Towards Freedom and Democracy," *News From Within* 15, no. 4 (April 1999): 3–9 [Hammami's first name is usually spelled "Rema."]; see also Giacaman and Odeh, "Palestinian Women's Movement." Cheryl Rubenberg, in a recent study, points to the role women themselves have played in perpetuating the nationalist priority and its concomitant factionalism by highlighting class and urban-rural cleavages among Palestinian women. Cheryl Rubenberg, *Palestinian Women: Patriarchy and Resistance in the West Bank* (Boulder and London: Lynne Rienner Publishers, 2001), 225–28.

17. Rosemary Sayigh, "Looking Across the Mediterranean," *MERIP* 124 (June 1984): 26.

18. Chandra Talpade Mohanty, "Cartographies of Struggle: Third World Women and the Politics of Feminism," in *Third World Women and the Politics of Feminism,* edited by Mohanty, Ann Russo, and Lourdes Torres (Bloomington: Indiana University Press, 1991), 13.

19. Ibid., 11, 38.

20. Deniz Kandiyoti, "Contemporary Feminist Scholarship and Middle East Studies," in *Gendering the Middle East: Emerging Perspectives,* edited by Kandiyoti (Syracuse: Syracuse University Press, 1996), 17.

21. Marnia Lazreg, "Feminism and Difference: The Perils of Writing as a Woman on Women in Algeria," *Feminist Studies* 14 (spring 1988): 87.

22. Sharon Sievers, "Six (or More) Feminists in Search of a Historian," in *Expanding the Boundaries of History: Essays on Women in the Third World,* edited by Cheryl Johnson-Odim and Margaret Strobel (Bloomington: Indiana University Press, 1992), 326.

23. Lazreg, "Feminism and Difference," 101.

24. As Cynthia Enloe observes, "Coming face to face with a Vietnamese feminist of the 1920s . . . makes it less possible for British and American women to imagine that *their* foremothers were the creators of feminist ideas." Cynthia Enloe, *Bananas, Beaches and Bases: Making Feminist Sense of International Politics* (Berkeley: University of California Press, 1989), 61. Third World feminist scholars, particularly those who are Western trained, have necessarily been more self-conscious about the relationship between their own and Western feminism. See, e.g., Lazreg, "Feminism and Difference," and the Third World scholarship discussed below.

25. Janet Afary, *The Iranian Constitutional Revolution, 1906–1911: Grassroots Democracy, Social Democracy and the Origins of Feminism* (New York: Columbia University Press, 1996), 10.

26. Sievers, "Six (or More) Feminists," 325.

27. Karen Offen, "Defining Feminism: A Comparative Historical Approach," *Signs* 14, no. 1 (1988): 129–30, 120, 134.

28. Offen, "Defining Feminism," 136; emphasis in original.

29. Sievers, "Six (or More) Feminists," 326.

30. Offen, "Defining Feminism," 139.

31. Temma Kaplan, "Female Consciousness and Collective Action: The Case of Barcelona, 1910–1918," *Signs* 7, no. 3 (1982): 545.

32. I find Offen's characterization of relational feminism as "egalitarian" debatable, considering it is based upon the essentialization of gender differences that implicitly limit women's roles and functions in society.

33. Sayigh, "Looking Across," 23.

34. Julie Peteet, "Authenticity and Gender: The Presentation of Culture," in *Arab Women: Old Boundaries, New Frontiers*, edited by Judith E. Tucker (Bloomington: Indiana University Press, 1993), 50, 53. She is quoting Mina Davis Caulfield.

35. Definitions of these terms, however, are somewhat vague and confusing. McClintock does not define "nationalist feminism" beyond remarking that its "singular contribution . . . has been its insistence on relating the feminist struggle to other liberation movements." Badran simply defines "national feminism" as denoting "feminisms that existed in . . . colonized or semi-independent countries such as Egypt, Syria, India, and the like." McClintock, "No Longer," 121; Margot Badran, *Feminists, Islam, and Nation: Gender and the Making of Modern Egypt* (Princeton: Princeton University Press, 1995), 21.

36. The use of words such as "traditional" and "traditional society" is often unexamined, both by contemporary writers and later historians. The concept is less monolithic and more fluid than is assumed; "traditions" change along with social, political, and economic transformations that make it convenient to either discard or retain certain practices considered "traditional," particularly as related to gender. Traditions also varied from time to time, place to place: they had rural versus urban components, and differed according to class. For more on tradition, see Rema Hammami, "Commentary: Feminist Scholarship and the Literature on Palestinian Women," *Gender and Society Working Papers*, Women's Studies Program, Birzeit University, June 1995, 20–21; and Peteet, "Authenticity and Gender," 52.

37. I discuss the "new woman" more fully in later chapters. I note here, however, that the new woman of early twentieth-century India and other colonized societies differs markedly from the new woman in late nineteenth-century Britain and the United States. For descriptions of this androgynous, well-educated nonconformist, see Carroll Smith-Rosenberg, "Discourses of Sexuality and Subjectivity: The New Woman, 1870–1920," in *Hidden From History: Reclaiming the Gay and Lesbian Past*, edited by Martin Duberman, Martha Vicinus, and George Chauncey (New York: Meridian, 1989), 264–80.

38. McClintock, *Imperial Leather*, 359.

39. Partha Chatterjee, "The Nationalist Resolution of the Women's Question," in *Recasting Women: Essays in Indian Colonial History*, edited by Kumkum Sangari and Sudesh Vaid (New Brunswick: Rutgers University Press, 1990), 238–40, 248. See also his *The Nation and Its Fragments: Colonial and Postcolonial Histories* (Princeton: Princeton University Press, 1993).

40. This figure has become legendary. The mother of the "martyr" Muhammad Jumjum, who was condemned to death by the British for his role in the 1929 Wailing Wall incidents, is reported to have refused to accept condolences after his execution, saying, "Why are you weeping? I'm proud of my son who was awarded a great honor through martyrdom." Khadija Abu 'Ali, *Muqaddimāt hawla al-wāqi'a al-mar'a wa tajrībatihā fī al-thawra al-Filastīniyya* (Beirut: General Union of Palestinian Women, 1975), 45. For more discussion about the "mother of the martyr," see Julie Peteet, "Icons and Militants: Mothering in the Danger Zone," *Signs* 23, no. 1 (1997): 103–29; and also her *Gender in Crisis: Women and the Palestinian Resistance Movement* (New York: Columbia University Press, 1991), 184–86.

41. McClintock, "No Longer," 116; Samita Sen, "Motherhood and Mothercraft: Gender and Nationalism in Bengal," *Gender and History* 5, no. 2 (1993), 232.

42. Hasso, "The 'Women's Front,' " 442.

43. McClintock, "No Longer," 116.

44. Guida West and Rhoda Lois Blumberg, "Reconstructing Social Protest from a Feminist Perspective," in *Women and Social Protest*, edited by West and Blumberg (Oxford: Oxford University Press, 1990), 4.

45. Peteet, "Authenticity," 52.

46. For autobiographies, see, for example, 'Anbara Sallam al-Khalidi, *Jawla fī al-dhikrayāt bayna Lubnān wa Filastīn* (Beirut: dār al-nahār lil-nashr, 1978); Wadi'a Qaddura Khartabil, *Bahthān 'an al-amal wa al-watan: sittūn 'āman min kifāh imra'a fī sabīl Filastīn, 1936–1990* (Beirut: Bisān al-nashr wa al-tawzi', 1995); Hala Sakakini, *Jerusalem and I: A Personal Record* (Amman: Economic Press, 1990); and Fadwa Tuqan, *A Mountainous Journey: A Poet's Autobiography*, translated by Olive Kenny, poetry translated by Naomi Shihab Nye, edited by Salma Khadra Jayyusi (Saint Paul: Graywolf Press, 1990). The first two authors, who were actually Lebanese feminists married to Palestinian men, lived in Palestine and were active in the women's movement during the mandate period. See also Asma Tubi, *'Abīr wa majd* (Beirut: Matba'at Qalalat, 1966); it is an informative biographical dictionary of modern Arab women notables, written by a Palestinian woman. Memoirs include Said K. Aburish, *Children of Bethany: The Story of a Palestinian Family* (London: I. B. Taurus and Co., 1988); John Melkon Rose, *Armenians of Jerusalem: Memories of Life in Palestine* (London: Radcliffe Press, 1993); and Serene Husseini Shahid, *Jerusalem Memories*, edited by Jean Said Makdisi, with an introduction by Edward W. Said (Beirut: Naufal Group, 2000). An oral history of Yusra Salah is *Safahāt min al-dhākira al-Filastīniyya*, no. 3, "Tadhakurrāt Yusra Salah," interviewed by Lubna 'Abd al-Hadi (Bir Zeit: The Center for Studies and Documentation of Palestinian Society, 1992). Some oral histories are also included in Orayb Najjar, with Kitty Warnock, *Portraits of Palestinian Women* (Salt Lake City: University of Utah Press, 1992); and Kitty Warnock, *Land Before Honour: Palestinian Women in the Occupied Territories* (New York: Monthly Review Press, 1990).

47. The interesting exception, written in 1936, at the height of the 1936

strike and revolt, is by a participant in the women's movement, Matiel Mughannam. Although the book highlights women's participation in its title and in certain sections, the majority of the book deals with the Palestinian situation more generally. See Mogannam, *The Arab Woman*. Some of the few scholarly historical treatments of Palestinian women are Judith E. Tucker, *In the House of the Law: Gender and Islamic Law in Ottoman Syria and Palestine* (Berkeley: University of California Press, 1998); Tucker, "*Muftis* and Matrimony: Islamic Law and Gender in Ottoman Syria and Palestine," *Islamic Law and Society* 1, no. 3 (1994): 265–300; and Tucker, "Ties That Bound: Women and Family in Eighteenth- and Nineteenth-Century Nablus," in *Women in Middle Eastern History*, edited by Nikki Keddie and Beth Baron (New Haven: Yale University Press, 1991); Iris Agmon, "Women, Class, and Gender: Muslim Jaffa and Haifa at the Turn of the Twentieth Century," *International Journal of Middle East Studies* 30, no. 4 (1998): 477–500; Yvonne Haddad, "Palestinian Women: Patterns of Legitimation and Domination," in *The Sociology of the Palestinians*, edited by Khalil Nakhleh and Elia Zureik (London: Croom Helm, 1980). Annelies Moors uses a historical approach in her anthropological study, *Women, Property and Islam: Palestinian Experiences, 1920–1990* (Cambridge: Cambridge University Press, 1995). My own work, all of it written after most of the research for this book was completed, focuses on Palestinian women's history. See Ellen Fleischmann, "Jerusalem Women's Organizations During the British Mandate, 1920s-1930s" (Jerusalem: Palestinian Academic Society for the Study of International Affairs, 1995); "Crossing the Boundaries of History: Exploring Oral History in Researching Palestinian Women in the Mandate Period," *Women's History Review* 5, no. 3 (Oct. 1996): 351–71; "Selective Memory, Gender and Nationalism: Palestinian Women Leaders in the British Mandate Period," *History Workshop Journal* 47 (April 1999): 141–58; "Nation, Tradition, and Rights: The Indigenous Feminism of the Palestinian Women's Movement (1929–1948)," in *Women's Suffrage in the British Empire: Citizenship, Nation, and Race*, edited by Ian Fletcher, Philippa Levine, and Laura Mayhall (New York: Routledge, 2000), 138–56; and "The Emergence of the Palestinian Women's Movement, 1929–1939," *Journal of Palestine Studies* 29, no. 3 (spring 2000): 16–32.

48. Nahla Abdo, "Nationalism and Feminism: Palestinian Women and the *Intifada*—No Going Back?" in *Gender and National Identity: Women and Politics in Muslim Societies*, edited by Valentine Moghadam (London and Atlantic Highlands, N.J.: Zed Press; Karachi: Oxford University Press, 1994), 148.

49. See Sayigh, "Femmes palestiniennes," 15.

50. Haddad, "Palestinian Women," 147.

51. The Israel State Archives contains the papers and records of numerous Palestinian individuals, such as George Antonius, and institutions ranging from the Supreme Muslim Council to the YWCA. The Hebrew University National Library, the Israeli equivalent to the Library of Congress, contains almost all of the Palestinian Arabic newspapers published during the mandate and before. It was (and remains) extremely difficult for Palestinians without Western pass-

ports to gain access to their own historical material. In 1993, when I attempted to enter the Israel State Archives with a Palestinian colleague from the West Bank, we were detained and almost ejected from the building until an archivist who recognized me angrily reprimanded the security guards. It is doubtful that my colleague would have been allowed entry without my accompanying her. When Hala and Dumya Sakakini visited the Hebrew University Library after 1967, they saw their father's extensive collection of books, which had been confiscated after their family's flight to Egypt during the fighting in Jerusalem in 1948. They even recognized his handwriting on the margins of the pages but were not allowed to recover the books; Hala and Dumya Sakakini, interview with the author, Sept. 28, 1992. As of this writing, Palestinians without an Israeli identity card or special permit are prohibited from entering Jerusalem or Israel proper, which is the location of many archival materials.

52. Nuha Abu Daleb, "Palestinian Women and Their Role in the Revolution," *Peuples méditerranéens* 5 (Oct.-Dec. 1978): 36.

53. For works on women in the national liberation struggle prior to the intifada, (including writings on women in diaspora communities and the Occupied Territories), see "Al-haraka al-nisā'iyya," *al-mawsū'a al-Filastīniyya*, vol. 2 (Damascus: ha'iyya al-masū'a al-Filastīniyya, 1984), 211–19; Ghazi al-Khalili, *Al-mar'a al-Filastīniyya wa al-thawra* (Beirut: PLO Research Center, 1977); Khadija Abu 'Ali, *Muqaddimāt;* Warnock, *Land Before Honour;* Peteet, *Gender in Crisis;* Najjar, *Portraits of Palestinian Women;* Soraya Antonius, "Fighting on Two Fronts: Conversations with Palestinian Women," *Journal of Palestine Studies* 8 (1979): 26–49; Giacaman and Odeh, "Palestinian Women's Movement"; Abu Daleb, "Palestinian Women"; Rosemary Sayigh and Julie Peteet, "Between Two Fires: Palestinian Women in Lebanon," in *Caught Up In Conflict,* edited by Rosemary Ridd and Helen Callaway (New York: New York University Press, 1987), 106–37; Hamida Kazi, "Palestinian Women and the National Liberation Movement: A Social Perspective," in *Women in the Middle East,* edited by the Khamsin Collective (London: Zed Press, 1987), 26–39.

For works on women during and after the intifada, a select list includes Islah Jad, "From Salons to Popular Committees: Palestinian Women, 1919–1989," in *Intifada: Palestine at the Crossroads,* edited by Jamal R. Nassar and Roger Heacock (Birzeit and New York: Birzeit University and Praeger Press, 1991); Jad, "Tatawwur al-dawr al-sīyāsī lil-mar'a al-Filastīniyya hatta al-intifāda," *Shu'ūn al-mar'a,* May 1991, 94–107 (pt. 1), and January 1992, 75–83 (pt. 2); Jad, "Claiming Feminism, Claiming Nationalism: Women's Activism in the Occupied Territories," in *The Challenge of Local Feminisms: Women's Movements in Global Perspective,* edited by Amrita Basu (Boulder: Westview Press, 1995), 226–50; Abdo, "Nationalism and Feminism"; Rita Giacaman and Penny Johnson, "Building Barricades and Breaking Barriers," in *Intifada: The Palestinian Uprising against Israeli Occupation,* edited by Zachary Lockman and Joel Beinin (Boston: South End Press, 1989), 155–70; Rita Giacaman with Islah Jad and Penny Johnson, "For the Common Good? Gender and Social Citizenship in Palestine," *Middle East Report* 26, no. 1 (Jan.-March 1996): 11–17; Rema Hammami, "Women, the Hijab and the Intifada," *Middle East Report* 20 (May-Aug. 1990): 24–28; "From Immodesty to Collaboration: Hamas, the Women's Movement, and National Identity in the Intifada," in *Political Islam: Essays from Middle East Report*, edited by Joel Beinin and Joe Stork (Berkeley: University of California Press, 1997), 194–210; Philippa Strum, *The Women Are Marching: The Second Sex and the Palestinian Revolution* (Chicago: Lawrence Hill Books, 1992); Elise Young, *Keepers of the History: Women and the Israeli-Palestinian Conflict* (New York: Teacher's College Press, 1992); Augustin, *Palestinian Women*; Sherna Berger Gluck, *An American Feminist in Palestine: The Intifada Years* (Philadelphia: Temple University Press, 1994); Simona Sharoni, *Gender and the Israeli-Palestinian Conflict: The Politics of Women's Resistance* (Syracuse: Syracuse University Press, 1995); Amal Kawar, *Daughters of Palestine: Leading Women of the Palestinian National Movement* (Albany: State University of New York Press, 1996); Hasso, "The 'Women's Front' "; Rabab Abdulhadi, "The Palestinian Women's Autonomous Movement: Emergence, Dynamics, and Challenges," *Gender and Society* 12, no. 6 (1998): 649–73; Hammami and Kuttab, "The Palestinian Women's Movement"; Suha Sabbagh, ed., *Arab Women: Between Defiance and Restraint* (New York: Olive Branch Press, 1996) and also (ed.), *Palestinian Women of Gaza and the West Bank* (Bloomington: Indiana University Press, 1998); and Rubenberg, *Palestinian Women*.

54. McClintock, *Imperial Leather*, 367.
55. *Al-mawsūʻa*, 212; Abu ʻAli, *Muqaddimāt*, 43.
56. Khalili, *al-marʼa al-Filastīniyya*, 80.
57. See, e.g., *Al-mawsūʻa*, Khalili, *Al-marʼa al-Filastīniyya*; and Abu ʻAli, *Muqaddimāt*. Swedenburg observes that contradictions in historical interpretations result from the fact that "official" historiography (i.e., produced by the PLO) "has had to invoke popular mobilizations of the past in order to motivate the populace of the present." He notes a similar tendency in historicizing the role of the peasantry, who are both exalted for their heroism and sacrifice and reduced to "bit players and ancillaries." Ted Swedenburg, *Memories of Revolt: The 1936–1939 Rebellion and the Palestinian National Past* (Minneapolis: University of Minnesota Press, 1995), 20. For a discussion of how nationalist discourse distorts popular memory of women's political role, see my "Selective Memory, Gender and Nationalism."
58. The list of works (in both English and Arabic) that barely refer to and do not even contain index references to women is too extensive to cite here. Perhaps more valuable to highlight are the exceptions that mention women more than in passing, or contain information on them in special sections. These include Ylana Miller, *Government and Society in Rural Palestine, 1920–1948* (Austin: University of Texas Press, 1985); Ann Mosely Lesch, *Arab Politics in Palestine, 1917–1939: The Frustration of a Nationalist Movement* (Ithaca: Cornell University Press, 1979); and Bayan Nuwayhid al-Hut, *Al-qīyādāt wa al-muʼassasāt al-sīyāsī fī Filastīn, 1917–1948* (Beirut: dār al-huda, 1986). Several works that notably discuss women in some depth are Akram Zuʻaytir, *Yawmiyyāt Akram Zuʻaytir: al-haraka al-wataniyya al-Filastīniyya 1935–*

1939 (Beirut: Palestine Studies Association, 1980); and Swedenburg, *Memories of Revolt*.

59. Vestiges of the movement, drastically transformed, still existed at the time of my research, 1992–99. A number of the major women's organizations that were part of the women's movement during the period under study—specifically, the AWA and the AWU—were still extant in Jerusalem, Ramallah, and Bethlehem.

60. See, e.g., West and Blumberg, *Women and Social Protest*; Nira Yuval-Davis and Floya Anthias, eds., *Woman-Nation-State* (New York: St. Martin's Press, 1989); Miranda Davies, *Third World/Second Sex: Women's Struggles and National Liberation* (London: Zed Books, 1983); Sara Evans, *Personal Politics: The Roots of Women's Liberation in the Civil Rights Movement and the New Left* (New York: Vantage Books, 1979); Richard Stites, *The Women's Liberation Movement in Russia* (Princeton: Princeton University Press, 1978); Kaplan, "Female Consciousness"; Jean Quaertert, *Reluctant Feminists in German Social Democracy, 1885–1917* (Princeton: Princeton University Press, 1979); Lizabeth Paravisini-Gebert, "Decolonizing Feminism: The Home-Grown Roots of Caribbean Women's Movements," in *Daughters of Caliban: Caribbean Women in the Twentieth-Century*, edited by Consuelo López Springfield (Bloomington: Indiana University Press, 1997); and Elizabeth Wood, *The Baba and the Comrade: Gender and Politics in Revolutionary Russia* (Bloomington: Indiana University Press, 1997).

61. Paul Connerton, *How Societies Remember* (Cambridge: Cambridge University Press, 1989), 2; Popular Memory Group, "Popular Memory: Theory, Politics, Method," in *Making Histories: Studies in History Writing and Politics*, edited by Richard Johnson, Gregor McLennan, Bill Schwarz, and David Suttow (Minneapolis: University of Minnesota Press, 1982), 205–52.

62. For a discussion of the collision between the Palestinian and Israeli interpretations of history, see Swedenburg, *Memories of Revolt*, especially ch. 1.

63. Sayigh recounts how an older woman activist, Umm Samir, when denounced by young women at a lecture for being a member of the "generation of the disaster," commented, "they forgot that it was we who opened the way for them." Sayigh, "Femmes palestiniennes," 18.

64. See, e.g., Philip Mattar, *The Mufti of Jerusalem* (New York: Columbia University Press, 1988); Yehoshua Porath, *The Emergence of the Palestinian-Arab Nationalist Movement: 1918–1929* (London: Frank Cass, 1974); and Porath, *The Palestinian Arab National Movement: From Riots to Rebellion, 1929–1939* (London: Frank Cass, 1977); Issa Khalaf, *Politics in Palestine: Arab Factionalism and Social Disintegration, 1939–1948* (Albany: State University of New York Press, 1991); Muhammad Muslih, *The Origins of Palestinian Nationalism* (New York: Columbia University Press, 1988); Hut, *Al-qīyādāt*; Kamil Mahmud Khilla, *Filasṭīn wa al-intidāb al-Barīṭānī, 1922–1939* (Beirut: PLO Research Center, 1974); ʿAbd al-Qadir Yassin, *Kifāḥ al-shaʿab al-Filasṭīnī qabla al-ʿām 1948* (Beirut: PLO Research Center, 1975); Subhi Muhammad

Yassin, *Al-thawra al-'Arabiyya al-kubra* (Cairo: dār al-kātib al-'Arabī, 1967); Akram Zu'aytir, *Yawmiyyāt;* Lesch, *Arab Politics.*

65. Joan Wallach Scott, *Gender and the Politics of History* (New York: Columbia University Press, 1988), 15–17. Scott's descriptions of these new categories are accompanied by extensive bibliographical notes.

66. One interesting phenomenon has been the evolution of a whole new subspecialty that examines the historical experiences of European and Western women in imperialist and colonial projects in Third World societies. See, e.g., Margaret Strobel, *European Women and the Second British Empire* (Bloomington: Indiana University Press, 1991); Billie Melman, *Women's Orients: English Women and the Middle East, 1718–1918: Sexuality, Religion and Work* (London: Macmillan, 1992); Nupur Chaudhuri and Margaret Strobel, eds., *Western Women and Imperialism: Complicity and Resistance* (Bloomington: Indiana University Press, 1992); Antoinette Burton, *Burdens of History: British Feminists, Indian Women, and Imperial Culture, 1865–1915* (Chapel Hill: University of North Carolina Press, 1994); Kumari Jayawardena, *The White Woman's Other Burden: Western Women and South Asia During British Rule* (New York: Routledge, 1995); Helen Callaway, *Gender, Culture and Empire: European Women in Colonial Nigeria* (London: Macmillan, 1987); Claudia Knapman, *White Women in Fiji, 1835- 1930: The Ruin of Empire?* (Sydney: Allen & Unwin, 1986); and McClintock, *Imperial Leather.* Scholars working within this new specialization self-consciously expose and confront the "historical racism of middle-class Western feminism," yet it contributes unintentionally to a continuation of Western feminists' "history of centralizing themselves in order to marginalize the Other." It thus "runs the risk of reproducing the imperialist effects that it hopes to critique," by focusing its lens, once again, on Western women, and their agency, however critically these subjects are framed. Burton, *Burdens of History,* 23, 32. The result is that, in much of this literature, indigenous women are objectified or barely present as subjects or agents of their own history, either reverting back into historical nonentities or reinforcing the victim status they have occupied in previous historical genres. For a critique of this, see Jane Haggis, "Gendering Colonialism or Colonizing Gender? Recent Women's Studies Approaches to White Women and the History of British Colonialism," *Women's Studies International Forum* 13, nos. 1–2 (1990): 105–15.

67. A very partial list of some of the studies that do exist includes Ruth Roach Pierson and Nupur Chaudhuri, eds., *Nation, Empire, Colony: Historicizing Gender and Race* (Bloomington: Indiana University Press, 1998); Chela Sandoval, "U.S. Third World Feminism: The Theory and Method of Oppositional Consciousness in the Postmodern World," *Genders* 10 (spring 1991): 1–24; Kumari Jayawardena, *Feminism and Nationalism in the Third World* (London: Zed Press, 1986); Mohanty et al., *Third World Women* ; and Johnson-Odim and Strobel, *Expanding the Boundaries.* There is a growing corpus on women from specific Third World societies, such as Bharati Ray, ed., *Seams of History: Essays on Indian Women* (New Delhi: Oxford University Press, 1995); Nina Mba,

Nigerian Women Mobilized: Women in Southern Nigerian Political History, 1900–1965 (Berkeley, Calif.: Institute of International Studies, 1982), to cite just a few. Much of the work, however, is not in the field of history, but rather, anthropology, literary criticism, comparative literature, and sociology, which seem to have made greater strides in attracting Third World women as both scholars and subjects of study. David Prochaska makes a similar point about postcolonial studies. "What is striking about the recent efflorescence of postcolonial studies," he writes, "is the degree to which the intellectual lead has been taken not by historians but by other academics." David Prochaska, "History as Literature, Literature as History: Cagayous of Algiers," *American Historical Review* 101, no. 3 (June 1996): 671.

68. Indeed, British colonial officials in Palestine explicitly drew upon their experiences in India (and other colonial projects such as Egypt, Iraq, and Nigeria), directly applying similar colonial policies and legislation. In this, they falsely assumed a certain homogeneity of "Muslim culture," often exchanging civil servants "between the administrations . . . where the same approach prevailed." Robert H. Eisenman, *Islamic Law in Palestine and Israel: A History of the Survival of Tanzimat and Sharīʿa in the British Mandate and the Jewish State* (Leiden: E. J. Brill, 1978), 6.

69. Rajeswari Mohan, "The Crisis of Femininity and Modernity in the Third World," in *Genders 19: "Sexual Artifice: Persons, Images, Politics,"* edited by Ann Kibbey, Kayann Short, and Abrouali Farmanfarmaian (New York: New York University Press, 1994): 229.

70. Chandra Talpade Mohanty, "Under Western Eyes: Feminist Scholarship and Colonial Discourse," *Boundary Two* 12, pt. 2 (1984): 336–37, 344, 339.

71. Mohanty, "Under Western Eyes," 339.

72. McClintock (referring to Mohanty), *Imperial Leather*, 384.

73. I borrow Anne McClintock's phrase (referring to her objections to use of the term "postcolonialism." See my note 8, above); McClintock, *Imperial Leather*, 15.

74. Scott, *Gender*, 40, 49, 42.

75. Moors, *Women, Property and Islam*, 6. Rosemary Sayigh reminded me that "even within the category 'rural' you have bedouin, semi-sedentary . . . different types of village, and differences of status within villages, all sources of difference between women." Personal communication, January 7, 1996. See also Rubenberg, *Palestinian Women*.

76. Indeed the books on women and gender in Middle East history are too numerous to include here, something that has changed considerably since I began this research in 1992.

77. Margaret L. Meriwether and Judith E. Tucker, introduction to *A Social History of Women and Gender in the Modern Middle East*, edited by Meriwether and Tucker (Boulder: Westview Press, 1999), 8–9.

78. Although written in 1983, Judith E. Tucker's critique of the field still applies to a great extent; see her "Problems in the Historiography of Women in the Middle East: The Case of Nineteenth-Century Egypt," *International Jour-*

nal of Middle East Studies 15 (1983): 321–36. She ascribes the discipline's "general backwardness" to its "concentration on visible political institutions, diplomatic events and intellectual currents of the high, as opposed to popular, culture [that] effectively wrote all but upper-class males out of the historical process." She also mentions Middle East history's isolation from both intellectual exchange with other historians and developments in the historiography of other regions as one of the problems (321).

79. West and Blumberg, "Reconstructing," 4.

80. This was illuminated for me on numerous occasions. When I asked Samah Nusseibeh, head of the Arab Ladies Association, if the organization did "nationalist work as well as social work," she responded: "National work—what do you mean? In politics, you mean"; Samah Nusseibeh, interview with the author, Nov. 23, 1993.

81. A Palestinian feminist in Gaza stated that Palestinian women have "concentrated on the political struggle and not on women's issues" because they define the main problem as the "occupation, not social problems." *New York Times,* July 17, 1994.

82. West and Blumberg, "Reconstructing," 8.

83. Although this general categorization emerged from the sources, both sexes are represented to an extent in all three.

84. There are some references to Palestinian women in the *Palestine Post* and *Bulletin,* which were Zionist owned. Not knowing Hebrew, I was limited to Arabic, English, and European language sources. My impression, offered cautiously here, is that Palestinian Arab women were not a subject of much interest to the Jewish community during this period.

85. For more on the problems of choosing interviewees, see my "Crossing the Boundaries of History."

86. Rosemary Sayigh's well-turned phrase. Rosemary Sayigh, *Too Many Enemies: The Palestinian Experience in Lebanon* (London: Zed Books, 1994), 6.

87. For a detailed discussion of these, see my "Crossing the Boundaries."

88. Robert Coles, *The Call of Stories: Teaching and the Moral Imagination* (Boston: Houghton Mifflin, 1989), 7; emphasis in original.

89. Connerton, *How Societies Remember,* 19.

90. Popular Memory Group, "Popular Memory," 228.

91. Joyce Appleby, Lynn Hunt, and Margaret Jacobs, *Telling the Truth About History* (New York and London: W. W. Norton & Co., 1994), 231.

92. Frances E. Mascia-Lees, Patricia Sharpe, and Colleen Ballerino Cohen, "The Postmodernist Turn in Anthropology: Cautions From a Feminist Perspective," *Signs* 15, no. 1 (spring 1989): 15. The authors attribute this observation to Nancy Hartsock, "Rethinking Modernism," *Cultural Critique* 7 (fall 1987):187–206.

93. I sidestep here the issue of the inherent complexities of the historian as the interpreter and producer of oral history. For excellent discussions of the ambivalent and often unequal power relationships between the scholar/historian and the subject/coauthor, the "history-giver," see the essays in Sherna

Berger Gluck and Daphne Patai, eds., *Women's Words: The Feminist Practice of Oral History* (New York and London: Routledge, 1991); Popular Memory Group, "Popular Memory"; and Rosemary Sayigh, "Researching Gender in a Palestinian Camp: Political, Theoretical and Methodological Issues," in Kandiyoti, ed., *Gendering*, 145–67.

94. Luisa Passerini, *Fascism in Popular Memory: The Cultural Experience of the Turin Working Class*, translated by Robert Lumley and Jude Bloomfield (Cambridge: Cambridge University Press, 1987), 2.

95. Hind al-Husayni, interview with the author, Feb. 15, 1993.

96. Swedenburg, *Memories of Revolt*, 22; Popular Memory Group, "Popular Memory," 211. I owe what follows to Swedenburg's astute dissection in his book of the meanings and contestations of national memory.

97. Susan Slyomovics, "The Memory of Place: Rebuilding the Pre-1948 Palestinian Village," *Diaspora* 3, no. 2 (1994): 158.

98. Swedenburg, *Memories of Revolt*, 5.

99. This phenomenon occurred often when I interviewed older women who were still involved in charitable work. They seemed either not to understand my interest in history or wished to avoid the topic. Instead they directed the conversation to their current work, and showed me around their institutions, proudly displaying their buildings, activities, and clients.

100. See, e.g., Neville Mandel, *The Arabs and Zionism Before World War I* (Berkeley: University of California Press, 1976); Yusuf Khuri, *Al-sihāfa al-'Arabiyya fī Filastīn, 1876–1948* (Beirut: Palestinian Studies Association, 1976); Ya'qub Yahushua, *Tārīkh al-sihāfa al-'Arabiyya al-Filastīniyya fī bidāyat 'ahd al-intidāb al-Brītānī 'ala Filastīn 1919/1929* (Haifa: Applied Scientific Research Co., University of Haifa, 1981); Qustandi Shumali, "Al-sihāfa al-Filastīniyya fī 'ahd al-intidāb, jarīdat 'Mirāt al-sharq', 1919–1939," *Shu'ūn Filastīniyya* 221–22 (Sept. 1991): 73–86.

101. This last is a classification of documents at the Israel State Archives; it contains files on marriage, divorce, and some disputes before different *shari'a* courts. The Israel State Archives categorized most British government documents according to the latter's own system.

102. Amin Maalouf, *The Rock of Tanios*, translated by Dorothy S. Blair (New York: George Braziller, 1994), 144.

103. An example of this was the women's labor union organizing in the 1940s, for which I could only find limited information (eight articles) in the Arabic press. See Chapter 7 for more discussion of this. (When I returned to the region for additional research in 1999, I tried to question older labor leaders and leftists such as Emile Touma about the women's labor unions. Unfortunately, he was very ill and could not see me. However, Dr. Butrus Abu Manneh later asked him questions on my behalf, eliciting the comment that no such effort had existed, or if one had, he did not recall it.) See also Chapter 6 for discussion on the problem of determining names and founding dates for the women's organizations due to the vague and partial nature of the sources.

104. Because there are so few documentary sources on poorer urban and

peasant women, oral history offers the most promising route for scholars. It is not a straightforward, unproblematic methodology, however. One of its major difficulties is convincing women they deserve to be interviewed; most peasant women I did talk to were self-deprecating and denigrated their own capabilities in offering valuable information. But now the major obstacle in obtaining oral information is simply the passage of time and the passing away of the peasant women and men of the mandate generation who could theoretically tell historians about the period. With each year fewer potential history-givers are still alive, and often the memory of those that are, is impaired from extreme age and/or illness.

CHAPTER 2. PALESTINIAN WOMEN AND THE RULE OF THE BRITISH MANDATE

1. Many of the Palestinians interviewed for this research conveyed this impression. See also Hala Sakakini, *Jerusalem and I: A Personal Record* (Amman: Economic Press, 1990), 79.

2. For a history of the development of Palestinian national identity and consciousness, see Rashid Khalidi, *Palestinian Identity: The Construction of Modern National Consciousness* (New York: Columbia University Press, 1997).

3. Beshara Doumani, *Rediscovering Palestine: Merchants and Peasants in Jabal Nablus, 1700–1900* (Berkeley: University of California Press, 1995), 8.

4. Ibid., 49, 153; Haim Gerber, *Ottoman Rule in Jerusalem, 1890–1914* (Berlin: Klaus Schwarz, 1985), 7.

5. Iris Agmon, "Women, Class, and Gender: Muslim Jaffa and Haifa at the Turn of the Twentieth Century," *International Journal of Middle East Studies* 30 (1998): 482.

6. Alexander Scholch, "European Penetration and the Economic Development of Palestine, 1856–1882," *Studies in the Economic and Social History of Palestine in the Nineteenth and Twentieth Centuries*, edited by Roger Owen (Carbondale: Southern Illinois University Press, 1982), 55.

7. Alexander Scholch, "Jerusalem in the Nineteenth Century (1831–1917 AD)," in *Jerusalem in History*, edited by K. J. Asali (Brooklyn: Olive Branch Press, 1990), 233.

8. Doumani, *Rediscovering Palestine*, 235–36.

9. Gerber, *Ottoman Rule*, 215.

10. Kenneth Stein, *The Land Question in Palestine, 1917–1939* (Chapel Hill: University of North Carolina Press, 1984), 19.

11. This oft-repeated generalization has become a subject of debate in Ottoman scholarship recently. Donald Quataert warns, "The pattern of landholding at the end of the Ottoman Empire derived from a complex interaction among a long list of variables . . . it is clear that there was not a single pattern of landholding in the Ottoman Middle East." Yet there is some consensus on the development in the wake of the 1858 Ottoman Land Code of larger, consolidated estates in the Syrian provinces of which Palestine was a part. See Suraiya Faro-

qhi, Bruce McGowan, Donald Quataert, and Ševket Pamuk, *An Economic and Social History of the Ottoman Empire*, vol. 2 (Cambridge: Cambridge University Press, 1994), 860, 867.

12. Doumani, *Rediscovering Palestine*, 49, 29.

13. Annelies Moors, "Gender Hierarchy in a Palestinian Village: The Case of Al-Balad," in *The Rural Middle East: Peasant Lives and Modes of Production*, edited by Kathy and Pandeli Glavani (London: Zed Press, 1989), 199; Moors, *Women, Property and Islam: Palestinian Experiences, 1920–1990* (Cambridge: Cambridge University Press, 1995), 28–29, 40; Rema Hammami, "Between Heaven and Earth: Transformations in Religiosity and Labor Among Southern Palestinian Peasant or Refugee Women, 1920–1993" (Ph.D. diss., Temple University, 1994), 224.

14. Judith E. Tucker, "*Muftis* and Matrimony: Islamic Law and Gender in Ottoman Syria and Palestine," *Islamic Law and Society* 1, no. 3 (1994): 269.

15. I thank Rosemary Sayigh for making this point. Granqvist also mentions that sometimes, if the father was not present, the mother would arrange a marriage in consultation with the nearest male relative. Hilma Granqvist, *Marriage Conditions in a Palestinian Village*, vol. 1 (Helsingfors: Akademische Buchhandlung, 1931), 46.

16. Judith Tucker, *Women in Nineteenth-Century Egypt* (Cambridge: Cambridge University Press, 1985), 195; Granqvist, *Marriage Conditions*, 1:94.

17. For a useful and thorough discussion of the complexities and ambiguities of property as a source of power for Palestinian women, see Moors, *Women, Property and Islam*.

18. C. T. Wilson, *Peasant Life in the Holy Land* (London: John Murray, 1906), 103. This is an often-repeated theme in common conversation, literature, and documentary sources. While working on this book in Jordan, I attended a dinner party among Palestinian friends who discussed the greater freedom of peasant women, stating that they had "never veiled" and had always been harder-working than men. See also 'Izzat Daraghma, *Al-haraka al-nisā'iyya fī Filastīn* (Jerusalem: maktab al-Diya' lil-dirasāt, 1991), 16.

19. Judith Tucker, "Ties That Bound: Women and Family in Eighteenth- and Nineteenth-Century Nablus," *Women in Middle Eastern History*, edited by Nikki Keddie and Beth Baron (New Haven: Yale University Press, 1991), 236.

20. Sophia Sabanakh (b. 1904), interview with the author, Mar. 5, 1993; Wadi'a Khartabil, *Bahthān 'an al-amal wa al-watan: sittūn 'āman min kifāh imrā' fī sabīl Filastīn, 1936–1990* (Beirut: Bisān lil-nashr wa al-tawzi', 1995), 43; Hilda Ridler, "The Palestine I Knew, 1918–1948," *The Journal of the B.M.H.S.*, Nov. 7, 1949, Hilda Ridler Papers, MEC.

21. Geoffrey Furlonge, *Palestine is My Country: The Story of Musa Alami* (New York: Praeger Publishers, 1969), 16.

22. See, e.g., Tucker, *Women in Nineteenth Century Egypt*. Undoubtedly, the types of work poorer urban women in nineteenth-century Egypt performed were similar to those of Palestinian women.

23. Yvonne Haddad, "Palestinian Women: Patterns of Legitimation and

Domination," in *The Sociology of the Palestinians*, edited by Khalil Nakhleh and Elia Zureik (London: Croom Helm, 1980), 156.

24. Musa al-Husayni (her son), interview with the author, Jan. 24, 1993.

25. Leila Ahmed, *Women and Gender in Islam: Historical Roots of a Modern Debate* (New Haven: Yale University Press, 1992), 133. See also Khaled Fahmy, "Women, Medicine and Power in Nineteenth-Century Egypt," in *Remaking Women: Feminism and Modernity in the Middle East*, edited by Lila Abu-Lughod (Princeton: Princeton University Press, 1998), 35–72.

26. Until the restoration of the Ottoman Constitution in 1908, there were no government elementary schools for girls in Palestine. See Asma Tubi, *'Abīr wa majd* (Beirut: matba'at qalalat, 1966), 35, 21–22.

27. Khartabil, *Bahthān 'an al-amal*, 54.

28. This word (*rā'ida*) is much-used in Arabic sources on women. See, e.g., *'Abīr wa majd*.

29. Information from her nieces, Hala and Dumya Sakakini, interview with the author, Sept. 11, 1992. The Russian Orthodox Church established a number of teacher training colleges in cities and towns with significant Christian populations, such as Bethlehem and Nazareth.

30. John Melkon Rose, *Armenians of Jerusalem: Memories of Life in Palestine* (London: Radcliffe Press, 1993), provides a vivid account of his aunt's work as a midwife and nurse during the last years of the Ottoman Empire.

31. Matiel Mogannam, *The Arab Woman and the Palestine Problem* (London: Herbert Joseph, 1937), 45; Frances E. Newton, *Fifty Years in Palestine* (London: Coldharbour Press, Ltd., 1948), 147; Ridler, "The Palestine I Knew, 1918–1948."

32. Ahmed, *Women and Gender in Islam*, 133–68.

33. Sabanakh, interview.

34. This year indicates when the League of Nations allotted the mandate to Great Britain and converted military rule to a civilian government but the specific conditions of the mandate did not formally come into operation until September 29, 1923, due to discussions of the draft text that delayed its final submission to the League of Nations. See *A Survey of Palestine Prepared in December 1945 and January 1946 for the Information of the Anglo-American Committee of Inquiry*, Vol. 1, 3–4.

35. As Barbara Smith points out, there is an institutionalized inequality in the very language of the statement, in which "facilitating" has a positive connotation, whereas "safeguarding" is inactive. Barbara J. Smith, *The Roots of Separatism in Palestine: British Economic Policy, 1920–1929* (Syracuse: Syracuse University Press, 1993), 13.

36. Robert H. Eisenman, *Islamic Law in Palestine and Israel: A History of the Survival of Tanzimat and Shari'a in the British Mandate and the Jewish State* (Leiden: E. J. Brill, 1978), 74. Class A mandates, such as existed in Iraq and Syria, called for eventual independence of the territories.

37. Ylana Miller, *Government and Society in Rural Palestine, 1920–1948* (Austin: University of Texas Press, 1985), 27.

38. Miller, *Government and Society*, 71.
39. Eisenman, *Islamic Law in Palestine and Israel*, 76.
40. Jane Lewis, *The Politics of Motherhood: Child and Maternal Welfare in England, 1900–1939* (London: Croom Helm Ltd., 1980), 15.
41. Palestine Women's Council Annual Report [hereafter PWC Report I], 1921–1922, ISA, RG 65 3117.
42. Newton, *Fifty Years*, 152; Barbara Board, *Newsgirl in Palestine* (London: Michael Joseph, 1937), 230.
43. PWC Report I.
44. Robert R. Nathan, Oscar Gass, and Daniel Creamer, *Palestine: Problem and Promise: An Economic Study* (Washington: Public Affairs Press, 1946), 338.
45. Smith, *Roots of Separation*, 47.
46. Economic Survey of the Colonial Empire, 1937, PRO, CO 733 463/3. Another government report notes: "It is not an uncommon experience in dealing with Palestine matters to be surprised and shamed by ... the extent to which the Palestine Government has failed to provide services on a scale comparable with other colonial territories of similar resources." Report of Committee of Development and Welfare Services, 1941, PRO, CO 733 447/2.
47. Nathan, Gass, and Creamer, *Palestine: Problem and Promise*, 348.
48. PWC Report I.
49. Newton, *Fifty Years*, 148–49.
50. Ruth Woodsmall, a YWCA official visiting Palestine in the 1930s, notes that the council still existed, but is "less active." Woodsmall, *Moslem Women Enter a New World* (New York: Round Table Press, 1936), 334. In its Annual Report, 1923–1924, it admits, somewhat defensively, that "circumstances have rendered the work of the Council less obvious to the outside world" and that "progress has been inevitably slower" due to changes among various officials in the government. I found little evidence that it was active among the majority Arab population much beyond its initial years of existence. Palestine Women's Council Annual Report [hereafter PWC Report II], 1923–1924, ISA, RG 65 3117.
51. In referring to "the British" or "British officials," I recognize that this term implies a homogeneity and unity among the colonial community that did not necessarily exist. Ann Stoler warns students of colonialism of the fallacies of assuming that colonial discourse expressed "a shared European mentality, the sentiments of a unified, conquering elite" and of conflating the "makers of metropole policy" with its "local practitioners." She points to the complex, often contradictory and contentious interests within the colonial culture itself. See Ann Laura Stoler, "Rethinking Colonial Categories: European Communities and the Boundaries of Rule," *Comparative Studies in Society and History* 31 (1989): 135.
52. Sarah Graham-Brown, *Images of Women* (London: Quartet Books, Ltd., 1988), 70–81.
53. Annie Van Sommer and Samuel Zwemer, eds., *Our Moslem Sisters: A*

Cry of Need From Lands of Darkness Interpreted by Those Who Heard It (New York: Revell Press, 1907), 152, 164, 170.

54. A few pro-Arab sympathizers such as Beatrice Erskine and Frances Newton, who lived in Haifa during the mandate period, portray Arab women in a more nuanced and less biased manner, yet both of these women were products of their time and of British colonial mentalities. They were not above self-promotion and congratulation about their own and the government's role in improving the status of Arab women. (Which is interesting, considering their often hostile relationships with the British government over the issue of Palestine. Newton was served by an exclusion order of the government in 1938 and deported. Police Report, Metropolitan Police, Special Branch, Scotland House, Nov. 7, 1938, PRO, CO 733 372/11.) See Beatrice Erskine, *Palestine of the Arabs* (London: George B. Harrap, 1935); and Newton, *Fifty Years*.

55. Woodsmall, *Moslem Women Enter*, 40.

56. Hilda Ridler, "Special Problems in the Training of Women Teachers in the Near East," *Government of Palestine Department of Education Annual Report for the Scholastic Year 1926–1927* (Jerusalem: 1928), 29.

57. "Fine Mothers of Fine Sons—Why Arab Leader Admires Englishwomen," *The Star*, March 31, 1930, ISA, RG 65 2603.

58. Ruth Woodsmall, *Moslem Women*, 191, 52.

59. Natal (South Africa) prime minister Sir John Robinson, quoted in Deborah Gaitskell, "Race, Gender and Imperialism: A Century of Black Girls' Education in South Africa," in *Benefits Bestowed: Education and British Imperialism*, edited by J. A. Mangan (Manchester: Manchester University Press, 1988), 151.

60. Sakakini, *Jerusalem and I*, 27–28. Curiously, although British women materialize repeatedly as subjects and actors in the historical record, their voices in the documents are muted and few.

61. Moors, *Women, Property and Islam*, 4.

62. PWC Report I.

63. Joan N. Burstyn, *Victorian Education and the Ideal of Womanhood* (London: Croom Helm, 1980), 11.

64. Frederick Cooper and Ann L. Stoler, "Tensions of Empire: Colonial Control and Visions of Rule," *American Ethnologist* 16, no. 4 (Nov. 1989): 610.

65. Annual Education Report, 1934–1935, PRO, CO 733 291/4.

66. Ridler, "The Palestine I Knew, 1918–1948."

67. Stoler, "Rethinking Colonial Categories," 141.

68. Draft memo entitled "Propaganda. Combative Propaganda conducted by a foreign power in Palestine," n.d. (probably late 1930s), CZA, RG 25S 22717.

69. Thomas Babington Macaulay (1800–1859), *Speeches by Lord Macaulay: With His Minute on Indian Education*, as quoted by Gayatri Chakravorty Spivak, "Can the Subaltern Speak?" in *Marxism and the Interpretation of Culture*, edited by Cary Nelson and Lawrence Grossberg (Urbana and Chicago: University of Illinois Press, 1988), 282.

70. Nathan, Gass, and Creamer, *Palestine: Problem and Promise*, 355.

71. Annual Report to the Permanent Mandates Commission, 1940, PRO, CO 733 439/23.

72. Annual Education Report, 1934–1935, PRO, CO 733 291/4; Annual Report, 1938, PRO, CO 733 399/23; Annual Report to the PMC, 1940, PRO, CO 733 439/23.

73. Department of Education Table provided by the principal of the WTC, Miss Ridler, Jan. 3, 1937, PRO, CO 733 346/17.

74. The government explicitly required women applying for certain posts to be single and under age thirty-five. This was particularly true for higher level postings, where the applicant had to have British educational qualifications, which often de facto indicated "no Arabs need apply." Over time, as some Arab women achieved these educational levels, the British were faced with problems of racial discrimination. These restrictions made the positions even more difficult to fill. Revised advertisement, Inspector of Girls Schools 1936, ISA CO 733/309.

75. Anna Davin, "Imperialism and Motherhood," *History Workshop* 5 (1978): 21.

76. Comments on the Palestine Matriculation Exam, Report on the Anglican Schools in Palestine, J. W. Headlam-Morley, July 6, 1927, PRO, CO 733 155/6.

77. Ridler, "Special Problems," 29; Annual Education Report, 1934–1935, PRO, CO 733 291/4.

78. Interestingly, in Egypt, feminist organizations criticized the (Egyptian) Ministry of Education for creating a curriculum that resulted in "ignorance on the part of our girls about the woman's duty toward her family, children, and society," demanding courses in "domestic science," child care, home economics, and the like. Sometimes colonialist and indigenous educational priorities coincided. See Na'imah al-Ayyubi, quoted (in 1937) in Margot Badran, *Feminists*, 147.

79. Comments on the Palestine Matriculation Exam, PRO, CO 733 155/6; H. E. Bowman, Director of Education, "The Education of Girls in Palestine," *The Palestine Bulletin*, Feb. 6, 1927.

80. Bowman, "The Education of Girls in Palestine."

81. Annual Education Report, 1934–1935, PRO, CO 733 291/4.

82. Ibid., 30.

83. Department of Education Table on the WTC, provided by Miss Ridler, principal, Jan. 3, 1937, PRO, CO 733 346/17; *Government of Palestine Junior Service Staff List* [hereafter *JSS List*] (Alexandria: Whitehead Morris, Ltd., 1931); Sa'id B. Himadeh, "Industry," *Economic Organization of Palestine*, edited by Sa'id B. Himadeh (Beirut: American Press, 1938), 283.

84. *Safahāt min al-dhākirā al-Filastīniyya*, no. 3, Tadhakurrāt Yusra Salah, interview by Lubna 'Abd al-Hadi (Bir Zeit: Center for Studies and Documentation of Palestinian Society, 1992), 11.

85. Annual Education Report, 1938, PRO, CO 733 399/23.

86. Like the WTC students, the RTC students also performed all the menial

work at the center. Despatch from the OAG to the SSC, June 7, 1935, CO 733 270/4.

87. Letter to the SSC (Cunliffe-Lister) from the HC (Wauchope), March 30, 1935, PRO, CO 733 270/4.

88. Issa Khalaf, *Politics in Palestine: Arab Factionalism and Social Disintegration, 1939–1945* (Albany: State University of New York Press, 1991), 36–37.

89. Nimra Tannus, interview with the author, Jan. 26, 1993.

90. Ellen Mansur, interview with the author, Sept. 5, 1992.

91. Sa'ida Jarallah, interview with the author, Apr. 19, 1994; Nafisa was her sister.

92. Petition, Oct. 16, 1928, PRO, CO 733 162/13.

93. Millicent Garett Fawcett, *Six Weeks in Palestine*, 2 vols. (London: Women's Printing Society, 1921–22), 2:52–53.

94. The judge had seven daughters and two sons, all of whom were educated; Jarallah, interview.

95. "Rural Education in the Near and Middle East," *Journal of the Royal Central Asian Society* (July 1939): 414, from the Humphrey Ernest Bowman Papers, MEC.

96. "Palestine Royal Commission: Notes of Evidence Taken on Friday, Nov. 27, 1936," Bowman Papers, MEC.

97. As quoted in Woodsmall, *Moslem Women*, 196.

98. Mogannam, *The Arab Woman*, 255. The influence of the private and missionary schools is an interesting subject that is, unfortunately, beyond the scope of this work.

99. Of the almost seventy people interviewed for this research, almost everyone brought up the subject of women and education.

100. Miller, *Government and Society*, 95.

101. *al-Difāʻ*, Mar. 25, 1946.

102. Hind al-Husayni, interview with the author, Feb. 15, 1993.

103. "The Education of Girls in Palestine," *al-Jāmʻia al-Islamiyya*, Oct. 30, 1934.

104. Jerome Farrell, "The Distribution of Educational Benefits in Palestine" [marked confidential], Dec. 17, 1945, Jerome Farrell Papers, MEC.

105. A. L. Tibawi, *Arab Education in Mandatory Palestine: A Study of Three Decades of British Administration* (London: Luzac & Co., 1956), 228; Papers of Farrell, "Distribution of Educational Benefits."

106. Mr. J. Farrell to Mr. C. W. M. Cox, June 7, 1945, PRO, CO 733/459/3.

107. Tibawi, *Arab Education*, 243, 244.

108. Almost every Palestinian woman interviewed for this research emphasized the role of education in forming her identity and sense of self.

109. Widad Qaʻwwar, interview with the author, Jan. 23, 1993.

110. Fadwa Tuqan, *A Mountainous Journey: A Poet's Autobiography*, translated by Olive Kenny, poetry translated by Naomi Shihab Nye, edited by Salma Khadra Jayyusi (Saint Paul: Graywolf Press, 1990), 45.

111. Yvonne Kardosh, interview with the author, Apr. 27, 1993.

112. Hind al-Husayni, interview. The Nasir sisters were the aunts of Hanna Nasir, the president of Bir Zeit University. Their sister, Nabiha Nasir, founded Bir Zeit College, a secondary school, which eventually became Bir Zeit University. After being moved when she observed young girls begging in the streets, Elizabeth established a school for girls, Rawdat al-Zuhur, in Jerusalem. The school originally provided vocational education for poor girls. Samia Khuri (the niece of Elizabeth Nasir), interview with the author, May 16, 1994.

113. *Safahāt*, 19.

114. One of its most renowned graduates is Hanan 'Ashrawi, who captured international headlines as a spokesperson for the PLO during the Madrid Conference in 1991. Other noteworthy institutions attended by the women from my interviews included Schmidt's Girls School (Jerusalem), Bir Zeit College (Bir Zeit), the Sisters of Zion (Jerusalem), Jerusalem Girls' College, and the English High School (Haifa).

115. "Big Meeting of the [female] Students and Their Capable Hands," *al-Difā'*, May 5, 1936; Sir Kenneth Blackbourne, Assistant District Commissioner of the Galilee, from a diary kept by himself and others, entry dated May 11, 1936, Sir Kenneth William Blackbourne Papers, RH.

116. Originally called the American Junior College (AJC), its name was changed in the late 1940s when it began to offer a four-year program; Margaret Bianchi, administrative assistant, Lebanese American University (formerly BCW), telephone interview with the author, New York, Mar. 23, 1995; Edith A. S. Hanania, "Access of Arab Women to Higher Education," *Arab Women and Education* (Beirut: Beirut University College, 1980), 50. Now coeducational, the university is called the Lebanese American University.

117. Hala and Dumya Sakakini, interviews with the author, Sept. 28, 1992; Apr. 30, 1993; Hala Sakakini, *Twosome* (Jerusalem: Habesch Press, 1993), 8–21.

118. Hanania, "Access of Arab Women," 50.

119. *Safahāt*, 21.

120. Hanania, "Access of Arab Women," 50.

121. Hala and Dumya Sakakini, interviews; *Safahāt*, 18.

122. *Safahāt*, 18.

123. Alexandra 'Aboud, interview with the author, Apr. 28, 1993; Yvonne Kardosh, interview; and Henriette Siksik, interview with the author, June 16, 1993.

124. 'Wafi'a al-Duzdar, interview with the author, Mar. 21, 1993.

125. Hala Sakakini, interview with the author, Nov. 21, 1992. Her own memoirs provide an account of how the upheavals affected her own and her family's life; see *Jerusalem and I*. Alexandra 'Aboud, who lived in the Galilee region, where the 1936–39 strike and revolt were the most prolonged and intensively fought, graphically describes the disruptions of normal life during this period. She was moved from Haifa to Nazareth because of the dangers and bombing incidents in the former; Alexandra 'Aboud, interview with the author.

126. Samah Nusseibeh, interview with the author, Nov. 23, 1993.

127. Amy Aramki, interview with the author, Nov. 26, 1992.

128. Nahid 'Abduh al-Sajjadi, interview with the author, Jan. 28, 1993. The word "aware"—*wa'ī*—is frequently used by Palestinians, signifying to be politically conscious or sophisticated.

129. Bowman, "The Education of Girls."

130. Henriette Siksik, interview with the author.

131. Woman from the Eastern Quarter of Nazareth (a neighborhood of refugees from pre-1948 destroyed villages), interview by Zuheira Sabbagh on the author's behalf, July 1993. (This woman did not wish to give her name in the interview because of her Communist Party affiliation.)

132. Woman from the Eastern Quarter, interview.

133. Women from Zeita, interviews with the author, May 10, 1993.

134. Rosemary Sayigh, "Femmes palestiniennes: une histoire en quête d'historiens," *Revue d'études palestiniennes* 23 (spring 1987): 23.

135. Woman from the Eastern Quarter, interview.

136. Selma Botman, "The Experience of Women in the Egyptian Communist Movement, 1939–1954," *Women's Studies International Forum* 2, no. 2 (1988): 125.

137. *Report of the High Commisioner on the Administration of Palestine, 1920–1925*, "An Ordinance to Supplement the Criminal Law With Regard to Offences Against Women," *The Palestine Bulletin*, May 6, 1925; Despatch to the SSC from the HC, May 1933, PRO, CO 733 245.

138. Fannie Fern Andrews, *The Holy Land Under Mandate*, vol. 1 (Boston: Houghton Mifflin Co., 1931), 83.

139. Palestine Department of Welfare Annual Report, 1944, ISA, RG 2 E/SW/20/47; *Palestine Press Review*, Public Information Office, 1942.

140. Fannie Fern Andrews, *Holy Land*, 2:216.

141. Lewis, *Politics of Motherhood*, 18.

142. Alice Mekhalian, "Service in the City," *Jerusalem Girls College Magazine*, June 1933, MEC.

143. Lewis, *Politics of Motherhood*, 65. Anna Davin analyzes British government concerns about its own population's poor health and hygiene in the early twentieth century and how these were linked to the imperial project and overall welfare of the nation, undercutting its ability to provide healthy workers and soldiers. She notes, too, how the individualistic targeting of the "ignorant" mother as the source of the problem "obscured to an extent which now seems astonishing the effects on child health of poverty and environment." See Davin, "Imperialism and Motherhood," 12.

144. PWC Report I, 5.

145. The 1938 Annual Report on Public Health reported the following infant mortality rates per 100,000: Muslims: 127.61; Christians: 103.98; Jews: 58.22; Others: 90.18. The last category is unclear (probably European Christians); the British differentiated on a "racial" basis between Arab Christians and European Christians; PRO, CO 733 399/24.

146. Ibid.

147. Lewis, *Politics of Motherhood*, 20.

148. Vera Petropoulos, "The Work I Love," Old Girls Guild Sixth Annual Report, 1929–1930, Jerusalem Girls College, MEC.

149. Lewis notes that "child and maternal welfare policies often discouraged already existing patterns of mutual aid between women." See *Politics of Motherhood*, 20.

150. For example, see letter to DMS from Sir Arnold Rowntree, Nov. 11, 1934, ISA, RG 10 73/2; it discusses the lack of a woman doctor at a government hospital; see also Advanced Proposal for 1948/49 Estimates for Department of Social Welfare, ISA, RG 2 E/SW/20/47, in which it is stated that it was "essential to have one post of Assistant Director which should be filled by a woman officer" in order to encourage "social work among women—a most important field of service in a predominantly Moslem country." .

151. Letter to DMS from Rowntree, Nov. 11, 1934; emphasis in original.

152. Bertha Vester, *Our Jerusalem* (Jerusalem: American Colony, 1988), 327.

153. Petropoulos, "The Work I Love."

154. Nathan, Gass, and Creamer, *Palestine: Problem and Promise*, 348, 21.

155. As provided in Jacob Metzer, *The Divided Economy of Mandatory Palestine* (Cambridge: Cambridge University Press, 1998), 119.

156. Himadeh, *Economic Organization*, 234; *Labor Conditions in Palestine, Voluntary Report* 100, American Consul in Jerusalem, Jul. 22, 1937, U.S. Department of State, Division of Near East Affairs, 867N.504/27.

157. *Labor Conditions in Palestine, Voluntary Report* 100, American Consul in Jerusalem, Jul. 22, 1937, U.S. Department of State, Division of Near East Affairs, 867N.504/35.

158. The major source for much of what follows is the *JSS List*, which contains much rich and detailed information. Unfortunately, the documentation on women's labor is scarce, and limited for the most part to the governmental sector.

159. Despatch from HC (Chancellor) to SSC (Passfield), Dec. 24, 1929, PRO, CO 733 182/5.

160. *JSS List;* comments on proposed new grades for the education department [signature illegible], June 20, 1930, PRO, CO 733 182/5; Despatch of the HC to the SSC, Dec. 24, 1929, PRO, CO 733 182/5.

161. *JSS List*. My statistics should be used as general guidelines. I determined which women were Arab by their names. Armenian women are included with Arab women since the distinction between Armenians and Christian Arabs during this period was nebulous, as the two groups intermarried freely. On Arab-Armenian relations, see Melkon Rose, *Armenians of Jerusalem*.

162. During the 1930s, the average dollar equivalent of the Palestinian pound, which was tied to the pound sterling rate, was $4.61; this average is calculated on the years 1931–39. The average for 1940–44 was $4.04. See Nathan, Gass, and Creamer, *Palestine: Problem and Promise*, 300.

163. Letter from the Postmaster General to the Chief Secretary, Mar. 22, 1929, ISA, RG 2 U/359/31.

164. Despatch to SSC (Cunliffe-Lister) from HC (Wauchope), Aug. 17, 1933,

ISA, RG 2 U/359/31. One of the major governmental concerns was paying pensions to women.

165. Jerome Farrell for CS, Oct. 9, 1934, ISA, RG 2 U/359/31.

166. Yvonne Kardosh mentions the rule against employing married women, interview with the author, Apr. 27, 1993. Advertisements for positions for women frequently stipulated that applicants be single and under the age of thirty-five. Despatch from OAG to SSC, May 10, 1935, PRO, CO 733 270/4; Inspector of Girls School Vacancy 1936, PRO, CO 733 309.

167. Annual Education Report, 1934–1935, PRO, CO 733 291/4; Annual Education Report, 1938, PRO, CO 733 399/23. Women teachers in French Mandate Lebanon and Syria were also "forced to leave their jobs when they married." See Elizabeth Thompson, *Colonial Citizens: Republican Rights, Paternal Privilege and Gender in French Syria and Lebanon* (New York: Columbia University Press, 2000), 89.

168. The battle between the male medical establishment and midwives in colonial Palestine was a reflection—even a replication—of similar rivalry and competition that had played itself out earlier on the domestic front in Great Britain from the late seventeenth to the early twentieth century. British midwives were increasingly regulated, controlled, and circumscribed for a complex variety of reasons, one of the most important of which included professional jealousy on the part of the more powerful male medical establishment. The Midwives Act of 1902, which established the first formal state regulation of midwives, was followed by further statutory elaborations (including restrictions) over the course of the century. For an account of this struggle, see Jean Donnison, *Midwives and Medical Men: A History of Inter-Professional Rivalries and Women's Rights* (New York: Schocken Books, 1977). The situation in Palestine contained another complicated layer due to the fact that the medical establishment comprised a hierarchy based on "race" and not just gender. (In Britain, class was also a factor that came into play in the contestation over which medical practitioners had the privilege to control childbirth procedures and, most importantly, the payment differentials among themselves.) The British-dominated medical establishment in Palestine was probably attempting to follow the example "back home" in their regulation, certification, and training of midwives.

169. Letter to the Hebron Medical Officer from the SMO, Mar. 20, 1941, ISA, RG 10 75/4.

170. The superintendent of midwifery wrote voluminously on this subject to the Senior Medical Officer; Great Britain Colonial Office, *Report on the Administration of Palestine, 1920–1921*, 54.

171. Letter to Miss Bahiya Afify from Dr. D. Boulos, SMO, Aug. 19, 1941, ISA, RG M/28/40.

172. Memorandum to the SMO of Hebron from Mrs. Rogers, Superintendent of Midwifery, Dec. 12, 1946, ISA, RG 10 75/4.

173. Letter from Adib Ahmad Shehada to SMO, Jerusalem, Nov. 28, 1940, ISA, RG 10 75/4.

174. The Superintendent of Midwifery and Child Welfare wrote to the SMO requesting that he appoint three women whose deceased mothers had been midwives, for example; letter to the SMO, Jerusalem, from the Superintendent of Midwifery and Child Welfare, Oct. 22, 1942, ISA, RG 10 75/4.

175. Report on Investigations Regarding the Dearth of Arab Nurses, n.d. (included in the minutes of the meeting of the Social and Moral Welfare Committee of the United Missionary Council held Jan. 21, 1944; report requested by the UMC in November 1942), ISA, RG 65 3118.

176. Memorandum to the Matron, Government Hospital, Jerusalem, from the CMO, June 9, 1931, ISA, RG 10 76.

177. Government of Palestine, Particulars of the Office of Lady Medical Officer in the Department of Health Now Vacant in the Government of Palestine n.d. (c. 1940), ISA, RG 2 U/365/40. Unless otherwise noted, all information on Dr. Saba is from one file in RG 2 U/365/40.

178. Confidential memorandum to the Chief Secretary from the DMS, Aug. 6, 1940.

179. Curiously, there is no record of any applications before five years had passed. This may well have been due to the war.

180. Telegram from SSC to OAG, Jan. 4, 1945, ISA, RG 2 U/365/40.

181. DMS to CS, n.d.; letter to CS from DMS, Feb. 22, 1945.

182. Cable from the SSC to the OAG, July 17, 1945.

183. Letter to F. G. Farley from Dr. J. McQueen, July 24, 1945. It seems that locally recruited Palestinian doctors usually started out in the lower-level clinical assistant position before reaching the position of medical officer. Another Palestinian woman, Dr. Salwa Khuri, who qualified at AUB, followed this route in the 1930s and eventually became an LMO in the mid-1940s; Palestine Civil Service List 1939; Memorandum from SMO to DMS, Jerusalem, Aug. 5, 1943, and letter from SMO to DMS, Sept. 23, 1946, ISA RG 10 76/15.

184. HC to DMS, Aug. 8, 1945; telegram from HC to SSC, Aug. 24, 1945.

185. HC to SSC, Oct. 8, 1945.

186. In 1948, a new DMS recommended hiring Saba as a part-time MO at 240 pounds per annum, but there is no evidence as to whether or not she accepted; DMS to Civil Service Commission, 1948. Asma Tubi writes that Saba ran a clinic in Jaffa in 1948, and lectured on medicine and family health. Tubi asked many other women what had happened to her, but received confusing replies. She may have moved to England. See Tubi, 'Abīr wa majd, 90.

187. Margaret Strobel, *European Women and the Second British Empire* (Bloomington: Indiana University Press, 1991), xi. Palestinian Arab men were thus discriminated against on a racial basis. One of the only reasons that Ahmad Samih al-Khalidi was approved as the head of the Government Arab College in Jerusalem, instead of an Englishman, was because "an Arab would be cheaper to hire." Bernard Wasserstein, *The British in Palestine: The Mandatory Government and the Arab-Jewish Conflict, 1917–1929*, 2nd ed. (London: Basil Blackwell, Ltd., 1991), 175.

188. Helen Callaway, *Gender, Culture and Empire: European Women in Colonial Nigeria* (London: MacMillan Press, 1987), 52.

189. See, for example, literature on British colonialist practices in India: Kumari Jayawardena, *Feminism and Nationalism in the Third World* (London: Zed Press, 1986), 83; Kumkum Sangari and Sudesh Vaid, "Recasting Women: An Introduction," in *Recasting Women: Essays in Indian Colonial History*, edited by Sangari and Vaid (New Brunswick: Rutgers University Press, 1990), 16.

190. Anisa Audi, *From Ramallah, Palestine, to Lake Wales, Florida, and In-Between* (New York: Vantage Press, 1992), 6. Anisa Audi had numerous government jobs, working also in the Department of Lands and the Women's Training College.

191. "Moslem Ladies Appear With Faces Uncovered," *Palestine Bulletin*, July 29, 1929.

192. Ridler, "Special Problems," 29.

193. Akram Zu'aytir, *Yawmiyyāt Akram Zu'aytir, al-haraka al-wataniyya al- Filastīniyya, 1935–1939* (Beirut: Palestinian Studies Association, 1980), has five photographs of the delegates to the Eastern Women's Conference on Behalf of Palestine in 1938. Almost every woman is unveiled. None wears a face veil.

194. Alexandra 'Aboud, interview with the author, Apr. 28, 1993; Evelyn Baramki, interview with the author, Feb. 20, 1993.

195. Duzdar, interview.

196. Sajjadi, interview. Wadi'a Khartabil's husband encouraged her to become involved in charitable associations in Tulkarm, for example. See Wadi' Khartabil, *Bahthān 'an al-amal*, 71.

197. Jarallah, interview.

198. Tuqan, *A Mountainous Journey*, 98–99.

199. Said K. Aburish, *Children of Bethany: The Story of a Palestinian Family* (London: I. B. Taurus and Co., 1988), 36–37.

200. Ruth Woodsmall, *Moslem Women*, 100–101, 196. Woodsmall praises the Supreme Muslim Council as "an effective instrument of reform" because of its support for midwifery training and a later marriage age. In fact, the SMC supported a minimum age of eighteen for marriage of girls, whereas the government decided to establish fourteen years as the minimum age. See *Great Britain Colonial Office Report on the Administration of Palestine and Transjordan, 1933*.

201. According to Khalaf, between 1922 and 1944, Palestine's Arab population shifted from 20 to 25 percent urban to 30 to 35 percent urban. By 1944, 80 percent of the Christian population was urban. See Khalaf, *Politics in Palestine*, 23. The Muslim Arab population went from 23.2 percent urban in 1922 to 30.5 percent urban in 1946. Deborah S. Bernstein, *Constructing Boundaries: Jewish and Arab Workers in Mandatory Palestine* (Albany: State University of New York Press, 2000), 27.

202. Fadwa Tuqan, *Mountainous Journey*, 99.

203. Hala Sakakini, interviews with the author, Sept. 28, 1992; May 6, 1994.

204. Unorganized peasant women resisted Zionist settlement; see Chapters 4, 5, and 6.

205. Women mentioned this in interviews. Wafi'a al-Duzdar contradicts herself, saying that women did not work, remove the veil, or receive a "proper education" until after 1948, yet she herself did all three before then. (She never wore the veil.) Lydia 'Arraj said that the atmosphere in 1948—the "neediness"—made people more open to change, and that the exodus of 1948 caused women to seek work outside the home and in different domains than the usual teaching or nursing. Lydia 'Arraj, interview with the author, Nov. 30, 1992.

CHAPTER 3. THE "WOMAN QUESTION" IN PALESTINE AND THE DEBATE IN THE ARABIC PRESS

1. This phrase (*qadiyyat al-mar'a*) was not used much in the articles surveyed for this research. Yet it is appropriate to use it, I believe, because it was the implicit, underlying framework for all of the discussions related to women and gender in the Palestinian press. The phrase was used elsewhere in the Arabic press, and much earlier as well.

2. I have provided the articles' translated titles in the citations for the most part, although in some cases I have only cited the newspaper. When an author's name is designated in the original, I provide it in the citations as well. Not much is known about the authors—even those who are named—other than the small tidbits of information that sometimes accompanied their byline.

3. The latter I have included as one category because these concepts are inextricable and even synonymous in various writers' discourse. The analysis that follows is based upon a selected sampling from articles published in the press in the period from 1924 to 1938. (See Appendix I).

4. Leila Ahmed, *Women and Gender in Islam: Historical Roots of a Modern Debate* (New Haven: Yale University Press, 1992), 128.

5. Beth Baron, "The Making and Breaking of Marital Bonds in Modern Egypt," *Women in Middle Eastern History*, edited by Nikki Keddie and Beth Baron (New Haven: Yale University Press, 1991), 279–80. She discusses how changing economic conditions in Egypt affected notions of marriage (and by implication women) at the turn of the twentieth century, trends that are discernible in Palestinian society in the 1920s and 1930s.

6. Kumari Jayawardena, *Feminism and Nationalism in the Third World* (London: Zed Press, 1986), 12, 14.

7. Ahmed, *Women and Gender*, 144, 130.

8. I include Egypt as part of the Mashriq here, primarily based on cultural considerations. Egypt, of course, was exceptional in other ways, as it alone of the Arab countries has maintained a geographical, if not national, integrity that predates the rest of most of the Arab world.

9. Intellectual influence and exchange also flowed between the Mashriq and other parts of the Middle East, notably Iran and late-Ottoman Turkey, the pages of whose journals and magazines carried similar debates. (Unfortunately, analy-

sis of their press is beyond the scope of the discussion here.) There was a sense of consanguinity, based partially on linguistic affinity, discernible in the pages of the Arabic-language press, whose readers and writers crossed politically artificial boundaries. Thus one finds, for example, not only numerous articles *about* Syria and Syrians in the Palestinian press, but also letters and articles written *by* Syrians. (This was also the case for other Arab countries.) See, e.g., "The Marriage Crisis," part 9, *Filastīn*, Dec. 9, 1927.

10. Ahmed, *Women and Gender*, 148.

11. Beshara B. Doumani, *Rediscovering Palestine: Merchants and Peasants in Jabal Nablus, 1700–1900* (Berkeley: University of California Press, 1995), 68.

12. Beth Baron, *The Women's Awakening in Egypt: Culture, Society, and the Press* (New Haven: Yale University Press, 1994); and Elizabeth Thompson, *Colonial Citizens: Republican Rights, Paternal Privilege, and Gender in French Syria and Lebanon* (New York: Columbia University Press, 2000), 120–22, 214–18. For an incisive questioning of the term "women's press," see Marilyn Booth, "*Woman in Islam:* Men and the 'Women's Press' in Turn-of-the-Twentieth-Century Egypt," *International Journal of Middle East Studies* 33, no. 2 (2001): 171–201. Her point is that "the 'women's press' was full of men: editors, writers, publishers, funders" (171). Much of the discourse of this press was as much about men and masculinity—gender—as opposed to "women." (I take up this point below.) Her critique, however, does not detract from the fact that women in the Middle East exercised a remarkable degree of agency and developed a significant voice through their involvement in a press that was defined (rightly or wrongly) as a "women's press."

13. Thomas Phillipp, "Demographic Patterns of Syrian Immigration to Egypt in the Nineteenth Century: An Interpretation," *Asian and African Studies* 16 (1982): 171–95.

14. Aida Najjar, "The Arabic Press and Nationalism in Palestine, 1920–1948" (Ph.D. diss., University of New York, Syracuse, 1975), 30.

15. Ibid.

16. Ami Ayalon, "*Sihafa:* The Arab Experiment in Journalism," *Middle Eastern Studies* 28, no. 2 (April 1992): 265–66. In Palestine some journals ceased publication only to reappear later under a new name. Yusuf Khuri, *Al-sihāfa al-'Arabiyya fī Filastīn, 1876–1948* (Beirut: Palestinian Studies Association, 1976), 3–6.

17. Najjar, "The Arabic Press," 54, 58.

18. Ami Ayalon, *The Press in the Arab Middle East* (Oxford: Oxford University Press, 1995), 99.

19. Allison Wilke, "Portraying Nationalists: Palestinian Women and the Press, 1929–39" (Ph.D. diss., Oxford University, in progress).

20. Ahmed, *Women and Gender*, 144. Until 1908, there were only four papers established in Palestine. See Khuri, *al-sihāfa al-'Arabiyya*, 3–6.

21. Amin is cited and quoted at length in a number of articles in the Palestinian press. See, e.g., *Filastīn*, April 9, May 21 and 28, 1927; *Sahīfat al-Nisā', al-Karmil*, Aug. 22, 1926. A number of scholars have recently and incisively

attacked Amin's feminist credentials and especially his "rearticulation in native voice of the colonial thesis of the inferiority of the native and Muslim and the superiority of the European." See Ahmed, *Women and Gender*, 162. See also Lila Abu-Lughod, "The Marriage of Feminism and Islamism in Egypt: Selective Repudiation as a Dynamic of Postcolonial Cultural Politics," in *Remaking Women: Feminism and Modernity in the Middle East*, edited by Abu-Lughod (Princeton: Princeton University Press, 1998), 255–61. Yet we cannot underestimate the impact of his writings on his contemporaries in the Middle East. Certainly by contemporary standards his "feminism" (if one can call it that) does not hold up to scrutiny. The fact that he was widely read, translated, quoted, and even reinterpreted indicates the importance of his role in instigating debate on issues of gender, however retrograde his position might seem, and however scathing the attacks against him. He also did have supporters, and he was a potent symbol of ostensibly progressive and provocative new views. See Afsaneh Najmabadi, "Crafting an Educated Housewife in Iran," 100–101; and Omnia Shakry, "Schooled Mothers and Structured Play: Child-rearing in Turn-of-the-Century Egypt," 131–32, in *Remaking Women*. As Marilyn Booth observes, "It was commentators at the time, not simply historians writing later, who gave [Amin's] books precedence." See Booth, "Woman in Islam," 178.

22. For differing points of view see Neville J. Mandel, *The Arabs and Zionism Before World War I* (Berkeley: University of California Press, 1976), 126; and Rashid Khalidi, *Palestinian Identity: The Construction of Modern National Consciousness* (New York: Columbia University Press, 1997), 53–56. Khalidi, for example, says that "among the many influences on cultural and intellectual life during the last few years of Ottoman rule, the press had perhaps the most widespread impact on society (53)." Mandel, on the other hand, disputes even the existence of public opinion during the pre–World War I period, and questions whether the press reflected public opinion or molded it (126).

23. Rashid Khalidi, introduction to *The Origins of Arab Nationalism*, edited by R. Khalidi, Lisa Anderson, Muhammad Muslih, and Reeva Simon (New York: Columbia University Press, 1991), ix.

24. Booth, "Woman in Islam," 177.

25. See Najjar, "The Arabic Press," 64, 87, 103. Up until 1920, the press was controlled by the British military government and freedom of expression was limited. During the 1930s—especially during the strike and revolt of 1936–39—newspapers were often prohibited from publishing by the government for long stretches of time. In June 1936, for example, all of the Arabic newspapers were banned for ten days. See CID Police Summary, June 2, 1936, PRO, FO 371 20018. See also an anonymous report, "The Arabic Daily Press," n.d., CZA, RG S25 22760.

26. Ayalon, *The Press in the Arab Middle East*, 100.

27. Relying on the 1931 census, the director of education reported the following illiteracy levels: 865 per thousand for Muslims, 445 for Christians, and 166 for Jews. See Despatch from OAG to SSC, Sept. 28, 1935, from an enclosure entitled "Memorandum on the Continued Expansion of Education in Arab Vil-

lages of Palestine," by H. E. Bowman, director of education, PRO, CO 733 282/11.

28. Report of the Commission on the Palestine Disturbances of August 1929, 29, as quoted in Fannie Fern Andrews, *The Holy Land Under Mandate*, vol. 2 (Boston: Houghton Mifflin Co., 1931), 205. It was fairly common in the Middle East for newspapers to be read out loud in various milieus, thus facilitating their consumption by the illiterate. See James L. Gelvin, *Divided Loyalties: Nationalism and Mass Politics in Syria at the End of Empire* (Berkeley: University of California Press, 1998), 237.

29. See, e.g., an article about demonstrations against the Balfour Declaration, *Filastīn*-English, Nov. 16, 1929.

30. "The Arabic Daily Press"; Ayalon, *The Press in the Middle East*, 99.

31. At the end of an article entitled "Women's Rights and Her Duties," the editors of *Filastīn* remark, "The pages of the press—and *Filastīn* is among them—are open to publishing woman's view and theories. What is good among them will be received with encouragement. What isn't, we'll criticize with evidence." See *Filastīn*, Mar. 4, 1927. For this research, I surveyed more than nineteen selected years of *Filastīn* between 1921 and 1948, and found over 1,100 articles on women.

32. *Al-Karmil* was owned by Najib Nassar, an Orthodox Christian from Haifa, and *Mirāt al-Sharq* was owned and published by Boulos Shihada, also an Orthodox Christian, in Jerusalem. See Mandel, *The Arabs and Zionism*, 130–33, for discussion of the articulation between the religious identity of editors and publishers and politics.

33. James Gelvin, in *Divided Loyalties*, questions the concept of a unifying, secular, "modern" Arab nationalism. He criticizes historians' acceptance of an "essentialized 'Arab nationalism'" that assumes a "retrospective homogeneity and coherence . . . that it never achieved in actuality," and scholars' eliding of fundamental ideological differences among Arab nationalists. See *Divided Loyalties*, 5, 7.

34. For example, "Gifts of the Ladies to the Prisoners and Detainees on the Occasion of the [Prophet's] Birthday," *Filastīn*, May 4, 1939.

35. The discourse of the documents is instructive in demonstrating how the British authorities endowed certain characteristics and sentiments to the subjects under investigation. Such testimony is highly subjective, bordering on racist. In the intelligence reports such as the one from which this is cited, individuals are described in very personal terms: their appearance is "sinister and Levantine" or "strikingly Arab," or their "main defect is emotionalism," clearly a negative attribute according to British notions of proper behavior. See "The Arabic Daily Press."

36. Thomas Phillipp, "Women in the Historical Perspective of an Early Arab Modernist (Gurgi Zaidan)," *Die Welt Des Islams* 18, nos. 1–2 (1977–78): 76–79 (I use a different transliteration of Zaydan than Phillipp); *Filastīn*, May 26, 1927.

37. Hala Sakakini, interview with the author, Nov. 21, 1992. This theme of shared culture was repeated in many other interviews.

38. One cannot discount the sometimes real tensions that arose and existed between Muslims and Christians. But it must be said that these often occurred more in the political realm than the personal. (See, e.g., Yehoshua Porath, *The Emergence of the Palestinian-Arab National Movement: 1918–1929* [London: Frank Cass, 1974], 299–300). In interviews, narrators uniformly stressed amicable Christian-Muslim relations. Although one must take some personal recollections with a grain of salt, I nonetheless personally witnessed the genuinely warm Christian-Muslim relationships among this generation in the way of visits, friendships, support, and neighborliness.

39. Zuheira Sabbagh, a researcher and librarian, and Mansur Kardosh, head of a human rights group, interviews with the author, May 20, 1993. They also commented on the fact that the Orthodox, being Eastern-based, were less susceptible to Protestant and Catholic missionaries from the West.

40. These trends were common in the Arabic press elsewhere as well. See Marilyn Booth, "Exemplary Lives, Feminist Aspirations: Zaynab Fawwāz and the Arabic Biographical Tradition," *Journal of Arabic Literature* 26 (1995): 122n9. Booth notes the ambivalent appropriation by Arab women writers and journalists of Western models via the "'famous woman' ... genre"–one that the Palestinian press imitated and experimented with. Elizabeth Thompson, writing about the Lebanese and Syrian press during the French Mandate, observes that the women who appeared on the front pages of the press "tended to be foreign and featured precisely for their atypical activities." See Thompson, *Colonial Citizens*, 214.

41. For example, "Turkish Ladies in the New Civil Law," *Filastīn*, Nov. 9, 1926; "Women's Revival and Unveiling" (in Iran), *Filastīn*, May 27, 1932; "The Sa'adist Egyptian Ladies Committee," *al-Jāmʿia al-ʿArabiyya*, Aug. 27, 1931; and "The Ladies Demonstrate [in Damascus]," *al-Difāʿ*, Nov. 23, 1933.

42. For example, "The French Woman and Her Place in Society," *Filastīn*, Dec. 25, 1932; and "The American Woman's Influence in America," *Filastīn*, Nov. 21, 1938.

43. I warmly thank Ela Greenberg for generously providing me with her material, including translations, from *al-Karmil*, particularly from the 1920s. Henceforth, I will attribute her translations with [EG] after the article reference.

44. On the few occasions I did find photographs of Arab women, they accompanied announcements of achievements; one was of an Arabic teacher who lectured at a club, for example, and another of the first Muslim woman dentist to graduate from the American University in Beirut. See *Filastīn*, July 10 and Sept. 4, 1932.

45. For more biographical information about Nassar, see Chapter 5.

46. "Ladies Magazine," *Filastīn*, Dec. 10, 1921. This article is about the founding of a women's magazine in Egypt by Rose Haddad (née Antun).

47. In Syria, unveiled women, or women who were "deemed insufficiently covered or who wore European-style clothing" were attacked in the streets in the 1920s and 1930s, for example. Some men threw acid on these women.

Women were also assaulted for attending the cinema. See Thompson, *Colonial Citizens*, 136, 138, 210, 262.

48. There are a few, somewhat obscure references in the press in the 1940s to unveiled women in Jaffa being attacked (see Chapter 7). There was also a kind of backlash against women's involvement in the 1936 revolt (see Chapter 5). But the documentary record on these somewhat isolated developments is scanty and rather obscure. A possible explanation for the seeming difference between Palestine and Syria (the lack of violent incidents in the former) might be that Palestinian women did not unveil to the same extent and as early as Syrian (and Lebanese) women, and thus did not provoke such clashes. Also, the Syrian and Lebanese women's movements were arguably more militant in their demands for social change and reforms in women's legal and political status than were their Palestinian counterparts, thus contributing to a more hostile environment against signs of change such as unveiling and women's appearing in public in Syria and Lebanon.

49. Lebanon's population was also small but more literate than Palestine's (and Syria's). Furthermore, Lebanon had a major cosmopolitan city, Beirut. Thompson gives the following figures for levels of literacy in the early 1930s: Lebanon's overall literacy rate was 60 percent; Syria's was 37 percent. In Beirut, there were twenty-three thousand literate men and sixteen thousand literate women. In Damascus, the literacy figures were fifty-eight thousand for men and fifty-five thousand for women. See Thompson, *Colonial Citizens*, 212. [See my note 27, above, for Palestine's literacy rates in this period.]

50. *Al-Karmil*, June 20, Aug. 1, Dec. 5, 1926; Mar. 34, 1932.

51. I borrow definitions of "modernist" and "conservative" from Barbara Stowasser, "Women's Issues in Modern Islamic Thought," in *Arab Women: Old Boundaries, New Frontiers*, edited by Judith E. Tucker (Bloomington: Indiana University Press, 1993), 3–4.

52. For example, *al-Jāmiʻa al-Islāmiyya* followed with great interest individual cases of conversion, such as one of a young woman converting to Christianity, as well as another where a young Christian woman converted to Islam; Jan. 15 and Apr. 3, 1933. *Al-Jāmiʻa al-ʻArabiyya* published an article about the "Bolsheviks," in which it sounds the alarm about their attempt to "destroy tradition and Islamic culture" through attempts to liberate women by calling for unveiling; Jan. 24, 1929. An article in *al-Sirāt al-Mustaqīm*, entitled "Oh for Shame—Muslim Women in Tel Aviv," describes how missionary schools attempt to "exterminate" Eastern customs by promoting unveiling and mixing with men; how Muslim women are beginning to go to the cinema and dance with foreign men in hotels, and so forth; the writer concludes by calling for the formation of an organization to protect Muslim women; Mar. 21, 1932. In a Mar. 24, 1932, article, the author chides women's organizations in Jaffa, saying that "even if our women are liberal and modernized, they should not forget their morals and virtue."

53. Indeed, the residual friction was such that, in the summer of 1928, the

editors of *Filastīn* wrote a disclaimer at the beginning of an article about the controversial, recently published book *Unveiling and Veiling* by the young Syrian woman Nazira Zayn al-Din, saying, "We are not going to judge the book so as not to provoke a fuss such as the one we faced last year." See Thompson, *Colonial Citizens*, 127–40, for more on Zayn al-Din.

54. In addition to Basisu's article, quite a few of the articles in *Filastīn* reply to articles previously published by *al-Sirāt al-Mustaqīm*: Amin al-Rihani, "Woman and Unveiling—the Hat and the Tarbush," "To He Who Said the Veil Must Stay," and "A Christian Opinion on Unveiling," *Filastīn*, May 7, 19, and 26, 1927. Unfortunately, the 1927 edition of *al-Sirāt al-Mustaqīm* seems to have disappeared. (I could not find it in three different archives in Jerusalem, Jordan, and Lebanon.)

55. Although numerous articles that were published about other subjects included comments on veiling, these fifteen were explicitly part of the series, in which they responded to other articles in the series. Out of this number, three of the writers were strongly opposed to unveiling, one advocated gradual unveiling, and three were ambivalent or unclear. See Rihani, "Women and Unveiling."

56. In the first edition that published Sa'id's article, the editors note that, although they have received many articles on the subject (of wearing the tarbush and hats instead of the *iqāl*, as well as the veil), they have chosen only articles written by "our Muslim brothers" on these topics since Christians wear wide-brimmed hats and do not veil, and thus their opinions are "less valuable." Over time, however, articles by Christians were included. As mentioned in Chapter 2, it is not necessarily true that all Christian women did not veil. See "The Hat and the Tarbush," *Filastīn*, Apr. 19, 1927.

57. Mata Lani, "Contentious Traditions: The Debate on *Sati* in Colonial India," *Recasting Women: Essays in Indian Colonial History*, edited by Kumkum Sangari and Sudesh Vaid (New Brunswick: Rutgers University Press, 1990), 116.

58. Phillipp, "Women in the Historical Perspective," 65.

59. Lani, "Contentious Traditions," 90.

60. Deniz Kandiyoti, "Some Awkward Questions on Women and Modernity in Turkey," in *Remaking Women*, 271.

61. "A Word on the Arab Woman," *Filastīn*, May 14, 1927; "The Impact of Woman Among the Arabs, Past and Present," *al-Karmil*, Dec. 12, 1926.

62. *Filastīn*, June 23, 1931.

63. The Arabic word *jihād* has an explicitly Islamic connotation, as "holy struggle." See *Al-Difā'*, July 15, 1936.

64. *Filastīn*, Apr. 21, 1927.

65. He contributed four articles to the series, describing himself as a member of a well respected and pious Muslim family that gave him a traditional religious education. See "Veiling and Unveiling," part 4, *Filastīn*, June 4, 1927.

66. "Between Veiling and Unveiling," *Filastīn*, May 10, 1927. In this, Karami concurs with Leila Ahmed. See *Women and Gender*, chs. 1 and 2.

67. "To He Who Said the Veil Must Stay," *Filastīn*, May 19, 1927; "A Word on the Arab Woman," *Filastīn*, May 14, 1927.
68. "The Veil and the Necessity to Lift It," *Filastīn*, Apr. 19, 1927.
69. "Between Veiling and Unveiling."
70. As I note, some of the men who contributed to the series wrote more than once. Many signed their names and gave some bit of information about themselves, but unfortunately, we have little or no personal data on most of them.
71. Ghalib al-Sa'id, "The Veil and the Necessity to Lift It," *Filastīn*, Apr. 19, 1927.
72. 'Abd al-Ghani al-Karami, "Veiling and Unveiling," *Filastīn*, May 24, 1927.
73. "The Veil and the Necessity to Lift It."
74. Ibid.
75. Wasfi Basisu, "A Call for Harmony and Solidarity in Action," *Filastīn*, May 21, 1927.
76. "Woman and Unveiling—the Hat and the Tarbush," *Filastīn*, May 7, 1927.
77. 'Abd al-Ghani al-Karami, "Veiling and Unveiling."
78. The Arabic word used in the Palestinian press for the process or act of "westernization" is from the root *"farnaja,"* literally, "to become Europeanized." See Hans Wehr, *A Dictionary of Modern Written Arabic*, edited by J. Milton Cowan (Beirut: Libraire du Liban, 1980), 710. The Arabic root is widely believed to derive from the word "Frank," used to denote foreigner (*al-ifrānji*) during the Crusades, and still utilized in parts of the Arab world to this day.
79. "The Arab Women in the National *Jihād*," *Filastīn*, Aug. 30, 1931.
80. "The Muslim Woman Today and Yesterday," *al-Sirāt al-Mustaqīm*, Apr. 3, 1933.
81. *Filastīn*, May 14, 1927.
82. "The Marriage Crisis" and Wadih Da'das, "The Talk of Palestine—the Marriage Crisis in Palestine—What Are the Reasons for It and What is the Remedy?" *Filastīn*, Aug. 22 and Aug. 9, 1931, both part of the series on the marriage crisis.
83. Su'ad Khuri, "Schools and Woman," *al-Difā'*, July 22, 1935.
84. "On the Palestinian Woman," *Filastīn*, Apr. 9, 1927.
85. "What Can Women Do to Work?" *al-Karmil*, June 28, 1934.
86. Raf'ul Sa'ada, "The Influence of Woman," *Filastīn*, Sept. 11, 1931.
87. *Filastīn*, May 21, 1927.
88. See, e.g., "Women's Renaissance in Palestine—A Conversation With the Esteemed Educator, Miss Zakiyya 'Abd al-Hamid Sulayman," *Filastīn*, June 21, 1927.
89. *Al-Jāmi'a al-Arabiyya*, Aug. 21, 1931. The article is on the program at the Eastern Women's Conference, which scheduled a discussion on what to take and what to reject from the two civilizations, East and West.
90. "Councils of Ladies," *Mirāt al-Sharq*, June 16, 1927.

91. "Woman and Her Influence Upon the Social Structure," *Filastīn*, June 23–25, 1931 (three part serial).
92. *Filastīn*, May 21, 1927.
93. Shakry, "Schooled Mothers and Structured Play," 135.
94. Hashim al-Saba'a, "Freedom of Woman," *Filastīn*, May 31, 1927.
95. "What Can Women Do to Work?" *al-Karmil*, June 28, 1934.
96. There were riots in Jaffa in 1921, resulting in the deaths of forty Jews; in 1929 rioting broke out in Jerusalem and spread throughout the country. Many Arabs and Jews were killed and an international commission was sent to investigate. (See Chapter 5).
97. "You [f.] are responsible," *al-Karmil*, Oct. 16, 1929 [EG].
98. Su'ad Khuri, "Schools and Woman."
99. Subhiyya Miqdadi, "Woman's Education and Upbringing," *Filastīn*, May 29, 1931.
100. "Education of Girls and the Iskandariyya College in Haifa," *al-Karmil*, Jan. 23, 1926.
101. Qasim Amin, *The Liberation of Women*, translated by Samiha Sidhom Peterson (Cairo: American University Press, 1992), 71.
102. Basisu, "A Call for Harmony."
103. "Some Aspects of Rural Education in Palestine" [article proof for *Asiatic Review*, n.d.] by Humphrey Bowman, Director of Education in Palestine 1920–1936, Humphrey Ernest Bowman Papers, MEC.
104. Qasim Amin, *Liberation*, 47.
105. He is no libertine, however; he does not advocate removing the veil in "one fell swoop," but, rather, recommends it as an intermediate step, preparing girls for contact with men under supervision of male relatives and foreigners. Yusuf Haykal, "The Veil Impairs a Girl's Education," *Filastīn*, Apr. 30, 1927.
106. "Women's Renaissance in Palestine."
107. "The Veil and the Necessity to Lift It."
108. "Women's Education and Upbringing."
109. Bishara Mansur, "The Marriage Crisis," *Filastīn*, Aug. 22, 1931; "The Influence of Woman."
110. "Women's Education and Upbringing."
111. Margot Badran, *Feminists, Islam and Nation: Gender and the Making of Modern Egypt* (Princeton: Princeton University Press, 1995), 63.
112. Najmabadi, "Crafting An Educated Housewife," 94, 109.
113. In Egypt and Syria, also, there was outcry over the "marriage crisis" in the 1930s. An entire book, *Azmat al-zawāj fī Misr* (The marriage crisis in Egypt) was devoted to this topic and published in 1933. See Badran, *Feminists, Islam, and Nation*, 136; and Thompson, *Colonial Citizens*, 220. In Palestine, there were signs of it before the 1930s. See "The Marriage Crisis," *al-Karmil*, Dec. 23, 1928.
114. "The Marriage Crisis," part 3, *Filastīn*, Aug. 6, 1931.
115. "The Marriage Crisis," part 6, *Filastīn*, Aug. 20, 1931.

116. "Expenses of Marriages in the Villages," *al-Sirāt al-Mustaqīm*, Dec. 1, 1930.

117. Bishara Mansur, "The Marriage Crisis," *Filastīn*, Aug. 22, 1931; Daʻdas, "The Talk of Palestine."

118. Daʻdas, "The Talk of Palestine"; ʻAbd al-Fattah Jabr, "The Marriage Crisis," *Filastīn*, Aug. 8, 1931; Bishara Nasura, "The Strike on Marriage—A Dangerous Social Epidemic and It Must be Solved Quickly," *Filastīn*, Dec. 18, 1932.

119. Kandiyoti, "Some Awkward Questions," 280.

120. "The Marriage Crisis," part 3.

121. See Baron, "Making and Breaking," for a discussion about new notions of marriage and the issues of choice, love, and companionate marriage in late-nineteenth–early twentieth-century Egypt.

122. Saʻid Al-Baba, "The Marriage Crisis in Palestine," part 2, *Filastīn*, Aug. 5, 1931. See also ʻAbd al-Fattah Jabr, "The Marriage Crisis," part 3, *Filastīn*, Aug. 8, 1931, for comments about parents' control. It is difficult to ascertain whether the complaints were about parents' control or fathers' control, since the Arabic word usually used—*ābā'*—can mean either.

123. "Women's Page," *al-Karmil*, Aug. 22, 1926 [EG].

124. Muhammad Ismaʻil, "The Necessity to Liberate Women," *Filastīn*, Apr. 21, 1927.

125. Matiel Mughannam, "The Arab Woman's Political Awakening," *al-Difāʻ*, Feb. 13, 1935.

126. "Women's Rights and Her Duties," *Filastīn*, Mar. 4, 1927.

127. "The Highest Model for the Eastern Woman," Huda Shaʻrawi, *Filastīn*, Jan. 1, 1932.

128. "A Word on the Arab Woman."

129. "Depriving Women and the *Sharīʻa*: A View of That Matter," *al-Sirāt al-Mustaqīm*, Nov. 1, 1934.

130. "A Word on the Arab Woman"; Hashim al-Sabaʻa, "The Freedom of Woman," *Filastīn*, May 31, 1927.

131. Mary Shihada, "Woman and Her Influence on the Social Structure."

132. Badran, *Feminists*, 91, 240.

133. Antoinette Burton, *Burdens of History: British Feminists, Indian Women, and Imperial Culture, 1865–1915* (Chapel Hill: University of North Carolina Press, 1994), 55.

134. Literally, "*balāsh yā qawm, kalām fārigh.*" See "Our Women and the Leader," *al-Karmil*, May 2, 1936.

135. "On Behalf of the Revival . . . the Palestinian Woman, Socially, Politically and Scientifically," *Filastīn*, Aug. 11, 1938.

136. Mary Shihada, "We Women Are Not Less Nationalistic Than Men," *Mirāt al-Sharq*, Oct. 15, 1929. The boycott of foreign goods was part of a nationalist campaign during this period to encourage the "national" economy. (See Chapter 5.)

137. See Khalidi, "Ottomanism and Arabism in Syria before 1914: A

Reassessment," in *The Origins of Arab Nationalism*, 64, for a discussion of the new social classes and "classes in embryo" beginning to form in the late Ottoman period that challenged the power and influence of the old-style notable class.

138. Marilyn Booth suggests that one of the reasons why Qasim Amin's work provoked such anxiety was "because it highlighted *men's* unmet responsibilities and therefore raised questions about what it was to be manly." See Booth, "*Woman in Islam*," 178.

139. Deniz Kandiyoti, "End of Empire: Islam, Nationalism and Women in Turkey," *Women, Islam and the State*, edited by Kandiyoti (London: Macmillan, 1991), 26.

140. Thomas Phillipp, "Women in the Historical Perspective," 66.

141. The Palestinian experience in dealing with the contradictions of westernization brought about through colonialism parallels that of India. One scholar "suggests that the concern with the social condition of women was far less an indicator of such ideological preference for liberalism and more an expression of certain 'acute problems of interpersonal adjustments within the family' on the part of . . . western educated males." See Sumit Sarkar cited by Partha Chatterjee, "The Nationalist Resolution of the Women's Question" in *Recasting Women*, 235.

142. Jayawardena, *Feminism and Nationalism*, 14.

143. Lila Abu-Lughod, "Introduction: Feminist Longings and Postcolonial Conditions," *Remaking Women*, 16.

144. For example, Wasfi Basisu, Su'ad Khuri, and Subhiyya Miqdadi were all students at the American University of Beirut.

145. *Al-Karmil*, Dec. 12, 1926.

146. *Filastīn*, Mar. 16, 1928.

CHAPTER 4. THE ROOTS OF MOVEMENT

1. For accounts of Egyptian women's organizations, see Margot Badran, *Feminists, Islam and Nation: Gender and the Making of Modern Egypt* (Princeton: Princeton University Press, 1995); and Beth Baron, *The Women's Awakening in Egypt: Culture, Society, and the Press* (New Haven: Yale University Press, 1994). For Lebanon and Syria, see ʿAnbara Sallam al-Khalidi's memoir, *Jawla fī al-dhikrayāt bayna Lubnān wa Filastīn* (Beirut: dār al-nahār lil-nashr, 1978); Hanifa al-Khatib, *Tārīkh al-tatawwur al-haraka al-nisāʾiyya fī Lubnān wa irtibātiha bīl-ʿālam al-ʿArabī, 1800–1975* (Beirut: dār al-hadatha, 1984); and Elizabeth Thompson, *Colonial Citizens: Republican Rights, Paternal Privilege and Gender in French Syria and Lebanon* (New York: Columbia University Press, 2000). On Iranian's women's organizations, see Parvin Paidar, *Women and the Political Process in Twentieth-Century Iran* (Cambridge: Cambridge University Press, 1995); Janet Afary, "On the Origins of Feminism in Early Twentieth-Century Iran," *Journal of Women's History* 1, no. 2 (fall 1989): 65–87; and Eliz Sansarian, *The Women's Rights Movement in Iran: Mutiny, Appeasement, and*

Repression, from 1900 to Khomeini (New York: Praeger, 1982). For a historical overview on Middle Eastern women's movements, see my "The Other 'Awakening': The Emergence of Women's Movements in the Modern Middle East, 1900–1940," in *A Social History of Women and Gender in the Modern Middle East*, edited by Margaret Lee Meriwether and Judith E. Tucker (Boulder: Westview Press, 1999).

2. In the United States, women began to form voluntary associations in the nineteenth century, establishing benevolent, social welfare, abolitionist, temperance, literary, and missionary organizations and various women's clubs. In Europe, women also became involved during the nineteenth century in similar associations and issues such as feminism, prostitution, and public health. See Anne Firor Scott, *Natural Allies: Women's Associations in American History* (Urbana: University of Illinois Press, 1991); Lori Ginzberg, *Women and the Work of Benevolence: Morality, Politics, and Class in the Nineteenth-Century United States* (New Haven: Yale University Press, 1990); and Paula Giddings, *When and Where I Enter: The Impact of Black Women on Race and Sex in America* (New York: Bantam Books, 1988). The literature on European women is too extensive to cite here. A good historical overview is Karen Offen, "Liberty, Equality, and Justice for Women: The Theory and Practice of Feminism in Nineteenth-Century Europe" in *Becoming Visible: Women in European History*, edited by Renate Bridenthal, Claudia Koonz, and Susan Mosher Stuart, 2d ed. (Boston: Houghton-Mifflin, 1987), 335–73. In the Third World, women began to establish women's organizations somewhat later, as was the case in India, for example, when women became involved in issues such as nationalism, feminism, and birth control in the first few decades of the twentieth century. Again, the literature is too extensive to cite here, but for some accounts, see Gail Minault, ed., *The Extended Family: Women and Political Participation in India and Pakistan*, (Delhi: Chanakya Publications, 1981); Suruchi Thapar, "Women as Activists, Women as Symbols: A Study of the Indian Nationalist Movement," *Feminist Review* 44 (summer 1993): 81–96; Kumkum Sangari and Sudesh Vaid, eds., *Recasting Women: Essays in Indian Colonial History* (New Brunswick: Rutgers University Press, 1990); Kumari Jayawardena, *Feminism and Nationalism in the Third World* (London: Zed Press, 1986); and Ruth Woodsmall, *Moslem Women Enter a New World* (New York: Round Table Press, 1936).

3. See Kumari Jayawardena, *The White Woman's Other Burden: Western Women and South Asia During British Rule* (New York: Routledge, 1995); and Antoinette Burton, *Burdens of History: British Feminists, Indian Women, and Imperial Culture, 1865–1915* (Chapel Hill: University of North Carolina Press, 1994).

4. This tended to be the case more for the wealthy, who could afford many servants. I reiterate that this is of course a broad generalization; the situation of women varied among different cultures and societies and depended upon the availability of cheap domestic labor. As I mentioned in Chapter 2, Arab middle-class housewives, for example, often worked alongside their servants. Sibylle Meyer cautions that the common assumption that middle-class European

women left the domestic work entirely to servants and had much idle time on their hands obscures the reality of many housewives' lives. The same held true for middle- and upper-class Arab women. As Meyer notes, "Keeping up bourgeois appearances forced the invisibility of housework. Making this work invisible became in itself work . . . what appears at first glance to be idleness is revealed, on closer examination, to be difficult and tiresome work." See Meyer, "The Tiresome Work of Conspicuous Leisure: On the Domestic Duties of the Wives of Civil Servants in the German Empire (1871–1918)," in *Connecting Spheres: Women in the Western World, 1500 to the Present*, edited by Marilyn J. Boxer and Jean H. Quataert (Oxford: Oxford University Press, 1987), 164.

5. Afaf Lutfi al-Sayyid Marsot, "The Revolutionary Gentlewoman in Egypt," in *Women in the Muslim World*, edited by Lois Beck and Nikki Keddie (Cambridge: Harvard University Press, 1978), p. 264.

6. Guida West and Rhoda Lois Blumberg, "Reconstructing Social Protest from a Feminist Perspective," in *Women and Social Protest*, edited by West and Blumberg (Oxford: Oxford University Press, 1990), 5, 9.

7. See, e.g., Rashid Khalidi, *Palestinian Identity: The Construction of Modern National Consciousness* (New York: Columbia University Press, 1997); Rashid Khalidi, Lisa Anderson, Muhammad Muslih, and Reeva Simon, eds., *The Origins of Arab Nationalism* (New York: Columbia University Press, 1991); Muhammad Muslih, *The Origins of Palestinian Nationalism* (New York: Columbia University Press, 1988); and Rashid Khalidi, "Arab Nationalism: Historical Problems in the Literature," *American Historical Review* 96 (1991):1363–73.

8. Asma Tubi, *'Abīr wa majd* (Beirut: matba'at qalalat, 1966), 115.

9. Jayawardena, *Feminism and Nationalism*, 10.

10. Scott, *Natural Allies*, 1. For discussions on how focusing on the nationalist issue has affected the contemporary women's movement in Palestine/the Occupied Territories, see Rima [sic] Hammami and Eileen Kuttab, "The Palestinian Women's Movement: Strategies Towards Freedom and Democracy," *News From Within* 15, no. 4 (April 1999): 3–9; Penny Johnson and Rita Giacaman, "The Palestinian Women's Movement in the New Era," *Middle East Report* 186 (1994): 22–25; and Rita Giacaman and Muna Odeh, "Palestinian Women's Movement in the Israeli-Occupied West Bank and Gaza Strip," in *Women of the Arab World*, edited by Nahid Toubia (London: Zed Press, 1988), 57–67.

11. Ruth Woodsmall, *Moslem Women*, 362. Woodsmall, despite sharing some orientalist conceptions common to many Westerners in this period, reveals in her writings a strong sympathy and sincere interest in the women she met, interacted with, and observed in her varied travels, which included Iraq, Iran, India, Egypt, Palestine, Syria, and Turkey.

12. The word *nahda* can mean revival, renaissance, or awakening. It is most frequently translated as "awakening." See Fleischmann, "The Other 'Awakening',"127n37.

13. Woodsmall, *Moslem Women*, 355.

14. I only came across one reference to "the nationalist women's movement" in all of the sources I consulted for this research. *Al-Karmil,* c. 1934 [n.d., edition number 1840] .

15. Rosemary Sayigh, ""Palestinian Women: Triple Burden, Single Struggle," *Peuples méditerranéens* 44–45 (1988): 249.

16. Ylana Miller, *Government and Society in Rural Palestine: 1920–1948* (Austin: University of Texas Press, 1985), 115.

17. Ginzberg, *Women and the Work,* 11; Qasim Amin, *The Liberation of Women,* translated by Samiha Sidhom Peterson (Cairo: American University Press, 1992), 74.

18. Tubi, '*Abīr wa majd,* 117, 118.

19. On women and *waqf,* see Mary Ann Fay, "Women and Waqf: Toward a Reconsideration of Women's Place in the Mamluk Household," *International Journal of Middle East Studies* 29, no. 1 (Feb. 1997): 33–51; Carl Petry, "Class Solidarity Versus Gender Gain: Women as Custodians of Property in Later Medieval Egypt," in *Women in Middle Eastern History,* edited by Nikki Keddie and Beth Baron (New Haven: Yale University Press, 1992), 122–42; and Gabriel Baer, "Women and *Waqf:* An Analysis of the Istanbul Tahrir of 1546," *Asian and African Studies* 17, nos. 1–3 (1983): 9–28.

20. Marsot, "The Revolutionary Gentlewoman," 264.

21. "Ladies Revival," *Filastīn,* Dec. 10, 1921.

22. *Al-Sirāt al-Mustaqīm,* Feb. 6, 1931.

23. Joan C. Williams, "Domesticity as the Dangerous Supplement of Liberalism," *Journal of Women's History* 2, no. 3 (1991): 69, 78.

24. Badran, *Feminists,* 47.

25. In fact, it was the mixing of women from both Muslim and Christian backgrounds, with secular pursuits paramount among their objectives, that distinguished some of the later, politically and reformist-oriented women's organizations during the mandate period from their more charitably oriented predecessors.

26. I do not wish here to enter the evolving debate over the public/private dichotomy and its appropriateness as "a universal explanation for the lower status of women vis-à-vis men." See Mary Ann Fay, "Women and Households: Gender, Power and Culture in Eighteenth-Century Egypt" (Ph.D. diss., Georgetown University, 1993), 36. I would like to assert, however, that the act of women who had generally been segregated and secluded from the rest of society in leaving their homes for "outdoors," be it to enter other women's houses or institutions such as schools, was a social innovation connoting entry into the "public sphere."

27. Comparing the actions of Chinese female nationalists in the early twentieth-century to Palestinian women's early organizational efforts are instructive in considering this question, although Chinese women took a different route from Palestinian women in inserting themselves as national actors by directly and self-consciously linking their education to nationalist participation. Joan Judge observes that the early female nationalists (students in this case) "were

circumspect in their criticism of patriarchal institutions and masculine culture. They realized they could not afford to offend male activists if they wanted to be recognized as national actors, and they understood that transgender alliances were crucial to national salvation." See Joan Judge, "Talent, Virtue, and the Nation: Chinese Nationalism and Female Subjectivities in the Early Twentieth Century," *American Historical Review* 106, no. 3 (June 2001): 797.

28. Scott, *Natural Allies*, 2.

29. Ibid.

30. Sayigh, "Palestinian Women," 249. Marsot points out that upper-class Egyptian women of the harem developed some of these skills, such as managing people and delegating authority, through running large households. See Marsot, "The Revolutionary Gentlewoman," 267. She actually uses the phrase "manipulate people," which I interpret as "manage."

31. Ginzberg, *Women and the Work*, 67.

32. Henriette Siksik, interview with the author, June 15, 1993.

33. Khalidi, *Jawla*, 190.

34. Scott, *Natural Allies*, 82.

35. Wadi'a Khartabil, interview by Julie Peteet and Rosemary Sayigh, March 1982. While talking to me about her aunt Zlikha al-Shihabi, Madiha Nusseibeh described the work of Shihabi's organization, the Arab Women's Union as "political but under the veil of social." Madiha Nusseibeh, interview with the author, Apr. 25, 1999.

36. Attempting to compile a comprehensive list and delineate the origins of women's organizations in Palestine is perhaps an impossible task. Sources, although available, are few, and the inconsistencies and contradictions among them create confusion. They often differ on information such as the actual names of the groups, dates of seminal events, and the leaders or founders. Part of the problem stems from the fact that information comes from both Arabic and English-language sources; the British were often slipshod about translating. For example, they often used different names to refer to the same group. But also, not surprisingly, perceptions varied widely as to the groups' objectives and histories. Wherever possible, I prefer to rely on Palestinian sources, since their producers were sometimes actively and directly involved in the groups themselves; also their terminology in Arabic tends to be more consistent. These sources pose their own set of problems as well, however, and do not always correspond with one another. For example, *Filastīn* mentions a meeting of the Arab Ladies Society (ALS) in Jaffa on Jan. 1, 1929, whereas Adele 'Azar, who was one of its founding members, states in her memoirs that it was founded in her home in 1939. Another article in *Filastīn* on Sept. 11, 1936, announces the official registration of the ALS in Jaffa. There are numerous articles in the press about the society in the late 1920s and early 1930s, many of which feature 'Azar herself.

37. Laila Jammal, *Contributions by Palestinian Women to the National Struggle for Liberation* (Washington: Middle East Publications, 1985), 12; Matiel Mogannam, *The Arab Woman and the Palestine Problem* (London: Herbert Joseph, 1937), 60–61; and Tubi, *'Abīr wa majd*, 122–28.

38. Elizabeth Thompson notes that this "seems quite late for the start of women's charity organizations; much later than Syria, Lebanon and Egypt." Personal communication, March 10, 2000. I am not sure why this is. Depictions of Palestine in the mid-nineteenth century, which is when the first women's charitable societies in Lebanon were established, give the impression of a less urban and developed society, comparatively speaking. See, e.g., Mary Eliza Rogers, *Domestic Life in Palestine* (London: Kegan Paul International, 1962). As discussed in Chapter 3, Palestine was somewhat of a "backwater" compared to other Mashriq societies. In this case, I suspect the difference can be attributed to its lack of real cities before the early twentieth century, since most of the earlier organizations (if not all) were founded in towns and cities.

39. Tubi, *'Abīr wa majd*, 122–23.

40. Adele 'Azar, untitled memoir, 1965, translated by Hilary Rantisi, kindly provided to the author by Hana Nasir. Hereafter referred to as "Memoir." Women were motivated to seek and develop education for themselves early on in Palestinian history. On an exploratory visit to Palestine in the mid-nineteenth century, one of the founders of the Friends (Quaker) Girls School in Ramallah was "accosted" in the streets of the town by a young girl who asked him to found a school for girls. When he asked who would be the teacher, she replied, "I will." Rosa Lee, "The Story of the Ram Allah Mission," *Holy Land Missions and Missionaries* (New York: Arno Press, 1977), 8–10.

41. *Watanī* (masculine; *wataniyya* is the feminine) is also translated as "patriotic."

42. 'Azar, Memoir.

43. Ibid.

44. Tubi, *'Abīr wa majd*, 126.

45. Miryam Hashim was the founder of the Nablus Women's Union in 1921. (See below.)

46. Nahid 'Abduh al-Sajjadi, interview with the author, Jan. 28, 1993.

47. Ibid.

48. Ibid.

49. Information from Hala and Dumya Sakakini, nieces of Melia Sakakini, and Madiha Nusseibeh, niece of Zlikha al-Shihabi, interviews with the author, April 23 and 25, 1999.

50. Nuha Abu Daleb, "Palestinian Women and Their Role in the Revolution," *Peuples méditerranéens* 5 (Oct.–Dec. 1978): 37; see Musa K. Budeiri, *The Palestine Communist Party, 1919–1948: Arab and Jew in the Struggle for Internationalism* (London: Ithaca Press, 1979); Zachary Lockman, *Comrades and Enemies: Arab and Jewish Workers in Palestine, 1906–1948* (Berkeley: University of California Press, 1996); and Lockman, "Railway Workers and Relational History: Arabs and Jews in British-Ruled Palestine," *Comparative Studies in Society and History* (1993): 601–27.

51. Tubi, *'Abīr wa majd*, 127–28.

52. Ibid., 129.

53. Bernard Wasserstein, *The British in Palestine: The Mandatory Govern-*

ment and the Arab-Jewish Conflict, 1917–1929, 2d ed. (London: Basil Blackwell Ltd., 1991), 2.

54. What, precisely, this last activity comprised is not entirely clear from the texts, whose authors are rather delicate about specifics. The council founded a home for girls and young "female offenders"—perhaps prostitutes—so the reference may be to "vice." See Bertha Vester, *Our Jerusalem*, new ed. (Jerusalem: Ariel Publishing House, 1988), 288; Fannie Fern Andrews, *The Holy Land Under Mandate*, vol. 1 (Boston: Houghton Mifflin Co., 1931), 83–84. The Social Service Association, unlike the Palestine Women's Council, was still in existence in 1940, collecting clothes for the needy and providing shelter for destitute women and girls. The Arab women on its committee at this time included two Muslims and two Christians. See Social Service Association, pamphlet, 1940, ISA RG 65 3117. (See Chapter 2 for more information about the Palestine Women's Council.)

55. Henriette Siksik Farradj, *A Glimpse Into the Life of Katherine Siksik, A Life of Light and Love From 7th April 1894 to 3rd May 1973*, pamphlet (Jerusalem: March 16, 1992).

56. Leila J. Rupp, *Worlds of Women: The Making of an International Women's Movement* (Princeton: Princeton University Press, 1997), 58.

57. Jammal, *Contributions*, 8. This book is one of the few that provides detailed, interesting information about Palestinian women's activity before 1967; however, most of the data is unattributed or uncited, which makes its reliability problematic. Another reference to the 1884 incident in Affula, to which Jammal refers, is contained in Hamida Kazi, "Palestinian Women and the National Liberation Movement: A Social Perspective," *Women in the Middle East*, edited by the Khamsin Collective (London: Zed Press, 1987), 27. She does not cite a primary source.

58. Letter to the Chief Administrator, O.E.T.A., from Arab Women in the North, Mar. 23, 1920, ISA, RG 2 30/I.

59. Ann Mosely Lesch, *Arab Politics in Palestine, 1917–1939: The Frustration of a Nationalist Movement* (Ithaca: Cornell University Press, 1979), 200.

60. Intelligence Report by Col. Commandant J. Byron and Captain C. D. Brunton, May 12, 1921, PRO, CO 733 13; Lesch, *Arab Politics in Palestine*, 205.

61. *Al-Karmil*, Dec. 17, 21, and 31, 1921.

62. *Al-Karmil*, Nov. 8, 1922. I thank Ela Greenberg for this reference.

63. For an exploration of why dates and clear "facts" about the women's organizations and leaders are elusive, see my "Selective Memory, Gender and Nationalism: Palestinian Women Leaders in the British Mandate Period," *History Workshop Journal* 47 (April 1999): 141–58.

64. I found no primary sources to confirm this. The issue of names continually surfaces. (See note 7, Chapter 1.) Many contemporary writers refer to the Palestinian Women's Union, an appellation that was never used during the mandate period (especially not in Arabic sources). Furthermore, these writers bestow this name on the organization in retrospect, since the organization started out as the Arab Women's (or Ladies) Association and the "union" (*itti-*

hād) designation only appeared when it split into two groups in 1938–39. The following all state that either a Palestinian Women's Union or Arab Women's Society, or merely a "women's group," was established in 1921: Khadija Abu 'Ali, *Muqaddimāt hawla wāqi' al-mar'a wa tajribatihā fī al-thawra al-Filastīniyya* (Beirut: GUPW, 1975), 44; Margot Badran, *Feminism*, 224; Julie Peteet, *Gender in Crisis: Women and the Palestinian Resistance Movement* (New York: Columbia University Press, 1991), 44; Ghazi al-Khalili, *Al-mar'a al-Filastīniyya wa al-thawra* (Beirut: PLO Research Center, 1977), 77; Kazi, "Palestinian Women and the National Liberation Movement," 27; Abu Daleb, "Palestinian Women and Their Role in the Revolution," 36; and Jammal, *Contributions*, 13. None cites primary sources. Another common assumption is that the organization, whatever it was called, was founded by Melia Sakakini and Zlikha al-Shihabi, who eventually became the long-term president of the Arab Women's Union. This is also difficult to confirm or refute; it seems unlikely, however, since al-Shihabi was born in 1903 and would have been a teenager in 1920 or 1921. Furthermore, her own "organ," the AWU, does not mention this in its jubilee pamphlet.

65. Palestine Women's Council, Annual Report, 1921–1922, ISA, RG 65 3117; Mogannam, *Arab Woman*, 55; Arab Women's Union, *Al-Ittihād al-nisā'ī al-'Arabī bīl-Quds fī yūbīlī al-dhahabī* [hereafter *Yūbīlī*], 1980, 1983, 18.

66. *Yūbīlī*, 18. Mughannam says it established an infant welfare center in 1931; see Mogannam, *Arab Woman*, 56. It is unclear how (and whether) she distinguishes this group from the Arab Women's (Ladies) Association, which was established in 1929. (See Chapter 5 for a detailed account of its formation.)

67. *Jam'iyyat al-ittihād al-nisā'ī-al-'Arabī bī Nāblus, Bayān 'ām 'an ā'mal al-jam'iyya wa mashārī'ha wa mu'assasātuha wa nashātātuha ma' al-taqrīr al-sanawī li-'ām 1966*.

68. Tubi, *'Abīr wa majd*, 115.

69. *YWCA of Ramallah*, pamphlet, n.d. Adele 'Azar, of Jaffa, joined the YWCA in 1899.

70. When the YWCA was about to form in Amman in 1941, one of the officers remarked that she thought it "a little strange" that the majority of the group starting it would be Muslim. Letter from M. Marianne Mills to Margaret Speirs, Secretary of the Council of the YWCA in Palestine, Apr. 10, 1941, ISA, RG 65 3117.

71. Julia 'Awad, interview with the author, Mar. 6, 1993. Mrs. 'Awad first became involved with the YWCA in Jerusalem, and later was general secretary of the Amman branch. She was in her early nineties when interviewed.

72. Samira Khuri, interview with the author, Apr. 27, 1993; 'Awad, interview. The poet Fadwa Tuqan took English classes at the YMCA in Jerusalem. See Tuqan, *Mountainous Journey: A Poet's Autobiography*, translated by Olive Kenny and edited by Salma Khadra Jayyusi, translated by Olive Kenny (Minneapolis: Graywolf Press, 1990), 98.

73. Letter to Margaret Davies, General Secretary of the YWCA, Jerusalem, from Clara S. Roe, YWCA office in Geneva, Mar. 4, 1938, ISA, RG 65 1325. The

YMCA-YWCA relations were sometimes tense. In her letter, Miss Davies mentions attempting to "enter into and maintain a cooperative instead of competitive relationship with the YMCA," saying there should be "an equal concern [on the part of the whole community] for the welfare of its women and girls."

74. *Al-Jām'ia al-'Arabiyya,* Apr. 28, 1933.

75. Yvonne Kardosh, interview with the author, Apr. 27, 1993.

76. Khuri, interview. The leafleting was not sponsored or approved by the YMCA but rather, the organizers targeted it as a place to reach young people.

77. Tubi, *'Abīr wa majd,* 135.

78. Palestine Association of University Women, The Secretary's Annual Report, 1932–1933, 1935–1936, and 1936–1937 (the last from ISA, RG 65 3117).

79. For example, *al-Karmil,* Dec. 17, 1921; *al-Sirāt al-Mustaqīm,* Nov. 15, 1929.

80. See Chapter 5 for information about girl students mobilizing for nationalist purposes and forming [female] student unions during the 1936 revolt.

81. Andrews, *Holy Land,* 80.

82. Humphrey Ernest Bowman, "A Review of Educational Policy, 1920–1932," Humphrey Ernest Bowman Papers, MEC. Bowman reports that the "'Guiders' . . . have shown enthusiasm in attending training camps and carrying out their duties" but neglects to mention what these were.

83. *Filastīn,* May 7, 1936; 'Abd al-Jawad Salih, the renowned nationalist (former) mayor of the West Bank town of Al-Bira (and current Palestinian National Council member) mentioned in an interview that his membership in a Boy Scout troop was one of the factors that contributed to his politicization as a youth. Interview, Jan. 24, 1993. See Yehoshua Porath, *The Palestinian Arab National Movement: From Riots to Rebellion, 1929–1939,* Vol. 2 (London: Frank Cass, 1977), 122–23, for a discussion of the nationalist character of the Boy Scout movement in the 1930s.

84. Samiha al-Khalil—"Umm Khalil"—renowned founder and head of *in'āsh al-usra,* a major women's charitable society in the West Bank town of Al-Bira, epitomized the intricate intersection between women's so-called social work and politics. Since *in'āsh al-usra*'s inception in 1965, she established herself as an important political personage (*shakhsiyya*) in West Bank social and political circles, having developed the society into an impressive institution with an array of projects. She was elected secretary general of the General Union of Palestinian Women, the representative body for women in the PLO, at its first convention in Jerusalem in 1965, and became something of a symbol of exemplary Palestinian womanhood, constantly extolled as a nationalist leader. Sharif Kan'ana and 'Abd al-Latif Barghuti, *Munādila Filastīn: dirāsa hayāt wa nidāl* (Al-Bira: *jam'iyyat in'āsh al-usra,* 1992), 174. While I was seeking older women to interview for this research, she was invariably the first and often only woman suggested for me to contact, despite the fact that she was too young to be active during the mandate period. (She subsequently died in 1999 during the writing of this book.)

85. Islah Jad, "Tatawwur al-dawr al-sīyāsī lil-mar'a al-Filastīniyya hatta al-intifāda," Shu'ūn al-mar'a, pt. 1 (May 1991): 94–95.
86. Woodsmall, Moslem Women, 355.
87. Minutes of the 52nd Meeting of the Council of the YWCA in Palestine, Feb. 9, 1944, ISA, RG 65 01353.
88. Woodsmall, Moslem Women, 404–5. Interestingly, in the same paragraph, she notes that Muslim women appeared unveiled before the high commissioner to protest Zionism.

CHAPTER 5. WOMAN IS ALL THE NATION

1. Mary Shihada, delivering a speech reported in Filastīn, June 23, 1931.
2. The Jerusalem Arab Women's Association (AWA) split into two organizations around 1938; the splinter group was the Arab Women's Union (AWU). See Chapter 6 for more discussion of this event.
3. William B. Quandt, Fuad Jabber, and Ann Moseley Lesch, The Politics of Palestinian Nationalism (Berkeley: University of California Press, 1973), 21–22.
4. For various accounts of this incident, see Yehoshua Porath, The Emergence of the Palestinian-Arab National Movement: 1918–1929 (London: Frank Cass, 1974), 258–73; David Hirst, The Gun and the Olive Branch, 2d ed. (London: Futura Publications, 1983), 64–74; and Bernard Wasserstein, The British in Palestine: The Mandatory Government and the Arab-Jewish Conflict, 1917–1929, 2d ed. (London: Basil Blackwell, Ltd., 1991), 225–38.
5. This rejuvenation was short-lived, however, as it dissolved in 1934. For more about the AE and factional politics in Palestine during the 1930s, see Ann Mosely Lesch, Arab Politics in Palestine, 1917–1939: The Frustration of a Nationalist Movement (Ithaca: Cornell University Press, 1979); and Yehoshua Porath, The Palestinian Arab National Movement: From Riots to Rebellion, 1929–1939 (London: Frank Cass, 1977).
6. Porath, Palestinian Arab, 127; Lesch, Arab Politics, 105.
7. Sayigh, "Palestinian Women: Triple Burden, Single Struggle," Peuples méditerranéens 44–45 (1988): 248; emphasis in original.
8. Numbers vary according to the source and depending upon their particular political agenda. The chief secretary (CS) of the mandate government estimated participants at between 150 and two hundred women, CS to Parkinson, Apr. 14, 1932, PRO, CO 733/221. Palestinian sources estimated two to three hundred women. See Filastin-English, Nov. 2, 1929; and Matiel Mogannam, The Arab Woman and the Palestine Problem (London: Herbert Joseph, 1937), 70; Filastīn, Oct. 29, 1929; Khadija Abu 'Ali, Muqaddimāt hawla wāqi'a al-mar'a wa tajribatihā fī al-thawra al-Filastīniyya (Beirut: GUPW, 1975); Ijlal Khalifa, al-mar'a wa qadīyyat Filastīn (Cairo: Modern Arab Press, 1974), 38; Ghazi al-Khalili, al-mar'a al-Filastīniyya wa al-thawra (Beirut: PLO Research Center, 1977), 77; al-mawsū'a al-Filastīniyya, vol. 2 (Damascus: ha'iyya al-mawsū'a al-Filastīniyya, 1984), 211. 'Issam 'Abd al-Hadi, the president of the

General Union of Palestinian Women, clearly exaggerating, claimed eight hundred women attended; interview with the author, Jan. 27, 1993. *The Palestine Bulletin*, a Zionist-owned newspaper, provides attendance figures of one hundred, Oct. 27, 1929.

9. Sir John Chancellor to Lord Passfield, Colonial Secretary, Oct. 31, 1929, Sir John Robert Chancellor Papers, RH.

10. Much detail and intelligence were provided in Chancellor's papers. See also Petition of the Palestine Arab Women Congress to the President of the Permanent Mandates Commission (PMC), Jan. 28, 1932, and its accompanying memorandum from Chancellor to the PMC, PRO, FO 371/106052.

11. *Al-ittihād al-nisā'ī al-'Arabī bīl-Quds, al-ittihād al-nisā'ī al-'Arabī bīl-Quds fi yūbīlī al-dhahabī 1980* (The Arab Women's Union of Jerusalem's Golden Jubilee 1980) [hereafter *Yūbīlī*] (Jerusalem: 1983), 20; *Filastin*-English, Oct. 26, 1929.

12. Mogannam, *Arab Woman*, 69–70. This book is one of the few firsthand accounts of the early years of the Palestinian women's movement. Mughannam was a founder and active participant in the movement in the 1930s.

13. Mogannam, *Arab Woman*, 70–76; *Filastīn*, Oct. 29, 1929; *al-Sirāt al-Mustaqīm*, Oct. 28, 1929; *Mirāt al-Sharq*, Oct. 28, 1929; *Mawsū'a*, 2:212; and Julie Peteet, *Gender in Crisis: Women and the Palestinian Resistance Movement* (New York: Columbia University Press, 1991), 44–47.

14. In making this claim, I am necessarily privileging certain sources (newspaper reports) that predated or appeared on the actual date of the congress; e.g., "Ladies to Hold a Nationalist Conference on Saturday," *Mirāt al-Sharq*, Oct. 23, 1929. This article describes a preparatory meeting during which a "temporary administrative committee" was elected and specifies the protests (i.e., resolutions) the women planned to present to the government. See also *Filastin*-English, Oct. 26, 1929, which provides the same details, except that it calls the committee the Arab Women's Executive. Both articles provide the names of the committee members who were ultimately elected at the congress. These articles and British government documents are the only primary sources I found that documented the details of the congress.

15. Mogannam, *Arab Woman*, 73–74. Another interesting discrepancy concerns reports in *Yūbīlī* (p. 21) and an interview with an older staff member of the AWU that the women "threw off their veils" at the meeting with Chancellor. Hassan Istambuli stated "the first idea" of the Arab ladies was to "raise the *hijāb*." Interview with the author, Apr. 22, 1993. This is not corroborated in any other primary sources.

16. Chancellor to Passfield, Oct. 31, 1929; *Filastīn*, Oct. 29, 1929. Mughannam contradicted her own version of this event in her book (see above) in an interview years later, corroborating Chancellor's recollections that negotiations occurred over what kind of demonstration the women were permitted to hold. Interview with Julie Peteet and Rosemary Sayigh, Aug. 10, 1985.

17. *Filastīn*, Oct. 29, 1929; Matiel Mughannam, interview. In the interview

and in *Arab Woman*, Mughannam puts the number of cars at 120, while other sources report sixty or eighty. See *Palestine Bulletin*, Oct. 27, 1929.

18. Chancellor to Passfield, Oct. 31, 1929; *Mirāt al-Sharq*, Oct. 28, 1929. See Mogannam, *Arab Woman*, 70–75, for the complete list of resolutions. The *Palestinian Encyclopedia* states that they pledged to support the resolutions of the Palestine Arab Congress, *al-mawsūʿa*, 2:212; the last one held was in June 1928. See Porath, *Emergence*, 251–54, 265.

19. *Mirāt al-Sharq*, Oct. 28, 1929.

20. Guida West and Rhoda Lois Blumberg, "Reconstructing Social Protest from a Feminist Perspective," in *Women and Social Protest*, edited by West and Blumberg (Oxford: Oxford University Press, 1990), 13.

21. The Arab Women's (or Ladies') Association was also referred to as the Arab Women's (or Ladies') Committee; the two were initially one and the same. Various sources such as the press and British government officials used the two names interchangeably. The women themselves used these names. In the only two Arabic copies I found of their letters, they call themselves *"lajnat al-sayyidāt al-ʿArabiyyāt"* (literally, Arab Ladies Committee) in 1937, and *"jamʿiyyat al-sayyidāt al-ʿArabiyyāt"* (Arab Ladies Association) in 1944; ISA, RG2 POL/5/44. See discussion of this also in Chapter 4.

22. Abu ʿAli, *Muqaddimāt*, 45. The founding dates of most of these branches are elusive, and the sources tend to contradict themselves and vary widely. Haifa women, for example, were in the process of forming a "branch association" from the congress in November 1929. Speech of Amina Chenje, Nov. 7, 1929, PRO, CO 733 178/76510. The situation of the Nablus Women's Union, however, demonstrates the confusion in attempting to date the establishment of these groups. In a pamphlet, it dates its founding in 1921. *Al-Ittihād al-nisāʾī al-ʿArabī bī-Nablus, Bayān ʿām ʿan āʿmāl al-jamʿīyya wa mashārīʿha wa mūʾassasātiha wa nashātātuha maʿ al-taqrīr al-sanawī li-ʿām 1966* (Nablus: 1966), 3. An article in *al-Sirāt al-Mustaqīm*, however, reports a meeting at which the founding of the Nablus Women's Association took place on Nov. 24, 1929. To confuse things even further, in 1935, the women from Haifa apparently went to Nablus and helped form a branch of the women's union there. *Al-Sirāt al-Mustaqīm*, March 14, 1935. It is possible, but unlikely, that these are different groups. I have not been able to figure out why such discrepancies—common with other branches as well—exist. Rosemary Sayigh suggests that "it's possible that groups became inactive, either through the death of a founding member, or intra-clique rivalries, but that, given the pressures of national crisis, new people would seek to re-establish it. The old name would be used to re-mobilize former members, or recall the reputation of the founder. Another reason for reviving an old name could be the existence of a permit." Personal communication, June 4, 1994. Another explanation could be that groups predated the congress in slightly different forms (as charitable organizations, for example), but after the convening of the congress, reorganized along more politically oriented lines, sometimes with new names. It is also possible that the press paid less attention

to the earlier, more charitable incarnations, and thus, belatedly and/or mistakenly reported their establishment. Sayigh's speculation seems one of the most plausible: that groups experienced ebbs and flows of activity during this period, and thus, seemed to be "founded" several times, when in fact, these numerous "foundings" constituted rejuvenations of moribund organizations. All of this is conjecture, however; without archives or the accounts of the founders themselves, it is unlikely we will be able to reconcile all of these puzzling incongruities in the sources.

23. *Mirāt al-Sharq*, Nov. 16, 1929.

24. Mogannam, *Arab Woman*, 77. *Al-Sirāt al-Mustaqīm* reported the purposes of the AWA: "from the political perspective, to support the nationalist demands of the men's executive committee, and from the social perspective, to support Arab women's affairs," Nov. 17, 1929. It is interesting to note the different juxtaposition of priorities between Mogannam's (later) account and a contemporary newspaper account. Mogannam's version is less explicitly political in tone.

25. Because of the ambiguity in distinguishing the separate identities of the AWA and AWE, I will occasionally use this dual acronym. See Chapter 6 for discussion of their overlap.

26. Lesch, *Arab Politics*, 225; Walid Khalidi, *Before Their Diaspora: A Photographic History of the Palestinians, 1876–1948* (Washington, D.C.: Institute for Palestine Studies, 1991), 191. During the revolt over five thousand Palestinians were detained, out of a population of less than one million. Considering that there were "no more than a total number of between 1,000–1,500 permanently active rebels broken into smaller bands," this indicates that the British arrested large numbers of people for noncombatant charges. See Tom Bowden, "The Politics of the Arab Rebellion in Palestine, 1936–1939," *Middle Eastern Studies* 11, no. 2 (1975): 156.

27. *Al-Jām'ia al-'Arabiyya*, May 18, 1930; *Filastīn*, Feb. 18, 1931; *Yūbīlī*, 23.

28. *Palestine Bulletin*, June 17, 1931; Porath, *Palestinian Arab*, 9. Originally, there had been calls for an annual "Palestine Day" to commemorate the martyrs through a national strike and day of prayer.

29. This according to Rosemary Sayigh, "Palestinian Women," 265n5.

30. Memorandum from the Executive Committee of the First Arab Women's Congress to the President of the PMC (via the HC), Jan. 28, 1932, PRO, CO 733 221. This memo (and others) demonstrates the AWE's understanding of the technicalities of mandatory policy and law; specifically, that residents of mandated territories could neither present their case directly nor send petitions to the PMC, but rather, had to send written appeals to the high commissioner, who was supposed to forward them to the responsible government with his own comments attached. The criticized government then presented the appeals and had the right of rebuttal, "thereby diluting the impact of any criticisms." See Lesch, *Arab Politics*, 38.

31. *Filastīn*, June 3, Sept. 4 and 9, 1932; Nov. 19, 1933; Central Intelligence Department Summary, Dec. 19, 1933, PRO, FO 371 17878. (For a rich descrip-

tion of the 1932 Arab Exhibition, see Hala Sakakini, *Jerusalem and I: A Personal Record* [Amman: Economic Press, 1990], 49–51); Porath, *Emergence*, 15–17.

32. "Ladies of Nablus Hold a Big Demonstration," *Al-Jām'ia al-'Arabiyya*, Aug. 25, 1931. For more on the Nablus unrest, see Weldon Matthews, "The Arab Istiqlal Party in Palestine, 1927–1934" (Ph.D. diss., University of Chicago, 1998), 122–31.

33. "Ladies of Nablus Hold a Big Demonstration"; Great Britain Colonial Office, *Report on the Administration of Palestine and Trans-Jordan, 1931;* "Intelligence from the Joint Bureau" [Hebrew], 24 Aug., 1931," CZA, RG S25/3557. Thanks to Don Matthews for bringing this to my attention and translating it for me. As he notes in his dissertation, "this [the woman killing a policeman] was not mentioned in other sources," which is corroborated by my research. See Matthews, "The Arab Istiqlal Party in Palestine," 129n84.

34. Mogannam, *Arab Woman*, 93–100; "Arab Ladies' Wonderful March in Jerusalem in Rejection of the Mandate Government's Repressive Policy," *Filastīn*, Apr. 15, 1933.

35. CID Report, Apr. 22, 1933, PRO, FO 371 16926.

36. HC to Cunliffe-Lister (SSC), Oct. 23, 1933, PRO, CO 733 239/5 Pt. I.

37. "The Ladies Participate in the Demonstrations," *Filastīn*, Oct. 14, 1933.

38. Inspector-General of Police to Chief Secretary, Oct. 14, 1933, PRO, CO 733 239/5 Pt. II; HC to Cunliffe-Lister; *Palestine Gazette Supplement: Report of the Commissioner, Feb. 7, 1934* [hereafter *Palestine Gazette*], PRO, CO 733 346/8.

39. Mogannam, *Arab Woman*, 228.

40. "Disturbances at Jaffa on October 27th and Events Leading up to and Following it" [unsigned government report], PRO, CO 733 239/5; *Palestine Gazette*.

41. Mogannam, *Arab Woman*, 228. A police report, oddly, states that the women "did not take part in the procession." See CID Report, Nov. 15, 1933, PRO, FO 371 16926.

42. *Filastīn*, Oct. 31, 1933; Nov. 8 and 28, 1933; Porath, *Palestinian Arab*, 45.

43. Porath, *Palestinian Arab*, 45. The events of 1933 were somewhat overshadowed by the revolt that followed, and thus tend to receive less emphasis in historiography on the mandate period.

44. The arms, which fell out of a broken barrel of cement while being unloaded, were consigned to a Jewish merchant in Tel Aviv. The government never discovered his identity, nor did they find those responsible for the shipment. See Porath, *Palestinian Arab*, 141.

45. *Al-Difā'*, Oct. 24, 1935.

46. *Al-Difā'*, Nov. 14, 1935; diary, Apr. 23, 1938, Sir Thomas Scrivenor Papers, RH. This tactic, used during the revolt, was revived during the intifada in 1987, when young men would sometimes coerce shopkeepers to observe strikes.

47. Subhi Muhammad Yassin, *al-thawra al-'Arabiyya al-kubra* (Cairo: dār al-kātib al-'Arabī, 1967), 30.

48. James P. Jankowski, "The Palestinian Arab Revolt of 1936–1939," *Muslim World* 63 (1973): 223.

49. Quotes from Porath, *Palestinian Arab*, 137; ʿAbd al-Qadir Yassin, *Kifāh al-shaʿab al-Filastīnī qabla al-ʿām 1948* (Beirut: PLO Research Center, 1975), 158. Yassin (a Marxist) states that the Qassamiyya movement signified the first time that a revolutionary movement took place that was not under the control of the traditional (by which he means reactionary) leadership of the nationalist movement.

50. Porath, *Palestinian Arab*, 131. "Hebrew labor" refers to the Zionist policy of Jews hiring only other Jews in industry and agriculture.

51. Ibid., 159. See also pp. 143–59 for an account of how the proposal for a legislative council for Palestine was circumvented, increasing Arab frustrations.

52. Letter to Chief Secretary from Sergeant H. P. Rice, CID, Dec. 14, 1935, CZA, RG 25S 22735.

53. Every major town quickly formed national committees to "carry on the strike movement and to lead the people." See Porath, *Palestinian Arab*, 163, 173. The different factions formed political parties in 1935. These included the Palestine Arab Party affiliated with the mufti, the Nashashibi-allied National Defense Party, and the Reform (Islah) Party.

54. Porath, *Palestinian Arab*, 172. Hind al-Husayni, interview with the author, Feb. 15, 1993.

55. Laila Jammal, *Contributions by Palestinian Women to the National Struggle for Liberation* (Washington, D.C.: Middle East Publications, 1985), 8; *Filastin*-English, Nov. 16, 1929.

56. Rosemary Sayigh, "Femmes palestiniennes: une histoire en quête d'historiens," *Revue d'études palestiniennes* 23 (spring 1987): 14.

57. Peteet, *Gender in Crisis*, 54–55.

58. Ted Swedenburg, *Memories of Revolt: The 1936–1939 Rebellion and the Palestinian National Past* (Minneapolis: University of Minnesota Press, 1995), 180.

59. Khalili, *Al-marʿa al-Filastīniyya*, 78.

60. Elizabeth Ann Finn, *Palestine Peasantry: Notes on Their Clans, Warfare, Religion, and Laws* (London: Marshall Brothers, 1923), 27. Mrs. Finn lived in Palestine from 1825 until 1921 as the wife of the British consul, and observed many battles.

61. "Military Lessons of the Arab Rebellion in Palestine 1936," General Staff Headquarters, British Forces in Palestine and Trans-Jordan, Feb. 1938, PRO, WO 282 6.

62. Daily Intelligence Summary (Police) of June 1, 1936, CZA, RG 25S 22733.

63. Telegram from Wauchope to SSC, May 25, 1936, PRO, CO 733 310. Women stoned and wounded troops in the villages of Halhul and Bayt Fajjar. See Intelligence Summary, May 16, 1939, CZA, RG 25S 22714.

64. *Al-Difāʿ*, Apr. 5 and Aug. 30, 1937.

65. Woman from the Eastern Quarter of Nazareth and Umm Fathi, inter-

views by Zuheira Sabbagh for the author July 1993. Al-Mayat was reportedly "very strong," but could not kill the collaborator, whom the rebels later assassinated.

66. British sources report women killed in circumstances that point to their being involved in skirmishes. A woman accompanying an armed band near Azzum, in the Qalqilya area, was mortally wounded in an ambush and later died in the hospital, for example. See *The Times*, June 29, 1936; *al-Difā'*, June 29, 1936. (This must have been Fatma Ghazzal. See above.) Three women were reported killed in the siege of the village of Shifr 'Amr. Despatch from the Officer Administering the Government (OAG) to the SSC, Nov. 24, 1938, CZA, RG 25S 22769.

67. Zuheira Sabbagh (personal communication from her interviews of villagers in the Galilee region, July 1993).

68. Letter to the HC from the Arab Women Committee [sic], July 25, 1936, PRO, FO 371 20929; telegram from Arab Women Committee, July 1, 1936, PRO, CO 733 310/2. Jammal says that Ghazzal was killed on June 26, 1936; it is conceivable that she is the anonymous woman referred to by the AWA. See *Contributions*, 17.

69. Monthly Administrative Report for August 1938, Sept. 2, 1938, Sir Kenneth William Blackbourne Papers, RH.

70. I found eleven cases of women's arrests on charges of arms smuggling or weapons possession as reported in the press from the period 1936–39. This probably does not accurately indicate the extent of their involvement in this activity, since many did not get caught. There are numerous references in other sources to women assisting the revolt in this way. Even a British woman played her part on behalf of the rebels, hiding cash thrust to her by a man sitting behind her on a bus when it was stopped for a police search. H. M. Wilson Papers (she was a schoolteacher in the village of Bir Zeit), 1938–39, MEC.

71. "Military Lessons of the Arab Rebellion in Palestine 1936," General Staff Headquarters, British Forces in Palestine and Trans-Jordan, Feb. 1938, PRO, WO 282 6; H. J. Simpson, *British Rule and Rebellion* (Edinburgh: William Blackwood, 1937), 227.

72. *Palestine Post*, Sept. 20, 1936; June 14, 1938.

73. Sayigh, "Femmes palestiniennes," 27.

74. Tharwa 'Abd al-Karam Hassan, interview by Zuheira Sabbagh, July 1993.

75. *Palestine Post*, Feb. 22, 1938.

76. *Palestine Post*, Oct. 23, 1936; Dec. 16, 1937; Feb. 17, Apr. 12, 1938. It is interesting that the Jewish-owned *Palestine Post* reported arrests and trials of women in detail whereas the Palestinian Arabic press often did not report these cases at all.

77. Sayigh, "Femmes palestiniennes," 28n45. This comment is indicative of revisionist historical analyses characteristic of younger generations (1970s on) of Palestinian leftist intellectuals who have attempted to reinscribe the lower classes—particularly peasants—into the historical narrative. As such, it is a

rejection of an older historiography in which the peasantry is depicted as having had a passive historical role; rather, the notable classes were perceived as the major actors. To a certain extent, the new intellectuals bend over backwards to rectify class biases in history writing. See, e.g., 'Yassin, *Kifāh*. For an interesting analysis of the confluence of class and nationalism in the image of the peasantry in Palestinian historiography, see Ted Swedenburg, "The Palestinian Peasant as National Signifier," *Anthropological Quarterly* 63, no. 1 (1990): 18–30.

78. *Palestine Post*, Dec. 23, 1937. Interestingly, in the next edition of the *Post* a disclaimer appears, stating that this woman is not a member of the noted Jerusalem Khalidi family.

79. Kitty Warnock, *Land Before Honour: Palestinian Women in the Occupied Territories* (New York: Monthly Review Press, 1990), 145.

80. Peteet, *Gender in Crisis*, 55.

81. Report, Sept. 14, 1936, CZA, RG 25S 22761. (The DO hastily delivered the money to a member of a local notable family instead.)

82. Peteet, *Gender in Crisis*, 54.

83. In 1937, the Royal (Peel) Commission, dispatched after the first stage of the revolt to investigate the reasons for the disorders, recommended partitioning Palestine into two states, Arab and Jewish. The militancy of the people from the north and the Galilee area during the revolt is ascribed to the fact that much of the Galilee was slated to be included in the Jewish-controlled area. See Porath, *Palestinian Arab*, 220–32.

84. As Ted Swedenburg remarks, "It is largely thanks to this correspondence that a documentary record exists that documents British abuses." See Swedenburg, *Memories of Revolt*, 176.

85. *Al-Difāʿ*, May 2, 1936. The women in this article were named as "the wife of," perhaps to garner nationalist credit for their husbands, as the tone of all of the articles in early May are proudly nationalist and hyperbolic.

86. *Al-Difāʿ*, May 4, 9, 21, 25, 1936.

87. Sayigh, "Femmes palestiniennes," 26.

88. CID Summary, July 12, 1936, PRO, FO 371 20018.

89. Diary, May 12, 1936, Blackbourne Papers, RH. See also entries from Apr. 28, May 2, 4, 11, 14, and 18, 1936. Throughout the country, most of the government schools went on strike and closed down, and the students formed their own strike committee, joining forces among different schools. These committees harassed students who did not observe the strike, particularly those attending missionary schools. Letter [anonymous] to the Jerusalem Mission, Nov. 6, 1936, Jerusalem Mission Papers Box LXI, "Political Situation in Palestine," MEC.

90. *Al-Difāʿ*, May 5 and 6, 1936. The members of the executive committee were Hind al-Husayni (English College), Fatima al-Budayri (Schmidt School), Zarifa al-Hakim (Schmidt), Sirin al-Husayni (Friends School; she was Jamal and Naʿimati's daughter), ʿAʾisha al-Dajani (National School-Bethlehem), Naʾifa Abu al-Saʿud (National Islamic School), Nafisa al-Husayni (Maʿmuniyya School), and Khadija al-Farʿayun (St. Joseph's).

91. *Al-Difāʻ,*, May 7, 1936; *Filastīn,* May 8, 1936. Some of the older women also accompanied the students.

92. *Filastīn,* May 15 and 14, 1936.

93. Salma al-Husayni, interview with the author, Apr. 19, 1993. She pointedly remarked that the British did not use hot water in a strong stream, like the Israelis did. See also John Melkon Rose, *Armenians of Jerusalem: Memories of Life in Palestine* (London: Radcliffe Press, 1993), 153–54.

94. Hala Sakakini, *Jerusalem and I* (Amman: Economic Press, 1990), 57; Hala and Dumya Sakakini, interview with the author, Nov. 21, 1992. When they finally could not bear to maintain the strike any longer, they went to see a film during a visit home from junior college in Beirut, sheepishly creeping in late to remain invisible in the dark; they subsequently discovered that they had sat down right beside Salma.

95. Jammal, *Contributions,* 18.

96. *Al-Difāʻ,* July 29, 1936.

97. *Filastīn,* Jan. 28, 1939.

98. Telegram from the HC to the SSC, June 6, 1936, ISA, FO 371 20033; diary of Sir Thomas Scrivenor, Apr. 23, 1938, Scrivenor Papers, RH; *Palestine Post,* Apr. 24 and 26, 1938. The women in Jerusalem also enforced the strike through intimidation. Telegram from HC to SSC, July 23, 1936, PRO, CO 733 310.

99. Musa al-Husayni (her son), interview with the author, Jan. 24, 1993; "Military Lessons of the Arab Rebellion in Palestine, 1936," General Staff, British Forces, Palestine and Trans-Jordan, Feb. 1938, PRO, WO 282 6.

100. The man, who was a cousin of Hind's, was concealing his identity by using a false name and pretending to be a villager. He had no sisters. (I heard numerous stories about men being imprisoned in dry wells during the revolt but never read anything about this practice in written sources.) Husayni, interview.

101. Telegram from the HC to the SSC, Apr. 1, 1939, CZA, RG 25S 22793.

102. Ibid.; draft letter to Mrs. Corbett-Ashby of the International Alliance of Women for Suffrage and Equal Citizenship (IAWSEC) from Creasy, n.d. [probably March 1939], PRO, CO 733 398/17 75156; Sir Thomas Scrivenor, diary entry, Mar. 24, 1939, Scrivenor Papers, RH.

103. Mogannam, *The Arab Woman,* 62.

104. Rosemary Sayigh, personal communication, Aug. 1, Nov. 22, 1992.

105. Rosemary Sayigh, "Femmes palestiniennes," 29.

106. Asma Tubi, *ʻAbīr wa Majd* (Beirut: Matbaʻat Qalalat, 1966), 170.

107. Najib Nassar was born in 1865. In 1939, when Sadhij Nassar was detained, their son Faruq was ten years old and Najib was seventy-four. We do not have Sadhij Nassar's birth date, but it would be safe to assume she was no older than thirty-five to forty-five years old when arrested. See Yaʻqūb al-ʻAwdat, *Min ʻālam al-fikr wa al-ādab fī Filastīn* (Amman: wakāla al-tawzīʻ al-Urdunī, 1987), 632; Letter from Shahinda Duzdar and Matiel Mogannam to the HC, June 19, 1939, PRO, CO 733 398/17 75156; Hanna Abu Hanna, interview

with the author, May 19, 1993; interview by Latifa Muyis Dubari, July 1993; *Al-Difāʿ*, interview by Zuheira Sabbagh, Jan. 25, 1934.

108. Palestine: General Strike Finances 14th July (1936), CZA, RG 25S 22768; Letter to Chief Secretary from Deputy Inspector-General, CID, n.d. [probably 1938], CZA, RG 25S 22732.

109. *Al-Sirāt al-Mustaqīm*, June 1, 1936; Intelligence Report to Chief Secretary from CID, Aug. 18, 1936, PRO, FO 371 20018. (The Palestinian pound was worth $4.97 in 1936.) Iranian women also donated their jewelry for nationalist purposes (to create a national bank) during the Constitutional Revolution of 1906–11. See Janet Afary, "The Debate on Women's Liberation in the Iranian Constitutional Revolution, 1906–1911," in *Expanding the Boundaries of Women's History: Essays on Women in the Third World*, edited by Cheryl Johnson-Odim and Margaret Strobel (Bloomington: Indiana University Press, 1992), 105.

110. Intelligence Summary from CID to Chief Secretary, Aug. 18, 1936, PRO, FO 371 20018; *Al-Difāʿ*, May 21, Aug. 7, Oct. 18, 1936; Intelligence Summary, Aug. 5, 1938, CZA, RG 25S 22732.

111. Swedenburg, *Memories of Revolt*, 181. He cites Sayigh's "Femmes palestiniennes."

112. Ibid., 182. For a particularly cogent discussion of the *kufiya* as a signifier of differentiation in Palestinian society, see especially pp. 31–35.

113. Despatch from MacMichael (HC) to MacDonald (SSC), Nov. 24, 1938, CZA, RG 25S 22769.

114. Secret Despatch to MacDonald from HC, Oct. 24, 1938, CZA, RG 25S 22671. During the revolt, the rebels set up their own judicial system, with courts, judges and their own "fairly refined and graded system of punishments, fines, and even incarceration." See Swedenburg, *Memories of Revolt*, 133–35.

115. *The Times*, Oct. 5, 1938; MacMichael to MacDonald, Sept. 13, 1938, PRO, CO 733 366/4 75156.

116. Alexandra ʿAboud, interview with the author, Apr. 28, 1993; Latifa Muyis Dubari, interview by Zuheira Sabbagh, July 1993; Evelyn Baramki, interview with the author, Feb. 20, 1993. Alexandra ʿAboud's actual words are revealing: "During the revolt the Muslims forced the Christians to wear black veils on their heads when they went out. The veils were to look like the one the Muslims wore. They didn't want the Christians to look like Jews when they went out. This act was both religious and national."

117. The leaders in the women's movement were able to transcend for the most part the intense factionalism of the male-led national movement, but the cracks began to surface in the mid-1930s. See Chapter 6 for a detailed discussion of this topic.

118. Sayigh, "Femmes palestiniennes," 28; translation Swedenburg (also citing Sayigh), *Memories of Revolt*, 181.

119. Swedenburg, *Memories of Revolt*, 181.

120. Ibid.

121. Ibid., 182. He quotes the chant of a popular poet and singer, Nuh

Ibrahim: "And you, the Arab woman, march into step with your sisters the warriors (*mujāhidāt*) of the villages. Stop using your make-up, stop going to the cinema and other kinds of entertainment. Rise to the level of your sisters who carry water jugs on their heads, joining the warriors, singing and cheering them and so easing their death." Citing Yuval Arnon-Ohanna, *Falahin Bamered Ha'ravi Be'retz Israel, 1936–1939*, translated by Maswari-Gault (Tel Aviv: Papirus, Tel Aviv University, 1982), 44–47.

122. Swedenburg, *Memories of Revolt*, 182.
123. Ibid., 184.
124. Peteet, *Gender in Crisis*, 54.
125. Women and men of Zeita, interview with the author and Farid Kamal, May 10, 1993.
126. Porath, *Palestinian Arab*, 299.
127. Samira Khuri, interview with the author, Apr. 27, 1993.

CHAPTER 6. THE POLITICS OF THE WOMEN'S MOVEMENT

1. *Mirāt al-Sharq*, Oct. 28, 1929; Matiel Mogannam, *The Arab Woman and the Palestine Problem* (London: Herbert Joseph, 1937), 55.
2. Mogannam, *The Arab Woman*, 53–55.
3. Ibid., 54.
4. Rita Giacaman and Muna Odeh, "Palestinian Women's Movement in the Israeli-Occupied West Bank and Gaza Strip," in *Women of the Arab World*, edited by Nahid Toubia (London: Zed Books, 1988), 61.
5. Wadi'a Khartabil, interview by Julie Peteet and Rosemary Sayigh, 1981; Matiel Mughannam and her daughter, Layla, also made this point when interviewed by same, 1985.
6. Yusra Berberi, "Active in Politics and Women's Affairs in Gaza," in *Palestinian Women: Identity and Experience*, edited by Ebba Augustin (London: Zed Books, 1993), 52.
7. Anne McClintock, "'No Longer in a Future Heaven': Women and Nationalism in South Africa," *Transition* 51 (1991): 105.
8. Nira Yuval-Davis and Floya Anthias, introduction to *Woman-Nation-State*, edited by Yuval-Davis and Anthias (New York: St. Martin's Press, 1989), 6; emphasis in original.
9. It is, however, still puzzling the extent to which Palestinian women differed on the issue of women's rights—explicitly, suffrage—when they undoubtedly were aware of the unsuccessful suffrage struggles of their Arab sisters in Syria and Egypt in the 1920s. See Margot Badran, *Feminists, Islam, and Nation: Gender and the Making of Modern Egypt* (Princeton: Princeton University Press, 1995), 207–9; and Elizabeth Thompson, *Colonial Citizens: Republican Rights, Paternal Privilege and Gender in French Syria and Lebanon* (New York: Columbia University Press, 2000) 117–26.
10. Samah Nusseibeh, interview with the author, Nov. 23, 1993.
11. Su'ad Khuri, "Schools and Woman," *al-Difā'*, July 22, 1935.

12. Partha Chatterjee, "The Nationalist Resolution of the Women's Question," in *Recasting Women: Essays in Indian Colonial History*, edited by Kumkum Sangari and Sudesh Vaid (New Brunswick: Rutgers University Press, 1990), 238–48.

13. Matiel Mughannam, quoted in *Filastīn*-English, Oct. 26, 1929; and in "Women of the Arab World" by G. P. Dickson, *Arab World Review*, vol. 1 (Sept. 1947), CO 733 482/1.

14. Rosemary Sayigh, *Palestinians: From Peasants to Revolutionaries* (London: Zed Press, 1979), 6.

15. *Filastīn*, Sept. 11, 1932; Théodore Sarrouf, "La situation de la Femme en Palestine," *L'Égyptienne*, no. 85 (Nov. 1932): 23.

16. Ruth Woodsmall, *Moslem Women Enter a New World* (New York: Round Table Press, 1936), 363.

17. James L. Gelvin, *Divided Loyalties: Nationalism and Mass Politics in Syria at the End of Empire* (Berkeley: University of California Press, 1998), 5, 143, 11.

18. Mogannam, *The Arab Woman*, 76.

19. An interesting article on the women's movement in Palestine in *al-Karmil* that traces its recent history from the "1929 revolution" also mentions the executive committee resigning after "the last revolution," criticizing this act for not being nationalistic. The article, however, is vague and ambiguous; it is undated (but probably c. 1934), and it is not clear from how it is written when it refers to the Haifa branch of the movement (which it discusses in some depth), or the national movement.

20. *Filastīn*, Oct. 29, 1929; *al-Jāmʿia al-ʿArabiyya*, July 21, 1930. Mughannam asserts that the Arab Women's Committee replaced the AWE but does not say when this happened. Because her book was published in 1937, it is likely to have occurred before 1936. See Mogannam, *The Arab Woman*, 81. See Chapter 5, note 21, for discussion about the confusion and interchangeability of names. The last source I found in which the AWE is mentioned is dated May 27, 1934, in *al-Difāʿ*. The term "executive committee" (*al-lajna al-tanfīdhiyya*) was also used with subsequent groups that formed, such as the women students who organized in 1936. (See Chapter 5.) Also, the Jaffa AWA had its own executive committee. (See *Filastīn*, June 15, 1934.) But this was clearly a local body and not the Arab Women's Executive, a national entity. Similarly, I found references to elections for an "administrative" board (*al-haʾiyya al-idāriyya*). See *Filastīn*, May 12, 1931.

21. Michael Dumper, *The Politics of Jerusalem Since 1967* (New York: Columbia University Press, 1997), 19.

22. This definition of "elite" overlaps with but also differs somewhat from that of Bayan Nuweihid al-Hout, who defines the (male) political elite as "men holding responsible positions in political institutions . . . [that are] . . . those parties and groups represented by members of the Palestinian Executive and Higher Committees in the mandate period who played a part in forming the political decisions taken in the name of the Palestinian people." See al-Hout,

"The Palestinian Political Elite During the Mandate Period," *Journal of Palestine Studies* 9, no. 1 (1979): 85. My definition of "elite" includes social and economic sources of power and prestige rather than solely political ones.

23. Ghazi al-Khalili, *Al-mar'a al-Filastīniyya wa al-thawra* (Beirut: PLO Research Center, 1977), 77; 'Abd al-Rahman Kayyali, interview with the author, Mar. 8, 1993.

24. Nahid 'Abduh al-Sajjadi, interview with the author, Jan. 28, 1993.

25. Suruchi Thapar makes this point about middle-class Indian women's involvement in the Indian nationalist movement. Some of the parallels between the Palestinian and Indian cases are striking. See Suruchi Thapar, "Women as Activists, Women as Symbols: A Study of the Indian Nationalist Movement," *Feminist Review* 44 (summer 1993): 89.

26. Although I interviewed more than forty different women from the mandate period, not all were active in women's groups, and virtually none of the major leaders was still alive.

27. Madiha Nusseibeh, interview with the author Apr. 25, 1999.

28. Sajjadi, interview; Hind al-Husayni, interview with the author, Feb. 15, 1993; Matiel Mughannam, interview.

29. Guida West and Rhoda Lois Blumberg, "Reconstructing Social Protest from a Feminist Perspective," in *Women and Social Protest*, edited by West and Blumberg (Oxford: Oxford University Press, 1990), 10.

30. Matiel Mughannam, interview.

31. See Alexander Schölch, *Palestine in Transformation, 1856–1882: Studies in Social, Economic and Political Development* (Washington, D.C.: Institute for Palestine Studies, 1993), 289–90, for an analysis of why intercommunal tension in late-nineteenth-century Palestine was not as severe as it was in Lebanon and Syria.

32. Hala and Dumya Sakakini, Lydia Arraj, Wedad Qawwar, Sa'ida Jarallah, 'Issam 'Abd al-Hadi, Siham Sukkar, interviews with the author of various dates. Ted Swedenburg notes that veterans of the 1936–39 revolt also minimized the significance of Christian-Muslim enmity in interviews. He attributes this partially to "current rhetoric (and practice) of sectarian unity ... [that] tended to obscure any recollection of instances of sectarian conflict that flared up in the past." See Ted Swedenburg, *Memories of Revolt: The 1936–1939 Rebellion and the Palestinian National Past* (Minneapolis: University of Minnesota Press, 1995), 90.

33. Sa'ida Jarallah, interview with the author, Apr. 19, 1994.

34. *Al-Difā'*, May 15, 1936; *al-Jām'ia al-'Arabiyya*, Apr. 16, 1933.

35. See, e.g., *Filastīn*, Jan. 28, 1933. (There are articles almost every year about such activities, which seem to have been a regular feature of the AWA.)

36. They were Melia Sakakini, Matiel Mughannam, Katrin Dib, and Mary Shihada. See Appendix II.

37. Approximately five members of the ten to fourteen women in the AWE were unmarried. It is difficult to obtain accurate biographical information about women in this period, but we do have the ages of some of the AWE members.

In 1929, of the unmarried women, Zlikha al-Shihabi (b. 1903) was twenty-six and Shahinda Duzdar (b. 1906) was twenty-three; of the married women, Matiel Mughannam (b. 1900) was twenty-nine and Na'imati al-Husayni (b. 1895) was thirty-four. Melia Sakakini (who was single) was born in 1890 and so at thirty-nine was older than most of her single colleagues. Shihabi, Duzdar, and Mughannam were active leaders during the 1930s.

38. This is my poetic rather than literal translation to reflect the rhyme in the original Arabic. A more literal translation is: "who don't have a house to escape and a spouse to hit." *Al-Karmil* no. 1840, "The Nationalist Women's Movement in Palestine," n.d. (probably 1934).

39. Selma Botman, "The Experience of Women in the Egyptian Communist Movement, 1939–1954," *Women's Studies International Forum* 2, no. 2 (1988): 122. She refers to young women who became involved in the Marxist movement in Egypt, but her observations are also applicable to Palestine in the 1930s. Married women sometimes avoided participating in the women's movement when their children were young. Evelyn Baramki told me she joined a women's organization when her children were a little older; similarly, some married women may have been involved before they had children. Evelyn Baramki, interview with the author, Feb. 20, 1993. Na'imati al-Husayni probably had small children during her involvement. A photograph taken in 1923 shows her with her daughter Sirin, who looks to be around three years old. (Na'imati was married in 1919). See Sarah Graham-Brown, *Images of Women* (London: Quartet Books, 1988), 115. Matiel Mughannam's children, all born in the 1920s, would have been quite small while she was active; phone interview, Theodore Mogannam (son), Sept. 28, 1995.

40. Samah Nusseibeh, interview. (Interestingly, she herself was a widow.)

41. *Filastīn*, Aug. 30, 1931; Mughannam and Tarab 'Abd al-Hadi spoke at demonstrations in April 1933, and Mughannam also delivered a speech at the October 1933 demonstrations. Mughannam and Wahida al-Khalidi are the main signatories on the written communications in the early 1930s.

42. There is an interesting dynamic at work in Palestinians' continual evocation of the name of Zlikha al-Shihabi as the "president" or "founder" of the women's movement during this period. (This is the case with both those who actually remember her and members of younger generations who have read or heard about her secondhand.) None of the documentary sources from the period indicates this. She was certainly involved in the movement from its inception, but, in fact, did not become president of the AWU until 1937. Up until then, she appears merely as one among many leaders in meetings with officials, articles in the press, and so on. Indeed, Matiel Mughannam and Shahinda Duzdar dominate the written sources up through 1938, yet they are barely remembered or mentioned in Palestinian secondary sources or by Palestinians today. It may be that this curious lacuna is related to factional struggles stirred up by the split in the ranks of the AWA circa 1938. (See below for discussion of the split.) A kind of reconstitution of history may have occurred, placing Shihabi in the forefront in retrospect because she represented the more popular faction that was also per-

ceived as more authentically nationalist. For further discussion of this, see my "Selective Memory, Gender and Nationalism: Palestinian Women Leaders in the British Mandate Period," *History Workshop Journal* 47 (April 1999): 141–58.

43. Nashashibi's successor, Samah Nusseibeh, was president from 1977 until 1993 (and possibly still is; she was president when I interviewed her in 1993). These lengthy tenures of office could also be indicative of a number of other factors, such as the lack of democratic structures in the organizations (i.e., no regular elections of officers) or the inability of the organizations to recruit fresh members to renew leadership positions. See the discussion below on the internal organization of the AWA and AWU.

44. This was particularly the case with the Jerusalem organizations. Married women were officers of the Jaffa and Haifa organizations; for example, Adele 'Azar (wife of Iftim Ya'qub 'Azar) was longtime secretary of the Jaffa AWA, and Sadhij Nassar (wife of Najib Nassar) was the secretary of the Haifa AWA for most of the mandate period.

45. In the later 1930s, especially, short press articles began to appear in which some male leaders acknowledged and extolled women's participation in nationalist activities.

46. Khalili, *Al-mar'a al-Filastīniyya*, 77.

47. In my analysis here, I infer this from my sources. As I have noted, virtually none of the most prominent leaders was still alive and thus able to be interviewed when I engaged in my research. Yet the tone in the language and impressions one gains from the newspaper accounts, archives, and interviews with relatives and acquaintances strongly suggest the excitement of the work and the strength of the women involved. When I interviewed Zlikha al-Shihabi's niece, Madiha Nusseibeh (whose sister Fatima was also present), both women remarked frequently about how these were exciting and interesting times. Madiha Nusseibeh said that all of the activities that surrounded her aunt were fun, and described her aunt as "vivid." Madiha Nusseibeh, interview.

48. This could perhaps be due to the fact that women who were married to men in the more prominent families that were active in the nationalist movement went into exile with them, a not uncommon occurrence during the mandate (especially in the late 1930s).

49. For example, Wahida al-Khalidi's husband, Husayn, a physician, was deputy director of public health and also the mayor of Jerusalem (elected 1934). Na'imati al-Husayni's husband, Jamal, was secretary of the Supreme Muslim Council (funded by the British government) from 1928 to 1930. This partially explains the AWA's interest in the situation of Arab officials, as delineated in detail in the memo they sent to the Permanent Mandates Commission in 1932. (See Chapter 5.) The memo deals with the grievances of Arab civil servants and goes into minutiae such as specific grades of pension and travel benefits. There is undeniably an element of self-interest in this memo. Memorandum from the Executive Committee of the First Arab Women's Congress to the President of the Permanent Mandates Commission, Jan. 28, 1933, PRO, CO 733 221.

50. Madiha Nusseibeh, interview.

51. Letter to HC from the Arab Women's Committee (signed by Matiel Mughannam, secretary), July 8, 1938, CZA, RG 25S 22793; CID Report 50/2/G/S, July 11, 1938, CZA, RG 25S 22731.

52. Kayyali, interview; Madiha Nusseibeh, interview.

53. I asked Samah Nusseibeh how the AWA was organized in the mandate period. One of the questions raised was about recruitment. I asked if there were memberships, if the AWA was open to the public, and how, exactly, women joined. Mrs. Nusseibeh replied, "It was open to the public, but . . . no one was interested in joining the society except the . . . well-known notables." Samah Nusseibeh, interview.

54. Julie Peteet, *Gender in Crisis: Women and the Palestinian Resistance Movement* (New York: Columbia University Press, 1991), 56.

55. Matiel Mughannam, interview.

56. *Jam'iyyat al-sayyidāt al-'Arabiyyāt al-Quds*, pamphlet prepared by Ya'qūb Al-'Ansari and Ibrahim al-Husayni (Jerusalem: 1980), 19.

57. Peteet says that nine of the women were married to AE members, but I could not confirm this after checking lists of the AE in Porath or al-Hut. See Peteet, *Gender in Crisis*, 48; Yehoshua Porath, *The Emergence of the Palestinian-Arab Nationalist Movement: 1918–1929* (London: Frank Cass, 1974), 383–87; Bayan Nuwayhid al-Hut, *al-qiyādāt wa al-mū'assasāt al-sīyāsiyya fī Filastīn, 1917–1948*, third printing (Beirut: dār al-huda, 1986), 866.

58. She may or may not have been a member of the AWE; see Appendix II. There is some confusion in the sources about when her involvement began. Several scholars claim that it was she and Shihabi who founded the Palestinian women's union in 1921, but none of them cites a source. I searched for but never found any primary sources on this subject. See, e.g., Khadija Abu 'Ali, *Muqaddimāt hawla al-wāqi'a al-mar'a wa tajribatihā fī al-thawra al-Filastīniyya* (Beirut: GUPW, 1975), 44; Nuha Abu Daleb, "Palestinian Women and Their Role in the Revolution," *Peuples méditerranéens* 5 (Oct.–Dec. 1978), 36; Khalili, *al-mar'a al-Filastīniyya*, 77; Peteet, *Gender in Crisis*, 44.

59. Other women may also have been sisters of AE members; because biographical data on the women is so elusive, I could not determine the exact extent to which the two groups were interrelated through relationships other than marriage.

60. She disappears from the records in the early 1930s, to reappear again, briefly, as a delegate to the Eastern Women's Conference held in Cairo in 1938. After signing many written missives with Mughannam in the first years of the AWE, she seems to have slipped into obscurity. According to her daughter, she stopped working with the AWE in 1939; Leila al-Khalidi, information provided to Rosemary Sayigh and kindly passed on to the author.

61. Husbands of other AWE members, and their affiliations, included 'Auni 'Abd al-Hadi, Istiqlal (Independence) Party; Subhi al-Khadra, Istiqlal; and Boulos Shihada, (sympathetic to) National Defense Party. Political affiliations could be fluid, however; loyalties shifted, wavered, and were transformed in the factional disputes during the 1920s and 1930s, so the political orientations of these

individuals and others were not necessarily stable or rigid. Some men belonged to more than one party. These men's tenure on the AE did not necessarily overlap one another. See Porath, *Emergence,* 383–87; al-Hut, *al-qiyādāt wa al-muʾassasāt,* 866. Other AWE members from the two rival *hamūla*s included Zahiya Nashashibi, Fatima al-Husayni, and Khadija al-Husayni; a Diya al-Nashashibi may have been an AWE member. (All of these women were single). See Appendix II.

62. Matiel Mughannam, interview.
63. "The Women's Movement," *al-Karmil,* Mar. 25, 1935.
64. *Al-Sirāt al-Mustaqīm,* Apr. 15, 1935.
65. See, e.g., Peteet, *Gender in Crisis,* 48–49. She posits the seeming lack of competition was due to the "elite politically active men" allowing their female relatives to work together "in order to maintain crucial social relations with rivals." As we shall see below, however, rivalries and competition did not necessarily always originate from relations between men, but rather, between women themselves. Rosemary Sayigh, who was the first to propose that the AWA was not affected by the factionalism in the national movement, speculates that women made a "conscious decision to uphold national unity." See Sayigh, "Palestinian Women: Triple Burden, Single Struggle," *Peuples méditerranéens* 44–45 (1988): 249. Both Peteet's and Sayigh's observations are true, I believe, but only partially so; the overall picture is more complex.
66. Information about the various branches of the AWA/AWU, unfortunately sketchy and sporadic, is contained primarily in the press and British government documents, which have tended to record the activities only of the most prominent individuals and groups. (See previous chapters' discussions of the problem of lack of concrete data.)
67. For example, issues of *Filastīn* mention the establishment of ladies associations in Jaffa (1921) and Ramla (April 1929). See *Filastīn,* Dec. 10, 1921; Apr. 30, June 6, 1929.
68. *Al-Jāmʿia al-ʿArabiyya,* Jan. 1, 1930; *al-Sirāt al-Mustaqīm,* Mar. 14, 1935.
69. *Filastīn,* May 1, 1931.
70. *Filastīn,* Aug. 27 and 29, 1931. This mutual aid was typical; the Haifa AWU sent aid to victims in Nablus via the Nablus AWU in 1939 during the revolt, for example; *Filastīn,* Jan. 28, 1939.
71. *Filastīn,* Oct. 27, 1933. This was particularly true of the coastal cities' branches (see below) and occurred in a wide range of activities. Acre and Jaffa met to organize a joint theatrical benefit, for example. See *Filastīn,* Apr. 9, 1940.
72. *Al-Sirāt al-Mustaqīm,* Feb. 6, 1931; *Filastīn,* Jan. 13, 1940.
73. "Leading" here does not equate being president or "the head of" a particular affiliate. In fact, to my knowledge, Nassar was never president of the Haifa AWU, holding instead the position of secretary; but the various offices women held did not necessarily correspond to the intensity (or lack thereof) of their actual involvement or to their leadership role. Matiel Mughannam, extremely active during the 1930s, was also secretary, not president, of the

AWE. Indeed, sometimes the presidents seemed more titular than other officers. (This was not the case with Zlikha al-Shihabi, however.)

74. I have already mentioned above that Haifa women smashed shop windows and intimidated shopkeepers; in another incident, they poured paraffin over the vegetables of merchants who did not comply with the strike. See *Palestine Post*, June 7, 1936.

75. *Al-Karmil*, Nov. 8, 1933.

76. Without other sources, it is difficult to ascertain whether the skewed picture of regional activity reflects a certain reality or the interests of the sources themselves. Most of the newspapers were published from the coastal cities or Jerusalem. Documentary sources reflect the same focus on the coastal cities, Jerusalem, and Nablus, as does the press.

77. *Filastīn*, May 14, 1936; Jan. 28, 1939; Daily Intelligence Summary, CID, Aug. 1, 1938, CZA, RG 25S 22732.

78. Letter to the HC from the Acre Women's Committee, Aug. 9, 1938, CZA, RG 25S 22793.

79. Rosemary Sayigh, personal communication, Nov. 22, 1992.

80. I could not ascertain if this power struggle was the same one that placed Mrs. Khartabil at the head of the organization.

81. *Al-Difāʿ*, Mar. 25, 31, and Apr. 3, 1935. It is not coincidental that these letters appeared at the same time as the founding conference of the Husayni-dominated Palestine Arab Party (Mar. 26–27), some four months after the Nashashibi faction had established its own party, the National Defense Party. The very air quivered with factionalism during this period. See Yehoshua Porath, *The Palestinian Arab National Movement: From Riots to Rebellion, 1929–1939* (London: Frank Cass, 1977), 49–77.

82. Although I have not mentioned her, Khalil (whose full name was al-Khalil ʿAwida) was president of the Haifa chapter for many years. Although less flamboyant than Nassar, she was nonetheless very active and apparently developed a close relationship with Nassar; in 1935, Nassar refused to attend the International Women's Conference in Istanbul without her (she was indisposed); *al-Sirāt al-Mustaqīm*, Apr. 22, 1935.

83. Matiel Mughannam, interview (with her daughter, Layla, present).

84. The actual date is difficult to ascertain, since women from the different groups apparently worked together on and off even after the split. (See below.)

85. See Swedenburg, *Memories of Revolt*; and Fleischmann, "Selective Memory, Gender and Nationalism."

86. Hassan Istambuli and Amina al-Kadhimi, interview with the author, Jerusalem, Apr. 22, 1993; Madiha Nusseibeh, interview; Jarallah, interview. Samah Nusseibeh (interview) commented that during the strike, the women began to "have political differences" and "divided . . . they [the AWU] . . . wanted to make politics." This was the most specific answer I could get to the question of what caused the split. Major leaders who remained with the AWA were Shahinda Duzdar and Zahiya Nashashibi; those who allied with the AWU were Zlikha al-Shihabi, Melia Sakakini, and most of the Husayni women.

87. The phrase "social work" derives from contemporary Palestinian political terminology, whereby the Arabic translation of "social work" (*'amal ijtīmā'ī*) means "benevolent," or "charitable work." Among the younger generation of Palestinian feminists, this phrase has a certain pejorative connotation, due to their perception that the women's movement of the mandate generation was not "revolutionary." Older women, however, used it more descriptively.

88. Rosemary Sayigh, "Palestinian Women," 250.

89. *Palestine Post*, Dec. 7, 1936.

90. She wears the *hijāb*, however, on the cover of the Arab women's union golden jubilee pamphlet. For photographs, see it, *Al-ittihād al-nisā'ī, al-ittihād al-nisā'ī al-'Arabī bīl-Quds fī yūbīlī al-dhahabī* [Hereafter, *Yūbīlī*] (Jerusalem: 1983); and *Al-mar'a al-'Arabiyya wa qadiyyat Filastīn* (Cairo: 1938).

91. When I asked Madiha Nusseibeh about this issue, she said that women veiled depending upon their age. Interestingly, not one of the older women interviewed for this research wore any kind of head covering, and many criticized the reappearance of it among younger Palestinian women.

92. Khartabil, interview. Nahid al-Sajjadi mentioned that the women from Nablus tended to wear the *hijāb* more than women from other cities; Sajjadi, interview.

93. James Gelvin discusses how in Syria certain nationalists "articulated a nationalism that ostensibly reaffirmed 'traditional values' yet did so within the institutional and discursive framework of a modern national movement." See Gelvin, *Divided Loyalties*, 96.

94. *Filastīn*, Dec. 13, 1944.

95. Salma al-Husayni, interview with the author, April 19, 1993. Interestingly, men who were interviewed repeated a variation of the theme of Huda Sha'rawi's involvement, claiming that she "founded" the Palestinian women's movement.

96. Samah Nusseibeh, interview; *Al-mawsū'a al-Filastīniyya* (Palestinian Encyclopedia), vol. 2 (Damascus: Ha'iyya al-mawsū'a al-Filastīniyya, 1984), 216. The AWU says that by 1944 the AWU comprised seventeen organizations in seventeen different cities, *Yūbīlī*, 16.

97. The AWU, in its golden jubilee pamphlet, consistently projects the "union" appellation back in time to refer to the organization (to its founding, for example) when, in fact, this word was never used in the press or other sources until the late 1930s and 1940s. (This was not true with some local groups, however, such as Haifa, which used the word "union" to refer to its association before the AWU was formed.) *Yūbīlī*, 17. To confuse things even further, the AWA was also called the Arab Ladies' Association (or Society). See other discussions about names.

98. Arab women to the HC, March 20, 1940, PRO, CO 733 425/16.

99. Hassan Istambuli and Amina Kadhimi; Sa'ida Jarallah; *mawsū'a*, 216. Samah Nusseibeh stated that the two groups worked separately after 1939.

100. Letter to HC from Shahinda Duzdar and Matiel Mogannam, June 19, 1939, PRO, CO 733 398/17 75156. Mughannam, as previously noted, was

aligned with the Nashashibi faction. Although not entirely clear, it seems she remained with the AWA. (Later she moved to Ramallah and became a founder of its AWU.) One gets the impression that she and Shihabi were competitors. In the AWU's golden jubilee pamphlet, she is not listed as a founding member, interestingly, although most of the other AWE members are on the roster. It seems as though some later political conflict between her and Shihabi may have resulted in the latter's excision of her from the AWU's official history. Nashashibi, Shihabi's ostensible rival for president, is included on this list. See *Yūbīlī*, 17. (The AWA's pamphlet, however, issued five years later, lists Mughannam as a founder; according to these two pamphlets, the two organizations shared six "founding members." See 'Ansari and Husayni, *Jam'iyyat al-sayyidāt al-'Arabiyyāt*, 2.) Mughannam, however, was an intensely political animal and willing (if not eager) to frequently appear in the limelight, as evidenced by the extensive documentation (in the press and otherwise) of her involvement in numerous protests, demonstrations, meetings with British officials, and so forth. Accounts of her activism decline after 1940. This might also be related to her increasing fears about personal safety in the wake of assassinations during the revolt, which she expressed during the 1938 Eastern Women's Conference in Cairo. (See Chapter 7.) It must have been personally difficult for her to have to change directions from her former political engagement toward "social work." The Ramallah Women's Union appears to have focused much of its energy on handiwork projects.

101. "Arab Women's Conference," *Davar* [n.d.], Press Review, ISA, RG 15 File 25. Mughannam, Duzdar, and other AWA leaders did not attend the 1944 conference. *Al- ittihād al-nisā'ī al-misrī, al-mu'tamar al-nisā'ī al-'Arabī* (Cairo: dār al-ma'rif, 1944), 41–42.

102. Husayni, interview.

103. *Mirāt al-Sharq*, Oct. 15, 1929.

104. I refer here to primary sources, for the most part, although this is true of secondary sources as well. There are some exceptions: Akram Zu'aytir indicates a high level of collaboration among the men and the women over the organizing of the 1938 Eastern Women's Conference in Cairo, in *Yawmiyyāt Akram Zu'aytir: al-haraka al-wataniyya al-Filastīniyya 1935–1939* (Beirut: Palestine Studies Association, 1980), 397–98, 451, 471–76. (See Chapter 7). The *Palestinian Encyclopedia* makes sweeping statements about women being a constituent part of the national movement, but with no reference to primary sources. See *mawsū'a*, 2:211–19.

105. Raja al-'Isa, interview with the author, Jan. 26, 1993; Hassan Istambuli, interview with the author, Apr. 22, 1993, said that there was no relationship between the AWU and the men, but some men worked for the AWU professionally. (As he did, both previously and at the time of our interview; he was their accountant.)

106. Samah Nusseibeh, interview; Samira Khuri, interview with the author, Apr. 27, 1993; Matiel Mughannam, interview; and Madiha Nusseibeh, interview.

107. Arabic Press Summary, Supreme Muslim Council, Jamal Husseini, 1929, PRO, CO 733/178/67500.
108. *Filastīn*, Oct. 29, 1929; *Mirāt al-Sharq*, Nov. 16, 1929.
109. *Filastīn*, Nov. 29, 1933; *al-Sirāt al-Mustaqīm*, Oct. 23, 1933. (Shuqayri's public declarations of support are interesting, considering that the opposition opposed the AE, which had planned and organized the demonstrations. His nationalist credentials have been called into question by historians. He did not always toe the line with the opposition, however, according to Porath. For more information about this contradictory figure, see Porath *Emergence*, 212; and *Palestinian Arab*, 224, 69. See also Ted Swedenburg, *Memories of Revolt*, 157–65.)
110. Sayigh, "Palestinian Women," 249.
111. *Al-Sirāt al-Mustaqīm*, Nov. 24, 1929.
112. *Al-Difāʿ*, May 14 and May 4, 1936; *Filastin*-English, Aug. 1, 1931.
113. Porath, *Palestinian Arab*, 2.
114. *Mirāt al-Sharq*, Oct. 15, 1929.
115. See, e.g., *Filastīn*, May 20, 1933, Mar. 26, 1939, Jan. 25, 1940; *al-Difāʿ*, Jan. 25, 1935, Nov. 22, 1936; *al-Sirāt al-Mustaqīm*, Mar. 14, 1935; *Mirāt al-Sharq*, Oct. 28, 1929.
116. *Al-Difāʿ*, Oct. 11, 1937; *al-Sirāt al-Mustaqīm*, Jan. 25, 1934; Apr. 15, 1935; ʿIsa, interview.
117. League of Nations Permanent Mandate Commission Minutes of the Thirty-Second (Extraordinary) Session Devoted to Palestine Held at Geneva from July 30 to August 18, 1937: Report of the Commission to the Council, Geneva, Aug. 18, 1937, PRO, CO 733/326/75031/3/37, 84.
118. *Filastīn*, Apr. 20, 1932.
119. *Filastīn*, Jan. 21, 1937.
120. "The Women's Movement," *al-Karmil*, March 25, 1935.
121. Matiel Mughannam, interview. Madiha Nusseibeh also mentioned that her aunt, Zlikha al-Shihabi, had close contact with men in the nationalist movement. Madiha Nusseibeh, interview.
122. "Items from the information of the United Bureau, 24 Aug., 1931," CZA, RG 25S/3557 (Hebrew).
123. CID Summary, Dec. 19, 1933, PRO, FO 371 17878.
124. *Mawsūʿa*, II, 212.
125. Layla Mughannam's word, in the interview with her mother.
126. Written in 1984, the *Encyclopedia* engages in what Ted Swedenburg describes as invoking "idealized images of the past . . . that work through 'mythicizing vagueness.'" Swedenburg, *Memories of Revolt*, 22. (I say "seems" because the sources upon which the *Encyclopedia* bases its information are obscure and uncited for the most part.) The *Encyclopedia* projects contemporary, official nationalist discourse back onto the past, idealizing historical events according to current needs and norms. Thus, when in 1984 the issue of national unity was of paramount importance to the Palestinian nationalist movement

(and female participation in the movement was perceived positively), it was important to represent the historical relationship between the male-led nationalist movement and the women's movement as harmonious and coordinated, regardless of evidence indicating otherwise. See also, Fleischmann, "Selective Memory, Gender and Nationalism."

127. *Al-Difāʿ*, Apr. 30, 1936. Articles frequently announced women's meetings to "look into the current situation" (*al-hāla al-hādira*). From the constant repetition of the phrase, it is clear that the "situation" over time became so complex and multifaceted that the reporters had no time, space, or inclination to delineate the phrase's meaning each time it was used, assuming collective political knowledge on the part of their readers. The phrase has evolved and endured over the years as a mnemonic signifier of the Arab-Jewish conflict and is in current usage in political discussions in Jerusalem, Gaza, and the West Bank.

128. Sayigh, "Palestinian Women," 248.

129. Matiel Mughannam, in a speech delivered to a mixed audience of Arab women and British officials' wives. *Filastin*-English, Aug. 1, 1931.

130. Chandra Talpade Mohanty, "Cartographies of Struggle: Third World Women and the Politics of Feminism," *Third World Women and the Politics of Feminism*, edited by Mohanty, Ann Russo, and Lourdes Torres (Bloomington: Indiana University Press, 1991), 20. Mohanty refers to a "collusion of colonialist and nationalist discourses." I have not found evidence of much willing collusion between the British government and male Palestinian nationalist leaders.

131. Rima [sic] Hammami and Eileen Kuttab, "The Palestinian Women's Movement: Strategies Towards Freedom and Democracy," *News From Within* 15, no. 4 (April 1999), 8.

132. "Note of Interview Granted by His Excellency the High Commissioner to a deputation of Arab Ladies on Monday, 30th October," PRO, CO 733 239/5.

133. Police Dispositions for Friday, October 27, 1933, Secret Despatch 3/99/s, J. M. Faraday Papers, MEC. The tactic of placing women either in front of or among men as "protection" was also utilized in both Syrian and Iranian nationalist demonstrations. See Philip Khoury, *Syria and the French Mandate: The Politics of Arab Nationalism, 1920–1945* (Princeton: Princeton University Press, 1987), 124; and Janet Afary, "The Debate on Women's Liberation in the Iranian Constitutional Revolution, 1906–1911," in *Expanding the Boundaries of Women's History: Essays on Women in the Third World*, edited by Cheryl Johnson-Odim and Margaret Strobel (Bloomington: Indiana University Press, 1992), 104–5. Iranian women protected striking clerics against government forces in demonstrations against the Shah by forming human barricades around the former.

134. See, for example, *al-Difāʿ* May 2 and 4, 1936; *al-Karmil*, May 2, 1936.

135. *Filastin*-English, Nov. 2, 1929 (my emphasis); *Filastīn*, Apr. 15, 1933; Interview granted by the OAG to the Arab Women's Committee on November 17, 1937, ISA, RG 2 Pol/5/44. See also "Interview," CO 733 239/5.

136. For 1929 examples of "first time," references, see below. Counting phrases appear in articles about the "first time ladies went out to demonstrate,"

"the first time" women were arrested, and the "second time during this war [World War II]" that women attended women's conferences in Cairo, to mention some examples. "A Splendid Demonstration of the Ladies of Tulkarm," and "The First Time . . . Arrest of Some Ladies and Children in Accusations of Violations of the Curfew in Jaffa," and "Women's Affairs . . . Women's Conference," *Filastīn*, May 4, 1936, Jan. 28, 1939, and Nov. 18, 1944.

137. "First Time in the History of Palestine—Conference of the Arab Ladies," *Filastīn*, Oct. 29, 1929; "For the First Time in History," *Filastin*-English, Nov. 2, 1929; *Mirāt al-Sharq*, Oct. 28, 1929; *al-Sirāt al-Mustaqīm*, Oct. 28, 1929.

138. *Filastīn*, Sept. 4, 1932; May 2, 1939; *al-Sirāt al-Mustaqīm*, Nov. 15, 1929; *Filastīn*, May 4, 1936; *al-Difāʿ*, May 4, 1936.

139. ʿIsa (son and nephew of the former owners and publishers of *Filastīn*), interview.

140. *Filastin*-English published for only three or four years, in the late 1920s and early 1930s. It ceased publication due to financial problems. The al-ʿIsa family, like the Mughannams, was also sympathetic to the National Defense Party, which supported the Nashashibis, another link that may have had a positive effect on press coverage of the Arab women, although the Arab Women's Executive Committee was nonpartisan. The AWE seems to have had a close relationship with both *Filastīns*, perhaps because of Mughannam's personal ties to the owners. An article appearing on Aug. 8, 1931, thanks the Arab women for their financial support.

141. In May 1936, the first month of the six-month general strike, there were more than fifty articles about women's involvement in *Filastīn* and *Al-Difāʿ* alone.

142. This is demonstrated by the hundreds of small articles whose headlines had these code words in them, and whose actual content sometimes consisted only of the information in the headline itself.

143. The child who held up the banner was the son of Sadhij Nassar. *Al-Difāʿ*, Jan. 25, 1934.

144. For example, in one article, the women praise the Arabic press and protest government censorship; *Filastīn*, Aug. 9, 1931. In surveying twenty-eight years of coverage among more than eight newspapers, I found only one or two articles that criticized the women's movement. This is not to deny that there were articles critical of *women*, however, which is another matter. (See Chapter 3.)

145. ʿIsa, interview.

146. "The Arab Woman in the National *Jihād*," *Filastīn*, Aug. 30, 1931. See Chapter 3, p. 79.

147. *Filastin*-English, Oct. 26, 1929.

148. It is perhaps telling that one of the few coeval, male chroniclers of the women's movement, Akram Zuʿaytir (b. 1909), was a member of the Istiqlal Party, and a bit of a "young Turk" within the Palestinian nationalist movement. The Istiqlal Party was, according to Weldon Matthews, "the first explicitly nationalist Palestinian Arab political association to undertake mass, populist

288 / Notes to Pages 165–167

political organization." It thus came into conflict with the Husayni leadership, which eventually undermined it. Zu'aytir for a brief period (Jan.–May 1930) was editor of *Mirāt al-Sharq*, until the British sentenced him to internal exile in his hometown of Nablus. More research has yet to be done on the attitudes of the Istiqlal toward women and gender. See Weldon Matthews, "The Arab Istiqlal Party in Palestine, 1927–1934" (Ph.D. Diss., University of Chicago, 1998), 91, 94.

149. For the somewhat byzantine relationships between the press and the different national factions, see Porath, *Palestinian Arab*, 65–66, 71; Anonymous Analysis of the Arabic Press n.d. (probably the late 1930s), CZA, RG 25S 22760; and Aida Najjar, "The Arabic Press and Nationalism in Palestine, 1920–1948" (Ph.D. diss., University of New York, Syracuse, 1975). To give an example of how convoluted things got, a 1934 CID report on the "newspaper wars" that, according to police files, began around 1933, comments, "'Al Jamia al Islamia' has joined pro-Majlis [i.e., Husayni] faction in boycotting 'Falastin.' 'Al Difaa' trying to steer a middle course. The proprietor of 'Al Difaa' is forced by his Istiqlal affiliation to support national activity, and by his friendship to Fakhri Nashashibi to manifest 'Opposition' sympathies." CID Periodical Appreciation Summary No. 11/34, Aug. 6, 1934, PRO, FO 371 17878. Later, papers switched sides: "The Nashashibi Party has won over to this side, it is reported, by subsidies, 'Falastin', 'El Difaa', and 'Jamia al Islamia', and all these journals (particularly the first named) have made it their policy to deprecate and discredit the leadership of the Husseini family." CID Periodical Appreciation Summary No.8/35, Apr. 20, 1935, PRO, FO 371 17957.

150. *An Appeal To Every British Woman Wherever She May Be*, June 3, 1936, ISA, RG 65 2/405/3624. Similarly, Mughannam took out an advertisement at her own expense in *Filastin*-English, entitled "To My Friends and Countrymen in the United States of America," in which she appealed for funds to combat "dangerous Zionist propaganda" and bring home "injustices done to the Arabs," Oct. 17, 1931. (Mughannam had been brought up in the United States before returning to the Middle East; she was actually Lebanese by birth.)

151. It must be noted that very few samples of the women's correspondence with the government exist in Arabic. The documentary records may therefore be English translations of the originals, although often it is impossible to tell whether or not they wrote a particular letter or memorandum in English. Since the women did have an English secretary, presumably some of their communications were in English. I found only two documents in Arabic (accompanying their English translations): two letters in files of the Israel State Archives. Comparisons of the Arabic and English versions reveal, however, that the translators were very capable in reproducing both tone and content. Arab Women's Committee to HC, Nov. 17, 1937, ISA, RG2 Pol/5/44. The substantial documentation of the women's correspondence in the Central Zionist Archives for the period 1936–39 comprised apparent copies (and possibly translations, as they are all in English) stolen by Zionist agents. Most of these documents do not appear in the British records held at the PRO and the Israel State Archives.

152. For example, letter to HC from the Arab Women's Committee, Mar. 23, 1938, CZA, RG 25S 22793. The letter protests torture of prisoners, among other matters.

153. Letter to HC from the Arab Women's Committee, Jan. 24, 1939, PRO, CO 733 406/14; same to same, Mar. 20, 1940, PRO, CO 733 425/16.

154. Letter [presumably to the HC but the heading is illegible] from the Arab Women's Committee, July 26, 1938, CZA, RG 25S 22793.

155. Letter to the OAG from the Arab Women's Committee, Nov. 17, 1937, CZA, RG 25S 22800.

156. This quote comes from a secret report by Musa ʿAlami, Arthur Wauchope's private secretary, on the "Present State of Mind and Feelings of the Arabs of Palestine," Secret Despatch to the SSC from the HC (Wauchope was HC from 1931–1937), Dec. 23, 1933, PRO, CO 733 257/11.

157. *Filastīn*, Dec. 21, 1944.

158. Telegram from the Arab Women Committee [sic] to Miss Farquharson, July 1, 1936, PRO, CO 733 313/6.

159. Speech delivered by Matiel Mughannam at a gathering in Bethlehem in honor of Captain Gordon-Canning, Nov. 10, 1929, PRO, CO 733 178/67510; *al-Sirāt al-Mustaqīm*, Nov. 15, 1929.

160. Julie M. Peteet, "Authenticity and Gender: The Presentation of Culture," in *Arab Women: Old Boundaries, New Frontiers*, edited by Judith E. Tucker (Bloomington: Indiana University Press, 1993), 52. Peteet's research on Palestinian women activists in the refugee camps in Lebanon demonstrates that this strategy of exploiting tradition continued to be utilized in the Palestinian women's movement.

161. A military report takes care to mention that "British troops had the very strictest of instructions to respect both mosques and women"; "Military Lessons of the Arab Rebellion in Palestine, 1936," General Staff, Headquarters, The British Forces, Palestine and Trans-Jordan, February 1938, PRO, WO 282 6.

162. Letter to the HC from the Arab Women's Committee, July 25, 1936, PRO, FO 371 20929.

163. "Interview," CO 733 239/5. (The women were protesting the police brutality and shooting deaths that occurred during the demonstrations. See above.) This statement is rather ironic, coming from Sakakini, as her brother, Khalil, was imprisoned by the Ottoman government during World War I.

164. Letter to SSC from Arab Ladies Committee, Dec. 16, 1938, PRO, CO 733 406/14. In a "comprehensive memo" to the HC from the women of Acre, Mrs. Fu'ad Saba, (whose husband had been deported to the Seychelles Islands), makes a point of saying that she hopes "as a Christian admirer of the spirit of British justice" that it will induce him to return the exiles, keeping the peace in order to spare the disappearance of the traditional friendship between the Arabs and the British. *Filastīn*, Apr. 12, 1938.

165. One unusual instance of their resorting to sexual segregation (as an organized group) came in 1936 when the house of the Economic Conference was emptied of men in order for them to hold a massive meeting to protest govern-

ment measures during the revolt. *Al-Difāʿ*, May 3, 1936. Such a move seems geared toward recruiting less actively involved (and possibly more conservative) women; the meeting had more than five hundred women attending, according to newspaper accounts.

166. "Interview," CO 733 239/5 pt. II; Inspector-General of Police to Chief Secretary, Oct. 14, 1933, PRO, CO 733 239/5 pt. II.

167. *Filastīn*, Nov. 8, 1933.

168. *Filastīn*, July 11, 1936.

169. It is also possible that the women used "tradition" to protect themselves from being considered too "Western," "modern," or "innovative," in order to appeal to more conservative male (and possibly, female) elements in Palestinian society as well. James Gelvin's description of the strategies of the nationalist popular committees in Faysali Syria (1918–20) is suggestive here. He comments, "The discourse employed by the popular committees facilitated social reconstruction and re-equilibration of gender roles by exhorting activities and values that were congruent with the new realities, while simultaneously protecting those activities and values from the imputation of innovation by wrapping them in the garb of 'tradition.'" See Gelvin, *Divided Loyalties*, 213.

170. The major purpose of the searches was to ferret out rebels who disguised themselves as women. Interestingly, in documents discussing procedures for and purposes of the searches, the British never admitted to women being the actual target of these operations—for example, in order to find concealed weapons. This indicates that, despite their frequent comments about (and irritation at) women engaging in such activities, they nonetheless did not take it as a serious enough threat for them to disrupt "tradition." We may never know the extent to which women took advantage of this attitude. (See Chapter 5.) Memorandum by the Secretary of State for War, "Hostile Propaganda in Palestine: Its Origin, and Progress in 1938," January 16, 1939, PRO, CO 733 387/1.

171. Letter to HC from Arab Ladies of Jerusalem, Feb. 5, 1938, PRO, FO 371 21875.

172. In a meeting with the AWA, the high commissioner said that "he had been reluctant to institute the searching of women, as it is disagreeable to the Moslems." (As though such searches would *not* be disagreeable to any woman, Christian, Muslim or Jew!) Interview of Arab Ladies with His Excellency, March 5, 1939, CZA, RG 25S 22793.

173. Draft Letter to the Censors of Jaffa and Haifa, District Commissioner's Office, Nov. 5, 1938, CZA, RG 25S 22760; emphasis in original. Extensive documentation of the government's problems in recruiting the appropriate (Armenian) women searchers exists in the Central Zionist Archives, and, to a lesser extent, the PRO.

174. *Al-Difāʿ*, Jan. 20, 1938.

175. Mogannam, *The Arab Woman*, 78.

176. Hammami and Kuttab, "The Palestinian Women's Movement," 9.

177. The invocation of motherhood has been used in other nationalist struggles in the Third World. South African women couched their protest against

pass laws in the 1950s "within the decorous language of domestic duty: 'As wives and mothers we condemn the pass laws and all that they imply.'" See McClintock, "'No Longer,'" 116. Hammami and Kuttab point to the effectiveness of the Mothers of the Plaza de Mayo in Argentina in challenging the Pinochet regime on the issue of the "disappeared." See Hammami and Kuttab, "Palestinian Women's Movement," 9.

178. "Interview," CO 733 239/5 pt. II. The women controlled when and how they behaved as peacemakers, however. When it suited their purposes, they rejected this role, as in the case cited above with the Acre women.

179. Daily diaries of Sir Kenneth William Blackbourne, May 4, 1936, Blackbourne Papers, RH.

180. A heavy police presence kept the crowds in control while the meeting convened, but after the women emerged, a demonstration broke out. *Filastīn*, May 14, 1936; *al-Difāʿ*, May 14, 1936.

181. Diary entry, Apr. 23, 1938, Sir Thomas Scrivenor Papers.

182. Ibid., diary entry dated Mar. 24, 1939.

183. "Interview," CO 733 239/5 pt. II; Chancellor to Passfield, Oct. 31, 1929, Chancellor Papers, RH.

184. A similar incident occurred in Nablus when women who had marched on the Saray refused coffee that was offered to them by the governor. *Filastīn*, Nov. 6, 1933.

185. Chancellor to Passfield. He notes that some of the women were embarrassed by the incident and later sent him word that the reason the two did not have coffee was stomach pain. The impression of the reader, however, is that the women made this gesture out of kindness and to save (his) face.

186. Letter to HC from Mrs. Corbett-Ashby, Mar. 28, 1939, CO 733 398/17 75156. See also letters from Miss Farquharson (a pro-Arab British personality), Lady Astor, an MP, and the Duchess of Atholl, responding to telegrams from the Arab Women's Committee about the British government's punitive demolition of the Old City of Jaffa during the revolt, July 1, 1936. PRO, CO 733 310/2.

187. Julia ʿAwad, interview with the author, Jan. 25, 1993.

188. See Fleischmann, "Selective Memory, Gender and Nationalism." The Nashashibi faction was widely considered pro-British and "moderate" (from the British point of view); from the Husayni and some other Palestinian points of view, these sympathies bordered on treason or collaboration.

189. Afsaneh Najmabadi, "Crafting an Educated Housewife in Iran," in *Remaking Women: Feminism and Modernity in the Middle East*, edited by Lila Abu-Lughod (Princeton: Princeton University Press, 1998), p. 113–15.

190. *Al-Difāʿ*, Oct. 26, 1939. Great Britain entered the war on Sept. 3, 1939.

CHAPTER 7. PAN-ARABISM AND THE 1940S

1. Yehoshua Porath, *The Palestinian Arab National Movement: From Riots to Rebellion, 1929–1939* (London: Frank Cass, 1977), 288.

2. Issa Khalaf, *Politics in Palestine: Arab Factionalism and Social Disinte-*

gration, 1939–1948 (Albany: State University of New York Press, 1991), 66. The members of the AHC themselves were divided; according to Kamil Khilla, the majority were in favor of accepting it but yielded to Hajj Amin and the "*mujāhidīn*" (fighting in the revolt), who opposed it. Kamil Mahmud Khilla, *Filastīn wa al-intidāb al-Baritānī, 1922–1939* (Beirut: PLO Research Center, 1974), 478.

3. Khalaf, *Politics*, 36–37, 49.

4. Hala Sakakini, *Jerusalem and I: A Personal Record* (Amman: Economic Press, 1990), 79.

5. Khalaf, *Politics*, 36–37.

6. Wafi'a al-Duzdar, interview with the author, Mar. 21, 1993.

7. Palestine Broadcasting Service Official Programs, 1936; *Filastīn*, Jan.–April, 1941. The lecturer in the latter series was a Syrian by marriage, Mrs. Salwa al-'Aid, daughter of the former mayor of Beirut.

8. Some of the women who broadcast included Fadwa Tuqan, Sa'ida Jarallah, 'Anbara Sallam al-Khalidi, Matiel Mughannam, Shahinda Duzdar, and Henriette Siksik, who narrated a "children's hour." Fadwa Tuqan, *A Mountainous Journey: A Poet's Autobiography*, translated by Olive Kenny and edited by Salma Khadra Jayyusi (Saint Paul: Graywolf Press, 1990), 98; *Filastīn*, Jan. 26, 1941; Sa'ida Jarallah, interview with the author, Apr. 19, 1994; Henriette Siksik, interview with the author, June 15, 1993. The PBS sponsored a training course for the Arabic service, out of which eight of the thirty applicants selected were women. "PBS News," Jan. 17, 1947, ISA, RG 15 File 33; HC to SSC, July 3, 1936, PRO, CO 733 398/12.

9. Sakakini, *Jerusalem and I*, 81, 83.

10. Khalaf, *Politics*, 163.

11. Ibid.

12. Ibid., 90.

13. Badran, *Feminists, Islam and Nation: Gender and the Making of Modern Egypt* (Princeton: Princeton University Press, 1995), 242.

14. See Ellen L. Fleischmann, "The Other 'Awakening': the Emergence of Women's Movements in the Modern Middle East, 1900–1940," in *A Social History of Women and Gender in the Modern Middle East*, edited by Margaret Lee Meriwether and Judith E. Tucker (Boulder: Westview Press, 1999); Martina Kamp, "Organizing Ideologies of Gender, Class and Ethnicity: The Pre-Revolutionary Women's Movements in Iraq," unpublished paper presented at the "Women and Gender in the Middle East: A Multidisciplinary Assessment of the State of Theory and Research" Conference, Bellagio, Italy, Aug. 27–31, 2001.

15. *Filastīn*, Dec. 15, 1944.

16. 'Izz al-Din al-Qassam, the quintessential hero of the 1936–39 revolt was of Syrian origin. He left Syria and immigrated to Palestine because of a death sentence for his participation in the 1920 Ibrahim Hananu revolt. See S. Abdullah Schleiffer, "The Life and Thought of 'Izz-Id-Din al-Qassam," *Islamic Quarterly* 23 (1979): 67. 'Anbara Sallam al-Khalidi, active in the Palestinian women's movement, relocated from her native Lebanon to Palestine in 1929 when she

married Ahmad Samih al-Khalidi. See ʿAnbara Sallam al-Khalidi, *Jawla fī al-dhikrayāt bayna Lubnān wa Filastīn* (Beirut: dār al-nahār lil-nashr, 1978).

17. *Al-Jāmʿia al-ʿArabiyya*, Apr. 20, 1930; *Filastīn*, Apr. 10, 1930. Elizabeth Thompson states that "the Eastern Women's conferences were not pan-Arab. The 1930 Beirut conference was staged by the Lebanese women's union; the one in Damascus that year (see below) was Nur Hamada's Eastern conference." Elizabeth Thompson, personal communication, March 10, 2000. I respectfully disagree, since the title "Eastern Arab women's conference" seems to indicate a certain pan-Arab consciousness. (This nomenclature comes from the Palestinian press, which admittedly could have gotten the name wrong, as they were rather imprecise in their use of names.) Furthermore, other Arab women (namely, Palestinian women) were invited and attended. The Palestinian women who attended (the reporter identified them only by their husbands' names): Mrs. Ahmad Samih al-Khalidi (ʿAnbara), Mrs. Jamal al-Husayni (Naʿimiti), Mrs. Dr. Husayn al-Khalidi (Wahida), Mrs. Shukri Dib (Katrin), Mrs. Mughannam Mughannam (Matiel), Mrs. Musa al-ʿAlami (Sadiyya), and the Misses Shahinda Duzdar and Melia Sakakini.

18. *Filastīn*, Apr. 26, 1930.

19. *Filastīn*, Apr. 29, 1930; Elizabeth Thompson, *Colonial Citizens: Republican Rights, Paternal Privilege, and Gender in French Syria and Lebanon* (New York: Columbia University Press, 2000), 143, 203.

20. *Al-Jāmʿia al-ʿArabiyya*, July 10, 1930. For some reason, Hanifa Khatib, in her history of the Lebanese women's movement, does not mention the 1930 conferences. Khatib, *Tārīkh tatawwur al-haraka al-nisāʾiyya fī Lubnān wa irtibātihā bīl-ʿālam al-ʿArabī, 1800–1975* (Beirut: dār al-hadātha, 1984), 111.

21. *Filastīn*, Oct. 18, 1932.

22. The women had made a direct request to "the palace" to hold the Baghdad conference. *Filastīn*, Oct. 2, 1932.

23. *Filastīn*, Oct. 30, 1932. Interestingly, the Egyptian women seem not to have attended.

24. *Al-Sirāt al-Mustaqīm*, Oct. 27, 1932.

25. Elizabeth Thompson, personal communication, March 10, 2000.

26. Joan Judge's phrase. See Joan Judge, "Talent, Virtue, and the Nation: Chinese Nationalism and Female Subjectivities in the Early Twentieth Century," *American Historical Review* 106, no. 3 (June 2001): 797.

27. Quoted in Thompson, *Colonial Citizens*, 144. The circumspect, almost defensive tone of the resolution hints at another complicated issue that may have played a part in its adoption. In contrast to contemporary Western feminists and women visitors in the region who harped constantly on the issue of veiling, some Arab women in this period placed as much (perhaps more) emphasis on a number of issues that were as compelling, and which directly affected their well-being, such as eradicating legal inequalities in marriage and property rights. The disjuncture between Arab women's and Western women's perceptions of what was required to improve Arab women's status was often discordant and proved to be an obstacle in their uniting on feminist issues. The issue

of veiling brought into relief the chasm, despite Arab women's own desires to unveil. Western women did not grasp that their attitudes of cultural superiority could produce an adverse reaction to the cause of feminism or improving women's rights. Arab women were not prepared to renounce their cultural attachments, as Western women seemed to be asking of them from the way they framed the issue of veiling, which highlighted Islam as an oppressive religion and cultural system. As Leila Ahmed points out, "adopting another culture as a general remedy for a heritage of misogyny within a particular culture is not only absurd, it is impossible." Leila Ahmed, *Women, Gender in Islam: Historical Roots of a Modern Debate* (New Haven: Yale University Press, 1992), 129.

28. The conference resolutions were submitted to "the government"—which one is unclear—for implementation.

29. *Filastīn*, Oct. 30, 1932.

30. *Filastīn*, Oct. 18, 1932. It is not clear whether or not Fatima Murad was Palestinian herself.

31. *Filastīn*, Oct. 18, 1932. Mrs. Hamada told the reporter that she had sent letters to "many Arab associations" and to 'Auni 'Abd al-Hadi and Rasim al-Khalidi, requesting them to ask Mrs. Fa'iz Haddad. From the muddled nature of the reports, it seems as though the women's groups in the early 1930s were less sophisticated in their communications than those in the later 1930s and the 1940s, possibly as a function of their organizational youth.

32. *Filastīn*, Oct. 30, 1932. A student at AUB, she wrote a long article entitled "Women's Education and Upbringing" in *Filastīn*, May 29, 1931. See Chapter 3. I do not have any biographical or background information on her.

33. *Filastīn*, Dec. 21, 1932.

34. The Syrian women even sent a telegram of protest on behalf of Palestine to the Daughters of the American Revolution. *Filastīn*, Aug. 27, 1931; Apr. 2, 1938; *al-Difā'*, May 8, 1938; *Filastīn*, June 3, 1938; *al-Difā'*, May 30, 1946; *Filastīn*, May 9, 1946. (See below for discussion of the recommendations of the Anglo-American Commission.)

35. *Filastīn*, Dec. 1, 1933; *Al-Sirāt al-Mustaqīm*, Nov. 30, 1933; *Mirāt al-sharq*, Dec. 1, 1933; *al-Difā'*, June 13, 1938. Although Alexandretta was not officially ceded until 1939, it took "two long years of haggling" up until then. See Philip Khoury, *Syria and the French Mandate: The Politics of Arab Nationalism, 1920–1945* (Princeton: Princeton University Press, 1987), 59.

36. *Filastīn*, Oct. 28 and 29; Nov. 8, 1944.

37. For example, the press reported on Arab women's demonstrations, economic boycotts of foreign goods, and the activities of women's groups. *Filastīn*, May 13, 1931; Nov. 23, 1933; May 31, 1934; *Al-Sirāt al-Mustaqīm*, Nov. 23 and 30, 1933; *Al-Jām'ia al-'Arabiyya*, Nov. 30, 1931. (The press also reported, albeit to a lesser extent, on women in Turkey, Iran, and India.)

38. The comments of *Fatāt al-Sharq*, in its October 1929 issue covering the First Arab Women's Congress, commented, "and thus the women of Palestine record their most glorious page in the history of the women's awakening." Cited in Ijlal Khalifa, *Al-mar'a wa qadiyyat Filastīn* (Cairo: Modern Arab Press,

1974), 41–42. For other coverage of Palestinian women, see also various issues of *L'Égyptienne*.

39. For example, a letter, dated April 25, 1938, from the Union Féministe Arabe in Beirut to the High Commissioner for Palestine, in which they express the union's "most vehement condemnations and protestations" against the "ruthless atrocities, ... merciless torture, deportations, exile, unwarranted arrests, and imprisonments" committed by the British authorities in Palestine. "We note that the most prominent traits in British statesmanship have always been sobriety, farsightedness, and fairplay [sic] ... the contradiction of these principles ... is becoming seriously detrimental to British prestige and good name." The letter was signed by the president, Ibtihaj Qaddura; PRO, CO 733 367/4.

40. In Arabic the IAW was usually called the "International Women's Union" (*al-ittihād al-nisāʾī al-dawlī*).

41. Quoted in Akram Zuʿaytir, *Yawmiyyāt Akram Zuʿaytir: al-haraka al-wataniyya al-Filastīniyya, 1935–1939* (Beirut: Palestine Studies Association, 1980), 394.

42. For more on this subject, see Badran, *Feminists, Islam and Nation*.

43. Zuʿaytir, *Yawmiyyāt*, 387–98, entry dated June 2, 1938; British Consul to Secretary of State for Foreign Affairs, June 8, 1938, PRO, FO 371 21878; same to same, July 2, 1938, PRO, FO 371 21877. The intellectual origins of the initiative remain somewhat unclear, due to divergent versions of the event. Khalifa describes how the officers of the Lebanese, Syrian, Palestinian, and Iraqi women's societies—Ibtihaj Qaddura, Buhayra al-ʿAzm, Zlikha al-Shihabi, and Nazik Jawdat, respectively—conceived of the idea to hold an Arab women's conference to look into a just solution to the Palestine problem. Khalifa, *Al-marʾa*, 112. In its golden jubilee pamphlet, the Arab Women's Union in Jerusalem states that the Palestinian Women's Executive Committee asked Shaʿrawi to issue a call to hold a conference of Arab women to "expose the British mandate policies and its plot to threaten Palestine." Shaʿrawi complied with their request. *Al-ittihād al-nisāʾī bīl-Quds fi yūbīlī al-dhahabī* [hereafter *Yūbīlī*] (Jerusalem: 1983), 23.

44. British Consulate in Damascus to Secretary of State for the Foreign Office, Viscount Halifax, July 2, 1938, no. 34, PRO, FO 371 21878/4049; British Consul to Secretary of State for Foreign Affairs, July 2, 1938, PRO, FO 371 21877.

45. Zuʿaytir provides the only detailed account of the 1938 conference. He reports daily events, exact dates, conversations, names of actors, and so forth. He does, however, tend to center himself in the affairs of the women. Regarding the men's involvement, he writes that various men were assigned to contact the different women's groups. (Syrian) Nabih Bey al-ʿAzm "called for" the forming of a Syrian women's association to defend Palestine, and "entrusted" his wife, Buhayra, to head it. Zuʿaytir was to contact the Iraqi women; Palestinian ʿAuni ʿAbd al-Hadi and (Lebanese Maronite) Asʿad Daghir, who were residing in Egypt, were to contact Huda Shaʿrawi. After various communications back and

forth, Zu'aytir writes, "Then I saw it was necessary to . . . bring together the noble women workers of the women's and nationalist movement in Syria to take charge of the negotiations [over the planning and organizing of the conference]." Zu'aytir, *Yawmiyyāt*, 398. (All of these men had histories of strong pan-Arab political involvement. Zu'aytir himself was active in the pan-Arab Istiqlal Party.)

46. Zu'aytir, *Yawmiyyāt*, 407.

47. Zu'aytir and Sha'rawi had a rather long argument over the name of the conference. He wanted it to be called the "Arab Women's Conference." He repeatedly, exacerbatedly refers to her "stubbornness." He tried various ways to convince her, first lecturing on Arab nationalism (*qawmiyya*); then observing, "India, Japan and China are all from the East, so where's the representation?" Finally, he resorted to flattery, saying, "My lady, you will be paid homage at this great, historic conference as a leader of Arab women and not as a leader of Eastern women." But Sha'rawi remained firm over this issue, and Zu'aytir, fearful of alienating her, surrendered. (He also notes that she would be bearing most of the costs of the conference.) He resolved, however, to ensure that the conference "be oriented towards Arabism." Zu'aytir, *Yawmiyyāt*, 471. (In her speech at the closing of the conference, Zlikha al-Shihabi, president of the Arab Women's Union in Palestine, referred to Sha'rawi as "the leader of the East." *Yūbīlī*, 24.)

48. Zu'aytir, *Yawmiyyāt*, 470–74. He was actively engaged in the proceedings, picking up the Palestinian delegation at the train station, and constantly at the beck and call of Mrs. Sha'rawi, who seems to have ordered him about.

49. Zu'aytir enigmatically comments that the assassination was an attack against him, *Yawmiyyāt*, 472. It was widely believed that Dajani was assassinated by rebel leader 'Arif 'Abd al-Raziq, considered a Husayni partisan. Ted Swedenburg, *Memories of Revolt: The 1936–1939 Rebellion and the Palestinian National Past* (Minneapolis: University of Minnesota Press, 1995), 102. Ironically, 'Abd al-Raziq sent a telegram of support to the women's conference. Badran, *Feminists*, 230.

50. One newspaper reported that she was ill and could not deliver her speech, which was read to the conference. *Filastīn*, Oct. 31, 1938. I have not found any corroboration for this, however; Zu'aytir describes her presenting her speech, after he had encouraged her to overcome her fear and reluctance (*Yawmiyyāt*, 488). The conference's official publication contains the text of her speech as well. (This publication distinguishes between the speeches delivered by delegates and the texts of speeches and letters of support received and read out to the conference.) *Al-mar'a al-'Arabiyya wa qadiyyat Filastīn* [hereafter *MAQF*] (Cairo, 1938), 174–78.

51. It is intriguing that, in her book, Mughannam devotes an entire chapter to "Political Divisions," yet the tone in which it is written is studiedly neutral and nonpartisan, despite the fact that her husband (as she notes) was a member of the National Defense Party. She states, "There is one aspect in the party system in Palestine which deserves special mention. All Arab parties are united in their national demands and in resisting the British mandate as embracing the

Zionist policy." She was obviously writing for external consumption. Matiel Mogannam, *The Arab Woman and the Palestine Problem* (London: Herbert Joseph, 1937), 244. In fact, the lines between the two factions among the women were fluid and blurred. A number of women worked with both the AWA and the Arab Women's Union (AWU); others tried to ignore the divisions. One indication of this is the interesting overlap of six women listed as the founders in the two groups' separate "official" histories, the AWU's *Yūbīlī* and the AWA's *Jam'iyyat al-sayyidāt al-'Arabiyyāt al-Quds*, compiled by Ya'qub al-'Ansari and Ibrahim al-Husayni (Jerusalem: 1985). See Chapter 6 for discussion of the split between the two organizations.

52. Zu'aytir earlier recounts an interesting episode during which he convinced Miss al-Qassam, who was afraid of being overcome by her emotions, to speak. He had a coaching session with her in his office. When the time came for her to deliver her speech before the conference, she did, indeed, become overwhelmed by her emotions and fainted. Sadhij Nassar rose with great presence of mind and took over the podium until Miss al-Qassam recovered amid a storm of applause, and resumed her speech. Zu'aytir, *Yawmiyyāt*, 484–85. (The whole tone of the fainting episode is reminiscent of Victorian literature.)

53. *MAQF*, 12.

54. *MAQF*, 171–73.

55. *Yūbīlī*, 24. (She invested the holy war with double sacredness by using the phrase "*al-jihād al-muqaddas*.")

56. The Palestinian women apparently did not become very involved with international women's groups. Jewish women sometimes attended international events as "Palestinian women," such as in 1926, when they sent a delegate to the International Women's Congress in Paris in 1926. *Palestine Bulletin*, June 14, 1926. Badran says that the International Alliance of Women (IAW) recognized the Jewish Women's Equal Rights Association in 1923, and admitted the Palestinian Arab Women's Union in 1935, thus implicitly recognizing "two 'entities' from the same country." She also reports, citing *L'Égyptienne*, that the Palestinian Arab women decided to send Sadhij Nassar to its conference in Istanbul in 1935. Badran, *Feminists*, 233, 225. According to the Palestinian press, Nassar refused to attend because Miryam Khalil, who was supposed to accompany her, did not go due to an injury. *Al-Sirāt al-Mustaqīm*, Apr. 22, 1935. (I could not find references to the Palestinian women joining the IAW in any Palestinian sources.) The Syrian women attended the Istanbul conference as new members, as did a Persian women's group. Adele Schreiber and Margaret Mathieson, *Journey Towards Freedom* (Copenhagen: International Alliance of Women, 1955), 47. In the only other reference to the 1935 conference in Palestinian sources, a reporter urged the women not to attend because there was a prohibition on discussing political matters. (In another article on the same day, the paper engages in a long harangue on the subject of Attaturk forbidding the Arab delegates to speak Arabic. I could not confirm this in any other source.) *Al-Awqāt al-'Arabiyya*, Apr. 12, 1935.

57. *Filastīn*, Oct. 20, 1938.

58. A delegation visited the British embassy in Egypt with a letter containing the resolutions, requesting that it be delivered to the prime minister. Telegram from Sir M. Lampson in Alexandria, Oct. 17, 1938; despatch from same to Lord Halifax, Oct. 21, 1938, FO 371 21882.

59. *The Times* (London), Oct. 18, 1938.

60. Badran, *Feminists*, 238. Badran freely translates "*nisāʾī*" as "feminist." Thus, she calls the women's unions (*al-ittihād al-nisāʾī*, sing.) "feminist unions," and the 1944 conference, which was called in Arabic "*al-muʾtamar al-nisāʾī al-ʿArabī*," the Arab Feminists Conference. I am not comfortable with this translation; few, if any, of the older activist women I interviewed for this research called themselves feminists, and the Palestinian women translate the name of their organization, *al-ittihād al-nisāʾī al-ʿArabī* as the Arab Women's Union. (Considering that, during this period, they often interchanged *sayyidāt* with *nisāʾī* in their various names, it is clear that they did not mean "feminist." Badran (244) refers to them as the "Palestinian Feminist Union," a phrase I have never read or heard elsewhere.)

61. *Filastīn*, Sept. 14, 1944.

62. For more on the divisions between the European and Arab women in the IAW on these and related issues, see Badran, *Feminists*, 232–36; and Leila J. Rupp, *Worlds of Women: The Making of an International Women's Union* (Princeton: Princeton University Press, 1997), 58–60. The overall East-West split came to a head at the 1939 international conference in Copenhagen.

63. The issue for contemporary feminists is not direct political imperialism per se, but rather, the domination of exclusive, narrow feminist ideologies that privilege Western concepts of "woman," and do not recognize Western cultural hegemony and its effects.

64. Leila J. Rupp, "Constructing Internationalism: The Case of Transnational Women's Organizations, 1888–1945," *American Historical Review* (Dec. 1994): 1587.

65. Al-Ittihād al-nisāʾī al-Misrī. *Al-muʾtamar al-nisāʾī al-ʿArabī* [hereafter *MNA*] (Cairo: dar al-mʿārif, 1944), 20..

66. Badran, *Feminists*, 239.

67. *MNA*, 32.

68. *MNA*, 330–34; see also Badran, *Feminists*, 238–44, for a detailed account of the conference.

69. *MNA*, 335–36.

70. *MNA*, 111–13. The Arabic press in Palestine highlighted proposals, speeches, and expressions of solidarity on the Palestine issue, while the English language press stressed the feminist content of the conference. The headlines alone reflect this. A sample from *Filastīn* reveals the following headlines: "The Arab Women's Conference in Cairo—Five Minutes of Applause and Cheering for the Cause of Palestine—Palestine in the Introductory Researches of the Conference and the Splendid Opening Party" (Dec. 13, 1944); "Representatives of Palestine at the Arab Women's Conference in Cairo—Demand to Confront the Jews with Their Same Tools" (Dec. 15, 1944); "The Conclusion of the Work

of the Arab Women's Conference in Egypt—the Conference Comes Up with a Practical Solution 'To Save the Arab Land in Palestine' " (Dec. 17, 1944). Compare this to the *Palestine Post:* "Arab Women Demand Rights" (Dec. 12, 1944); "Arab Women on Equality and Palestine" (Dec. 14, 1944); "Arab Women's First Step to Progress" (Dec. 25, 1944).

71. Unlike the terms of the Palestine mandate, which left ambiguous the ultimate status of the territory, the French Mandate for Syria and Lebanon was based upon the assumption of eventual independence of the territories. This is not to deny, however, the intensity of the nationalist struggle that ensued against the French; as Khoury points out, the mandate was perceived as "illegitimate" and imposed by force. Khoury, *Syria,* 4. In Egypt, the Egyptians had achieved a nominal independence from the British in 1923.

72. Thompson, *Colonial Citizens,* 272.

73. As quoted in the *Palestine Post,* Dec. 12, 1944. Another reporter, commenting on the conference, noted that "the views of the delegations from the various countries show differing tendencies . . . the idea of women going in for politics appears to be unacceptable in those Arab countries where the law of the Koran is still strictly applied." (He does not mention which countries those are.) *Palestine Post,* Dec. 14, 1944.

74. Matiel Mughannam and her daughter Leila, interview by Julie Peteet and Rosemary Sayigh, Aug. 10, 1985.

75. A number of observers remarked on Palestinian women's social conservatism as compared to other Arab women, particularly Egyptian women. (See, e.g., Ruth Woodsmall, *Moslem Women Enter a New World* [New York: Round Table Press, 1936], 381, 191–92.) Although I hesitate to endorse gross generalizations about, and comparisons of relative degrees of conservatism among, Arab women, I find it interesting that, although Badran says that nearly half the participants at the 1944 conference were single women, the Palestinian delegation was composed overwhelmingly of married women. Out of the twenty-six delegates, two were single; of the nine auditors, two were single. These figures might indicate that many Palestinian families were still reluctant to allow their single (usually young) women the mobility and personal independence that attendance at such an event required. Badran, *Feminists,* 239; *MNA,* 41–42.

76. *Filastīn,* reporting on an interview with Agence Presse Française, Dec. 13, 1944.

77. *Filastīn,* Jan. 19, June 18 and 23, 1940.

78. *Filastīn,* Oct. 11, 1944. Interestingly, the (rival) Arab Women's (Ladies) Association had just previously formed an executive committee to take charge of executive decisions and correspondence on the Palestine cause. *Filastīn,* Sept. 28, 1944.

79. Letter from Malcolm P. Hooper, American Consul in Jerusalem, to the Secretary of State, Nov. 10, 1945, U.S. NA 890B.

80. Neither of these efforts apparently got off the ground, or if they did, were short-lived. I never found other documentation about them.

81. *Filastīn,* Oct. 31, 1944.

82. *Filastīn* Oct. 14, 1944.
83. *Filastīn*, Nov. 15, 1944.
84. Thompson, *Colonial Citizens*, 272.
85. See above, and also, an article about the Cairo conference and women's formation of a "united front." *Filastīn*, Dec. 3, 1944; June 7, 1946; Jan. 16, Dec. 5, 1947.
86. The charitable organizations had always been involved in some of these arenas; however, the AWU makes a point of drawing attention to this "expanded" interest in its *Yūbīlī*, 26.
87. Could there, perhaps, have been subversive subtexts to these parties? One of the films shown was *The Rebellious Girl*. *Filastīn*, Dec. 11, 1942. In a play that was presented in Haifa and also toured Jerusalem and Jaffa, Sadhij Nassar performed the role of Salah al-Din. *Al-Difāʿ*, June 3, 1937.
88. Increased interest in sports and other types of clubs seems to have been characteristic of the 1940s. Men also organized sports clubs. Khalaf claims they were politically oriented, originating out of the dissatisfaction of younger men, who saw in clubs an alternative to the Mufti's Palestine Arab Party. They were fearful of openly antagonizing the Mufti by organizing explicitly political parties that would constitute competition to the PAP, although some efforts were made in this direction. Khalaf, *Politics*, 95–96.
89. Equipment was donated by doctors and pharmacists. In 1947, a Palestinian doctor who just returned from England started a pediatric department at the clinic. *Filastīn*, Jan. 10, 1946; June 12, 1947.
90. *Filastīn*, June 4, Sept. 27, 1942.
91. *Filastīn*, Oct. 30, 1940.
92. *Filastīn*, Jan. 25, 1940.
93. District Commissioner (DC) Intelligence Report, Jerusalem District, Mar. 16, 1940, PRO, CO 733 420/22; *Filastīn*, Jul. 17, 1940. In October 1941, the Gaza DC reported that a "deputation of 6 notables has protested strongly to me against the idea that women should be allowed to vote in Municipal or other elections. The reason they gave for objecting is that there are very few women in this district sufficiently educated." Intelligence Report No. 68, Oct. 17, 1941, PRO, CO 733 439/15.
94. DC Report, Lydda District, Jaffa, Apr. 19, 1941, PRO, CO 733 439/15.
95. One article linked the attacks on unveiled women to "a movement to enforce stricter observance of Moslem traditions," including forcing merchants to close their shops on Friday. *Palestine Post*, Dec. 12, 1944; *Filastīn*, Oct. 11, 1944.
96. *Filastīn*, Feb. 28, July 25, 1946. Women and men attended some cultural functions together in the 1930s, also, albeit not frequently.
97. *Filastīn*, June 30, 1942.
98. *Filastīn*, July 30, 1942. The government apparently took journalists on a tour of the facilities in its "undisclosed location," where certain details were not divulged.
99. *Filastīn*, Sept. 25, 1942. Hala and Dumya Sakakini commented that

women who joined the British army were few and "not very popular for it." Interview with the author, May 6, 1994.

100. They also advertised that some of the meetings would be held without men present. *Filastīn*, Nov. 14, 1942.

101. The information below was obtained from a visit to Asia and Sofiyya Halabi in Jerusalem, May 28, 1993. Most of the details in this interview came from Sofiyya, Asia's sister.

102. I heard persistent rumors that Ms. Halabi was the high commissioner's personal driver, but I could never confirm this.

103. Raja al-'Isa, interview with the author, Jan. 26, 1993.

104. Asia Halabi's very uniqueness shielded her from potential criticism for collaborating with the British. Many Palestinians of the mandate period remember her with pride, holding her up as a distinguished Arab woman of her generation, implicitly according her recognition for being a "pioneer."

105. Asma Tubi states it was founded in 1942. Tubi, *'Abīr wa majd* (Beirut: Matba'at Qalalat, 1966), 167.

106. A 1942 intelligence report from Gaza described it as a "movement" called "The Friends of Freedom and Democracy": "It is organized in small groups of people . . . who meet to discuss the news on the basis of a commentary issued by Headquarters of the Organization. In this way they confirm each other *in the faith* and acquire confidence to spread their views among the apathetic and *unbelieving*. The only condition of membership is that one should be friendly to *the cause*." Gaza Intelligence Report No. 90, Oct. 3, 1942, PRO, CO 733439/16; emphasis mine. It is rather striking that the British felt they had to organize some kind of secret society and imbue it with an almost religious tinge. Nowhere is it indicated in any documents what, precisely, "the faith" or "cause" was.

107. Martina Kamp describes a similar, earlier effort initiated by the British traveler, journalist, and writer Freya Stark in Iraq in 1938, to "promote the debate on 'democratic values.'" The same organizing strategies of targeting the young educated middle and upper classes, and the same names, "Brotherhood of Freedom" and "Sisterhood of Freedom," were used. She says, "The *Sisterhood of Freedom*, centered in Baghdad, set up several local clubs in Ba'quba, Diwaniya, Amara, and Basra. The British consulate in Basra financed a woman's journal in Arabic to assist the women's clubs, but was cut short when the British support for the organization ended and it dissolved in 1946. Although it was substantially funded, the lectures to a female elite as a modernizing factor within Iraqi society—as it seems—, did not attract many women of the Iraqi upper-class, who had already set up well run charitable associations." Kamp, "Organizing Ideologies."

108. Letter from Major Scaife, Area Officer, Ikhwan al-Hurriya, to Chief Secretary (CS), Aug. 10, 1943, ISA, RG 2 SF/90/43.

109. Note by H.R., Mar. 15, 1947, ISA, RG 2 SF 90/43; secret memo [draft] of the CS, n.d. [probably 1943], ISA, RG 2 SF/90/43.

110. Secret memo, ISA, RG 2 SF/90/43.; Major Scaife, letter to CS, Oct. 4,

1943; handwritten notes at the beginning of the file, ISA, RG 2 SF/90/43. This (unsigned) note seems to be some kind of report from one of Abu al-Huda's superiors.

111. The society received a grant of five hundred Palestinian pounds every three months from the Social Welfare Department, and had three employees. Report on the Women's Social Endeavor Society n.d. [probably later than 1944], ISA, RG 65 3117. [The Palestinian pound was worth $4.04 in 1944.] There was acrimony over funding and jurisdiction of the society, indicating political differences within the government over its function, purpose and effectiveness. Letter, Acting Director of Social Welfare, Mar. 10, 1948, ISA, RG 2 SF/90/43. Ultimately, the society seems to have become semi-independent, its funding by the government phasing out over time.

112. Note, signed H.R., Mar. 15, 1947, ISA, RG 2 SF/90/43.

113. Such attitudes corresponded closely with missionaries' (ostensibly) religious strategies, as developed during the nineteenth century in the Middle East (and elsewhere), to reach "heathen" society through its women and children. See my "'Our Moslem Sisters': Women of Greater Syria in the Eyes of American Protestant Missionary Women," *Islam and Christian-Muslim Relations* 9, no. 3 (1998): 307–23.

114. Tubi, *'Abīr wa majd*, 167.

115. Tubi, *'Abīr wa majd*, 167. A number of women from prominent families became involved with the society, including Hind al-Husayni, the founder of *Dār al-tifl al-'Arabī*, the orphanage for children from Dayr Yassin; Nahid 'Abduh al-Sajjadi; Sa'ida Jarallah, the daughter of Husam al-Din Jarallah, the prominent Jerusalem *'ālim;* and others from the Jarallah and 'Abd al-Hadi clans. (The Jarallahs were particularly active in the association; for example, in Jerusalem and Jaffa.) In my interviews, some of these women seemed unaware of the British role in establishing the organization. The extent and duration of Abu al-Huda's association with the group in Palestine is unclear. She represented Trans-Jordan at the Arab Women's Conference in Cairo in 1944 and became increasingly identified as a Jordanian women's activist. *MNA*, 37.

116. Tubi, *'Abir wa majd*, 167. Women in interviews usually referred to it this way, in both Arabic and English.

117. An article in *Filastīn* on Dec. 5, 1947, says that the society "wants to mention that [it] participated in the women's demonstration" held in Jaffa the day before. It apparently did not participate in the big national women's conference on saving the land in July 1947. (See below.)

118. "Notice from the Women's Social Solidarity Society," *al-Difā'*, May 7, 1946.

119. *Filastīn*, Dec. 5, 1947.

120. Rosemary Sayigh, from interviews with older nationalist women in Lebanon. Personal communication, Jan. 14, 1992.

121. Public Information Office, Review of the Palestine Press; *Filastīn*, Apr. 13, 1943.

122. Khalaf, *Politics*, 38; Zachary Lockman, *Comrades and Enemies: Arab*

and Jewish Workers in Palestine, 1906–1948 (Berkeley: University of California Press, 1996), 283. The government's efforts, however, were geared toward "peaceful conciliation and cooperation between Arab employees and employers," emphasizing the long-standing policy of the mandate government toward maintaining "social order and harmony and minimum intervention," rather than aggressive defense of workers' rights and changes in social policy. Khalaf, *Politics*, 42.

123. Lockman, *Comrades and Enemies*, 333.
124. Khalaf, *Politics*, 39.
125. *Al-Difāʿ*, Jan. 29, 1946.
126. One can determine this by their names. The women were Farida Nasir, Eileen Habib, Marguerite Najjar, Mary Haddad, Rose ʿAsfur (the wife of Hana ʿAsfur, a member of the PAWS Executive Committee), Linda Wakim, Victoria Salfiti, Isabel Qubti, and Lutfiyya Sulayman. *Filastīn*, Feb. 5, Feb. 27, 1946; *al-Difāʿ*, Jan. 29, Feb. 22, Feb. 27, 1946. It seems that more Christian than Muslim women entered the workforce. This was also true of government clerical workers and teachers in other parts of the country. See, e.g., Ylana Miller, *Government and Society in Rural Palestine: 1920–1948* (Austin: University of Texas Press, 1985), 106.
127. *Al-Difāʿ*, Feb. 22, 1946.
128. *Filastīn*, Sept. 11, 1942; *al-Difāʿ*, Jan. 29, 1946.
129. A district commissioner in the Galilee area reported that "in Acre fears are expressed that now that the army are employing women as well as men and increasing wages by way of allowances, sufficient olive pickers will not be available to cope with this year's crop." DC Report for period ending 31 Oct. 1942, Nov. 7, 1942, PRO, CO 733 439/15.
130. Khalaf, *Politics*, 108.
131. Khalaf, *Politics*, 109.
132. *Filastīn*, Dec. 23 and 24, 1947.
133. See Khalaf, *Politics*, especially 133–58.
134. Women of Iraq, Lebanon, Egypt, and Syria all protested with telegrams, meetings, and demonstrations. Letter from Huda Shaʿrawi (June 5, 1946) and telegram from the Arab Women's Federation of Syria (May 4, 1946) to the British Prime Minister and the Queen of England, PRO, CO 733 463/17. The women of Syria also fired off salvos to the king of England, President Truman, the Daughters of the American Revolution, American women's associations, and the Executive Committee of the Indian Women's Congress. *Filastīn*, May 23, 11, and 9, 1946; *al-Difāʿ*, Mar. 13, May 6, 1946.
135. It is also intriguing that Shihabi and Mughannam seemed to be reunited in common political activity, despite evidence of some falling-out since 1938. (See discussions of the AWU/AWA split in Chapter 6; the AWA "bloc" of the movement did not attend the 1944 women's conference.)
136. Letter from General Arab Women's Union, May 21, 1946, and letter from Ladies of Acre to Galilee District Commissioner, May 25, 1946, PRO, CO 733 463/17; *Filastīn*, Mar. 1, May 7 and 8, 1946; *al-Difāʿ*, May 6, 7, and 12, 1946.

It was in the midst of all this activity that the Women's Solidarity Society issued its notice in the paper denying its relationship to the British government.

137. Khalaf, *Politics*, 112, 107, 151; Benny Morris, *The Birth of the Palestinian Refugee Problem, 1947–1949* (Cambridge: Cambridge University Press, 1987), 37. The brutal bombing of the King David Hotel by the Irgun, a signal event in the escalating tension, occurred in February 1946.

138. Letter to the CS from the Haifa DC, Jan. 26, 1946, ISA, RG 2 POL/1/46. There was "an increasing tempo of representations on behalf of" Jamal al-Husayni's release in this period; he returned to Palestine in February and immediately became deeply involved in strained efforts among feuding political personalities to form a cohesive, effective entity to lead the national movement and the nation, something which never happened. Khalaf, *Politics*, 117.

139. *Palestine Press Review*, Public Information Office, "Where are those torches?" Mar. 4, 1946.

140. *Filastīn*, June 19, July 9, 1947. This new incarnation of the AHC was formed after acrimonious power struggles among the national leadership at a meeting held in Bludan in June 1946, under the guidance of Arab rulers. See Khalaf, *Politics*, 122–24. (This body is not to be confused with the AHC of the revolt.) The AHC of the 1940s was named the Arab Higher Executive, but was usually referred to as the Arab Higher Committee.

141. *Palestine Press Review*, Public Information Office, "Three conferences," June 18, 1947.

142. Ibid.

143. *Filastīn*, July 17, 1947.

144. Khalaf, *Politics*, 146.

145. *Filastīn*, June 13, 1947.

146. Morris, *Birth*, 29.

147. *Filastīn*, Dec. 5, 1947.

148. *Filastīn*, Dec. 19, 1947. At this point in time, the military situation in the country was critical, and many Palestinian organizations attempted to coordinate with one another in efforts to deal with the problems resulting from the escalating armed conflict.

149. Nahid al-Sajjadi, interview with the author, Jan. 28, 1993; Tubi, *'Abīr wa Majd*, 313–14. Tubi comments that the *zahrāt al-uquhān* wanted to enter the battle alongside the male volunteers, and when refused, demanded to know the reasons why. (She does not report the answer they were given.)

150. "The Arab Women's Union on Palestine" from *The Arab Press*, Jan. 6, 1948; "Arab Women's Union on Terrorism" [*al-Difa'*], Jan. 9, 1948; and "Arab Women's Union Memorandum to G.O.C." [*The Arab Press*], Feb. 22, 1948. *Palestine Press Review*, Public Information Office.

151. Laila Jammal, *Contributions by Palestinian Women to the National Struggle for Liberation* (Washington: Middle East Publications, 1985), 18.

152. For her account of this, see my "Young Women in the City: Mandate Memories," *Jerusalem Quarterly File* 2 (winter 1998): 37–38.

153. Hind al-Husayni, interview with the author, Feb. 15, 1993.

154. Domesticity certainly was not challenged, nor had concepts about married women's responsibilities changed. One of the resolutions at a preparatory meeting for the conference on saving the land was that "girls without domestic responsibilities" form committees to supervise the boycott and other activities of the movement. *Filastīn*, June 27, 1947.

155. Mogannam, *Arab Woman*, 217.

156. Soraya Antonius, "Fighting on Two Fronts: Conversations with Palestinian Women" *Journal of Palestine Studies* 8 (1979): 37.

157. Orayb Aref Najjar, "Between Nationalism and Feminism: the Palestinian Answer," in *Women Transforming Politics: Worldwide Strategies for Empowerment*, edited by Jill M. Bystydzienski (Bloomington: Indiana University Press, 1992), 145; Judith P. Butler, *Gender Trouble: Feminism and the Subversion of Identity* (New York: Routledge Press, 1990).

158. *Al-Difāʿ*, Mar. 25, 1948.

159. Minutes of the Members Council of the YWCA, March 8, 1946, ISA, RG 65 1391.

160. Thus Palestine is distinguished from Algeria, for example, where an independent French Algerian state was not the explicit policy of the colonists. The colonists envisioned, rather, "assimilation" of Algeria to France. See John Ruedy, *Modern Algeria: The Origins and Development of a Nation* (Bloomington: Indiana University Press, 1992), 86.

161. Memo of the Arab Women's Higher Committee to the HC enclosed in despatch from Malcolm Hooper, American Consul to Jerusalem, to Secretary of State, Nov. 10, 1945, U.S. NA 890B.

162. Quoted by Ruth Woodsmall, *Moslem Women*, 197.

163. Sharon Sievers, "Six (or More) Feminists in Search of a Historian," in *Expanding the Boundaries of History: Essays on Women in the Third World*, edited by Cheryl Johnson-Odim and Margaret Strobel (Bloomington: Indiana University Press, 1992), 325.

164. Leila Mughannam in interview with her mother, Matiel.

165. Lydia ʿArraj, interview with the author, Nov. 30, 1992.

166. Temma Kaplan, "Female Consciousness and Collective Action: The Case of Barcelona, 1910–1918," *Signs* 7, no. 3 (1982): 547, 546.

167. Christian women involved in the movement expressed a kind of solidarity with Muslim women based upon common culture and historical pride. Matiel Mughannam (a Christian) wrote that women "had benefited greatly through the awakening which swept through the Arab peninsula with and after the birth of Islam. Islam secured to the woman that advancement which is usually only attained by long and persistent endeavors." Mogannam, *Arab Woman*, 20.

168. Mogannam, *Arab Woman*, 65.

169. Sajjadi, interview.

170. Kaplan, "Female Consciousness," 547.

171. Sajjadi, interview. Muhammad ʿAbduh and Jamal al-Din al-Afghani, Islamic reformers, died in 1905 and 1897, respectively.

172. Frances S. Hasso, "The 'Women's Front': Nationalism, Feminism, and Modernity in Palestine." *Gender and Society* 12, no. 4 (1998): 442.

173. Marie-Aimeé Hélie-Lucas, as quoted in Cynthia Enloe, *Bananas, Beaches and Bases: Making Feminist Sense of International Politics* (Berkeley: University of California Press, 1989), 45.

174. The famous quote of Golda Meir that "there was no such thing as Palestinians ... they did not exist" combined with recent campaigns to discredit Edward Said's "Palestinian-ness" demonstrate that it was, and continues to be, incumbent upon Palestinians to "prove" their own existence as a people. *The New York Times,* June 16, 1969; Justus Weiner, "'My Beautiful Old House' and Other Fabrications by Edward Said," *Commentary* 108, no. 2 (Sept. 1999): 23–31.

175. I thank Julie Peteet for this insight. Personal communication, March 2000.

176. Guida West and Rhoda Lois Blumberg, "Reconstructing Social Protest from a Feminist Perspective," in *Women and Social Protest,* edited by West and Blumberg (Oxford: Oxford University Press, 1990), 15.

177. Orayb Najjar, discussing the contemporary Palestinian women's movement, warns, "Unless the women's committees take the threats conservatives pose to women's self-determination as seriously as they take the Israeli threat to Palestinian self-determination, Palestinian women's groups will lose most of the gains women have made since the founding of the first women's committee in 1978." See Najjar, "Between Nationalism," 159.

178. Najjar, "Between Nationalism," 159; emphasis in original.

179. Rita Giacaman and Muna Odeh, "Palestinian Women's Movement in the Israeli-Occupied West Bank and Gaza Strip," In *Women of the Arab World,* edited by Nahid Toubia (London: Zed Press, 1988), 58.

180. For an excellent account of Palestinian women's involvement in this period, see Julie Peteet, *Gender in Crisis: Women and the Palestinian Resistance Movement* (New York: Columbia University Press, 1991).

APPENDIX II. MEMBERS OF THE ARAB WOMEN'S
EXECUTIVE COMMITTEE

1. Not all of these sources overlap and contain the same list of members of the AWE, so there are discrepancies.

2. There is confusion about this person. One source lists her as Miss Budayri, and another as Mrs. Kamal Budayri. *Filastin*-English, Oct. 26, 1929; *Mirāt al-Sharq,* Oct. 28, 1929.

Bibliography

ARCHIVES

Central Zionist Archives (CZA), Jerusalem, Record Group (RG) 25S, Political Affairs Files
Israel State Archives (ISA), Jerusalem
   RG 2, Chief Secretary's Office
      K: Moslem Affairs
      M: Health and Vital Statistics
      E: Education
      P: Post, Telephones, Broadcasting and Press
      SF: Secret Files
      U: Civil Service Commission
      X: High Commissioner, Executive and Advisory Council
      O: Police and Prisons
   RG 8 Education
   RG10 Health
   RG13 Labor
   RG15 Public Information Office
   RG23 Jerusalem District Commissioner's Office
   RG65 George Antonius papers
Public Records Office (PRO), London
   Colonial Office (CO), Palestine Correspondence 733
   Foreign Office (FO), Political 371
   War Office (WO), 282
Middle East Centre (MEC), Private Papers Collection, St. Antony's College, Oxford
   Humphrey Ernest Bowman Papers
   Miss E. Emery letters
   J. M. Faraday Papers
   Jerome Farrell Papers
   Jerusalem Girls College Papers

Hilda Ridler Papers
Miss H. M. Wilson Papers
Rhodes House (RH), Bodleian Library, Oxford
William Denis Battershill Papers
Sir Kenneth William Blackbourne Papers
Sir John Robert Chancellor Papers
Charles Campbell Ross Papers
Sir Thomas Scrivenor Papers
U.S. National Archives
American Consulate General, Jerusalem 890B

GOVERNMENT DOCUMENTS

Government of Palestine. Civil Service List. Alexandria: Whitehead Morris, Ltd., 1931, 1935, 1937.
Government of Palestine. Department of Education Annual Report for the Scholastic Year 1926–1927. Jerusalem, 1928.
Government of Palestine. Department of Labor Annual Reports. Jerusalem, 1942–46.
Government of Palestine. Junior Service Staff List. Alexandria: Whitehead Morris, Ltd., 1931.
Government of Palestine. Office of Statistics. Special Bulletin No. 8. Statistics of Wage Rates, Wage Census. March 1942.
Government of Palestine. Office of Statistics. Survey of National Income of Palestine. C. G. Wood, Government Statistician. 1943.
Great Britain Colonial Office Blue Books for Palestine, 1926–1939. London.
Great Britain Colonial Office Education Reports for Palestine, 1926–1939. London.
Great Britain Colonial Office Reports on the Administration of Palestine and Trans-Jordan, 1920–1921, 1929, 1931, 1933, 1936.
Palestine Broadcasting Service. Official Programs. 1936, 1938.
Palestine Press Review. Public Information Office, Jerusalem, 1946–48.
A Survey of Palestine Prepared in December 1945 and January 1946 for the Information of the Anglo-American Committee of Inquiry. Vol. 1. Washington: Institute of Palestine Studies, 1991.

INTERVIEWS

All the interviews were conducted by the author (1992–99) unless otherwise indicated.

'Ali 'Abbas, Amman, 1993.
'Issam 'Abd al-Hadi, Lydia al-'Arraj, and Siham Sukkar, Jan. 27, 1993, Amman.
Lawahaz 'Abd al-Hadi, June 8, 1994, Nablus.

Alexandra ʿAboud, Apr. 28, 1993, Nazareth.
Bahjat Abu-Gharbiyya, Jan. 29, 1993, Amman.
Hanna Abu Hanna, May 19, 1993, Nazareth.
Miryam Abu Nuwwar, Apr. 27, 1993, Nazareth.
Umm Ibrahim Abu Saʿud, Jan. 28, 1993, Amman.
Amy Aramki, Nov. 26, 1992, Bir Zeit.
Lydia al-ʿArraj, Nov. 30, 1992, Beit Jala.
Nasir ʿAuda, Apr. 28, 1993, Nazareth.
Julia ʿAwad, Mar. 6, 1993, Amman.
Evelyn Baramki, Feb. 20, 1993, Bir Zeit/Ramallah.
Margaret Bianchi, Mar. 23, 1995, New York (telephone).
Georgette Bishara, May 19, 1993, Nazareth.
Wedad Bulos, Jan. 27, 1993, Amman.
Muhammad Ahmad Bustami, May 16, 1993, Nablus.
Myasir Dahir, Apr. 28, 1993, Nazareth.
Yusuf Dawadiya, Jan. 23, 1993, Amman.
Umm Joseph Dib, May 19, 1993, Nazareth.
Latifa Muyis Dubari, July 1993, Nazareth. Interviewed by Zuheira Sabbagh.
Wafiʿa al-Duzdar, Mar. 21, 1993, Al-Bira.
Negar Bahai Emsellem, Apr. 24, 1999, Haifa.
Umm Fathi, July 1993, Nazareth. Interviewed by Zuheira Sabbagh.
Subhi Ghosha, Jan. 27, 1993, Amman.
Asia and Sofiyya Halabi, May 28, 1993, Jerusalem.
Tha-wa ʿAbd al-Karam Hassan, July 1993. Interviewed by Zuheira Sabbagh.
Hind al-Husayni, Feb. 15, 1993, Jerusalem.
Musa al-Husayni, Jan. 24, 1993, Amman.
Rema al-Husayni, Jan. 24, 1993, Amman.
Salma al-Husayni, Apr. 19, 1993, Jerusalem.
Raja al-ʿIsa, Jan. 26, 1993, Amman.
Hassan Istambuli and Amina Kadhimi, Apr. 22, 1993, Jerusalem.
Saʿida Jarallah, Apr. 19, 1994, Jerusalem.
Salma Khadra Jayyusi, July 1, 1996, Boston (telephone).
Augustine Jouzy, Mar. 1, 1993, Amman.
Mansur Kardosh, May 20, 1993, Nazareth.
Yvonne Kardosh, Apr. 27, 1993, Nazareth.
ʿAbd al-Rahman Kayyali, Mar. 8, 1993, Amman.
Wadiʿ Khartabil, Beirut, 1981. Interviewed by Julie Peteet and Rosemary Sayigh.
Ibtihaj Khuri and Salwa Musa, May 20, 1993, Acre.
Samira Khuri, Apr. 27, 1993, Nazareth.
Ellen Mansour, Sep. 5, 1992, Ramallah.
Farida Saleh Mayer, Mar. 6, 1993, Amman.
Rabiha Dajani Miqdadi, Mar. 4, 1993, Amman.
Matiel Mughannam, Washington, D.C., 1985. Interviewed by Julie Peteet and Rosemary Sayigh.
Theodore Mughannam, Sep. 28, 1995, Arlington, Virginia (telephone).

Hazzim Nusseibeh, Feb. 1, 1993, Amman.
Madiha Nusseibeh, Apr. 25, 1999, Jericho.
Samah Nusseibeh, Nov. 23, 1993, Jerusalem.
People from 'Asira Shamaliya, May 26, 1993, 'Asira Shamaliya.
Mary and Widad Qa'wwar, Jan. 23, 1993, Amman.
Dr. Suhayla Rimawi, Jan. 25, 1993, Amman.
Sophia Sabanakh, Mar. 5, 1993, Amman.
Lulu Sabbagh, May 19, 1993, Nazareth.
Zuheira Sabbagh, May 20, 1993, Nazareth.
Muhammad Bashir al-Saffuri, July 1993, Nazareth. Interviewed by Zuheira Sabbagh.
Nahid 'Abduh al-Sajjadi, Jan. 28, 1993, Amman.
Hala and Dumya Sakakini, Sep. 11, Sep. 28, Nov. 21, 1992; Apr. 30, June 21, Oct. 14, Dec. 13, 1993; May 6, June 10, 1994, Ramallah.
Doris Salah, Feb. 17, 1993, Jerusalem.
'Abd al-Jawad Salih, Jan. 24, 1993, Amman.
Nimr Sarhan, Jan. 30, 1993, Amman.
Sereen al-Husayni Shahid, Mar. 2, 1999, Beirut.
Henriette Siksik, June 15, 1993, Jerusalem.
Sabah al-Tabari, July 1993, Nazareth. Interviewed by Zuheira Sabbagh.
Nimra Tannus, Jan. 26, 1993, Amman.
Rema Nasir Tarazi, June 21, 1993, Ramallah.
Women from Eastern Quarter (who requested anonymity), July 1993, Nazareth. Interviewed by Zuheira Sabbagh.
Women and men from Zbaabde, May 29, 1993, Zbaabde.
Women and men from Zeita, May 10, 1993, Zeita (requested anonymity). Interviewed by author and Farid Kamal.
Akram Zu'aytir, Jan. 24, 1993, Amman.
Hanna Zureik, May 19, 1993, Nazareth.

UNPUBLISHED WORKS

'Azar, Adele. Untitled memoir. 1965.
Farradj, Henriette Siksik. *A Glimpse Into the Life of Katherine Siksik, A Life of Light and Love From 7th April 1894 to 3rd May 1973.* Pamphlet. Jerusalem: March 16, 1992.
Fay, Mary Ann. "Women and Households: Gender, Power and Culture in Eighteenth-Century Egypt." Ph.D. diss., Georgetown University, 1993.
Hammami, Rema. "Between Heaven and Earth: Transformations in Religiosity and Labor Among Southern Palestinian Peasant or Refugee Women, 1920–1993." Ph.D. diss., Temple University, 1994.
Kamp, Martina. "Organizing Ideologies of Gender, Class and Ethnicity: The Pre-Revolutionary Women's Movements in Iraq." Paper presented at the conference "Women and Gender in the Middle East: A Multidisciplinary Assessment of the State of Theory and Research," Bellagio, Italy, Aug. 27–31, 2001.

Matthews, Weldon. "The Arab Istiqlal Party in Palestine, 1927–1934." Ph.D. diss., University of Chicago, 1998.
Najjar, Aida. "The Arabic Press and Nationalism in Palestine, 1920–1948." Ph. D. diss., University of New York-Syracuse, 1975.
al-Shihabi, Zlikha. Unpublished paper. N.d.
Wilke, Allison. "Portraying Nationalism: Palestinian Women and the Press, 1929–39." D.Phil. diss. in progress, Oxford University.

NEWSPAPERS

Arabic

Al-Awqāt al-'Arabiyya (Jerusalem), 1935.
Al-Difāʿ (Jaffa), 1934–39, 1945–46.
Al-Fatāt (Haifa), selections.
Fatāt al-Sharq (Cairo), selections.
Filastīn (Jaffa), 1921–40, 1942, 1944, 1946, 1947.
Al-Jām'ia al-'Arabiyya (Jerusalem), 1929–33.
Al-Jām'ia al-Islamiyya (Jaffa), 1933.
Al-Karmil (Haifa), 1920–39.
Mirāt al-Sharq (Jerusalem), 1921–37.
Al-Sirāt al-Mustaqīm (Jaffa), 1929–42.

English

Filastin (Jaffa), 1929–31.
Palestine Bulletin (Jerusalem), 1925–32.
Palestine Post (Jerusalem), 1932–39, 1944.
The Times (London), 1936–38.

French

L'Égyptienne (Cairo), selections.

BOOKS AND ARTICLES

Abdo, Nahla. "Nationalism and Feminism: Palestinian Women and the Intifada—No Going Back?" In *Gender and National Identity: Women and Politics in Muslim Societies,* edited by Valentine Moghadam. London and Atlantic Highlands, N.J.: Zed Books; Karachi: Oxford University Press, 1994.
Abdulhadi, Rabab. "The Palestinian Women's Autonomous Movement: Emergence, Dynamics, and Challenges." *Gender and Society* 12, no. 6 (1998): 649–73.
Abu ʿAli, Khadija. *Muqaddimāt hawla al-wāqiʿa al-marʾa wa trajribatihā fī al-thawra al-Filastīniyya.* Beirut: General Union of Palestinian Women, 1975.
Abu Daleb, Nuha. "Palestinian Women and Their Role in the Revolution." *Peuples méditerranéens* 5 (Oct.–Dec. 1978): 35–47.

Abu-Lughod, Lila, ed. *Remaking Women: Feminism and Modernity in the Middle East.* Princeton: Princeton University Press, 1998.
Aburish, Said K. *Children of Bethany: The Story of a Palestinian Family.* London: I. B. Taurus and Co., 1988.
Afary, Janet. "On the Origins of Feminism in Early Twentieth-Century Iran." *Journal of Women's History* 1, no. 2 (fall 1989): 65–87.
———. "The Debate on Women's Liberation in the Iranian Constitutional Revolution, 1906–1911." In *Expanding the Boundaries of Women's History: Essays on Women in the Third World,* edited by Cheryl Johnson-Odim and Margaret Strobel. Bloomington: Indiana University Press, 1992.
———. *The Iranian Constitutional Revolution, 1906–1911: Grassroots Democracy, Social Democracy and the Origins of Feminism.* New York: Columbia University Press, 1996.
Agmon, Iris. "Women, Class, and Gender: Muslim Jaffa and Haifa at the Turn of the Twentieth Century." *International Journal of Middle East Studies* 30, no. 4 (1998): 477–500.
Ahmed, Leila. *Women and Gender in Islam: Historic Roots of a Modern Debate.* New Haven: Yale University Press, 1992.
al-'Amd, Salwa. "Mulāhazāt hawla wāqi' al-mar'a fī al-thawra al-Filastīniyya." *Shu'ūn Filastīniyya* 113 (April 1981): 9–20.
Amin, Qasim. *The Liberation of Women.* Translated by Samiha Sidhom Peterson. Cairo: American University Press, 1992.
Amin, Samir. *The Arab Nation: Nationalism and Class Struggle.* London: Zed Press, 1983.
Andrews, Fannie Fern. *The Holy Land Under Mandate.* 2 vols. Boston: Houghton Mifflin Co., 1931.
al-'Ansari, Ya'qub, and Ibrahim al-Husayni. *Jam'iyyat al-sayyidāt al-'Arabiyyāt al-Quds.* Jerusalem: 1985.
Antonius, Soraya. "Fighting on Two Fronts: Conversations with Palestinian Women." *Journal of Palestine Studies* 8 (1979): 26–45.
Appleby, Joyce, Lynn Hunt, and Margaret Jacobs. *Telling the Truth About History.* New York and London: W. W. Norton & Co., 1994.
Arab Women and Education. Beirut: Institute for Women's Studies in the Arab World, Beirut University College, 1980.
Asali, K. J., ed. *Jerusalem in History.* Brooklyn: Olive Branch Press, 1990.
Audi, Anisa. *From Ramallah, Palestine, to Lake Wales, Florida, and In-Between.* New York: Vantage Press, 1992.
Augustin, Ebba. *Palestinian Women: Identity and Experience.* London: Zed Books, 1993.
Al-Awdat, Ya'qub. *Min 'ālam al-fikr wa al-ādab fī Filastīn.* Amman: wakāla al-tawzī' al-Urduniyya, 1987.
Ayalon, Ami. "*Sihafa:* The Arab Experiment in Journalism." *Middle Eastern Studies* 28, no. 2 (April 1992): 258–80.
———. *The Press in the Arab Middle East.* Oxford: Oxford University Press, 1995.

Badran, Margot. *Feminists, Islam, and Nation: Gender and the Making of Modern Egypt*. Princeton: Princeton University Press, 1995.
Baer, Gabriel. "Women and Waqf: An Analysis of the Istanbul Tahrir of 1546." *Asian and African Studies* 17, nos. 1–3 (1983): 9–28.
Baron, Beth. "The Making and Breaking of Marital Bonds in Modern Egypt." In *Women in Middle Eastern History*, edited by Nikki Keddie and Beth Baron. New Haven: Yale University Press, 1991.
———. *The Women's Awakening in Egypt: Culture, Society, and the Press*. New Haven: Yale University Press, 1994.
Bentwich, Norman and Helen. *Mandate Memories: 1918–1948*. New York: Schocken, 1965.
Berberi, Yusra. "Active in Politics and Women's Affairs in Gaza." In *Palestinian Women: Identity and Experience*, edited by Ebba Augustin. London: Zed Books, 1993.
Bernstein, Deborah S. *Constructing Boundaries: Jewish and Arab Workers in Mandatory Palestine*. Albany: State University of New York Press, 2000.
Board, Barbara. *Newsgirl in Palestine*. London: Michael Joseph, 1937.
Booth, Marilyn. "Exemplary Lives, Feminist Aspirations: Zaynab Fawwāz and the Arabic Biographical Tradition," *Journal of Arabic Literature* 26 (1995): 120–45.
———. "'May Her Likes Be Multiplied': 'Famous Women'. Biography and Gendered Prescription in Egypt, 1892–1935." *Signs* 22, no. 41 (1997): 827–90.
———. "Women in Islam: Men and the 'Women's Press' in Turn-of-the-Twentieth-Century Egypt." *International Journal of Middle East Studies* 33, no. 2 (May 2001): 171–201.
Bosch, Mineke, with Annemarie Kloosterman. *Politics and Friendship: Letters from the International Woman Suffrage Alliance, 1902–1942*. Columbus: Ohio State University Press, 1990.
Botman, Selma. "The Experience of Women in the Egyptian Communist Movement, 1939–1954." *Women's Studies International Forum* 2, no. 2 (1988): 117–26.
Bowden, Tom. "The Politics of the Arab Rebellion in Palestine, 1936–1939." *Middle Eastern Studies* 11 no. 2 (1975): 147–74.
Brownfoot, Janice. "Sisters Under the Skin: Imperialism and the Emancipation of Women in Malaya, c. 1891–1941." In *Making Imperial Mentalities*, edited by J. A. Mangan. Manchester: Manchester University Press, 1990.
Budeiri, Musa K. *The Palestine Communist Party, 1919–1948: Arab and Jew in the Struggle for Internationalism*. London: Ithaca Press, 1979.
Burstyn, Joan N. *Victorian Education and the Ideal of Womanhood*. London: Croom Helm, 1980.
Burton, Antoinette. *Burdens of History: British Feminists, Indian Women, and Imperial Culture, 1865–1915*. Chapel Hill: University of North Carolina Press, 1994.
Busailah, Reja-e. "The Fall of Lydda, 1948: Impressions and Reminiscences." *Arab Studies Quarterly* 3, no. 2 (spring 1981): 124–51.

Butler, Judith P. *Gender Trouble: Feminism and the Subversion of Identity.* New York: Routledge Press, 1990.

Callaway, Helen. *Gender, Culture and Empire: European Women in Colonial Nigeria.* London: MacMillan Press, 1987.

Chatterjee, Partha. "Colonialism, Nationalism, and Colonized Women: The Contest in India." *American Ethnologist* 16, no. 4 (1989): 622–33.

———. "The Nationalist Resolution of the Women's Question." In *Recasting Women: Essays in Indian Colonial History,* edited by Kumkum Sangari and Sudesh Vaid. New Brunswick: Rutgers University Press, 1990.

———. *The Nation and Its Fragments: Colonial and Postcolonial Histories.* Princeton: Princeton University Press, 1993.

Chaudhuri, Nupur, and Margaret Strobel, eds. *Western Women and Imperialism: Complicity and Resistance.* Bloomington: Indiana University Press, 1992.

Coles, Robert. *The Call of Stories: Teaching and the Moral Imagination.* Boston: Houghton Mifflin Co., 1989.

Connerton, Paul. *How Societies Remember.* Cambridge: Cambridge University Press, 1989.

Cooper, Frederick, and Ann L. Stoler. "Tensions of Empire: Colonial Control and Visions of Rule." *American Ethnologist* 16, no. 4 (Nov. 1989): 609–21.

Courtney, Roger. *Palestine Policeman: An Account of Eighteen Dramatic Months in the Palestine Police Force During the Great Jew-Arab Troubles.* London: Herbert Jenkins, 1939.

Daraghma, 'Izzat. *Al-haraka al-nisā'iyya fī Filastīn.* Jerusalem: maktab al-Diya' lil-dirasāt, 1991.

Davies, Miranda. *Third World/Second Sex: Women's Struggles and National Liberation.* London: Zed Books, 1983.

Davin, Anna. "Imperialism and Motherhood." *History Workshop Journal* 5 (1978): 9–65.

Donnison, Jean. *Midwives and Medical Men: A History of Inter-Professional Rivalries and Women's Rights.* New York: Schocken Books, 1977.

Doumani, Beshara B. "Rediscovering Ottoman Palestine: Writing Palestinians Into History." *Journal of Palestine Studies* 82 (winter 1992): 5–28.

———. *Rediscovering Palestine: Merchants and Peasants in Jabal Nablus, 1700-1900.* Berkeley: University of California Press, 1995.

Dumper, Michael. *The Politics of Jerusalem Since 1967.* New York: Columbia University Press, 1997.

Eisenman, Robert H. *Islamic Law in Palestine and Israel: A History of the Survival of Tanzimat and Shari'a in the British Mandate and the Jewish State.* Leiden: E. J. Brill, 1978.

Enloe, Cynthia. *Bananas, Beaches and Bases: Making Feminist Sense of International Politics.* Berkeley: University of California Press, 1989.

Erskine, Beatrice. *Palestine of the Arabs.* London: George B. Harrap, 1935.

Evans, Sara. *Personal Politics: The Roots of Women's Liberation in the Civil Rights Movement and the New Left.* New York: Vantage Books, 1979.

Fahmy, Khaled. "Women, Medicine and Power in Nineteenth-Century Egypt."

In *Remaking Women: Feminism and Modernity in the Middle East*, edited by Lila Abu-Lughod. Princeton: Princeton University Press, 1998.

Faroqhi, Suraiya, Bruce McGowan, Donald Quaertert, and Ševket Pamuk. *An Economic and Social History of the Ottoman Empire.* Vol. 2. Cambridge: Cambridge University Press, 1994.

Fawcett, Millicent Garett. *Six Weeks in Palestine.* 2 vols. London: Women's Printing Society, 1921–22.

Fawzy, Didar. "Palestinian Women in Palestine." In *Women of the Mediterranean*, edited by Monique Gadant. London: Zed Books, 1986.

Fay, Mary Ann. "Women and Waqf: Toward a Reconsideration of Women's Place in Mamluk Households." *International Journal of Middle East Studies* 29, no. 1 (Feb. 1997): 33–51.

Finn, Elizabeth Ann. *Palestine Peasantry: Notes on Their Clans, Warfare, Religion, and Laws.* London: Marshall Brothers, 1923.

Fleischmann, Ellen. "Jerusalem Women's Organizations During the British Mandate, 1920s–1930s." Jerusalem: Palestinian Academic Society for the Study of International Affairs, 1995.

———. "Crossing the Boundaries of History: Exploring Oral History in Researching Palestinian Women in the Mandate Period." *Women's History Review* 5, no. 3 (Oct. 1996): 351–71.

———. "Young Women in the City: Mandate Memories." *Jerusalem Quarterly File* 2 (winter 1998): 31–39.

———. "'Our Moslem Sisters': Women of Greater Syria in the Eyes of American Protestant Missionary Women." *Islam and Christian-Muslim Relations* 9, no. 3 (1998): 307–23.

———. "Selective Memory, Gender and Nationalism: Palestinian Women Leaders in the British Mandate Period." *History Workshop Journal* 47 (April 1999): 141–58.

———. "The Other 'Awakening': The Emergence of Women's Movements in the Modern Middle East, 1900–1940." In *A Social History of Women and Gender in the Modern Middle East*, edited by Margaret Lee Meriwether and Judith E. Tucker. Boulder: Westview Press, 1999.

———. "Nation, Tradition, and Rights: The Indigenous Feminism of the Palestinian Women's Movement (1929–1948)," in *Women's Suffrage in the British Empire: Citizenship, Nation, and Race*, edited by Ian Fletcher, Philippa Levine, and Laura Mayhall. New York: Routledge, 2000.

———. "The Emergence of the Palestinian Women's Movement, 1929–1939," *Journal of Palestine Studies*, vol. 29, number 2 (spring 2000), 16–32.

Furlonge, Sir Geoffrey. *Palestine is My Country: The Story of Musa Alami.* New York: Praeger Publishers, 1969.

Gaitskell, Deborah. "Race, Gender and Imperialism: A Century of Black Girls' Education in South Africa." In *Benefits Bestowed: Education and British Imperialism*, edited by J. A. Mangan. Manchester: Manchester University Press, 1988.

Gelvin, James L. *Divided Loyalties: Nationalism and Mass Politics in Syria at the End of Empire.* Berkeley: University of California Press, 1998.

Gerber, Haim. *Ottoman Rule in Jerusalem, 1890–1914.* Berlin: Klaus Schwarz, 1985.

Giacaman, Rita, and Penny Johnson. "Building Barricades and Breaking Barriers." In *Intifada: The Palestinian Uprising against Israeli Occupation,* edited by Zachary Lockman and Joel Beinin. Boston: South End Press, 1989.

———, and Muna Odeh. "Palestinian Women's Movement in the Israeli-Occupied West Bank and Gaza Strip." In *Women of the Arab World,* edited by Nahid Toubia. London: Zed Press, 1988.

———, with Islah Jad and Penny Johnson. "For the Common Good? Gender and Social Citizenship in Palestine." *Middle East Report* 26, no. 1 (Jan.–March 1996): 11–17.

Giddings, Paula. *When and Where I Enter: The Impact of Black Women on Race and Sex in America.* New York: Bantam Books, 1988.

Ginzberg, Lori. *Women and the Work of Benevolence: Morality, Politics, and Class in the Nineteenth-Century United States.* New Haven: Yale University Press, 1990.

Gluck, Sherna Berger. *An American Feminist in Palestine: The Intifada Years.* Philadelphia: Temple University Press, 1994.

———, and Daphne Patai, eds. *Women's Words: The Feminist Practice of Oral History.* New York and London: Routledge, 1991.

Gouda, Frances. "Teaching Indonesian Girls in Java and Bali, 1900–1942: Dutch Progressives, the Infatuation with 'Oriental' Refinement, and 'Western' Ideas about Proper Womanhood." *Women's History Review* 4, no. 1 (1995): 25–62.

Graham-Brown, Sarah. *Images of Women.* London: Quartet Books Ltd., 1988.

Granqvist, Hilma. *Marriage Conditions in a Palestinian Village.* 2 vols. Helsingfors: Akademische Buchhandlung, 1931.

Grant, Elihu. *The People of Palestine.* Philadelphia: J. B. Lippincott, 1921.

Haddad, Yvonne. "Palestinian Women: Patterns of Legitimation and Domination." In *The Sociology of the Palestinians,* edited by Khalil Nakhleh and Elia Zureik. London: Croom Helm, 1980.

Haggis, Jane. "Gendering Colonialism or Colonizing Gender? Recent Women's Studies Approaches to White Women and the History of British Colonialism." *Women's Studies International Forum* 13, nos. 1–2 (1990): 105–15.

Hammami, Rema. "Women, the Hijab and the Intifada." *Middle East Report* 20 (May-Aug. 1990): 24–28.

———. "Commentary: Feminist Scholarship and the Literature on Palestinian Women." In *Gender and Society Working Papers.* Birzeit: Birzeit University Women's Studies Program, 1995.

———. "From Immodesty to Collaboration: Hamas, the Women's Movement, and National Identity in the Intifada." In *Political Islam: Essays from Middle East Report,* edited by Joel Beinin and Joe Stork. Berkeley: University of California Press, 1997.

Hammami, Rima [sic], and Eileen Kuttab. "The Palestinian Women's Move-

ment: Strategies Towards Freedom and Democracy." *News From Within* 15, no. 4 (April 1999): 3–9.
Hanania, Edith A. S. "Access of Arab Women to Higher Education." In *Arab Women and Education*. Beirut: Institute for Women's Studies in the Arab World, Beirut University College, 1980.
Hartsock, Nancy. "Rethinking Modernism." *Cultural Critique* 7 (fall 1987): 187–206.
Hasso, Frances S. "The 'Women's Front': Nationalism, Feminism, and Modernity in Palestine." *Gender and Society* 12, no. 4 (1998), 441–465.
Himadeh, Sa'id B., ed. *Economic Organization of Palestine*. Beirut: American University Press, 1938.
Hirst, David. *The Gun and the Olive Branch*. 2nd ed. London: Futura Publications, 1983.
Holy Land Missions and Missionaries. New York: Arno Press, 1977.
Al-Hout, Bayan Nuweihid. "The Palestinian Political Elite During the Mandate Period." *Journal of Palestine Studies* 9, no. 1 (1979): 85–111.
Al-Hut, Nuwayhid. *Al-qīyādāt wa al-mu'assasāt al-sīyāsiyya fī Filastīn, 1917–1948*. Beirut: dār al-huda, 1986, third printing.
al-Ittihād al-nisā'ī al-'Arabī bīl-Quds. Al-ittihād al-nisā'ī al-'Arabī fī yūbīlī al-dhahabī. Jerusalem: 1983.
al-Ittihād al-nisā'ī al-Misrī. Al-Mu'tamar al-nisā'ī al-'Arabī. Cairo: dar al-ma'rif, 1944.
Jad, Islah. "From Salons to Popular Committees: Palestinian Women, 1919–1989," in *Intifada: Palestine at the Crossroads*, edited by Jamal R. Nassar and Roger Heacock. Birzeit and New York: Birzeit University and Praeger Press, 1991.
———. "Tatawwur al-dawr al-sīyāsī lil-mar'a al-Filastīniyya hatta al-intifāda." *Shu'ūn al-mar'a*, May 1991, 94–107 (part 1), and January 1992, 75–83, (part 2).
———. "Claiming Feminism, Claiming Nationalism: Women's Activism in the Occupied Territories." In *The Challenge of Local Feminisms: Women's Movements in Global Perspective*, edited by Amrita Basu. Boulder: Westview Press, 1995.
Jam'iyyat al-ittihād al-nisā'ī al-'Arabī bī Nāblus. Bayān 'ām 'an ā'māl al-jam'iyya wa mashārī'ha wa mu'assasātuha wa nashātātuha ma' al-taqrīr al-sanawī li-'ām 1966.
Jam'iyya tadāmun al-mar'a al-'Arabiyya. Al-nadwa al-dawliyya lil-sihāfa al-nisā'iyya fī al-bilād al-'Arabiyya. (Conference proceedings.) Cairo: Jam'iyya tadāmun al-mar'a al-'Arabiyya, 1990.
Jammal, Laila. *Contributions by Palestinian Women to the National Struggle for Liberation*. Washington: Middle East Publications, 1985.
Jankowski, James P. "The Palestinian Arab Revolt of 1936–1939." *Muslim World* 63 (1973): 220–33.
Jayawardena, Kumari. *Feminism and Nationalism in the Third World*. London: Zed Press, 1986.

———. *The White Woman's Other Burden: Western Women and South Asia During British Rule.* New York: Routledge, 1995.
Johnson, Penny, and Rita Giacaman. "The Palestinian Women's Movement in the New Era." *Middle East Report* 186 (1994): 22–25.
Johnson-Odim, Cheryl, and Margaret Strobel, eds. *Expanding the Boundaries of Women's History.* Bloomington: Indiana University Press, 1992.
Jouzy, Augustin. *My Life.* N.p., n.d.
Judge, Joan. "Talent, Virtue, and the Nation: Chinese Nationalism and Female Subjectivities in the Early Twentieth Century." *American Historical Review* 106, no. 3 (June 2001): 767–803.
Kan'ana, Sharif, and 'Abd al-Latif Barghuti. *Munādila Filastīn: dirāsa hayāt wa nidāl.* Al-Bira: jam'iyyat in'āsh al-usra, 1992.
Kandiyoti, Deniz. "End of Empire: Islam, Nationalism and Women in Turkey." In *Women, Islam and the State*, edited by Deniz Kandiyoti. London: Macmillan, 1991.
———. "Identity and Its Discontents: Women and the Nation," *Millenium* 20, no. 3 (1991): 429–43.
———, ed. *Gendering the Middle East: Emerging Perspectives.* Syracuse: Syracuse University Press, 1996.
———. "Some Awkward Questions on Women and Modernity in Turkey." In *Remaking Women: Feminism and Modernity in the Middle East*, edited by Lila Abu-Lughod. Princeton: Princeton University Press, 1998.
Kaplan, Temma. "Female Consciousness and Collective Action: The Case of Barcelona, 1910–1918." *Signs* 7, no. 3 (1982): 545–66.
Kawar, Amal. *Daughters of Palestine: Leading Women of the Palestinian National Movement.* Albany: State University of New York Press, 1996.
Kazi, Hamida. "Palestinian Women and the National Liberation Movement: A Social Perspective." In *Women in the Middle East*, edited by the Khamsin Collective. London: Zed Press, 1987.
Keddie, Nikki, and Beth Baron, eds. *Women in Middle Eastern History.* New Haven: Yale University Press, 1991.
Khalaf, Issa. *Politics in Palestine: Arab Factionalism and Social Disintegration, 1939–1948.* Albany: State University of New York Press, 1991.
al-Khalidi, 'Anbara Sallam. *Jawla fī al-dhikrayāt bayna Lubnān wa Filastīn.* Beirut: Dar al-nahār lil-nashr, 1978.
Khalidi, Rashid. "Arab Nationalism: Historical Problems in the Literature." *American Historical Review* 96 (1991): 1363–73.
———. *Palestinian Identity: The Construction of Modern National Consciousness.* New York: Columbia University Press, 1997.
———, Lisa Anderson, Muhammad Muslih, and Reeva Simon, eds. *The Origins of Arab Nationalism.* New York: Columbia University Press, 1991.
Khalidi, Walid. *Before Their Diaspora: A Photographic History of the Palestinians, 1876–1948.* Washington, D.C.: Institute for Palestine Studies, 1991.
Khalifa, Ijlal. *Al-mar'a wa qadiyyat Filastīn.* Cairo: Modern Arab Press, 1974.

Al-Khalili, Ghazi. *Al-mar'a al-Filastīniyya wa al-thawra*. Beirut: PLO Research Center, 1977.
Khartabil, Wadi'a Qaddura. *Bahthān 'an al-amal wa al-watan: sittūn 'āman min kifāh imra'a fī sabīl Filastīn, 1936–1990*. Beirut: Bisān lil-nashr wa al-tawzi', 1995.
Khatib, Hanifa. *Tārīkh tatawwur al-haraka al-nisā'iyya fī Lubnān wa irtibātiha bīl-'ālam al-'Arabī, 1800–1975*. Beirut: dar al-hadatha, 1984.
Khilla, Kamil Mahmud. *Filastīn wa al-intidāb al-Barītānī, 1922–1939*. Beirut: PLO Research Center, 1974.
Khoury, Philip. *Syria and the French Mandate: The Politics of Arab Nationalism, 1920–1945*. Princeton: Princeton University Press, 1987.
Khuri, Yusuf. *Al-sihāfa al-'Arabiyya fī Filastān, 1876–1948*. Beirut: Palestinian Studies Association, 1976.
Knapman, Claudia. *White Women in Fiji, 1835–1930: The Ruin of Empire?* Sydney: Allen & Unwin, 1986.
Kupferschmidt, Uri M. *The Supreme Muslim Council: Islam Under the British Mandate For Palestine*. Leiden: E. J. Brill, 1987.
Kwon, Insook. "'The New Women's Movement' in 1920s Korea: Rethinking the Relationship Between Imperialism and Women." *Gender and History* 10, no. 3 (Nov. 1998): 381–405.
Lani, Mata. "Contentious Traditions: The Debate on Sati in Colonial India." In *Recasting Women: Essays in Indian Colonial History*, edited by Kumkum Sangari and Sudesh Vaid. New Brunswick: Rutgers University Press, 1990.
Lazreg, Marnia. "Feminism and Difference: the Perils of Writing as a Woman on Women in Algeria." *Feminist Studies* 14 (spring 1988): 81–107.
———. *The Eloquence of Silence: Algerian Women in Question*. New York and London: Routledge, 1994.
Lee, Rosa Lee. "The Story of the Ram Allah Mission." In *Holy Land Missions and Missionaries*. New York: Arno Press, 1977.
Lesch, Ann Mosely. *Arab Politics in Palestine, 1917–1939: The Frustration of a Nationalist Movement*. Ithaca: Cornell University Press, 1979.
Lewis, Jane. *The Politics of Motherhood: Child and Maternal Welfare in England, 1900–1939*. London: Croom Helm Ltd., 1980.
Lockman, Zachary. "Railway Workers and Relational History: Arabs and Jews in British-Ruled Palestine." *Comparative Studies in Society and History* (1993): 601–27.
———. *Comrades and Enemies: Arab and Jewish Workers in Palestine, 1906-1948*. Berkeley: University of California Press, 1996.
Maalouf, Amin. *The Rock of Tanios*. Translated by Dorothy S. Blair. New York: George Braziller, 1994.
Mandel, Neville J. *The Arabs and Zionism Before World War I*. Berkeley: University of California Press, 1976.
Mangan, J. A., ed. *Benefits Bestowed: Education and British Imperialism*. Manchester: Manchester University Press, 1988.

———, ed. *Making Imperial Mentalities*. Manchester: Manchester University Press, 1990.

Al-mar'a al-'Arabiyya wa qadiyyat Filastīn. Conference publication. Cairo 1938.

Marsot, Afaf Lutfi al-Sayyid. "The Revolutionary Gentlewoman in Egypt." In *Women in the Muslim World*, edited by Lois Beck and Nikki Keddie. Cambridge: Harvard University Press, 1978.

Mascia-Lees, Frances E., Patricia Sharpe, and Colleen Ballerino Cohen. "The Postmodernist Turn in Anthropology: Cautions From a Feminist Perspective." *Signs* 15, no. 1 (spring 1989): 9–33.

Mattar, Philip. *The Mufti of Jerusalem*. New York: Columbia University Press, 1988.

Al-mawsū'a al-Filastīniyya (Palestinian Encyclopedia). Vols. 2, 4. Damascus: ha'iyya al-mawsū'a al-Filastīniyya, 1984.

Mba, Nina. *Nigerian Women Mobilized: Women in Southern Nigerian Political History, 1900–1965*. Berkeley, Calif.: Institute of International Studies, 1982.

McClintock, Anne. "'No Longer In a Future Heaven': Women and Nationalism in South Africa." *Transitions* 51 (1991):104–23.

———. *Imperial Leather: Race, Gender and Sexuality in the Colonial Contest*. New York and London: Routledge, 1995.

Melkon Rose, John. *Armenians of Jerusalem: Memories of Life in Palestine*. London: Radcliffe Press, 1993.

Melman, Billie. *Women's Orients: English Women and the Middle East, 1718–1918: Sexuality, Religion and Work*. London: Macmillan, 1992.

Meriwether, Margaret Lee, and Judith E. Tucker, eds. *A Social History of Women and Gender in the Modern Middle East*. Boulder: Westview Press, 1999.

Metzer, Jacob. *The Divided Economy of Mandatory Palestine*. Cambridge: Cambridge University Press, 1998.

Meyer, Sibylle. "The Tiresome Work of Conspicuous Leisure: On the Domestic Duties of the Wives of Civil Servants in the German Empire (1871–1918)." In *Connecting Spheres: Women in the Western World, 1500 to the Present*, edited by Marilyn J. Boxer and Jean H. Quataert. Oxford: Oxford University Press, 1987.

Miller, Ylana. *Government and Society in Rural Palestine, 1920 -1948*. Austin: University of Texas Press, 1985.

Minault, Gail, ed. *The Extended Family: Women and Political Participation in India and Pakistan*. Delhi: Chanakya Publications, 1981.

Mogannam, Matiel. *The Arab Woman and the Palestine Problem*. London: Herbert Joseph, 1937.

Mohan, Rajeswari. "The Crisis of Femininity and Modernity in the Third World." In *Genders 19: "Sexual Artifice: Persons, Images, Politics,"* edited by Ann Kibbey, Kayann Short, and Abrouali Farmanfarmaian. New York: New York University Press, 1994.

Mohanty, Chandra Talpade. "Under Western Eyes: Feminist Scholarship and Colonial Discourse." *Boundary Two* 12, pt. 2 (1984): 333–58.

———. "Cartographies of Struggle: Third World Women and the Politics of

Feminism." In *Third World Women and the Politics of Feminism*, edited by Mohanty, Ann Russo, and Lourdes Torres. Bloomington: Indiana University Press, 1991.

———, Ann Russo, and Lourdes Torres, eds. *Third World Women and the Politics of Feminism*. Bloomington: Indiana University Press, 1991.

Moors, Annelies. "Gender Hierarchy in a Palestinian Village: The Case of Al-Balad." In *The Rural Middle East: Peasant Lives and Modes of Production*, edited by Kathy and Pandeli Glavanis. London: Zed Press, 1989.

———. *Women, Property and Islam: Palestinian Experiences, 1920–1990*. Cambridge: Cambridge University Press, 1995.

Morgan, D. J. *The Official History of Colonial Development. The Origins of British Policy, 1924- 1945*. Vol. 1. Atlantic Highlands, N.J.: Humanities Press, 1980.

Morris, Benny. *The Birth of the Palestinian Refugee Problem, 1947–1949*. Cambridge: Cambridge University Press, 1987.

Muhawi, Ibrahim, and Sharif Kanaana. *Speak, Bird, Speak Again*. Berkeley: University of California Press, 1989.

Muslih, Muhammad. *The Origins of Palestinian Nationalism*. New York: Columbia University Press, 1988.

Najjar, Orayb Aref. "Between Nationalism and Feminism: The Palestinian Answer." In *Women Transforming Politics: Worldwide Strategies for Empowerment*, edited by Jill Bystydzienski. Bloomington: Indiana University Press, 1992.

———, with Kitty Warnock. *Portraits of Palestinian Women*. Salt Lake City: University of Utah Press, 1992.

Najmabadi, Afsaneh. "Crafting an Educated Housewife in Iran." In *Remaking Women: Feminism and Modernity in the Middle East*, edited by Lila Abu-Lughod. Princeton: Princeton University Press, 1998.

Nassar, Jamal R., and Roger Heacock, eds. *Intifada: Palestine at the Crossroads*. New York: Praeger Publishers and Bir Zeit University, 1991.

Nathan, Robert R., Oscar Gass, and Daniel Creamer. *Palestine: Problem and Promise, An Economic Study*. Washington: Public Affairs Press, 1946.

Newton, Frances E. *Fifty Years in Palestine*. London: Coldharbour Press, Ltd. 1948.

Ni'ma, 'Asma'. "Dūr al-mar'a fī al-thawra al-Filastīniyya." *Shu'ūn 'Arabiyya* 54 (June 1988): 27–42.

Offen, Karen. "Liberty, Equality, and Justice for Women: The Theory and Practice of Feminism in Nineteenth-Century Europe." In *Becoming Visible: Women in European History*, edited by Renate Bridenthal, Claudia Koonz, and Susan Mosher Stuart, 2nd ed. Boston: Houghton-Mifflin, 1987.

———. "Defining Feminism: A Comparative Historical Approach." *Signs* 14, no. 1 (1988): 119–57.

Owen, Roger, ed. *Studies in the Economic and Social History of Palestine in the Nineteenth and Twentieth Centuries*. Carbondale: Southern Illinois University Press, 1982.

Paidar, Parvin. *Women and the Political Process in Twentieth-Century Iran.* Cambridge: Cambridge University Press, 1995.

Paravisini-Gebert, Lizabeth. "Decolonizing Feminism: The Home-Grown Roots of Caribbean Women's Movement." In *Daughters of Caliban: Caribbean Women in the Twentieth- Century,* edited by Consuelo López Springfield. Bloomington: Indiana University Press, 1997.

Parker, Andrew, Mary Russo, Doris Sommer, and Patricia Yeager, eds. *Nationalisms and Sexualities.* New York and London: Routledge, 1994.

Passerini, Luisa. *Fascism in Popular Memory: The Cultural Experience of the Turin Working Class.* Translated by Robert Lumley and Jude Bloomfield. Cambridge: Cambridge University Press, 1987.

Personal Narratives Group, ed. *Interpreting Women's Lives: Feminist Theory and Personal Narratives.* Bloomington: Indiana University Press, 1989.

Peteet, Julie M.. *Gender in Crisis: Women and the Palestinian Resistance Movement.* New York: Columbia University Press, 1991.

———. "Authenticity and Gender: the Presentation of Culture." In *Arab Women: Old Boundaries, New Frontiers,* edited by Judith E. Tucker. Bloomington: Indiana University Press, 1993.

———. "Icons and Militants: Mothering in the Danger Zone." *Signs* 23, no. 1 (1997): 103–29.

Petry, Carl. "Class Solidarity Versus Gender Gain: Women as Custodians of Property in Later Medieval Egypt." In *Women in Middle Eastern History,* edited by Nikki Keddie and Beth Baron. New Haven: Yale University Press, 1992.

Phillipp, Thomas. "Women in the Historical Perspective of an Early Arab Modernist (Gurgi Zaidan)." *Die Welt Des Islams* 18, nos. 1–2 (1977–78): 65–83.

———. "Demographic Patterns of Syrian Immigration to Egypt in the Nineteenth Century: An Interpretation." *Asian and African Studies* 16 (1982): 171–95.

Pierson, Ruth Roach, and Nupur Chaudhuri, eds. *Nation, Empire, Colony: Historicizing Gender and Race.* Indiana: Indiana University Press, 1998.

Popular Memory Group. "Popular Memory: Theory, Politics, Method." In *Making Histories: Studies in History Writing and Politics,* edited by Richard Johnson, Gregor McLennan, Bill Schwarz, and David Suttow. Minneapolis: University of Minnesota Press, 1982.

Porath, Yehoshua. *The Emergence of the Palestinian-Arab Nationalist Movement: 1918–1929.* London: Frank Cass, 1974.

———. *The Palestinian Arab National Movement: From Riots to Rebellion, 1929–1939.* London: Frank Cass, 1977.

Porter, Bernard. *The Lion's Share: A Short History of British Imperialism, 1850–1970.* London and New York: Longman Group, 1977.

Prochaska, David. "History as Literature, Literature as History: Cagayous of Algiers." *American Historical Review* 101, no. 3 (June 1996): 671–711.

Quaertert, Jean. *Reluctant Feminists in German Social Democracy, 1885–1917.* Princeton: Princeton University Press, 1979.

Quandt, William B., Fuad Jabber, and Ann Moseley Lesch. *The Politics of Palestinian Nationalism.* Berkeley: University of California Press, 1973.
Ray, Bharati, ed. *Seams of History: Essays on Indian Women.* New Delhi: Oxford University Press, 1995.
Rogers, Mary Eliza. *Domestic Life in Palestine.* London: Kegan Paul International, 1962.
Rubenberg, Cheryl. *Palestinian Women: Patriarchy and Resistance in the West Bank.* Boulder and London: Lynne Rienner Publishers, 2001.
Ruedy, John. *Modern Algeria: The Origins and Development of a Nation.* Bloomington: Indiana University Press, 1992.
Rupp, Leila J. "Constructing Internationalism: The Case of Transnational Women's Organizations, 1888–1945," *American Historical Review* 99 (Dec. 1994): 1571–1600.

———. "Challenging Imperialism in International Women's Organizations, 1888–1945," *National Women's Studies Association* 8, no. 1 (spring 1996): 8–27.

———. *Worlds of Women: The Making of an International Women's Movement.* Princeton: Princeton University Press, 1997.
Sabbagh, Suha, ed. *Arab Women: Between Defiance and Restraint.* New York: Olive Branch Press, 1996.

———, ed. *Palestinian Women of Gaza and the West Bank.* Bloomington: Indiana University Press, 1998.
Saddani, Nuriyya. *Al-haraka al-nisā'iyya al-'Arabiyya fī al-qarn al-'ashrīn 1917–1981.* N.p., 1982.
Safahāt min al-dhākira al-Filastīniyya, no. 3, "Tadhakkurāt Yusra Salah," interviewed by Lubna 'Abd al-Hadi. Bir Zeit: the Center for Studies and Documentation of Palestinian Society, 1992.
Sakakini, Hala. *Jerusalem and I: A Personal Record.* Amman: Economic Press, 1990.

———. *Twosome.* Jerusalem: Habesch Press, 1993.
Samuel, Edwin. *A Lifetime in Jerusalem: The Memoirs of the Second Viscount Samuel.* Jerusalem: Israel Universities Press, 1970.
Sandoval, Chela. "U.S. Third World Feminism: The Theory and Method of Oppositional Consciousness in the Postmodern World," *Genders* 10 (spring 1991): 1–24.
Sangari, Kumkum, and Sudesh Vaid, eds. *Recasting Women: Essays in Indian Colonial History.* New Brunswick: Rutgers University Press, 1990.
Sansarian, Eliz. *The Women's Rights Movement in Iran: Mutiny, Appeasement, and Repression, from 1900 to Khomeini.* New York: Praeger, 1982.
Sarrouf, Théodore. "La situation de la Femme en Palestine." *L'Égyptienne* no. 85 (Nov. 1932): 23.
Sayigh, Rosemary. *Palestinians: From Peasants to Revolutionaries.* London: Zed Press, 1979.

———. "Women in Struggle—Palestine." *Third World Quarterly* 5, no. 4 (1983): 880–86.

———. "Looking Across the Mediterranean." *MERIP* 124 (June 1984): 22–26.
———. "Femmes palestiniennes: une histoire en quête d'historiens." *Revue d'études palestiniennes* 23 (spring 1987): 13–33.
———. "Palestinian Women: Triple Burden, Single Struggle." *Peuples méditerranéens* 44–45 (1988): 247–68.
———. *Too Many Enemies: The Palestinian Experience in Lebanon*. London: Zed Books, 1994.
Sayigh, Rosemary. "Researching Gender in a Palestinian Camp: Political, Theoretical and Methodological Issue." In *Gendering the Middle East: Emerging Perspectives*, edited by Deniz Kandiyoti. Syracuse: Syracuse University Press, 1996.
———, and Julie Peteet. "Between Two Fires: Palestinian Women in Lebanon." In *Caught Up In Conflict*, edited by Rosemary Ridd and Helen Callaway. New York: New York University Press, 1987.
Schleiffer, Abdullah. "The Life and Thought of 'Izz-id-Din al-Qassam." *Islamic Quarterly* 23 (1979): 61–81.
Schölch, Alexander. "European Penetration and the Economic Development of Palestine, 1856–1882." In *Studies in the Economic and Social History of Palestine in the Nineteenth and Twentieth Centuries*, edited by Roger Owen. Carbondale: Southern Illinois University Press, 1982.
———. "Jerusalem in the Nineteenth Century (1831–1917 AD)." In *Jerusalem in History*, edited by K. J. Asali. Brooklyn: Olive Branch Press, 1990.
———. *Palestine in Transformation, 1856–1882: Studies in Social, Economic and Political Development*. Washington, D.C.: Institute for Palestine Studies, 1993.
Schreiber, Adele, and Margaret Mathieson. *Journey Towards Freedom*. Copenhagen: International Alliance of Women, 1955.
Scott, Anne Firor. *Natural Allies: Women's Associations in American History*. Urbana: University of Illinois Press, 1991.
Scott, Joan Wallach. *Gender and the Politics of History*. New York: Columbia University Press, 1988.
———, ed. *Feminism and History*. Oxford and New York: Oxford University Press, 1996.
Seikaly, May. *Haifa: Transformation of an Arab Society, 1918–1939*. London and New York: I. B. Tauris Publishers, 1995.
Sen, Samita. "Motherhood and Mothercraft: Gender and Nationalism in Bengal." *Gender and History* 5, no. 2 (1993): 231–43.
Shaaban, Buthaina. *Both Right and Left-Handed*. Bloomington and Indianapolis: University of Indiana Press, 1991.
Shafiq, Munir. "Mawdū'āt hawla nidāl al-mar'a." *Shu'ūn Filastiniyya* 62 (Jan. 1977): 200–28.
Shahid, Serene Husseini. *Jerusalem Memories*, edited by Jean Said Makdisi, with an introduction by Edward W. Said. Beirut: Naufal Group, 2000.
Sharaf, Randa. "Zlikha al-Shihabi fī dhimmat al-tārīkh: rā'idāt al-haraka al-

nisa'iyya fi Filastīn, mu'assasa al-ittihād al-nisā'ī al-'Arabī." *Al-mar'a* 13 (June 1992): 8–10.

Sharoni, Simona. *Gender and the Israeli-Palestinian Conflict: The Politics of Women's Resistance*. Syracuse: Syracuse University Press, 1995.

Shublaq, Ra'ifa. "Nidāl al-mar'a fi al-haraka al-wataniyya al-Filastīniyya." *Filastīn al-thawra* 124 (Dec. 29, 1974): 96–100.

Shumali, Qustandi. "Al-sihāfa al-Filastīniyya fi 'ahd al-intidāb, jarīdat 'Mirāt al-Sharq', 1919–1939." *Shu'ūn Filastīniyya* 221–22 (Sept. 1991): 73–86.

Sievers, Sharon. "Six (or More) Feminists in Search of a Historian." In *Expanding the Boundaries of History: Essays on Women in the Third World*, edited by Cheryl Johnson-Odim and Margaret Strobel. Bloomington: Indiana University Press, 1992.

Simpson, H. J. *British Rule and Rebellion*. Edinburgh: William Blackwood, 1937.

Slyomovics, Susan. "The Memory of Place: Rebuilding the Pre-1948 Palestinian Village." *Diaspora* 3, no. 2 (1994): 157–68.

Smith, Barbara J. *The Roots of Separatism in Palestine: British Economic Policy, 1920–1929*. Syracuse: Syracuse University Press, 1993.

Smith-Rosenberg, Carroll. "Discourses of Sexuality and Subjectivity: The New Woman, 1870–1920." In *Hidden From History: Reclaiming the Gay and Lesbian Past*, edited by Martin Duberman, Martha Vicinus, and George Chauncey. New York: Meridian Press, 1989.

Spivak, Gayatri Chakravorty. "Can the Subaltern Speak?" In *Marxism and the Interpretation of Culture*, edited by Cary Nelson and Lawrence Grossberg. Urbana and Chicago: University of Illinois Press, 1988.

Stein, Kenneth. *The Land Question in Palestine, 1917–1939*. Chapel Hill: University of North Carolina Press, 1984.

Stites, Richard. *The Women's Liberation Movement in Russia*. Princeton: Princeton University Press, 1978.

Stoler, Ann Laura. "Rethinking Colonial Categories: European Communities and the Boundaries of Rule." *Comparative Studies in Society and History* 31 (1989): 134–61.

———. "Making Empire Respectable: the Politics of Race and Sexual Morality in Twentieth-Century Colonial Cultures." *American Ethnologist* 16, no. 4 (1989): 634–60.

Stowasser, Barbara. "Women's Issues in Modern Islamic Thought." In *Arab Women: Old Boundaries, New Frontiers*, edited by Judith E. Tucker. Bloomington: Indiana University Press, 1993.

Strobel, Margaret. *European Women and the Second British Empire*. Bloomington: Indiana University Press, 1991.

Strum, Philippa. *The Women Are Marching: The Second Sex and the Palestinian Revolution*. Chicago: Lawrence Hill Books, 1992.

Swedenburg, Ted. "Problems in Oral History: The Palestine Revolt of 1936." *Birzeit Research Review* 2 (winter 1985/86): 30–41.

———. "The Palestinian Peasant as National Signifer." *Anthropological Quarterly* 63, no. 1 (1990): 18–30.

———. *Memories of Revolt: The 1936–1939 Rebellion and the Palestinian National Past*. Minneapolis: University of Minnesota Press, 1995.

Thapar, Suruchi. "Women as Activists, Women as Symbols: A Study of the Indian Nationalist Movement." *Feminist Review* 44 (1993): 81–96.

Thompson, Elizabeth. "Ottoman Political Reform in the Provinces: The Damascus Advisory Council in 1844–45." *International Journal of Middle East Studies* 25, no. 3 (1993): 457–75.

———. *Colonial Citizens: Republican Rights, Paternal Privilege, and Gender in French Syria and Lebanon*. New York: Columbia University Press, 2000.

Tibawi, A. L. *Arab Education in Mandatory Palestine: A Study of Three Decades of British Administration*. London: Luzac & Co., 1956.

Toubia, Nahid, ed. *Women of the Arab World*. London: Zed Press, 1988.

Tubi, Asma. *'Abīr wa majd*. Beirut: matba'at qalalat, 1966.

Tucker, Judith E." Problems in the Historiography of Women in the Middle East: the Case of Nineteenth-Century Egypt." *International Journal of Middle East Studies* 15 (1983): 321–36.

———. *Women in Nineteenth-Century Egypt*. Cambridge: Cambridge University Press, 1985.

———. "Ties That Bound: Women and Family in Eighteenth- and Nineteenth-Century Nablus." In *Women in Middle Eastern History*, edited by Nikki Keddie and Beth Baron. New Haven: Yale University Press, 1991.

———, ed. *Arab Women: Old Boundaries, New Frontiers*. Bloomington: Indiana University Press, 1993.

———. "*Muftis* and Matrimony: Islamic Law and Gender in Ottoman Syria and Palestine." *Islamic Law and Society* 1, no. 3 (1994): 265–300.

———. *In the House of the Law: Gender and Islamic Law in Ottoman Syria and Palestine*. Berkeley: University of California Press, 1998.

Tuqan, Fadwa. *A Mountainous Journey: A Poet's Autobiography*. Translated by Olive Kenny, poetry translated by Naomi Shihab Nye, edited by Salma Khadra Jayyusi. Saint Paul: Graywolf Press, 1990.

Van Sommer, Annie, and Samuel Zwemer, eds. *Our Moslem Sisters: A Cry of Need From Lands of Darkness Interpreted by Those Who Heard It*. New York: Revell Press, 1907.

Vester, Bertha. *Our Jerusalem*. New ed. Jerusalem: Ariel Publishing House, 1988.

Warnock, Kitty. *Land Before Honour: Palestinian Women in the Occupied Territories*. New York: Monthly Review Press, 1990.

Wasserstein, Bernard. *The British in Palestine: The Mandatory Government and the Arab-Jewish Conflict, 1917–1929*. 2nd ed. London: Basil Blackwell, Ltd., 1991.

Wehr, Hans. *A Dictionary of Modern Written Arabic*. Edited by J. Milton Cowan. Beirut: Libraire du Liban, 1980.

Weiner, Justus. "'My Beautiful Old House' and Other Fabrications by Edward Said." *Commentary* 108, no. 2 (Sep. 1999): 23–31.
West, Guida, and Rhoda Lois Blumberg, eds. *Women and Social Protest*. Oxford: Oxford University Press, 1990.
Williams, Joan C. "Domesticity as the Dangerous Supplement of Liberalism." *Journal of Women's History* 2, no. 3 (1991): 69–88.
Wilson, C. T. *Peasant Life in the Holy Land*. London: John Murray, 1906.
Wood, Elizabeth. *The Baba and the Comrade: Gender and Politics in Revolutionary Russia*. Bloomington: Indiana University Press, 1997.
Woodsmall, Ruth. *Moslem Women Enter a New World*. New York: Round Table Press, 1936.
Yahushua, Ya'qub. *Tārīkh al-sihāfa al-'Arabiyya al-Filastīniyya fī bidāyat 'ahd al-intidāb al-Brītāni 'ala Filastīn 1919/1929*. Haifa: Applied Scientific Research Co., University of Haifa, 1981.
Yassin, 'Abd al-Qadir. *Kifāh al-sha'ab al-Filastīnī qabla al-'ām 1948*. Beirut: PLO Research Center, 1975.
Yassin, Subhi Muhammad. *Al-thawra al-'Arabiyya al-kubra*. Cairo: dār al-kātib al-'Arabī, 1967.
Yazbak, Mahmud. *Haifa in the Late Ottoman Period, 1864–1914: A Muslim Town in Transition*. Leiden: E. J. Brill, 1998.
Young, Elise. *Keepers of the History: Women and the Israeli-Palestinian Conflict* New York: Teacher's College Press, 1992.
Yuval-Davis, Nira, and Floya Anthias, eds. *Woman-Nation-State*. New York: St. Martin's Press, 1989.
YWCA of Ramallah. Pamphlet. N.d.
Zeidan, Joseph T. *Arab Women Novelists: The Formative Years and Beyond*. Albany: State University of New York Press, 1995.
Zu'aytir, Akram. "Awwal mu'tamar nisā'ī 'Arabī fī al-tārīkh li-nasra al-qadiyya al-Filastīniyya 'ām 1938." *Tārīkh al-'Arab wa al-'alam* 1, no. 12 (1979): 4–14.
———. *Yawmiyyāt Akram Zu'aytir: al-haraka al-wataniyya al-Filastīniyya 1935–1939*. Beirut: Palestine Studies Association, 1980.

Index

'Abd al-Hadi, 'Auni: 122, 280n61, 294n31, 295n45
'Abd al-Hadi, Tarab: 121, 122, 145, 146, 148, 214
'Abd al-Majid, Fa'iza: 67, 168
Abdo, Nahla: 11
'Abduh, Muhammad: 30, 65, 87
Abdallah (King of Jordan): 41
'Aboud, Alexandra: 46, 59, 240n125, 274n116
Abu al-Huda, Luli: 194
Abu Durra: 127
Acre: 29, 104, 119, 150, 151, 152, 199
Affula: 125
Ahmed, Leila: 64–65
'Alami, Musa: 28
'Ali, Muhammad: 29
Allenby, General: 121
American Colony Aid Association: 50, 51, 107
American Junior College (AJC): 240n116
American University of Beirut: 44, 45, 73, 250n44
Amin, Qasim: 30, 65, 67, 77, 82–83, 247n21, 256n138
Anglo-American Commission (AAC): 195, 198, 199, 204
Antonius, Katy: 177
Arab Executive (AE): 108, 116, 121, 148, 151, 156, 157, 158, 158, 161

Arab Higher Committee (AHC):124, 148, 175, 200, 201, 202, 292n2
Arab Ladies Society: 42, 46, 139, 195
Arab Orthodox School: 29
Arab Women's Association (AWA): 5, 109, 115, 139, 142, 143, 159, 161, 197, 198; and AWE: 142, 144, 147, 149–151, 166, 228n59, 290n172, 296n51; and the British administration: 168, 169, 172; and early years: 120, 121, 123; and founding: 109, 119, 220n7; and nationalism: 184; and Revolt of 1936–39: 123, 127–131, 132, 135, 136; and split: 152–156. See also Arab Women's Executive; Jerusalem
Arab Women's Conference (1944): 187–189
Arab Women's Congress (1929): 88, 105, 115, 116, 119, 145, 155, 163
Arab Women's Executive: 117, 118, 119, 120, 122, 131, 142–151, 156, 166, 171, 179, 200; and AWA: 142, 144, 147, 149–151, 166; and Christians: 144, 147; and leadership: 142–149. See also Arab Women's Association
Arab Women's Union (AWU): 5, 18, 99, 106, 109, 115, 131, 132, 142, 150, 151, 184, 186, 189, 190, 191, 195, 197, 200, 228n59, 286n51; and

329

Arab Women's Union *(continued)*
    founding: 155. *See also* Arab
    Women's Association
'Arraj, Lydia: 206–207, 246n205
Association of the Women's League:
    195
'Azar, Adele: 104, 105, 152, 260n36,
    279n45

Balfour Declaration (1917): 24, 31, 81,
    108, 118, 125, 185
Baramki, Evelyn: 59, 274n116
Basisu, Wasfi: 77, 79, 82
Bedouin: 48
Beersheba: 163
Bethlehem: 82, 132, 192
Beirut College for Women (BCW): 45
Bir Zeit University: 46, 210, 240n112
Bisan: 132, 201
Black Hand: 128
Booth, Marilyn: 247n12
Boy Scouts: 112, 162
"British character": 37–38, 168. *See
    also* "character"
"British justice": 24, 167–168, 170
British Mandate of Palestine: 31–4,
    53–54, 192–198, 249n35; and atti-
    tude toward women: 34–36, 57–58,
    61–62, 157, 160–161, 171–173
British Syrian Training College: 41, 45
Brotherhood of Freedom: 194

Callaway, Helen: 58
Catholic Club: 196
Central Economic Committee for the
    Boycott: 200
Central Intelligence Department: 124
Chancellor, Sir John: 116, 118, 144
"character": 37–38, 39, 45, 49. *See also*
    "British character"
charities: 5, 99–107, 264n84, 283n87;
    and British: 33–34; and Christian:
    104–108, 110; and Muslim: 106,
    109, 110; and nationalism: 98–99,
    108; and world phenomenon: 95–97;
    and Zionism: 95, 96, 98, 108. *See
    also* Christianity/Christians; Pales-
    tinian women's movement

Christianity/Christians: 26, 28, 29, 32,
    41, 45, 47, 59, 69–70, 79, 80, 81, 97,
    259n25, 103, 104–106, 131, 144,
    169, 170, 192, 193, 197, 199, 206,
    207, 242n161, 245n201, 252n52,
    252n56; and AWE: 144, 147; and
    charities: 104–108, 110; Palestinian
    women's movement: 144, 147; and
    the press: 69–70, 75. *See also* chari-
    ties; Arab Women's Executive; the
    press; Palestinian women's
    movement
class: 27–30, 47–48, 62, 102, 113, 123,
    257n4, 276n22. *See also* Revolt of
    1936–39; Palestinian women's
    movement
conferences: *See* Arab Women's
    Conference; Arab Women's Con-
    gress; Eastern Women's Conference;
    General Eastern Women's
    Conference
Communist Party: 48, 107, 110
Cunningham, Alan: 199

al-Dajani, Hassan Sidqi: 184
Dar al-Tifl al-'Arabi: 20, 43, 202
Dayr Yassin Massacre (1948): 20, 42,
    202
Demonstrations: 31, 121, 129, 130,
    135, 150, 151, 160–163, 170, 171,
    182, 195. *See also* Palestinian
    women's movement
Department of Education: 54, 81, 135,
    152, 175
Department of Health: 55–56
Dib, Katrin: 166, 214, 293n17
Dib, Shukri: 188
al-Difā': 67, 68, 73, 78, 135, 152, 175,
    267n20
domesticity: 10, 82–83, 100–101
dress and fashion: 34–35, 58–59, 134,
    153, 154. *See also* veiling *(hijāb)*
Duzdar, Shahinda: 145, 146, 152, 155,
    213–214, 278n37, 292n8, 293n17
Duzdar, Wafi'a: 46, 246n205

Eastern Women's Conference (1930):
    179–182, 293n17

Eastern Women's Conference (1938): 109, 154, 184–189, 280n60, 283n100, 284n104
education: 248n27; and British: 36–48, 195; and changing attitudes toward: 190, 195; and Ottoman: 29; and Palestinian attitude towards: 40–48; and Palestinian women: 43–48, 81–83. *See also* Ottoman Empire/heritage

Egyptian Feminist Union: 182, 184, 295n39
Egyptian Sa'adist Ladies Committee: 182
employment/labor: 28–30, 55–58, 105, 191, 192, 196, 197, 232n103, 238n74; and midwives: 48, 54–56; and nurses: 55–56
English College: 107
Erskine, Beatrice: 237n54

factionalism: 14, 118, 119, 149, 152–154, 155, 158, 174, 177, 184–185, 281n65, 282n81, 296n51; and press: 288n149
Farrell, Jerome: 43
feminism: 119, 137–141, 153, 154, 174–175, 204–209, 298n70; and definitions: 8, 14–16; and Palestinian history: 11–14; Pan-Arab: 178–189; and Third World studies: 5–11. 14–17. *See also* Palestinian women's movement
Filastīn: 67, 68, 69–70, 71, 73, 75, 84, 91, 92, 122, 130, 135, 163, 164, 165, 191, 193
Foreign Office: 21, 22, 199
Friends Girl School: 131

Galilee: 126, 129, 132
Gaza: 119, 138, 151, 190, 200, 202
Gelvin, James: 249n33, 290n169
General Eastern Women's Conference (1932): 181–182
General Syrian Women's Union: 180
Ghazzal, Fatma: 126, 171n66, 171n68
Girl Guides Association: 111–112, 130
Girl Scouts: 96, 111

Great Depression: 40

Haifa: 26, 29, 66, 109, 119, 122, 131, 132, 147, 149, 151, 152, 157, 164, 195, 197, 201, 279n44
Haifa Orthodox Club: 182
Halabi, Asia: 193
Halabi, Sultana: 196
Hamada, Nur: 180–181, 293n17
hamūla: 99, 149, 179
Hashim, Miryam: 152
Haykal, Yusuf; 79, 82
health: 32, 48–51, 76–77
Hebron: 60, 120, 129, 151
al-Husayni, 'Abd al-Qadir: 131, 154
al-Husayni, Hajj Amin: 124, 142, 149, 184, 185, 292n2
al-Husayni, Hind: 20, 42, 44, 124, 131, 202, 302n115
al-Husayni, Jamal: 109, 122, 156, 200, 279n49
al-Husayni, Na'imati: 122, 146, 148, 149, 214, 278n37, 279n49, 293n17
al-Husayni, Salma: 130
al-Husayni, Wajiha: 29
hygiene: 24, 31, 35, 39, 48–51

ikhlāq: 181
Indian National Congress: 150
inter-communal violence: 108, 115, 118, 121, 123, 147, 172, 254n96. *See also* Revolt of 1936–39
International Alliance of Women: 108, 183, 297n56
International Alliance of Women for Suffrage and Equal Citizenship: 173
al-'Isa family: 69, 164, 193
Islamic Council: 87
Islamic Legal Association: 84
Islamic Society: 151
Isma'il, Muhammad: 75, 86

Jabr, 'Abd al-Fattah: 84–85
Jaffa: 3, 26, 29, 30, 42, 60, 66, 69, 75, 76, 80, 82, 87, 104, 105, 108, 119, 122, 123, 129, 131, 145n44, 147, 150, 151, 152, 161, 170, 172, 191, 195, 200, 202, 204, 254n96

332 / Index

al-Jami'a al-'Arabiyya: 73, 110
al-Jami'a al-Islamiyya: 73
Jarallah, Sa'ida: 41–42, 59, 144
Jenin: 129, 199
Jerusalem: 24, 26, 29, 41, 46, 47, 55, 56, 59, 60, 61, 66, 87, 103, 106, 107, 109, 117, 121, 122, 143, 147, 152, 161, 171, 179, 186, 190, 195, 200, 203, 205; and AWA: 119, 142, 150, 151, 155, 156, 279n44
Jerusalem Executive Committee: 119
Jerusalem First Aid Committee: 190
Jerusalem Solidarity Society: 202
Jerusalem Women's Association: 119

Kaplan, Temma: 9
al-Karami, 'Abd al-Ghani: 76
Kardosh, Yvonne: 44
al-Karmil: 71, 72, 81, 86, 132, 149, 158, 163, 276n19
al-Khadra, Anisa: 131, 146, 148, 152; and background: 215
al-Khadra, Salma: 131, 273n94
al-Khalidi, 'Anbara Sallam: 177, 293n17
al-Khalidi, Wahida: 146, 148, 177, 279n49, 293n17; and background: 213
al-Khalil, Miryam: 152, 297n56
al-Khalil, Samiha: 264n84
Khartabil, Wadi'a: 138, 139, 152, 154
Khuri, Su'ad: 78–79, 81, 109
Khurshid, Nariman Nihad: 201
kufiya: 133, 134

Labor Department: 196
labor unions: 96, 111, and organizing women in Palestine: 196–198. See also Palestine Arab Workers Society
Ladies Anglican Society: 198
Ladies Arabic Club: 198
Lazreg, Marnia: 8
League of Nations: 31, 166, 182, 183

Mansur, Ellen: 41
marriage: 27–28, 42, 46, 53–54, 61, 145–147, 177, 245n200; and the "Marriage Crisis": 78, 84–86
McClintock, Anne: 221n8
memory: 18–21

Meriwether, Margaret: 17
midwives: 48, 55–56. See also employment/labor
Miqdadi, Subhiyya: 83, 181
Mirāt al-Sharq: 71, 73, 143, 163
missionaries; 26, 29
modernity/modernization:25, 29, 30, 34–36, 37, 54, 58, 72–75, 78, 79, 80, 90, 91, 140, 153–154, 160, 164, 174, 181, 182, 188, 194, 195, 206, 251n52, 290n169. 296n51
Mohan, Rajeswari: 15
Mohanty, Chandra Talpade: 15
motherhood: 10–11, 32, 35, 38–39, 49–50, 80–83, 91,171, 195, 224n40, 290n51
Mughannam, Matiel: 42, 67, 75, 86, 117, 118, 137, 138, 141, 145, 146, 147, 160, 164, 166, 168, 170, 173, 177, 199, 204, 207, 208, 220n7, 278n37, 283n100, 287n140, 288n150, 293n17; and AWA: 109, 121, 122, 148, 149, 152, 153, 155; and background: 216; Eastern Women's Conference: 184
Mughannam, Mughannam: 147
mujāhidāt: 182
mukhtar: 55, 191
Murad, Fatma: 181

Nablus: 31, 39, 40, 41, 46, 51, 60, 109, 119, 121, 122, 150, 151, 152, 153, 156, 158, 162, 170, 182, 287n148
nahda: 101
Najmabadi, Afsaneh: 83
nakba: 8, 24, 62, 107, 178, 209, 210
Nashashibi, Raghib: 147, 149
Nashashibi, Zahiya: 148, 217
Nashashibi family: 133, 156, 283n100
Nasir, Elizabeth: 44, 240n112
Nasir, Victoria: 45, 240n112
Nassar, Najib: 71, 72, 131, 132, 273n107, 279n44
Nassar, Sadhij: 67, 71, 72, 75, , 81, 131, 132, 151, 152, 155, 172, 173, 196, 204, 273n107, 279n44, 281n73, 297n56
National Committee: 129

National Defense Party (NDP): 147, 149, 158, 184, 282n81, 296n51
National Orthodox School: 104
nationalism: 9, 42, 67, 137–142, 154, 165, 170, 174, 187, 205, 208–209, 283n93. *See also* Palestinian women's movement
Nazareth: 29, 44, 70, 109, 119, 150, 192

Newton, Beatrice: 237n54
"new woman": 9–10, 25, 64, 76, 80–83, 92, 140–141, 160, 166, 206, 223n37
Nixon, Margaret: 33
nurses and nursing: 55–56. *See also* employment/labor
Nusseibeh, Samah: 46

Offen, Karen: 9
Orthodox Aid Society for the Poor: 104
Orthodox Charitable Society: 104
Orthodox Girls Society: 198
Orthodox Ladies Society: 104, 105
Orthodox Society for the Destitute Sick: 103, 108
Orthodox Youth Club: 80
Ottoman Empire/heritage: 25–31, 65–66, 69, 103–104, 110, 120

Palestine Arab Party: 149, 158, 282n81, 300n88
Palestine Arab Women's Union (PAWU): 190, 199, 200, 203
Palestine Arab Workers Society (PAWS): 196, 197
Palestine Association of University Women: 111
Palestine Broadcasting Service: 177, 182
Palestine Bulletin: 163
Palestine Liberation Organization (PLO): 31, 210, 240n114, 264n84
Palestine Matriculation Exam: 39, 42
Palestine Relief Fund: 33
Palestine Women's Congress: 5, 95
Palestine Women's Council: 33, 34, 49–50, 107, 109
Palestinian women's movement: 115–136, 137–175, 189–202, 260n36; and Christians: 144, 147; and civil rights: 86–89, 90, 204–206, 275n9; and class: 5, 140, 142–143, 148; and confusion over names: 220n7, 262n64, 267n21, 267n22, 282n97; and feminism: 204–209; and language: 11, 164–168; and male attitudes: 59–60, 148, 155–159, 162, 188, 200, 281n65; and motherhood: 31, 35, 290n177; and nationalism/pan-Arabism: 5, 9–10, 80–83, 120, 138–142, 148, 155–159, 164, 170, 178–189, 208, 227n57; and notable family politics: 146, 148–149, 153, 155, 156,185–186, 282n81, 288n149; and opposition: 88–89; press: 163–165; and relations with international women's movement: 88, 150, 154, 173, 174, 179–189; and tactics: 159–168; and tradition: 62, 169–171; and Westernization: 30, 84–86, 153–154, 164–165
Palestine Women's Union: 109
Palestinian Encyclopedia, The: 159
Passerini, Luisa: 19
patriarchy: 10, 15, 171–173
Permanent Mandates Commission (PMC): 120, 157, 166, 279n49
press: 21, 111, 159, 163–165, 186, 211–212; and censorship: 66, 68, 248n25; and Christians: 69–70, 75; and circulation: 68–69; concepts of rights in: 86–89; debate on veiling in: 73–80; and history and Islam: 75–76; history of Arab press: 63–66, 71–72; lack of women's press: 71–73; Westernization: 77–80; and Zionism: 74. *See also al-Difāʿ, Filastīn, al-Jāmiʿa al-ʿArabiyya, al-Jāmiʿa al-Islāmiyya, al-Karmil, Mirāt al-Sharq, Palestine Bulletin, al-Sirāt al-Mustaqīm*

al-Qassam, ʿIzz al-Din: 47–48, 123, 124, 185, 292n8
al-Qassam, Maymana: 185

Ramallah: 40, 58, 113, 131, 144
Ramla: 119, 151

Red Crescent Society: 106
Red Cross: 107, 108
Reform Party: 148
Revolt of 1936–39: 20, 24, 123–135, 145, 157, 171, 196; and elite women: 124, 128–133; and peasant women: 125–128
Ridler, Hilda: 34–35, 37
Rifaqāt al-Qassam: 129
rights: 24, 30, 31, 43,75,79,81, 90, 115, 120, 138–139, 140, 151, 154, 165, 170, 182, 275n9; concepts of (in press): 86–89
Royal Peel Commission: 158, 272n83
Rubenberg, Cheryl: 222n16
Rural Training Center for Women (RTC): 38

Saba, Charlotte: 56–58
Saba, Nicola: 56
al-Saʻid, Amina: 182
al-Saʻid, Ghalib: 76
St. Joseph School: 29
al-Sajjadi, Nahid ʻAbduh: 59, 106, 143, 207–208
Sakakini, Dumya: 45, 130–131, 273n94
Sakakini, Hala: 45, 46, 61, 70, 130–131, 240n125, 273n94
Sakakini, Khalil: 29, 70, 148
Sakakini, Melia: 29, 106, 143, 146, 148, 152, 169, 262n64, 277n36, 278n37, 280n58, 282n66, 293n17; and background: 215–216
Salah, Yusra: 40, 44, 45–46
San Remo Conference (1920): 31
Sayigh, Rosemary: 3, 47
Schmidt Girls School: 107
Scott, Joan Wallach: 14
Scrivenor, Thomas: 132
Shaʻrawi, Huda: 87, 88, 105, 154, 180, 184, 186, 187, 189, 208
shariʻa: 79, 87, 88, 123, 187
al-Shihabi, Zlikha: 18, 106, 143, 145, 146, 147, 152, 153, 154, 186, 189, 199, 203, 208, 216, 262n64, 278n42, 283n100
Shihada, Boulos: 71, 280n61

Shihada, Mary: 67, 71, 75, 80, 88, 148, 157; and background: 214–215
Shuqayri, Asʻad: 156
Siksik, Henriette: 46, 47, 102–103
Siksik, Katherine: 108, 292n8
al-Sirāt al-Mustaqīm: 67, 68, 73, 87, 150
Sisterhood of Freedom: 194
Social Service Association: 107
Social Welfare Department: 194, 195
Society of Saint Teresa: 110
Society of the Wounded Soldier: 106
sources: 17–23, 104, 282n76, 288n151
Sports and Literary Club: 190
Supreme Muslim Council: 60, 73, 110, 119, 156, 205
Swedenburg, Ted: 20

Taha, Sami: 196
al-Tahtawi, Rifaʻah Rafiʻ: 30, 65
Tannus, Nimra: 40–41
Taybi, ʻAziza: 92
Teachers Training College: 29
Tel Aviv: 85
Thabit, Labiba: 180
Thabit, Munira: 86
Third world: and feminism: 5–11, 187; and history: 14–16; women: 15–16
Tibawi, A.L.: 43
Totah, Khalil: 43
tradition: 9,10–11, 50–51,54, 73, 74, 75, 80, 86, 90, 91, 103, 117, 118, 119, 126, 127, 140, 141, 144, 153, 160, 161, 162, 166, 168–172, 173, 174, 201, 205, 207, 223n36, 283n93, 289n160, 290n169, 290n170
Tubi, Asma: 67, 71, 96, 99, 105, 107, 109, 152, 189, 195
Tucker, Judith: 17
Tulkarm: 103, 128, 129, 138, 152, 153, 154, 199
Tuqan, Fadwa: 44, 59, 60–61

ʻulama: 28, 142
United Nations: 199

veiling (*hijāb*): 30, 34, 46, 73, 106, 131, 133, 153, 191, 205, 234n18, 250n47,

251n48, 266n15, 274n116, 293n27; and debate over *hijāb*: 73. *See also* dress and fashion
Vester, Bertha: 51

Wadi Azzoun: 126
Wailing Wall Incident (1929): 24, 115, 118, 120, 136, 224n40
Wauchope, Arthur: 122
White Paper (1939): 136, 176, 198
Women's Council: 49
Women's Orthodox Society: 105
Women's Social Endeavor Society: 193–194, 196
Women's Solidarity Society: 106, 154, 194–195
Women's Suffrage Alliance Congress (1923): 88

Women's Training College (WTC): 36, 38–40, 44, 106, 110
Women's Volunteer Auxiliary Army: 192
World War I: 65, 66, 107–108, 141
World War II: 136, 175, 176, 177, 193, 197

YMCA: 45, 110, 121
YWCA: 35, 45, 110, 113, 173, 182, 204

Za'rour, Miryam: 191
Zionism: 20, 42, 95, 96, 98, 108, 112, 121, 124, 177, 187, 198, 205
Ziyada, May: 86, 200
Zu'aytir, Akram: 184, 200, 287n148, 295n43, 295n45, 296n47
Zurayq, Qustantin: 44

CPSIA information can be obtained at www.ICGtesting.com
Printed in the USA
BVOW07s0252020114

340660BV00002B/309/A

9 780520 237902